FROM *ENDANGERED SPECIES*

Joseph Heller:
Q—"I've read that you don't care if there's a God or not."
A—"I don't."
Q—"And you look upon death the same way you do root-canal work?"
A—"Exactly. People get through it, how difficult can it be?"

Elmore Leonard on fan letters: "I've got this one from a convict: 'I thought you might be interested in a report on your growing popularity among this prison's hardcore readers. . . . The Italians like you but they prefer Judith Krantz and Sidney Sheldon, anything about the lush life in New York City. Jamaicans read westerns, Africans read nonfiction, Indians and Pakistanis read the *Wall Street Journal*."

Joyce Carol Oates on the quantity of her output: "Maybe I shouldn't say this, but I've actually been writing while I'm being introduced to give a talk."

James Ellroy on his father's last words: "He said, 'Son, try to pick up every waitress who serves you.' A legacy I have fulfilled at moments in my life."

J. P. Donleavy on a strange talk-show appearance with Merv Griffin: "I can recall just turning when he asked me a question and looking at him, and instead of facing one of these bland cut-off kind of people, I found he was actually listening to what I was going to say—which so terribly threw me that I could hardly say a thing."

Alex Haley on how his famous *Playboy* interview with Miles Davis came about: "The invitation was clear: get in the ring with him or forget any hope of an interview. So I got in the ring and it didn't last all that long. . . . Afterwards we went to the showers. There's something about two guys under adjacent showerheads that's not terribly formal and he began to talk."

Neil Simon on his suggested epitaph: "Ssshh, he's writing."

ENDANGERED

SPECIES

OTHER BOOKS BY LAWRENCE GROBEL

Above the Line
Conversations with Capote
The Hustons
Conversations with Brando
Talking with Michener

ENDANGERED SPECIES

SPECIES

Writers Talk About Their Craft,
Their Visions, Their Lives

LAWRENCE GROBEL

DA CAPO PRESS

Portions of the following interviews were originally published in *Playboy:* Joyce Carol Oates (November 1993), Elmore Leonard (profile, May 1995), Saul Bellow (May 1997). © 1993, 1995, 1997 by Playboy Enterprises, Inc. Portions of the interview with James Ellroy appeared in *Playboy Japan* (June 1998); Joseph Heller in *Writer's Digest* (profile, October 1977); Allen Ginsberg in *Diversion* (introduction, June 1997); Andrew Greeley in *Modern Maturity* (May/June 1996); Ray Bradbury in *Newday's LI Magazine* (November 1975), *Los Angeles Free Press* (November/December 1975), *South Bay* (March 1981); Elmore Leonard in *Movieline* (July 1998).

First Da Capo Press edition 2001

Published by Da Capo Press
A Member of the Perseus Books Group
http://www.dacapopress.com

Da Capo Press books are available at special discounts for bulk purchases in the U.S. by corporations, institutions, and other organizations. For more information, please contact the Special Markets Department at the Perseus Books Group, 11 Cambridge Center, Cambridge, MA 02142, or call (617) 252-5298.

Cataloging-in-Publication data for this book is available from the Library of Congress.
ISBN 0-306-81004-2

Design by Jeff Williams
Set in 11-point Legacy Serif by Jane Raese

1 2 3 4 5 6 7 8 9—04 03 02 01

FOR MAYA AND HANA
READ, READ, READ!

CONTENTS

FOREWORD

by Robert Towne

A girlfriend of mine had, among her other complaints, an enduring one of a former boyfriend. When they were on the phone and she told him she loved him, he, perhaps because of the company he was keeping on his end, could not bring himself to respond in kind. He did, however, feel he had to say *something* and so he did: "Ditto."

This recollection occurs to me because the temptation is overwhelming, in reading Larry's interviews with these writers, to take Joyce Carol Oates's introduction to his earlier book, *Above the Line*, in which she begins, "If there is a Mozart of interviewers, Larry Grobel is that individual," write "Ditto," and be done with it.

As an interviewer Larry's all the things Joyce Carol Oates has said he is: prepared, adaptable, and graced with the intelligence needed to shoot the breeze and elicit intriguing responses from uncommonly gifted and often uncommonly suspicious subjects. After all, the Aboriginal's fear of having his soul stolen by the photographer and the author's suspicion that the interviewer is up to the same goddam no-good are not easily overcome. In this new collection, once again Larry has overcome. Being a good and capable thief, he has stolen a bit of the soul from each of twelve extraordinary writers and put it on paper. It's a gratifying accomplishment for the reader and, I think, for these writers.

The interviews capture and preserve just those moments in the authors' lives that otherwise would be lost to all but passing memory—priceless anecdotes, offhand remarks, feelings, and insights neither likely to find their way into their respective works or even out of their mouths without the aid of Larry Grobel's seemingly effortless provocations.

There's memorable shop talk on the process of writing and writers. Bellow's assessment, for example, of Capote's gifts relative to his own genius as "not being near the tail of the comet," is a wickedly inspired image in an interview that is truly sacred and profane.

Greeley's remark that the writer is particularly capable of identifying with God since both can create characters neither can control, says as much about writing and God in one sentence as I've ever read.

One way and another these pieces are filled with a rare order of gossip as well as wisdom: Elmore Leonard's recounting of story conferences with Pacino, Hoffman, and the usual Hollywood suspects achieves the sublime level of some sort of perverse Platonic form in capturing the essence of all such clusterfucks, if not from time out of mind, certainly from Ben Hecht to now. When Joyce Carol Oates talks about being trapped in a supermarket and having grocery slips thrust upon her to be autographed, she adds to the pain of writing the pain in the ass of being a writer, in one succinct image.

Finally these writers come to life so vividly because Larry Grobel senses there are no answers in life, only questions. Good ones.

PREFACE

People often ask me if I'm ever intimidated interviewing some of the people I've talked with over the years. Usually they are referring to actors, such as Marlon Brando, Barbra Streisand, Al Pacino, or Robert De Niro. I have a healthy respect for these artists and prepare for them accordingly, but it's not actors who make my pulse beat faster, it's writers. Writers have always been heroes to me, ever since I was a boy and first read "The Love Song of J. Alfred Prufrock," *Martin Eden, Tender Buttons, Great Expectations, Portrait of the Artist as a Young Man, Henderson the Rain King, On the Road, Catch-22, The Ginger Man,* "Howl," the *Esquire* essays of Norman Mailer, and the *Playboy* interviews of Alex Haley. The manipulation of words, the flow of ideas, the deftness of metaphors were as dazzling to me then as, perhaps, the wizardry of Kobe Bryant on a basketball court or Tiger Woods on a golf course are to young people today.

I don't know whether writers have the same power over us now as they once did, but I do know that we are somehow lessened by their not being recognized in the same way as rock stars, movie stars, or professional athletes.

Norman Mailer told me that writers may be an endangered species. Saul Bellow noted that, "The country has changed so that what I do no longer signifies anything, as it did when I was young. There was such a thing as a literary life in this country and there were people who lived as writers. All that changed in my lifetime."

Most of the writers in this collection I read and studied during my formative years, that is, while in school. They are very different and distinctive, yet all have something in common: they are entertaining. They may be very serious or darkly humorous, in your face or off on flights of fantasy, full of themselves or self-effacing, but these are writers who have mastered their material, who are our cultural barometers. Among them they have been awarded every possible writing prize, including the Pulitzer, the National Book Award, the O. Henry, the Edgar Allan Poe Award, the Tony, the Rea, the Heideman, the Gold Medal, and the Nobel.

As a journalist I have been interviewing people for thirty years. When I'm sometimes asked what my "angle" is, I answer that I have none—that is, I try to be as broad, far-reaching, and incisive as I can be. My goal is to reveal the person: his thoughts, her work, his childhood, her personal life. What makes Joyce Carol Oates the prolific writer she is? What made Saul Bellow such a highly acclaimed writer? How did Neil Simon become the "Shakespeare of his time"? How did Alex Haley's *Playboy* interviews prepare him to research and write *Roots?* Why was it so easy for Allen Ginsberg to present himself as a gay writer in the fifties? What made Elmore Leonard understand the criminal mind? Joseph Heller the military mind? Andrew Greeley the Catholic mind? Bradbury the alien mind? What makes Norman Mailer run?

Mailer once expressed disappointment with the lack of stimulating questions asked him by college students and offered to pay $5 for each good question. I read about that and took it as a challenge. When he later asked me why I wanted to get into his motives for stabbing his second wife, I told him I knew about his offer and wanted to make sure he wasn't bored with me.

When I traveled to Tahiti to interview Marlon Brando, he asked me how long did I expect to be there. I answered, "for as long as it takes." Interviews can be stimulating if the subject is willing to sit for as long as it takes. Most of the time, however, an interview is unsatisfying because all the questions aren't asked; this happens because of time. When you only get a set amount of time to talk with someone, you try to cover whatever he or she is promoting, and touch on areas of general, topical, or timely interest. I've done a number of these and I know only too well what's been left out.

Yet, I've also been fortunate to have conducted in-depth conversations with no fixed time limits. This, obviously, is the preferred method of interviewing. It is also rare. How often is a major figure going to sit down for an in-depth conversation? When I first went to see James A. Michener in Florida in 1980, he said he could give me only a day of his time. I told him I had prepared fifty-six pages of questions, and five days and fifty hours later we were still talking. The same with Saul Bellow. It took nearly two years for him to agree to see me, and then the day before I flew to Boston he said he could only talk to me for one hour. I said it was impossible to cover all the topics I had prepared in an hour, and we wound up spending a full day and a few more hours over the phone in conversation.

I've spent two days interviewing Ray Bradbury for four different publications; a long afternoon in Tucson talking with Father Andrew Greeley for *Modern Maturity;* two hours with Joseph Heller for *Writer's Digest;* a day in Ireland at the home of J. P. Donleavy. For cable television I've spent between two and four hours talking with Allen Ginsberg, Norman Mailer, Alex Haley, and Neil Simon. None of these interviews ever ran more than eight minutes on the air, and none have ever before appeared in print. My interviews with Joyce Carol Oates, Elmore Leonard, and Saul Bellow had to be cut nearly in half for *Playboy* due to space limitations.

This book, then, presents the conversations with these dozen writers in full. Some are longer and go deeper than others owing to time, but all, I believe, offer insights into their creative processes.

How endangered are these writers? Ginsberg, Haley, and Heller are no longer with us; Bellow and Bradbury are in their eighties; Mailer, Leonard, Donleavy, Simon, and Greeley are between seventy-three and seventy-eight; Oates is sixty-three; Ellroy, fifty-three. "I've run out of youth," Yossarian says in Heller's *Closing Time* . . . "I'm not going to live forever, you know, even though I'm going to die trying." If we want to know where we're heading, we've got to know where we've been, and the collected wisdom of these writers can serve as a beacon to shine a light in even the darkest places.

SAUL BELLOW

Treading on the Toes of the Brahmans

IF WE JUDGE OUR ARTISTS BY THE AWARDS THEY RECEIVE, then Saul Bellow must be America's best living writer. He's won three National Book Awards (*The Adventures of Augie March*, 1953; *Herzog*, 1964; *Mr. Sammler's Planet*, 1970), the Pulitzer Prize (*Humboldt's Gift*, 1975), the Gold Medal for the Novel (1977), the National Institute of Arts and Letters Award (1952), the Friends of Literature Fiction Award, the James L. Dow, the Prix International, and Fomentor Award (for *Herzog*), the French Croix de Chavalier (1968), and the 1976 Nobel Prize for Literature. He's received a Guggenheim Fellowship, a Ford Foundation grant, and, in 1983, he was made a commander of the French Legion of Honor.

While Bellow has said that writers seldom wish other writer's well, other writers have come around to acknowledge his position among the great novelists of the world. Philip Roth calls him "the grand old man of American-Jewish writers," as well as "the country's most accomplished working novelist." John Updike thinks he is "the best portraitist writing American fiction." Irving Howe dubbed him the "most serious" and "the best living American novelist." Joyce Carol Oates considers him a genius and places him "off the scale of even Truman Capote, Thomas Pynchon or

Thomas Wolfe." Robert Alter in *The New Republic* noted, "at the top of his form he is the strongest American stylist since Faulkner." Stanley Crouch has called Bellow the "literary equivalent to Ted Williams" and compared the clarity and detail of his vision to that of Balzac.

While Bellow could read Hebrew before he entered kindergarten (his mother hoped he would be a Talmudic scholar), recognition of his talent didn't occur until he was in his mid-twenties, when *Partisan Review* first started publishing some of his stories. His parents were Russian emigrants who moved in 1913 with their two sons and a daughter to Lachine, a suburb of Montreal, Canada. Their third son, Saul, was born there on July 10, 1915. At the age of eight he was diagnosed with a respiratory infection and had to be hospitalized for six months. Not long after his recovery, the family moved to Chicago. His father worked in a bakery, sold wood scraps for fuel, and did some bootlegging. His mother died of cancer when he was seventeen, before Bellow entered the University of Chicago. After two years there, he transferred to Northwestern and majored in anthropology and sociology. In 1937, he married Anita Goshkin and got a job writing literary biographies for the federally funded WPA Writers Project. After that he began teaching, writing book reviews, and working on the Index of the Encyclopedia Britannica's *Great Books* series. During World War II he was classified 2A because of a hernia, and after surgery he joined the merchant marines. He sold a novel called *The Very Dark Trees*, but when the publisher delayed it because of the war, Bellow decided it wasn't good enough and destroyed it. He then wrote *Dangling Man*, about a young man waiting to be drafted, which earned him a $200 advance from his publisher, Vanguard, in 1944, the year his first son, Gregory, was born. There were vernacular words such as *nooky* and *darky* that his publisher wanted to excise, but Bellow refused to make any changes. Edmund Wilson, perhaps the most revered critic at the time, praised the novel, calling it "an excellent document on the experience of the noncombatant in time of war . . . one of the most honest pieces of testimony on the psychology of a whole generation who have grown up during the Depression and the war."

Another novel manuscript called *The Adventurers* was also destroyed but, in 1947, he wrote *The Victim,* which *Time* described as a novel "about a solemn and touchy Jew accused by a fanatic Gentile of having ruined him," and said that it "has troubling depths of meaning unusual among new novels." Alfred Kazin called it "one of the few really distinguished books . . . of my generation." Elizabeth Hardwick predicted that Bellow would become "the redeeming novelist of the period." Other critics favorably compared *The Victim* to the works of E. M. Forster and Graham Greene; but the book only sold 2,257 copies, and it would be six years before his next novel appeared.

As Tom Wolfe has noted, from the 1950s emerged a new golden age of the American novel, and the novel had become a nationwide tournament. J. D. Salinger's *The Catcher in the Rye* appeared in 1951, Ralph Ellison's *Invisible Man* in 1952, Bellow's *The Adventures of Augie March* in 1953, J. P. Donleavy's *The Ginger Man,* Vladimir Nabokov's *Lolita,* and William Gaddis's *The Recognitions* in 1955, Jack Kerouac's *On the Road* in 1957, Bellow's *Henderson the Rain King* in 1959. With such groundbreaking fiction it is impossible to say who came out on top, though in 1995 writer Martin Amis declared in the pages of *The Atlantic Monthly* that Bellow achieved with *Augie March* what has always been considered to be unachievable: having written The Great American Novel—a story about an optimistic, naive young man from Chicago who goes into the world seeking adventures and finds that "you do all you can to humanize and familiarize the world, and suddenly it becomes more strange than ever." "Search no further," Amis wrote. "All the trails went cold forty-two years ago. The quest did what quests very rarely do: it ended. . . . The Great American Novel was a chimera; this mythical beast was a pig with wings. Miraculously, . . . and uncovenantedly, Saul Bellow brought the animal home."

The poet and Bellow's friend Delmore Schwartz considered it a modern-day *Huckleberry Finn,* and Cynthia Ozick would later write that *Augie March* "struck out on a course so independent from the tide of American fiction that no literary lessons could flow from it . . . [it] was an eruption, a tumult, a marvel . . . a work that turned over American fiction, breaking through all restraints of language and range."

Many critics at the time it was published differed sharply with these assessments: because the novel broke new ground with its gush of language and description, they didn't know what to make of it. Norman Podhoretz considered the novel a failure; Anthony West wrote that Bellow's writing was wooden and dead. Norman Mailer called it "absurd . . . unconvincing . . . overcooked, overstuffed, unfelt, heaps of literary bull-bull." At its worst, Bellow's novel was "a travelogue for timid intellectuals," and Mailer dubbed Augie "an impossible character, and his adventures could never have happened, for he is too timid a man ever to have moused into more than one or two cruel corners of the world."

What seemed to upset them was that Bellow had so radically departed from his first two finely drawn and more confined novels, which he now calls his M.A. and Ph.D.

Bellow himself had undergone considerable changes between his second and third novel. He had gone from writing book reviews (for $5 to $10 a review) in Brooklyn to teaching at the University of Minnesota in Minneapolis for two years (1946–1948), receiving a Guggenheim Fellowship in 1948, and spending the next two years in Europe. Upon his return he taught evening classes at NYU (1950–1951), became a Creative Writing Fellow at Princeton (1952–1954), and a professor of American Literature at Bard College (1953–1954).

His next novel, *Seize the Day,* about a day in the anxiety-ridden life of a young man named Tommy Wilhelm, was called "one of the finest short novels in the language" by the *Guardian. The New Republic* said that "Bellow seems more suited by temperament and ability than any writer of his generation to create for America 'the uncreated conscience' of modern man."

The same year *Seize the Day* was published, 1956, Bellow married his second wife, Alexandra Tsachacbasov, and a year later his second son, Adam, was born. That marriage lasted only three years and ended around the time Bellow's picaresque hero, *Henderson the Rain King,* appeared. This comical one-man journey into the heart of a mythical Africa was compared to the *Odyssey* and *Don Quixote* by *Newsweek.* His hero, Eugene Henderson, seemed to echo his creator when he says, "I am a high-spirited kind of guy. And it's the destiny of my generation of Americans to go out in the world and try to find the wisdom of life."

As has been the case with each of his novels, the raves were balanced by the pans. Elizabeth Hardwick harshly condemned it in the influential *Partisan Review,* warning Bellow that he was trying too hard to be "an important American novelist." Dwight Macdonald came to Bellow's defense and condemned the magazine for publishing Hardwick's misguided review. Bellow's response to such controversy? "Oh well, I just write stories."

He married his third wife, Susan Glassman, in 1961, and their son Daniel was born in 1962. Bellow continued writing. His next novel, *Herzog,* about a sometimes suicidal intellectual who writes but never sends letters to world figures, wound up at the top of the *New York Times* best-seller list for twenty-nine weeks. Jack Ludwig, a professor, writer, close friend, and coeditor with Bellow of a literary magazine, *The Nobel Savage* (which lasted five issues in 1960) reviewed *Herzog* in *Holiday* magazine, describing it as a "summing up, fictionally, of everything Bellow has written." He compared it to Thomas Mann's *Dr. Faustus,* and Herzog's unsent letters were a "curious modification of Joyce's interior monologues in *Ulysses.*" Ludwig's praise, no matter how high, must have been difficult for Bellow to accept, as it was Ludwig who had had a secret affair with Bellow's second wife. Bellow learned of this after their separation and wrote about his hero–alter ego's adulterous wife in *Herzog.* As Ruth Miller wrote in her 1991 biography of Bellow, "The facts—reality!—came as a profound shock. After all the fireworks of his soul in search of a unique destiny . . . he was after all . . . the most commonplace of victims. His wife and his best friend, and he the last to know! . . . the story of his betrayal would become the basis for the plot of *Herzog.*"

Bellow's attempt to crack the theater world with his play *The Last Analysis* opened on Broadway the same year but closed after twenty-eight days. His collection of stories, *Mosby's Memoirs,* was published in 1969, and a year later came *Mr. Sammler's Planet,* about another cynical intellectual, which prompted the Sunday *Times* of London to proclaim Bellow "the most important writer in English in the second half of the twentieth century."

A 1965 *Book Week* poll of novelists and critics found Bellow to have written the "most distinguished fiction of the 1945–65 period." Among the six best novels of those postwar years, that poll found Bellow to have written three of them.

By this time Bellow had accepted a permanent position at the University of Chicago as a professor on the Committee on Social Thought and began writing *Humboldt's Gift,* about a failed dead poet and a successful novelist hounded by a gangster, a thinly veiled story about his relationship with Delmore Schwartz. The London *Times* pronounced Bellow to be "one of the most gifted chroniclers of the Western world" and the Swedish Academy agreed, awarding Bellow the Nobel Prize for Literature in 1976. The academy felt his body of work represented an emancipation of American writing from the "hard-boiled" style that had become "routine" in thirties literature; and for its mix of "exuberant ideas, flashing irony, hilarious comedy, and burning compassion."

Said Bellow in his Nobel lecture, "We writers do not represent mankind adequately." The intelligent public, he went on, waits "to hear from art what it does not hear from theology, philosophy, social theory, and what it cannot hear from pure science." And what is it they wait to hear? Whether mankind will endure or go under—and it is art, he concluded with a nod to Joseph Conrad, that attempts "to find in the universe, in matter as well as in the facts of life, what is fundamental, enduring, essential."

What is fundamental and enduring to Bellow are the subjects he chooses to write about, which he describes in an essay called "Distractions of a Fiction Writer": "Men and women, families and marriages, divorces, crime and flight, murders, weddings, wars, rises and declines, simplicities and complexities, blessedness and agony." His books deal with things that matter, be it an examination of prejudice, jealousy, or the exploration of the human soul. He writes about betrayal, despair, oppression, guilt, and suffering, as well as the "nameless things," as Tommy Wilhelm says in *Seize the Day,* "which it was the business of his life to carry about."

After winning the Nobel, Bellow's next book was his first of nonfiction, *To Jerusalem and Back,* his account of a visit to Israel. Three novels (*The Dean's December, More Die of Heartbreak, Ravelstein*), another book of stories (*Him with His Foot in His Mouth*), four novellas (*A Theft, The Bellarosa Connection, Something to Remember Me By, The Actual*), and a book of essays (*It All Adds Up*) were published within the last fifteen years.

"Bellow has always told me things I did not know," novelist and Bellow biographer Mark Harris has written.

He was a marvel at details . . . [and] of moments I remember beyond the wholeness of the books they inhabit: the woman physician saving the life of the circumcised Polish Jew, the Chassid on the airplane offering Bellow money to be kosher, the dead birds in the toilet at Ludeyville, the battlefield of the six-day Israeli war, Mr. Sammler and the pickpocket on the bus and afterward, . . . Henderson lifting Mummah clear off the ground, Cantabile and Citrine in the shithouse. . . . On and on, Bellow's language, formal and colloquial in the same stroke, wondrous in its timing, its infinite resourcefulness. . . . I rejoice in his hyperbole, his vision. I surrender myself to his style, try to imitate it, and so improve my own.

Bellow's descriptive gift is acute. In *The Dean's December* his Dean looks for the humanity in his disagreeable nephew: "It was as hard to see as the thin line of mercury in some thermometers." Bellow not only can describe a face so that the reader can distinguish it from all other faces, his laserlike powers of observation often pin his subject in a way uniquely his (as Cynthia Ozick observed, "he was on to something few moderns would wish to believe in: the human head as characterological map"). After detailing his character Mosby's face—his teeth, jaw, eyes, hair—he closes with a master painter's stroke, focusing on the "strong vertical grooves between the brows, beneath the nostrils, and at the back of the neck."

Bellow married his fourth wife, Alexandra Ionescu Tulcea, a mathematics professor, in 1975, and he dramatized her mother's illness and their trip to Rumania in his 1982 novel. "The good thing about *The Dean's December,*" wrote John Updike, is that "it is by Saul Bellow, and therefore possesses wit, vividness, tenderness, brave thought, earthy mysticism, and a most generous, searching, humorous humanity. The bad thing about it, or at least not so good: it is *about* Saul Bellow."

Despite his five marriages (yes, he married again to Janis Freedman, and at the age of eighty-four he became a father again) and frequent moves (he now divides his time between Boston and Vermont, where, he says, "the noisiest thing you hear is a woodpecker or a tractor down the road or a rifle shot about a mile away"), Bellow has not been distracted or separated from his talent. As a 1975 *Newsweek* profile noted, "He has not succumbed to any of the classic fates America seems to reserve for most of its major writers. He did not crack up, like Fitzgerald; he was not consumed by his own myth, like Hemingway; he did not suffer from long-delayed recognition, like Faulkner. Nor is Bellow a specimen of that other American phenomenon, the writer as show-biz personality or sudden superstar."

No saint by any means, Bellow can be cranky and cantankerous and admits to being irritable and aggressive. He bristles when critics label him a Jewish writer. "People who make labels should be in the gumming business," he has said.

Bellow has never been shy to say what he thinks about other writers. He found D. H. Lawrence to be repetitious and silly; Hemingway, a writer who had "succumbed to some of the democratic prejudices of the society"; Norman Mailer's seriousness "impossible to take seriously"; Solzhenitsyn "kinky"; Isaac Bashevis Singer's opinion of himself "so high he doesn't need anyone else's certification."

« «   » »

I remember reading *Henderson the Rain King* while still in high school and it had stayed with me when I joined the Peace Corps some years later and journeyed to Africa. I couldn't get Henderson's refrain—"I want I want I want"—out of my head. I too wanted, but didn't know what. As it turned out, what I wanted was experience. I got it from reading, now I wanted it from doing. Bellow's book—his ideas, his imagination—was a beam lighting the path I wanted to take as a writer.

When I first tried to contact Bellow for an interview I heard from his secretary saying that he had suffered an illness and was convalescing and couldn't talk with me. "I'll try again when he's better," I replied. "He's also trying to complete a novel he's been working on for nearly ten years," she warned me. "Frankly, I don't think he'll ever finish it."

Six months later I tried again, writing to Bellow care of the University Professors at Boston University. This time he responded, saying he was inclined to talk but not for another six months. Half a year later, in 1996, I flew to Boston.

I arrived fifteen minutes early at his office on the sixth floor of the Department of Theology and he pointed me to a chair and suggested I read a book while he finished some paperwork. As I looked around the large, gloomy office, hearing the traffic and street noise from Commonwealth Avenue, I thought how unpretentious it was compared to the plush offices of movie stars I have frequently visited. His solid brown desk was old, the windows behind it somewhat grimy, there were no couches to sink into, no paintings on the walls, just two flimsily framed pieces of paper: one his National Book Award for *Herzog,* the other the Harold Washington Literary Award. There were three black filing cabinets, one wall of books, and four cardboard boxes on the worn purplish carpet. It felt like the office of a cheap detective. At exactly our appointed time he put away his papers and I took a seat across a round table from him and we began our talk.

How sick have you been, and how are you now?
I've been very sick. I went down to St. Martin in the Caribbean with my wife to finish a book about a year and a half ago and ate some fish that was toxic and the toxin was very dangerous and often fatal. It attacks the nervous system. I wasn't aware of this at all at first. Then I began to feel rather odd. I couldn't work and I passed out one night in the bathroom. My wife sent for an ambulance but I wouldn't get in it, so she got me back to Boston somehow and got me over to the Boston University hospital just in time, because they told me I would have died that night. They thought I was going to die anyhow. I was in intensive care for five weeks and they didn't diagnose this strange ciguatera until I was out of intensive care. They thought it was Legionnaires' disease or dengue. First I had heart failure and then double pneumonia. And in between I also had a gall bladder operation, which set me back. Any one of these things at my age could have been fatal but I survived, though I've had a very hard time pulling myself together again.

After you recovered from this fish poisoning, were you able to write?
When I got out of the hospital I couldn't even sign my name. I couldn't manage my hand, I couldn't feed myself. They gave me a bowl of soup and a tablespoon and it was like beating the tom toms on the side of the dish. It's taken a little more than a year to recover.

So what can we expect from you next?
A novella called *The Actual*.

And what about the big novel you've been working on for the past ten years and which your former secretary believes you will never complete?
That's not accurate. Which is all I want to say about that for now.

What kinds of demands on your time are made with Boston University?
I have a special arrangement. I teach literature one term, the spring term. I don't teach writing classes.

Is it American, English, or world literature?
It's whatever I like. I just finished teaching freshmen about ambitious young men in the nineteenth century. We read Balzac's *Père Goriot*, Stendhal's *The Red and the Black*, Dickens's *Great Expectations*, and Dostoyevsky's *Crime and Punishment*.

You mean you don't teach graduate students?
No, I like to teach the younger ones because I think I should try to instill some feeling for literature.

If you were entering college today, what would you study?
I would study history and literature. But it would be hard to find anybody teaching literature anymore because the profession has decided

that we're better off without literature. The name of that trend is deconstructionism.

You've said that the teaching of literature has been a disaster. Why?
People now teach literature to expose the authors, no matter how ancient, as racist, colonialists, imperialists, chauvinists, misogynists, exploiters, parasites, et cetera. Sure you can do this to Shakespeare . . . but why should you?

Are you encouraged or discouraged by the students you see today, as compared to other generations?
If they've gone to reasonably decent schools they've been assigned good books. But those books are now in competition with the media and films. The challenge of a film is to reveal the inner lives of the people in it without really entering into their inner lives. The difference between a work of fiction and a movie is that the work of fiction is not just an account of actions, it's not just external, but internal. And it's that internal life that you're missing in movies.

And yet there are those who believe that movies are the art form of our time.
That's like mixing up the sign over a hock shop with bowling balls. Just because the things are round and look as if they might roll does not mean they are what they seem to be, okay? Commercially there's no contest between the movies and the novel because people feel there's something pretentious about high art and the novel as high art has been demoted by the movie as high art, and the movie people are promoting this view.

Do you go to many movies?
I go to movies quite a lot. I have a wife who's a great movie fan and she drags me off to see them.

Do the movies you see satisfy you or leave you empty?

I may be skeptical but I can be captivated. These emotions are and should be childlike. I was highly suspicious of *Schindler's List,* but I was moved by it just the same. I couldn't deny at the end I was carried away by some of the terrible things that had never been shown on film before, like the young woman presuming to offer advice, shot and killed right before your eyes. You can't help but be moved by that. Violently moved.

Were you also moved by Robin Williams's portrayal of Tommy Wilhelm in the PBS film of your novel, *Seize the Day*?
No, I didn't like it very much. I thought Robin had succumbed to the temptation to make Tommy Wilhelm a very schmaltzy Jewish hysterical character.

You once observed: "Give an actor a sentence with a subordinate clause and it kills him. He gets a hernia trying to heave it across the lights." Are there any actors you've seen who could make such a heave?
I like Jack Nicholson quite a lot, he's a very intelligent actor—that is to say, for an actor he's quite intelligent. He was interested in directing, not acting in, *Henderson the Rain King.* He had it under option for some years but then he never did it.

Did you meet with him?
Yeah, I enjoyed meeting him. I was very impressed by the fact that he didn't throw the roaches of his marijuana away but kept them in a little silver case.

Must have been very expensive dope.
Or they might have been auctioned as relics or something like that. Those guys are about as close to holy men as we get this removed from India.

Did you share a joint with Nicholson?
No, he didn't offer me any.

Have you ever used drugs to stimulate your thinking the way Huxley or Samuel Coleridge did?
No. If anything I'm overstimulated all the time.

Have you ever seen an actor you thought might be cast as one of your characters?
I don't really try to make that translation. The closest I ever got was to imagine Victor McLaglen playing *Henderson the Rain King*, he would have been ideal.

Didn't he win an Oscar in the title role of John Ford's *The Informer* back in 1935?
That's right. He goes back to the silent movies. He was something of a fascist in a sort of Hollywoody way; he trained with a group of horsemen, they were planning to be a cadre or some reactionary movement. He was just nutty.

Actors obviously amuse you, have you known any intimately?
The only actress that I ever knew well was Marilyn Monroe, whom I knew quite well in the days when she was married to Arthur Miller. She was like somebody who picked up a high voltage wire and then couldn't get rid of it. She was connected with a very powerful current but she couldn't disconnect herself from it. You often felt that she was supercharged. There were moments of wistfulness when you could see how willingly she would have cut off the charge if she'd been able to do it, but she couldn't. I don't even think she was aware of the superexcited state she was in. She was a very charming and really very beautiful woman.

Did she take your breath away, did she have that kind of presence?
Well, I felt no sexual attraction toward her. It may have been because Miller was a friend of mine and I had a fairly strong Jewish respect for any incest regulations. Somehow I felt that she was too beautiful to be real. She had a kind of curious incandescence under the skin, which is rare.

Did you know them during the time they were making *The Misfits* with John Huston out in Nevada?

Yeah. Arthur and I were divorced at the same time in Nevada, so we were living in the same group of shacks at Pyramid Lake, Nevada. That was where he got the idea for corralling the wild horses, which became *The Misfits*.

Were you able to get much work done when you lived in Nevada, establishing legal residency for your divorce?

I lived out there on the Piute Indian reservation at Pyramid Lake for nearly a year. I wrote *Seize the Day* and a story called "Leaving the Yellow House" out there.

Other than *Seize the Day* and *Henderson*, have any of your works been made into or optioned for the movies?

No, they're very seldom optioned. I'm considered to be a highbrow. But I was delighted when *Henderson the Rain King* was optioned, it gave me a small income and I never had to face the fact that it would become a picture.

MGM expressed interest in you after *Dangling Man* was published—but it wasn't to option the book, was it?

No. It was a guy named Goldwyn, not from the famous Goldwyns, who came to Chicago and called me up. I went downtown hoping that he wanted to buy the book; instead he told me that he'd seen pictures of me and he thought that I would do well as an actor.

Did you give it any consideration?

I was outraged [*laughs*]. I was wrong, I should have done it. In those days I was very proud of being a writer.

And you weren't thinking of making your fortune on the big screen?

I was never interested in being rich. Not in the slightest.

Years later you had your chance to appear, as yourself, in Woody Allen's *Zelig*. How'd he talk you into it?

That was a piece of foolishness. If I'd known what it was about I would never have done it. But Woody Allen made a great secret out of this. He wouldn't say what the film was about. All he said was that he was chatting up a certain number of intellectuals on an ill-defined subject. I knew some others who were doing it, including Bruno Bettelheim, whom I call the Bettelheim of the Republic, so I thought it might be a gas. He sent me some pages of dialogue. The circumstances were very amusing. It was being filmed in an old apartment on Central Park West. I walked around and ran into a solitary young man drifting from room to room. He told me that he had inherited the apartment from his parents and he couldn't maintain it so he rented it out to movie companies. I said, "What do you do?" He said, "I'm a novelist."

Was he aware who you were?

I don't think so.

Perhaps that's a fitting image of the writer: one who wanders aimlessly among the rented empty rooms of an apartment he cannot afford to maintain.

Nowadays when a young man thinks of becoming a writer, first he thinks of his hair style and then what clothes he should wear and then what whiskey he's going to endorse.

What did you think of when you first thought of becoming a writer?

It wasn't that I was going to be a glamorous person who would impress people. I had no idea what being a writer meant, really.

Did you know in grade school that you wanted to be a writer?

Oh yes, I definitely knew that I wanted to be a writer.

Did your parents try to discourage you?

My mother didn't interfere with me. Of course, she died when I was seventeen. She was concerned, as I later learned—she would talk to the neighbors and to her friends and to her dressmaker. But my parents came from St. Petersburg and they were fairly sophisticated people. They were readers. I didn't exactly introduce them to Tolstoy as a child, they knew all about that before I was born. In principle they wouldn't have had any objection to my being a writer, they just doubted that a child could be serious about this and whether he had the stuff for it. How were they supposed to know that?

When did you become aware of the power of the written word?
When I found myself in a hospital children's ward when I was eight.

Was that when you came down with tuberculosis?
It wasn't tuberculosis, it was something called empyema, which is an infection of the respiratory system which fills the lung cavity with fluid. I had to be tapped and I ran a fever every afternoon.

How long did that last?
Nearly a year.

It must have been a very formative year in your life.
Oh yes, it was indeed, because I was away from home for the first time. It was 1923, just after World War I, and it was a very restricted, old-fashioned place.

Were there kids a lot sicker than you? Did you witness children dying?
Yeah, it was quite upsetting. You'd see activity during the night, the nurses were running, a light would go on, a screen would be set up along somebody's bed, and in the morning it was an empty bed. And you knew the kid had died.

Did you think that you might die?
Yes.

Did it make you more determined to live, or were you resigned to possibly not making it?

Resigned? No, I would hunker down in my bed and make myself as small as possible.

So death couldn't find you?

Something like that. I met the world at the age of eight there in the hospital and I had never known it on those terms before.

And how did you spend your time?

Reading, though reading matter was very limited. There were the funny papers, which were very important then, with characters who don't exist anymore, like Happy Hooligan, Slim Jim, Mutt and Jeff, Boog McNutt.

That wasn't what introduced you to the power of the word, was it?

No. A lady brought me a copy of the New Testament. She was very solemn, grim, middle-aged, dressed with many layers of clothing, long skirts, laced boots, a big hat. She was connected with some missionary society. First she tested me to see if I could read well enough. I learned to read the Old Testament when I was four—I was reading Genesis in Hebrew, which was a very powerful influence. The New Testament made a big hit with me, I was terribly moved by the Gospels. The rest was off-putting, but I read about the life and death of Jesus and I realized that he was a Jew. I began to feel a responsibility for the crucifixion. I loved Jesus. I realized that I could not talk to my family when I got home about this, they would have been shocked and angry with me. So I kept it to myself. There were all kinds of things that I had to keep to myself. And that was what I learned in the hospital.

Jesus and masturbation?

I wasn't quite old enough for masturbation. I didn't start until pubic hair began to tickle me. When I began to have wet dreams. But there was no explicit sexual experience in the hospital. There was, though, quite a lot of anti-Semitism among the French Canadian kids.

Soon after you left the hospital your parents moved from Montreal to Chicago. Did you notice the difference between the cities?

Yes. Montreal was like a European city, Chicago was different in every possible way.

How did the Depression affect your family?

It was harder to make a living. During the Depression my father was in a business selling wood fuel to Jewish bakers; in those days they used scrap wood in their ovens, which he used to get from northern Wisconsin. I used to go around with him quite a lot, so I knew most of the Jewish bakers of Chicago. We were never hungry, we just didn't have any money.

Those who remember the Depression often consider it the most defining time of their lives.

It was defining in a very curious way. Instead of breeding crime and antagonism it bred compassion and solidarity between people, they were much less harsh or severe than in times of prosperity. Sometimes I thought that the greatest blow of the Depression was not lack of money as damage to the pride of honest working people who felt the Depression was a punishment somehow.

Did you feel something like that when your mother died when you were seventeen?

That was a terrible shock. It was a long drawn-out cancer death. I couldn't even imagine my mother being dead, it was the greatest challenge to my imagination when she died because I couldn't imagine existence without her. We were really a very close family, my two brothers, my sister, my parents.

How did her death affect your father?

He was devastated. He felt sexual privation of her long illness and he didn't do anything while she was alive, I know, but she hadn't been dead very long before he began to see ladies in the neighborhood. He remarried within two years.

Did you like your stepmother?
I liked her, but I liked her like a good joke. She was a very funny lady. I couldn't take her seriously though.

You've said that your father was violent, strong, and authoritarian.
He was. He'd beat all of us.

With a strap or with his hand?
Whatever came first.

Have you experienced much violence in your life?
Quite a bit. I've seen a lot of it—enough to make me feel fright at being in a state of nature again. Of having nothing but my naked self to depend upon.

Besides having seen it, have you ever physically been a victim, other than from the hands of your father?
I was abused when I was a child by a stranger in an alley.

Sexually?
Yeah.

How old were you?
Seven, six.

Did he make you cry?
He threatened me.

How far did it go?

It went pretty far. I don't want to go into detail on that. [*Pauses*] I'm amused when I read about child abuse today because it is exaggerated and an unsavory falling back on one's legal status. It's also fashionable to hate your parents. It's a nasty little vice encouraged by society. It's a sign that people are unable to shed their childhood, it's a way of remaining childish, of explaining your own defects, that you were unjustly punished or abused as a child. I've never found it to be much more than a racket. I've been in courtrooms enough to know that there is such a thing as genuine child abuse, but when the middle class began to horn in on this I said, uh-uh.

Did you follow the Lyle and Eric Menendez trial in California?
Yes, I did. The first trial was disgraceful. The court shouldn't have accepted this testimony about how their parents did them sexual harm. That the jury would take their word for it stank to high heaven.

Well, it was tried in California. . . .
Yeah. California's like an artificial limb the rest of the country doesn't really need. You can quote me.

Dare I ask you what you thought of the O. J. Simpson trial?
Trial by jury is in trouble everywhere, but in California the whole justice system is in deep trouble. It's no longer reliable. Everything is immediately transformed into a big TV show or spectacle. They are so narcotized by entertainment that they tend to transform everything from real life into entertainment terms. The whole thing's unreal.

I take it then you were shocked by the Simpson verdict?
Yes, I was shocked. I've never seen two murder victims so quickly forgotten. I could remember from my own childhood what an enormity a murder was. It was taken really very, very seriously. Now it's nothing to take a human life. It's like watching a comedy cartoon in which the hero falls in front of a steamroller and is rolled flat, then he's picked up and propped against the wall and in the next frame he's running again. So it had no reality.

More than half a century ago, in 1940, you were in Mexico when one of your heroes, Leon Trotsky, had fallen to an assassin's attack. Was that murder made more real to you when you saw Trotsky in his coffin?
Not in his coffin, just on a table in the hospital.

How did you manage that? Trotsky was an international figure, wasn't there security?
No, Mexican hospitals in those times, everybody went everywhere. I said I was an American journalist, so they let me in.

Were you moved at all seeing the man you so admired dead on a table?
He was wearing massive bloody bandages, his face and beard were smeared with blood. So that was that.

What enabled you to go to Mexico was the $500 you received from your mother's life insurance policy, which came to you seven years after her death. Your father, though, said the money should have been his. Did this cause a split between you and your father?
Briefly. After blowing his stack about it to my brothers and to his wife he just got over it.

Before you posed as a journalist you studied anthropology at Northwestern. Why anthropology?
Because Chicago was a melting pot and as close to being a primitive society as you can imagine. Chicago was a string of exotic villages threaded around various industries: the stockyards, the steel mills, laconic agricultural machinery, radio factories, printing plants.

So it was modern-day anthropology which fascinated you?
Yeah, well, you know. I also had a very influential professor, Melville Herskovitz, who had written a great deal about Africa.

Did the chairman of the English department there [William Frank Bryan] discourage you from majoring in English literature and from writing because you were Jewish?

Yeah, he put it to me very bluntly. He said that as a Jew I could never bring the right feeling to the subject.

And how did you handle such anti-Semitic sentiments?

My attitude was to hell with these bastards. Everything that concerned my higher life, as I called it, whether I was going to be a scholar or an artist, I was very defiant about. I would not let anybody interfere with it.

Sounds like critic Alfred Kazin was pretty astute when he wrote of you as a youth: "He was putting himself up as a contender . . . he was ambitious and dedicated in a style I had never seen in an urban Jewish intellectual; he expected the world to come to him. He had pledged himself to a great destiny. He was going to take on more than the rest of us were."

[*Laughing*] Some of that I attribute to the difference between Eastern Seaboard Jews and inland Jews. I was inland Jew. Inland Jews found it quite natural to see themselves as Americans. We didn't think of ourselves as set aside from the rest of the country, which the Eastern Seaboard Jews did; they were a much larger and more isolated community. I didn't feel the kind of pressures as the Jews of the Eastern Seaboard, who came from Philadelphia, Boston, New York.

You once remarked that the constant linking of your name with Bernard Malamud's and Philip Roth's reminded you of Hart, Schaffner, and Marx. How irritating is it to be called a Jewish novelist?

It's irritating only when you realize that the WASPs resent you or kind of dismiss you. I would gladly acknowledge all their charges and back down if they could come up with some really important piece of work.

Is being labeled a "Jewish" writer as annoying as Joyce Carol Oates complaining that she's often labeled a "woman" writer?
If you'll excuse me, anti-Semitism is not in the same class as what people might call misogyny or antifeminism. It's very different.

Would you rather not be called a Jew?
I don't mind being called a Jew, I am a Jew.

Yet you do think that you've been a disappointment to those Jews who, as you've noted, "expect Jewish writers to do good work for them and propagandize for them."
Do they really care very much about what writers say? They don't. At the moment the push-button reaction to me is that I'm a conservative, but that's just foolish labeling—they don't know whether I'm a conservative or not, they've just heard that. Everything is rumor, all opinion is rumor. People simply react to rumor by repeating it as though it were true. Nothing that I can do about that.

Is conservative a negative word?
In some quarters it is, in some it's a positive word. At *Commentary* magazine it's a positive word. But *Commentary* doesn't review my books, and if I'm a conservative, why are my books not reviewed at *Commentary?*

***Commentary* did review *Henderson the Rain King,* where a question was raised that might be asked of many of your works: "What is so far chiefly missing in Bellow's writing is an account of what his heroes want to be free from." Is that a fair question to ask you?**
There's an old Yiddish saying that translates: A fool throws a stone into the pond, ten sages go into the pond looking for it and can't find it. In other words, it takes almost nothing except a thoughtless tossing of a stone to motivate foolish people. Why should I answer that question? A dyspeptic book reviewer says something and now I have to answer him at this moment? I don't have to answer him.

Philip Roth has said that, unlike Elie Wiesel or Isaac Bashevis Singer, you are a figure of more importance to other Jewish writers than to the Jewish cultural audience. Is he right?
When *Herzog* went on the best-seller list, Hannah Arendt said it was because of the Jewish public. She was quite sensitive to that sort of thing. She had an interest in keeping me in the kike class. Philip Roth had no such interest, he's just wrong.

Was Kazin wrong when he observed that you were the first Jewish writer he had met who seemed as clever about every side of life as a businessman?
Alfred is a very strange critic. Alfred has more career smarts in his little finger than I have in my entire constitution. When I first knew Alfred he was working as an editor for the *New Republic*. Now, how he had gotten there, he knew something that I didn't know. Then he went to work for Henry Luce and Company—I was turned away from there when I tried to get a job at *Time*.

Was that when you were interviewed by Whittaker Chambers for the job of movie critic and got fired after one day?
Yes, but I was fired the *same* day. It was a gag, which I since discovered by comparing notes with John Berryman. We were both friends with Jim Agee and Agee was always being pitched by his Village pals for jobs. He would say, "Okay, I'll see what I can do." Then you came there and Mr. Chambers would be sitting behind his desk like the original man of destiny, brooding over the Hudson River facing the harbor from his skyscraper window. He would turn around in this huge leather chair to interview you and you could tell that he was a Victor Hugo or Dostoyevsky type of man, a historical figure. Then he'd ask you some trivial questions, like where were you educated and what did you study? He asked if I ever read Wordsworth and what kind of poet I thought he was. "What does that have to do with reviewing motion pictures?" I asked. "Just answer the question," he'd say. So I answered: Romantic poet. And he said, "There's no room for you in this organization." John Berryman had gone through exactly

the same process. So we understood that Agee had arranged all this to look like a good guy among his friends, and Chambers was very much enjoying this. Evidently it had happened many times before because there was a line of people in the corridor when I came out waiting to shake my hand and say, "Best thing to ever happen to you was not to get this job." It was a scam organized between Agee and Whittaker Chambers.

You once worked in your brother's coal yard for $12 a week, but he fired you. Why?
Because he was hot tempered and irascible and he didn't command from me the adoration and worship that he expected.

I heard it was because you were always late.
It was difficult not to be late because I had to go there on the streetcar.

You also wrote biographies about Middle Western authors for the WPA Writers Project. Who did you write about and do the manuscripts still exist?
I wrote about John Dos Passos, who was born in Chicago, and Sherwood Anderson. They never appeared anywhere and I'm sure they're lost.

Might they exist among your papers?
Never kept papers.

You never saved the early things you wrote?
No, never thought it was that important.

How about all the stories you submitted to magazines in the forties?
They were almost always rejected. Had no luck at all with stories.

John Huston said that getting a story accepted by the *American Mercury* and hearing from H. L. Mencken changed his life. Was it

that way for you when the *Partisan Review* published your first story in 1941?

I can understand that happening to Huston because Mencken was such a powerful figure in those days. He was *the* man in the literary world. Not only was he a terrific writer but he was a real literary figure and he knew everybody. He could call up Theodore Dreiser any time of the day. That was a big thing. I was excited that *Partisan Review* would print me, but it didn't have the national character that the *American Mercury* had. *Partisan Review* was just an avant-garde magazine, conspicuous on campuses. The *Mercury* was not avant-garde, it was genuinely a national popular magazine.

Seymour Krim wrote that he was "literally made, shaped, whetted and given a world with a purpose by the American realistic novel of the mid-to-late-1930s." Was it like that for you as well?

I think so. We all read Dreiser, Sinclair Lewis, Louis Bromfield, and their English counterparts like Archibald Cronin, Arnold Bennett, and H. G. Wells.

Was there any novel that got to you emotionally?

I found Dreiser's *An American Tragedy* hard to read because it was so extremely painful, almost unbearable. One of those books I didn't finish reading until much later.

What made it so painful?

Just the horror of having taken a pregnant woman out in a boat and murdering her.

Your own first novel, *The Very Dark Trees*, dealt with a white man who turned black. What happened to that?

It was accepted by a publisher in San Francisco, Colt Press, which had published Henry Miller's *The Colossus of Maroussi,* so I was impressed by that. I was only twenty-six or twenty-seven, and after I reread it I decided to destroy it.

Why?
I was ashamed to be associated with it. I threw it down the incinerator drop in the building where I lived.

How many manuscripts have you done that with over the years?
A few.

After spending so much time writing a novel, couldn't you figure out a way to salvage it rather than burn it?
It was artificial. There's nothing wrong with being artificial, but it was artificial without being genuinely interesting. It was a gimmick: How would a white man feel if he suddenly found himself changed to a black man and had to learn to live like a black man?

That "gimmick" was attempted by John Howard Griffin, who wrote the book *Black Like Me* in 1960.
I wish him well, but I didn't want to be connected with this.

You obviously had higher ambitions. In 1959 Norman Mailer wrote: "If I have one ambition above all others, it is to write a novel which Dostoyevsky and Marx; Joyce and Freud; Stendhal, Tolstoy, Proust and Spengler; Faulkner, and even old moldering Hemingway might come to read, for it would carry what they had to tell another part of the way." Did you have similar ambitions?
He deserved to fail with a fantasy like that. He wasn't thinking about writing a marvelous book, he was thinking of placing himself in a tradition. I never had such notions. And I doubt that many of those people had such notions. Mailer is an extraordinary writer of vigorous prose, but he doesn't have the kind of mind that goes with the kind of writing that he chose to do. He does have historical ideas about himself, but they're foolish ideas.

What writers among your peers do you feel had the talent to successfully pull off their ideas?

Among my contemporaries I very much like John Cheever. I admired and loved Faulkner. I like Wright Morris and J. F. Powers a lot. They're all people with much more modest aims, which doesn't mean that their novels are not good, they're first rate.

What about the novels of Nabokov, Jack Kerouac, William Gaddis, Gabriel García Márquez?

Nabokov was a very accomplished writer, but he was also a cold narcissist who invited the reader to join him. Jack Kerouac belonged to a movement—the Beat spirit of the country—and was a sort of cult writer. I never had much to do with that. William Gaddis is an excellent writer, I like him a lot. He's an original, a great user of the language. I liked García Márquez's *One Hundred Years of Solitude,* but all the others were just reruns of that. As you grow older you don't like to involve yourself in reckless reading of a great number of books, you want to limit yourself to the best that your generation has to offer.

Does that include Edmund Wilson, Kenzaburo Oë, Gertrude Stein?

Oë's too westernized for my taste. My favorite Japanese writer is Tanizaki, then Kawabata and Mishima. Edmund Wilson was not anything like an imaginative writer. His essays are marvelous but his novels are not. Gertrude Stein was not a writer, she was a maker of formulas. They were curiosities, verbal museum pieces. She was a kind of wit, but she believed that she was a very great writer and that her novel, *The Making of Americans,* should be classed with Mann's *The Magic Mountain,* Proust's *Remembrance of Things Past,* and Joyce's *Ulysses.* I don't think she belonged in that group.

Didn't Virginia Woolf also feel something like that?

She may have. Virginia Woolf was a more genuine writer, that is to say she had less literary ambition than Gertrude Stein, who wanted to be a monument. I never felt about Virginia Woolf that she was trying to be monumental.

What was your impression of Samuel Beckett, whom you met in Paris?

He was a very great person, you had a feeling about him that he was humanly significant, physically even, when he strolled across the boulevard to meet you and sat down at a café table near the Pont Royal Hotel. It gave me marvelous comfort to see and talk to him, he was so sane, so balanced, so quiet, so unpretentious.

Did you ever talk to him about James Joyce, whom he once worked for?

Yes, we often talked about Joyce. He said he was often taken to be an intimate of Joyce, which he was not. He was somebody to whom Joyce dictated because of his eyesight. So some kind of relationship developed, but he wouldn't call it a friendship.

Have you ever read Joyce's *Finnegans Wake*?

No. I'm waiting for the nursing home to read it.

Do you measure yourself against other writers?

Well, one does, you know. Recently I reread *Crime and Punishment* and I said to myself, "If only you could do this kind of thing, wouldn't it be great?"

We know your strengths as a writer, but what would you consider your weaknesses?

One of my weaknesses as a writer is that I was far too modest in my choice of subjects. If I was going to invest my talent more profitably I should have more ambitious themes than I allowed myself to have. I don't know why it was. But that would be the principle criticism that I have.

Can you be more specific? How could you have been more ambitious with some of the work you've done?

Well, *Augie March* was a very ambitious book, but it was ambitious in a very different way. It was ambitious in language because I wanted to invent a more energized language that would allow me to move much more freely than I had hitherto been able to move. I wanted to be able to do American society in a way in which it had never been done before and in part I succeeded in that book. But I failed because in the end I couldn't govern my discovery, I couldn't control it.

It's interesting that you consider it a failure, especially since you must be aware that forty-three years after its publication *The Atlantic Monthly* devoted thirteen pages to Martin Amis's essay making the case that *The Adventures of Augie March* is the Great American Novel.
That's because Amis himself is like me, devoted to the language of the novel to an extraordinary degree. In my case it was excessive.

Amis contradicted what he had written earlier, in 1982, when he said "for all its marvels, *Augie March*, like *Henderson the Rain King*, often resembles a lecture on destiny fed through a thesaurus of low-life patois." What do you think accounts for his coming around to calling it the Great American Novel?
Maybe he found more in it than he'd been able to find the first time. Sometimes one is not ready for the book that one picks up. It's happened to me many times. I don't know how many times I read *Pride and Prejudice* before I really saw it.

Cynthia Ozick considered *Augie* the second American prose revolution, after Hemingway. Did you have a sense of that?
I wanted to do it for myself; I had no idea of establishing a benchmark. I'm beginning to see that my ambitions were rather strangely limited. Not that I was modest, I've never been modest. But I set myself bounds and I had to liberate myself from those bounds. Augie March starts out as a naive person and I don't let him get too sophisticated—that's a limitation in the book.

***Augie March* also set off a storm of critical side taking. There were those, like Dwight MacDonald, who highly praised it, and**

Elizabeth Hardwick and Norman Podhoretz, who didn't like it at all. How do you deal with such mixed reviews?

You have to have a thick skin. I began to understand what I had done with *Augie March* that had upset so many people. I had unintentionally turned over a good many WASP apple carts. I had introduced a note into American fiction that was dangerous, it was undisciplined, it was awkward, it was jazzy, and it reflected immigrant and particularly Jewish points of view that were unwelcome to the WASP establishment. It had never occurred to me before that I might be treading on the toes of the Brahmans or the heirs of the Brahmans with an interest in controlling their undisciplined and disciplined unfortunate Jews who had not been sent to Harvard. *Augie March* was too unbuttoned, too red-skinned even for the redskins.

Do you feel that you succeeded in liberating the language and creating a truly original character with Augie?

Yes, I did. I felt that I had liberated the American novel from what was left of the English mandarin influence. And even from the Hemingway influence, because we did need liberation from that. Hemingway was a very marvelous and beautiful writer who was constricting, he produced novels with a very highly polished surface. You didn't want to mar the surface of his beautifully constructed and polished stories or novels. But then it was too narrowing because there were all kinds of experience which would never fit into that. Hemingway's personal attitudes intending to redefine American manhood were too constricting and too exclusive. But you could see what the social effects of Hemingway's books were.

Is Hemingway the only writer you can single out like this?

Every American writer of any consequence for a long time had really defined the American character to the educated American public. This has been going on since Walt Whitman, in fact since the days of Hawthorne and Fenimore Cooper.

Are writers defining the American character as much today?

This has been taken over by journalism. Magazines like *Playboy* and *Esquire* instruct young men in the way to be acceptably and successfully American: how to date, how to dress, how to buy a car, how to order a meal, how to prepare a salad dressing, how to take a holiday. Everything was prescribed starting on a high level and descending into the lower ranges. That's been the secret of the power in these important magazines. I had a grasp of this when I was younger and I resisted it all, I didn't want any part of it. Too many human ingredients were missing from each and every one of these formulas.

How much of your resistance came through therapy?
I was just lucky that the writer in me survived all of the therapy that I had.

Have you been through analysis?
At the insistence of one of my wives I went to a psychoanalyst for a while. I enjoyed talking with him but I was never analyzed.

What about Reichian therapy? It's been said that your experiences with this freed you to write *Augie March*.
That's an incorrect theory because I started writing *Augie March* in Paris two years before I ever heard of Reich.

So you're saying that Reichian sexual therapy wasn't responsible for changing your style of writing?
It would have been a disaster if it had. I protected my writing from the therapy, which I would call biological holistic therapy.

Reich wrote a book about orgasms and his orgone box. Did you ever use the box?
I would sit in it from time to time. I don't know what effect it had on me. It would heat me up quite a lot. It was agreeable to be in the box, because it shut off all kinds of outside influences and gave you a meditative hour, which never does any harm. But I never went beyond Reichian therapy—that was enough.

Why did you stop doing it?
Because it released very violent feelings which I then couldn't govern.
I'd lose my temper horrendously.

You never lost your temper like that before?
Not to the point of getting into fights.

Physical fights? With strangers?
Yeah. I'd be insulted on the subway, I'd be ready to fight.

Ever get your nose broken or eye blackened?
No, luckily I'd be dragged away. [*Laughs*]

Were you a good fighter?
Not that good. I had exaggerated ideas about my powers. I think
most men do.

**The New Journalists of the sixties and seventies would probably
agree with you. That was a period when writers like Tom Wolfe
were shouting that the novel had fallen and that journalists had
wiped out the novel as literature's main event.**
And here is Tom Wolfe making his fortune out of the novel some
years later. Seems prophetically inconsistent.

**Tom Wolfe was addressing you personally in his opening to *The
New Journalism* by saying it started the first new direction in
American literature in half a century. "Bellow, Barth, Updike . . .
Roth—the novelists are all out there right now ransacking the
literary histories and sweating it out, wondering where they
stand. Damn it all, Saul, the Huns have arrived . . . "**
Yes, and the Huns were taught to read English and then they bought
The Bonfire of the Vanities, which was a whole series of the most stunning billboards along the highway that I ever saw. Let me tell you
something: I'm a Jew, and when Jews hear the language of the Holocaust, because that's what it is—the world will be *Novelrein,* just as

Hitler wanted to make Germany *Judenrein,* okay?—so I say to myself,
it's all *meshuga.* I'm used to hearing this eliminationist talk.

**Are you also used to hearing the kind of assessment a writer like
Joyce Carol Oates has said of you, when she called you a genius
and "off the scale of even Truman Capote, Thomas Pynchon or
Thomas Wolfe"?**
I don't think that Truman Capote gets near the tail of the comet.
Pynchon I like but he is sort of an endless virtuoso, it's like listening
to twenty hours of Paganini. One would be plenty. I loved Thomas
Wolfe when I was young. I stayed up all night reading *Look Homeward
Angel* when I was nineteen and I remember in the morning how dev-
astated I was to have no more Thomas Wolfe to read.

Have you known many people of genius?
I've known a small number, but I'm not going to name names for fear
of offending those still alive who may think I believe them to be a
genius.

What is genius to you?
It's an extraordinary gift or capacity to put things together that are
just longing to be put together, it's to see connections that nobody
else has ever seen.

**Getting back to Oates's remark: Modesty aside, do you have that
sense about yourself and your work?**
I don't think in those terms. I tend to agree with her, but Lenin said,
when describing what happened in Russia in 1917, the power was lying in the street, I just picked it up. [*Laughs*] I do have that feeling
that, yes, I did do something. Not that anybody cares very much
nowadays about such things. The country has changed so that what I
do no longer signifies anything as it did formerly when I was young.
There was such a thing as a literary life in this country and there were
people who lived as writers. All that changed in my lifetime. Of
course, this is such an enormous country that sometimes I think that

if only one-tenth of one percent of the population were reading seriously, it would still mean a quarter of a million readers.

After receiving the second of your three National Book Awards in 1964 you said that unless novelists "make a clearer estimate" of their condition, "we will continue to write kid stuff, to fail in our function, we will lack serious interests and become truly irrelevant."
Yeah, that turned out to be true. Those are hard words to listen to.

How relevant is the novelist today? Do we need novelists?
Do we need them? Yes. Do we know it? No. Although, as I say, you will still find a quarter of a million supporters somehow or other around the country. These are people who have preserved themselves secretly like members of a lodge who are not allowed to give away the secret of the handshake. I used to play a game when I traveled around the country. I would stop in some town's library named after some multimillionaire like Andrew Carnegie and walk through the open stacks to see how many readers Proust had in Punksatawney, Pennsylvania. To my surprise, there were readers taking his books out. They were not the most used books on the shelves, but were not absolutely neglected. So there is something really going on, as if people were clinging to life by means of these books.

Did you also look to see if your own books were being read?
I looked occasionally.

If you had a crystal ball, what might you see for the future of the novel?
It's a bad time for the novel. What's going to happen to the novel is what's going to happen culturally to this country. The number of readers is diminishing. Family life today is not creating more readers. Partly because of TV, partly because of schooling, partly because of books prepared for schoolchildren that pretend to be stories and that are so ill-constructed and flat and corny that the kids have no regard

for them. The experience of literature is missing from the lives of the younger generation of readers and that's a bad deal. I don't think the classics are being read anymore. I know the Bible isn't being much read anymore, and the Bible is a great oceanic source for literature. When the Bible diminishes in stature, literature diminishes with it.

As the author of _Herzog_, who was such a voluminous letter writer, do you hear from your readers?
I do, and sometimes they're the most intelligent letters I get. John Cheever used to swear by them. He'd say, "If it wasn't for all those people writing me, I'm not sure that I would have the strength to do it anymore."

Do you respond to your mail?
As much as possible I do. I'm getting older, it's harder to do. I don't have the strength.

Do you get letters from prisoners, strike up any relationship as Norman Mailer did with John Abbott?
I've sometimes received letters from extraordinary prisoners, yes. But I don't try to get them released.

What about women? Does a novelist like yourself have literary groupies?
They do send pictures of themselves, often seductive.

Has it ever led to anything?
No, I've never tried it. I might have done better than I actually did.

Having married five times, you actually did quite a bit. What do you make of the institution of marriage and what have you learned about it that you can pass on to your grandchildren?
You should have asked me this serious question at first, when I was full of piss and vinegar. I learned that the sexual revolution is a very bloody affair, like most revolutions.

Divorces can be costly—to the soul and the pocket. Are the divorce laws fair?

I had one big lawsuit relating to a divorce. Let me put it this way: I never yet saw a judge on the bench whom I would trust to condemn a man to death, that's one of my arguments against capital punishment. I don't think that these people are humanly qualified very often to decide these legal questions or to interpret the law.

Were your marriages ever relationships where you loved too much . . . or not enough?

Most questions about marriage and love are silly. There are no formulas that I have to offer about love and marriage. They wouldn't be worth printing and they certainly aren't worth giving.

You have three sons from three of your marriages, has it been difficult for them?

Undoubtedly.

Any resentments by them, having you as their father?

Yeah, I guess so. However, let's get on with this.

Back to women then. Are there differences between the sexes?

There are ways of seeing the world that are distinctly feminine. Males have to learn about those.

Joyce Carol Oates has said that she couldn't think of many of her male colleagues who've written compellingly or convincingly about women. She cited you, Faulkner, Melville, and Shakespeare as great writers who never created any women characters of great depth. What writers have best captured the way a woman thinks and feels?

It's a question you should address to a lady, since evidently I'm down here as not a misogynist but as somebody who's missed the boat on the other sex. Is this for your lady readers—a sort of sop to throw them another victim? Somebody else to hate?

It's one thing to write about women in a time when women are happy to read about themselves, it's another thing in an ideological age when women read you in order to see whether you measure up ideologically to their standard.

John Gardner called you a male chauvinist pig. Are you?
What should I say, that I'm not a pig? There's an old Irish gag from Chicago that went: "Mike said you wasn't fit to live with pigs. But I stood up for you, I said you was." Why should I defend myself against charges by John Gardner or anybody else? They may well have been wrong. I never asked them to stand up to my charges.

Why do interviewers ask people questions that they wouldn't ask their neighbor for fear of being punched in the nose? Like "Why are your bowel movements such a strange color?" Or, "Why do you piss through your ears?" Some of these things, it's "Let's you and him fight." "So-and-so said about you the following, and what have you got to say?" I'm not responsible for what so-and-so said about me. I don't mind obliging you, I just don't like being put through the shredder.

In *More Die of Heartbreak* you write about a pain schedule one deals with toward the end of a life, and the hardest item of all has to do with love. You pose the question: "If love cuts them up so much, and you see the ravages everywhere, why not be sensible and sign off early?" Why not?
Well, why not? My challenge is to be very funny about these serious questions.

Why do so many people die of heartbreak?
They don't even know that their hearts are breaking. Might be a death, might be a disappointment. Might be a realization that one has made mistakes deep enough to split your life up or it may be just a hankering at something hardly realized or an objective that has now become hopeless, that you have no hope of reaching. All kinds of reasons why people die of that sort of disappointment.

Is monogamy a natural state for people, now that our life expectancies reach into the seventies?

The sexual revolution has made love virtually impossible because it destroyed the special status that love had enjoyed in our society for centuries. Of course, it was going downhill since the time of Rousseau anyhow—Rousseau described it as an illusion which the imagination *should* sustain and develop. The fact is, we become interchangeable, like commodities: you don't like the shoes you bought, you can return them and get a new pair. When once this element of consumerism appeared in the relations between men and women, it was over, for all intents and purposes, because there would always be comparisons made and there would always be efforts to improve on your original purchase. But love has become a consumerist phenomenon because we judge people as we judge commodities—we can do better, or we can get another one. We can always replace what's lost.

Salman Rushdie said in *Playboy* "at this moment in history the whole area of communication between the sexes is so fucked up." Do you feel that way?

That's what I'm saying. I'm blaming it on the sexual revolution. Look at the French Revolution in 1789—it was famous not just for Liberty, Fraternity, and Equality but by the time it got to 1793 it was the Reign of Terror, they were chopping each other's heads off. Well, the sexual revolution never had any 1789, it's had nothing except 1793, a Reign of Terror.

Do you think AIDS is part of that terror?

If I believed in God I would say that this is God's way of restoring the seriousness to the sexual connections. Because AIDS is a phenomenon that comes from promiscuity, which is wider among homosexuals than among heterosexuals.

Do you think it's God's way of thinning the population, the way wars have done in the past?

If He wanted to thin the population why did He start with homosexuals? They're the ones least likely to reproduce.

You said if you believed in God—meaning, you don't?
I don't really know what to think. I know what I thought about Him when I was a child—I had an image of God which over the years turned out to be the image of my big brother. He parted his hair in the middle and he had a round, moony sort of face, and he was not really benevolent.

Harold Bloom noted in *The Western Canon* that Kafka shared his unbelief in God with Freud, Woolf, Joyce, Beckett, Proust, Borges, and Neruda.
Harold Bloom has one of these souls that began to whither under the influence of too much education. He probably is the most overeducated person I've ever had anything to do with, and I don't say this only because he omitted all mention of me from his book.

He didn't completely ignore you—he included three of your novels—*Seize the Day*, *Augie March*, and *Herzog*—among those which deserved preserving.
Oh really? You see, that's what's wrong with people who imitate Moses the Lawgiver. He made room for everybody.

Can you find solace in a belief in God?
I'm not even asking for solace. I'm only asking for a certain kind of coherence in the deeper sense. First of all, that on this earth there is not nothing, but something. You and I are sitting here. If pushed we could give an account for the reasons why we are here. But ultimately it's too serious for either you or me to explain. It exceeds all explanation.

You've said in 1979 that modern literature has not dealt confidently with the intimations of the far side. "In Eastern Europe, people still talk about a spiritual life. We in the West

haven't gotten it." With all the recent books on angels and prophecies, has that changed at all?

I don't know whether it's changed or not. But when something like that happens in the United States it becomes a movement and it's very hard to distinguish the motive of the people who join the movement. Because they have prepared texts and they have gurus and they're not satisfied with intonations, they go directly to some doctrine.

In *Humboldt's Gift* you wrote: "We occupy a point within a great hierarchy that goes far far beyond ourselves." And in *Henderson the Rain King* you pose the question: "Do you think the world is nothing but an egg and we are here to set upon it? First come the phenomena. Utterly above all else." What phenomena are you talking about?

Very early in life I had sensations that never went away. It started almost before I could think. I sensed that I'd never been here before, and I also sensed that I would never be here again. And in the interim there were all these miraculous phenomena. The people to look at and to hear and see were extraordinary. I felt that they contained meanings that I was challenged to interpret. I never felt that I was getting anywhere as I grew older, but I really do think that my writing had something to do with that.

Would you call those early sensations a mystical experience?

I didn't see it as a mystical experience. I saw it as concrete. It was the extraordinary specificity of things that intrigued me.

And not the sense that in some past life you were really an Indian holy man or an English con artist?

No, because that would have included a doctrine of immortality. I didn't have any such thing as a child.

And now as a man, have you thought about an afterlife, immortality?

I think about those things all the time. There is nothing in death that science can tell you about with certainty. I find pretty good support in Plato because Socrates said it very clearly in the *Dialogues:* Either there is a life after death or there is none. If there is none then you go back to the state that you were in before you were born, oblivion. So it's either oblivion or immortality.

What's your intuition: oblivion or immortality?
My intuition is immortality. No argument can be made for it, but it's just as likely as oblivion.

If you could come back as something else, what would that be?
I haven't the slightest idea. I think of life as a course of instruction and education and I think of the soul as a student coming back time after time. So life is just a graduate study program. [*Laughs*]

In *Mr. Sammler's Planet,* Sammler categorizes people who threaten him into various animals. If you were to describe yourself as an animal, what would it be?
An orangutan. I like the idea of being an arboreal animal, hanging by my tail, eating a banana. Reminds me of a limerick:

> *There was a young man from Dundee*
> *who buggered an ape in a tree;*
> *The results were most horrid,*
> *all ass and no forehead,*
> *blue balls and a purple goatee.*

How many limericks do you know?
Oh, a lot of them.

Do you remember your short poem about a Polish girl which Mark Harris mentioned in his book about you but never quoted?
That's the one John Berryman fell in love with:

You can biff me, you can bang me,
but get it you'll never.
Think because I'm a Polish girl
   I fuck?
Kiss my ass, that's what you are.

Since we're back to young ladies, in *Henderson* you wrote: "She may have been a hot lay once, but among great beauties that is rare." Why is great sex rare with beautiful women?
Because great beauties tend to be very narcissistic. They don't give themselves freely because they're much too valuable.

Speaking of valuable, Mr. Sammler had a disdain for the rich, who were "usually mean." Are the rich any different from the rest of us?
It's an interesting subject. Fitzgerald said the rich are different, and Hemingway said they have more money. I can tell you what I think but I doubt that it will make much sense unless I wrote a whole chapter about it. There is an event in history called the Enlightenment, and the Enlightenment philosophers argued that man could make a heaven on earth and that man would devote the next centuries to conquering and overcoming nature. Well, the last few centuries *have* been devoted to the conquest of nature. And we've done a hell of a job, we really have in so many ways subdued the natural world. And through high tech we're transforming everything. We've transformed human life so that it doesn't begin to resemble what it used to be. And all the fairy tales of the past have come true. People read about them in the *Arabian Nights:* flying through the air, hearing voices from far away, being in two places at once, extraordinary events in exotic settings. All available to people now. And they don't really know how it happens. They push a button and get light, they turn a tap and get water—never happened before. Bread, which was the cause of so much suffering and famine and wars, is now super available in cheap forms. All of the basic commodities are very cheap, they're almost like free commodities, and the world has been totally transformed by them. The mean-

ing of everything has changed with this. We're getting near the place where pretty soon people are not going to have to do anything at all.

Whether people are aware of it or not, they really do live among tangible miracles and life has a miraculous character and nobody really understands it, but everybody presumes that it can be explained. So we are like primitive people feeling both the delight and dread of all those strange kinds of novelties. The earth has shrunk. We can go anywhere. You could make the mental decision to go to Buenos Aires tomorrow at 4 P.M. and it's pretty easy to do. So all these things that used to be impossible are now possible. Strangely possible. And the whole character of life has been altered. How much difference is there between the guy on welfare driving an old Cadillac and the rich man in the suburbs driving a Lexus? It's not all that much different, really. All this mobile luxury and comfort is now available on a fairly large scale. I don't really know what it means but I can see that it's happened. The conquest of nature has actually occurred to a pretty considerable extent, short of death, with unusual longevity and unusual rates of survival.

It's different, everything is different. Only our souls have not assimilated. We spend our time enjoying it and being comfortable in it. So the privileges of the rich . . . you go back and see how they lived three centuries ago and visit their estates, you wonder how they put up with so much discomfort, how they could bring themselves to put their behinds down on such cold carriage seats and the rest of that. That's no longer necessary. Except at Oxford.

So . . . how do you distinguish the rich from the masses today?
The rich really experience boredom because they prepare themselves all too well for what no human really knows how to do. You go down to Florida and you visit around and you see enormous wealth and all these resources and you feel nothing but boredom. Those beautiful golf courses resemble cemeteries all too much. People really don't know what to do with themselves. When you see a young Forbes running for president you can't help but think that his father was one of these multimillionaires who threw these lavish parties in North

Africa and brought everybody there by Concord. It doesn't mean anything anymore. What this great wealth does is to test the limits of meaning and experience meaninglessness, because what can you do actually with this wealth?

What has money meant to you?
I haven't got all that much money. I was married too many times to have much money.

Truman Capote once observed that what makes the rich different is that they eat tiny fresh vegetables and meats that are nearly unborn.
Truman hated me.

Why?
I don't know enough about homosexual psychology to be able to explain it. When I first knew Truman Capote he was a charming little boy whom I met in Richard Wright's Paris apartment. He didn't have any axe to grind then, though he monopolized the conversation talking about his society friends and his closeness to the House of Windsor and so on. But later on, he looked like a little shrunken Sidney Greenstreet and he was vicious about me.

He didn't think you deserved the Nobel Prize.
Maybe I didn't deserve the Nobel Prize, but it's a cinch he didn't even deserve the Pulitzer. I can't see what Truman deserved at all, except a kick in the ass.

He felt he created something new with *In Cold Blood*, the nonfiction novel.
I wasn't bowled over. And his early books were just Southern faded fabrics, that's all.

The stories he published in his uncompleted *Answered Prayers* certainly created a stir.

I read them. There was one story which he said Jews ought to be stuffed and put in museums. [*Laughs*] That's where it is: that's where the little fairies like that really belong, in Auschwitz on the General's staff; in the Auschwitz barracks with a swagger stick.

Capote thought that *Answered Prayers* would kill any chance he had of winning any great literary prize. Did the Nobel Prize mean a great deal to you?
I didn't give a hoot about it one way or the other. I don't exist for that sort of thing and I was very careful to see that it didn't affect my life too much.

How can it not?
It's just a prize, like any other. Proust didn't get it, or Tolstoy, Joyce. So it isn't as though you were in the royal line and you went to Stockholm for the coronation.

Is it really more of a political prize, each year given to a writer from a different part of the world?
There's a certain amount of politics connected with it.

Is there a downside to having won the prize?
Yes, people feel that you are a public functionary, that you have to produce a certain amount of cultural shrubbery on God's little acre. [*Laughs*]

So it didn't affect the way you write?
Not at all.

You said once that it's better to write a marvelous book than to get the Nobel Prize. Don't you have to write at least one marvelous book to get the prize?
I can think of writers who didn't write marvelous books and got the prize. But don't push me because I don't want to make more enemies than I already have.

Norman Mailer's been campaigning for it for years; think he should get it?

Well, I'd give it to him . . . if he had anything to trade. [*Laughs*]

You're already on record for saying that writers seldom wish other writers well. Did winning the Nobel widen the gulf between you and your peers?

I suppose that was Truman's problem. Maybe even Gore Vidal's problem. Gore never mentions me without treating my head like an ashtray, flicking his cigarette on it.

Hold on, Vidal said in *Palimpsest* that, with the exception of you, his "celebrated contemporaries all seem to have stopped learning in their twenties."

Well, that's true. But I looked up some of the references in his last book and they were not as kind as all that. He can't resist putting me down.

Is Vidal a better nonfiction or fiction writer?

His novels lack originality, his essays are much more interesting. Gore Vidal is a good writer, he's just not as good as he thinks he is. I often thought of Gore as a patrician who got trapped among plebeians and somehow he was condemned by his sexual preferences to live a level or two beneath the station to which he's entitled. And he's always resented it a great deal, he doesn't see why homosexuals should not also be the aristocrats. Well, he's right about that. He also thinks of himself as a great historical and social prophet and there I think he exaggerates quite a lot because his insights are really not as smashing as he seems to think that they are.

Do you read any of the younger generation of writers, like David Foster Wallace, William Vollmann, T. C. Boyle?

I've read a little of Boyle. I rather like him. There's this terrific, *mishuga* young American writer named Denis Johnson, who wrote *Resuscitation of a Hanged Man*.

**How about Don DeLillo, Cormac McCarthy, Joyce Carol Oates—
are they Nobel worthy?**

I like Don DeLillo, he's often very amusing and penetrating. And I
like McCarthy very much, grim as all get out—though I didn't like *All
the Pretty Horses* so well because it was a little more conventional. Joyce
Carol Oates offends people by being so prolific which is the wrong
reason to offend. On the whole, I'm for her, she's a very good writer. I
read again recently James Dickey's *Deliverance* and was knocked over
by it. It's one of the finest books of that generation of writers.

Did you ever see the movie?

No, I avoid movies based on novels that I like a lot, because I don't
like them to be damaged. I don't know how many times I've seen
films of *Anna Karenina* and they grow worse with every decade. The
fact that *Anna Karenina* has survived all these movies and is still infi-
nitely greater than any of them gives me hope.

**Back to future Nobel laureates: What about John Updike or
Philip Roth?**

I could see Philip Roth, he's a little buggy now and then, but a very
gifted writer.

And someone eight years your senior, James A. Michener?

I would rather see him get it than Toni Morrison, but I don't want to
get into that. I'm not here to give prizes.

**Geoffrey Wolff has written about how many writers drink and
how many are drunks and alcoholics, listing Fitzgerald, London,
Crane, Thomas Wolfe, Hammett, Capote, Williams, Berryman,
Lardner, Parker, O'Hara, Kerouac, Poe, Thurber, et cetera. He
also pointed out that five American Nobel Prize winners had the
problem: O'Neill, Faulkner, Steinbeck, Hemingway, and Sinclair
Lewis. How did you escape it?**

When we were in Canada my old man was a bootlegger. He had a still
and we used to go out there. I was just a little kid. Once he forgot the

keys, so he had to climb over the fence, and he'd get inside and pour some of the booze into a dish and set it afire. If it didn't all burn out and there was any fluid left in the bottom that wasn't fit to sell, he'd make me taste it. I don't know, I just got my intoxication out of reading poetry. I found *Macbeth* intoxicating.

Whose ideas in this century have intoxicated you? You've said that "There are only a few big ideas. I can think of only a very small handful of people in the twentieth century who were truly original." Who are they?

I think Kafka was truly original. Proust. Joyce. Probably Heidegger, although I don't care for him. Certain of our scientists, like Richard Feynman, who must have been a genuine original. Picasso was a real original. Matisse also. Hemingway. John Berryman. Eugene O'Neill.

What about Tennessee Williams?

No, I don't think so. He was cut from a cloth that you see quite a lot of.

Arthur Miller?

No.

Sigmund Freud?

I'm quite puzzled by Freud, I don't really think all that much of him. First of all, his literary influence isn't very clear to me, he is derivative, in a way. Secondly, Freud needed a theory of dreams so he dreamt all the dreams himself. He went into business using himself as stock. He was a Jewish businessman, whatever he needed he made at home. He was a home industry. He was extremely ingenious, obviously a man of great gifts. But then he narrowed everything down to his own explanations, with the erotic as the root. It's not erotic in the great sense in which Plato and Socrates had an Eros. Freud's Eros is much narrower and it's biologically determined. It's instinctual with us to have the Oedipus complex, you have it whether you wish it or not; so, in a way, you're sentenced and Freud sentences you from the bench to manifest these deep, vital motives which are all sexual in character and you can't get away from that. I don't like to be boxed in like that. It's *chutzpah* on his part.

Would you include Irving Berlin among the century's originals?
I love Irving Berlin, but I don't think of him as an artist at all, I think of him as an entertainer for the masses and at that he was very good.

Same with George Gershwin?
I like Gershwin but he doesn't stir or move my soul to awe.

Do any twentieth-century musicians or composers?
Dmitry Shostakovich. Igor Stravinsky sometimes.

Not the Beatles, or Elvis, or Barbra Streisand?
That's pop stuff. It's very good, charming, but pop is pop.

Can a pop master like Andy Warhol ever reach the status of a Matisse?
Well, Warhol is no longer here to sign tin cans. I don't know—I haven't seen all the tin cans assembled yet.

How about the Wright Brothers?
Yes, obviously men of genius. I think William James was a man of genius.

What about his brother, Henry?
He was an extraordinary writer, but he didn't have the same scope as William.

Bill Gates?
That's technical stuff.

Laurence Olivier?

Olivier was a great actor, he could do anything. I once saw Olivier doing Dreiser's *Sister Carrie*. He played the American hotel manager just like an American, you couldn't have distinguished him from any other Chicagoan at that time—absolutely an extraordinary performance. I thought he made a lousy Othello because he imported certain gimmicks—a laugh of despair in which Othello stuck out his tongue. He would have done better with his mouth shut.

That's what some people say about Marlon Brando.
Have you ever seen Marlon Brando playing Marc Antony in *Julius Caesar?* Doesn't make it.

What did you think of Brando's comment that the Jews run Hollywood and that they never allowed the image of the "kike" to reach the screen?
Well, I never thought he was a great thinker or a first-class philosophical character. I was a little surprised that he could be so foolish. Most people are much better at concealing their anti-Semitism than Marlon Brando. Anti-Semitism is extremely common; if you're still being shocked at the age of eighty by the random expressions of anti-Semitic views there's something wrong with you. In a century where we experienced the Holocaust and two world wars, shock is a little more difficult to find. I don't expect very much from a person like Marlon Brando. Why would I be shocked, because he appeared in *On the Waterfront?* He had a script.

Were you shocked over the Oklahoma bombing and the incarceration of those young men, Timothy McVeigh and Terry Nichols?
They're macho types, imaginary pioneers, militants, fighters in the cause of freedom, but really their minds have been poisoned by all kinds of ideological marijuana. There have always been these know-nothing movements in this country. I'm reading the life of Lincoln now and he obviously had to deal with it then.

In *Herzog* you described Moses Herzog as a person in a very agitated and almost mad state who is resisting everything, including his own intellectual life. That description could also apply to Ted Kaczynski, the Unabomber.

Maybe so, but having read Kaczynski's manuscript in the newspapers I would place him intellectually about 170 degrees vertically below Herzog. He just didn't have a mental life worth mentioning. It just shows how you could be a brilliant mathematician and otherwise be a high-IQ moron, which is how I see him.

Was there anything in his manifesto regarding the dangers of technology that struck you as accurate?

Of course technology is a very severe and serious problem, but to go into business as a private Luddite who mails bombs to people you dislike seems to me a pretty stupid way to deal with the problems of high technology.

Did it surprise you that he was once a professor at a university?

I don't put anything past professors, but what struck me most of all is that he was a professor of mathematics. Which means that as a mathematician you can be very brilliant without really qualifying on the elementary level for membership in the species.

In *The Dean's December* you said that it was a protest about the dehumanization of the blacks in big cities. What can be done about approaching that problem correctly?

The first important step is an accurate description of what is happening in the slums. Not the kind of baloney that one reads in the newspapers and in books. Somebody ought to seriously chronicle what is really happening there. Then you begin to think about it, you don't just throw money at it, and you don't announce as you face the problem that you're a person of good will and you want the best to happen for everybody and that you think welfare is better than workfare or whatever you think. But people are not really serious in the consideration of these problems, they just treat them as newspaper or TV issues which they discuss over dinner tables, they don't know what's really happening in the slums.

Do you feel we ever will?

I don't know, I'm not a prophet, I'm just a describer.

You've said that the blacks look like a doomed population to you.

They have the highest death by murder, homicide rate. They are the largest population in prisons on violent crimes and criminal charges. It's a terrible problem.

Where is there hope?

I'm a Bulls fan. After jazz, basketball is the greatest gift of the Negroes to the art of this country. I think of Michael Jordan and Scottie Pippin as great artists.

Ralph Ellison, another great artist who wrote *Invisible Man*, was a friend of yours. He never published another novel in his lifetime—do you know why?

We never discussed it. I felt he was having trouble enough without my prying into it, it would only irritate him. I had too much respect for him to push for answers to such questions, answers that possibly he didn't have himself. I didn't see much of Ralph the last twenty years of his life, so our intimacy stopped in the sixties.

We haven't touched on your own writing methods. Is it true that you rewrote *Herzog* twenty-five times?

Yes, but that was unusual. The reason is that the first chapter was the foundation and I couldn't make alterations later without shaking the whole structure, so I had to go back to the beginning each time. *The Victim* and *Dangling Man* were quite short books so they didn't present as many problems. *The Adventures of Augie March* was a long book, but it was very loosely organized so when I rewrote I didn't have to do it from the beginning. The reason why *Herzog* was rewritten so many

times was that I had to get rid of all the personal references. I just
didn't want them there. I know that it is viewed as an autobiographical book, but it's selectively autobiographical; it has very little to do
with the reality of my existence.

**Would you say that it's true of most novels, that they are
autobiographical?**
[Alberto] Moravia used to say that every novel was a form of higher
autobiography, but that doesn't mean that there's any one-to-one relation between the facts and the facts about your own life. In fact
nothing would be harder to write than a real autobiography.

Why? Because we can't face ourselves?
No, the point is much simpler. The novel is highly stylized. To be literally accurate about your life is to break through the stylization. A
novel has an aesthetic dress which may be good for some higher
truths that you're concerned with. Literal truth has very little to do
with it. The first paragraph, the opening pages of a novel usually set
the key, the tone for everything and establish a style for the behavior
of the characters and for the language in which they think. That's
why being literally truthful would be a daunting thing.

**But isn't it possible to set a stylistic tone that can work for a work
about oneself?**
I read Rousseau's autobiography recently. He was much more interested in the phenomenon called *sincerity*. He invented romantic sincerity, which was being rigorously truthful with yourself. It's not the
same as writing a novel. It is getting out all of the facts about your
life, including the very worst ones, and then showing how to live with
those terrible facts. That's not the objective of the novelist.

**Your pal Gore Vidal noted in his recent memoir that you were
one of the few novelists who managed to turn the events in your
life into art, "not the easiest task for someone writing in the
American realistic manner."**

Modern writers know well enough how badly writers who use their own lives as novelistic material get caught in various binds and would have been better off being less autobiographical. Tolstoy, for instance, writing about Levin in *Anna Karenina.* It's quite clear from recurrent themes in his life, like the temptation of suicide, who he's writing about, and it's far from the most successful part of the book. In fact, I couldn't bear to read an entire book about Levin, I would have thrown it away.

There have been quite a number of critical and biographical books about you; what do you think about being the subject of them, especially the more intimate ones by Mark Harris, Ruth Miller, and James Atlas?
It depends on the biographer. You have to judge as to whether the person writing the book is up to the job. Very often the person is not, in which case it's just an embarrassment. I have no comment yet on James Atlas. Mark Harris's book was more or less a joke, he meant it to be a friendly gag. Ruth Miller I couldn't read because it just went against the grain. I thought she didn't understand the subject very well. Secondly, she misunderstood the things that I said to her. There was no real communication between us. I also think biographies shouldn't be written until the subject is dead.

And when you're gone and the movie is made of your life, who should play you?
The archangel Michael. [*Laughs*]

Well, while we still have you around there are still more questions I'd like to ask. You've written about all sorts of victims; have you ever felt yourself to be one?
No, I don't feel myself to be a victim at all. I feel myself to be a winner, I always did. I was interested in victims as a subject.

Is evil more inherent in our characters than good?

You could read those pages in Thomas Hobbes's *Leviathan* in which he describes the human being in the state of nature: solitary, poor, nasty, brutish, and short—that was his view. I don't say that it's my view, but it is a prevailing view of mankind in our time.

Is it accurate to say that you imitated Rilke's *Journal of My Other Self* when you wrote *Dangling Man*; Dostoyevsky's *The Eternal Husband* when you wrote *The Victim*; and that Sherwood Anderson influenced *Augie March*?
No, I didn't imitate Rilke, I was very stirred by that book, it had a great effect on me and I thought I would write something in that manner. So I did. Dostoyevsky—yeah, I thought I might be able to use that plot to my own ends and in a way I did, there are similarities, but unfortunately, not similar enough. Sherwood Anderson had nothing to do with *The Adventures of Augie March* except what I might have been thinking about is that "Gee whiz, I'm just a naive kid" attitude. And he overdid it.

Are there any other influences for your other books?
No, I don't think so.

Are you glad to have lived at this time, or would you have preferred another time in history?
You have to take what you can get, not to make demands. That's what's so striking about Norman Mailer. That he sprang from his mother's womb with two fists filled with demands and requirements for what life was going to be.

What were the demands made of you back in 1970 when you were shouted off the stage at San Francisco State College?
There was a Mexican guy who had written a book and he stood up and denounced me. He said, "What do you want to listen to this old man for? His balls are dried up, he can't come, he's absolutely of no interest." I didn't know what to say, except, "I didn't thrust myself

upon you, I came here because I was invited to speak to you." They
booed me.

Your silence was their loss.
There's one thing I do know: When I'm tempted to say something
and I don't say it, I feel all the better for it. I feel I've gotten stronger.

**J. D. Salinger must feel like Superman—he's kept quiet for three
decades. In 1960 Philip Roth called J. D. Salinger the writer of the
age, because he didn't turn his back on the times. Do you have
any insight into why he turned silent?**
I don't know Salinger. I always liked his books, he's a very good
writer. I don't know why he became so embittered as to turn into a
hermit. I can understand it. I can even somewhat sympathize with it.
It's better not to be doing what you and I are doing here. From my
point of view.

From my point of view, however . . .
Right. I'm a public commodity. I'm listed on the AMEX.

**Commodities are what sell. What did you think of Sotheby's
auction of Jackie Onassis's estate?**
That was a travesty.

You mean you wouldn't pay $770,000 for Kennedy's golf woods?
I'm afraid not. I was not impressed by Kennedy. He was a charming
man, very intelligent, but he was no president. Besides, his father had
bought the office for him. And I don't see why, in a country as sensitive about plutocrats as this one, they should have cheered when he
became president.

Bill Clinton's a great admirer of JFK.
I don't think Clinton is anything like a president of this country. He
is a yuppie, a playboy. He's not serious, he's basically unserious. I
don't even know why he wants to be there.

Perhaps because he has a sense of history and feels he's a better alternative than Bob Dole?

If he has a sense of history he should clear out and let the job go to a man who knows what to do with it. Dole is not my idea of a great president, though at least he would take the business of government seriously. Dole does not inspire me with towering emotions. He is a very quiet person, he's not a backroom politician, he's a committee room guy, he's not used to public exposure. Clinton is far better with the public than Dole can ever be. Dole has no instinct for it. And television has made that now a requirement: some kind of showman should be the candidate. When Reagan ran against Carter that became obvious. It had to be somebody in show biz. Carter was really incapable of anything. Carter proved that the country doesn't need a president, and does just as well with a nonentity.

Have there been any postwar presidents who have impressed you?

I was impressed with Truman. And, in some ways, by Eisenhower.

Let's turn to literary politics. Is there a literary Establishment today?

No. There are poor shreds of it at the *New York Review of Each Other's Books.*

Norman Mailer said that William Burroughs changed the course of American literature. Oates said it was Walt Whitman who did that. What do you say?

If I have to choose between Walt Whitman and William Burroughs, I'm not going to choose Burroughs.

What did you think about Iran's fatwa on Salman Rushdie?

I thought it was horrendous, of course. But I also thought that since Rushdie had so westernized himself that he seems to have convinced himself, as so many writers do and have done since the twenties, since the time of *Ulysses,* that anything could be said in a novel and be accepted. If Joyce could treat the Catholic Church slightingly then

Rushdie thought that he could do the same with Islam. He felt that he was going to do with Islam what Joyce had done with Catholicism. He was wrong. Which means that he had lost touch with Islam and had become so thoroughly westernized that he didn't recognize that this was apt or likely to happen. Maybe it was inevitable. . . .

In 1995 Nigerian writer Ken Saro-Wiwa was executed. Rushdie observed that "all over the world, writers are being thrown in jail. They mysteriously die in police custody. It is open season on writers and it must stop." In America will it ever be dangerous to be a writer?

No. They may knock us to the ropes once in a while and give us a rabbit punch to the kidneys, but nobody takes us seriously enough to kill us.

RAY BRADBURY

The Skull Behind the Flesh

BRADBURY. MEN ON MARS. THE DINOSAUR WHO FELL IN love with a lighthouse. The otherworldly mushrooms that came in the mail and grew in your basement. The burning of books, the illustrated man, the ghosts of Poe and Shaw. The script of *Moby-Dick*.

He can sit on his couch in the living room of his home in Cheviot Hills in Los Angeles surrounded by the paintings that have appeared as covers on his paperback books, or at his basement desk where Mexican Indian masks hang from low overhead wooden beams, or at his overcrowded office overlooking Wilshire Boulevard where he works from 9 A.M. until 1 P.M., refusing ever to write under artificial light, and tell you with a completely straight face that some story he wrote is totally original and new in the entire history of literature. And you look back at him and ask yourself, Is he kidding? But you don't call him on it because you can see he's not. And you excuse him his hyperbole because he's been making such claims all his adult life. He gets away with it because he always articulates the case he's championing, punctuating his exuberant speech with examples from his own work, and talking with the force of a self-educated man who has been right more often than he's been wrong.

Bradbury has early childhood memories of picking Burns and Allen radio scripts from the garbage outside the CBS radio stu-

61

dios in Hollywood; even earlier ones of climbing trees and swinging from branch to branch in Waukegan, Illinois, where he was born in 1920 and where so many of his stories are set. Not one to hide his influences, his stories echo with homages to Edgar Allan Poe, Herman Melville, George Bernard Shaw, Shakespeare. He learned how to plot stories by reading comic strips. He developed his visual descriptive sense by cutting out photographs in magazines and writing poetry to match the pictures.

When he was twelve his family moved to Tucson, Arizona, for a year and Bradbury spent endless hours listening to the radio, imagining himself broadcasting stories one day like those he was hearing—Buck Rogers, Chandu the Magician. He even went to the local radio station and offered his services. "I hung around every night for two weeks," he recalls, "ran out for newspapers, emptied ashtrays . . . and it worked! Two weeks later I was on the radio reading the comics to the kiddies every Saturday night." A singular accomplishment for a twelve-year-old—but a good indication of what makes Bradbury run. No one's ever convinced him to slow down.

He's written novels, short stories, poems, plays, children's books, song lyrics, librettos, TV scripts, movies. *The Illustrated Man* starred Rod Steiger. François Truffaut directed *Fahrenheit 451*. John Huston directed his adaptation of *Moby-Dick*. Alfred Hitchcock presented some of his chilling tales on TV.

The Martian Chronicles made him famous in 1949, and when *Life* magazine commissioned him to write about the Apollo project before the first moon landing twenty years later, Bradbury sat quietly in the back of a briefing room filled with sixty astronauts. When it was mentioned that he was sitting there, "forty percent of the astronauts jumped an inch in their seats," according to Bradbury. He was the physical embodiment of all their dreams. When the briefing was over they surrounded him and many of them spent much of that night talking with him at the home of John Glenn. By the time the Apollo mission was over, a crater on the moon was named after one of his books.

When NASA was about to launch the Viking space shot to Mars, writer Harlan Ellison suggested to the scientists at the Jet Propulsion Laboratory in Pasadena that they hire Bradbury to publicize it. "Pay him whatever he wants," Ellison said, "five thousand, fifty thousand, whatever it takes to get him. He'll bring tears to the public's eyes, he'll make it sound like the greatest adventure in the history of mankind. Because he believes it. He's the greatest optimist in the world. And he's needed because of that."

Though he's never driven a car and his fear of flying has kept him from being a world traveler, in Los Angeles Bradbury is known as a crusader of the possible. He often lectures high school and college students on how to make a better future. He speaks to futurists on how not to forget the past and present. He consults with architects and city planners on how to turn cities into parks and rebuild communities more feasible for living. And during the annual UCLA/*Los Angeles Times* Festival of Books, he is the writer with the longest line of fans cradling copies of his books to be signed.

Do you have any idea how many stories you've written?

Oh God, I don't know. Millions and millions of words. Two or three thousand short stories; I've published around five hundred. Plus a couple of hundred articles. I've lost track.

Among these millions of words, do you have favorites?

My favorite novel is *Something Wicked This Way Comes*. It's sort of a metaphor for all of life. I didn't realize I was cramming so much into it. Being born, growing up, growing old, sickening, dying—all the metaphors are there to elate and terrify you. My father is the hero of the book. He died in the late 1950s but he still lives in the book, so I like to go back and browse through and find him. It's a very important book for me because of my love for my dad.

Have you always written what you wanted to write?

Always. You can never put yourself there; you must always be there, so no one ever controls you, you're in control of your own destiny, you do always what you want to do, starting when you're twelve. I've never been money-oriented and I've never cared about money. I get it as a reward for doing good work.

When you were young, did you see yourself where you are now?
No, I don't think I imagined I would be as fortunate as I have been. You go through a period for ten years or so when you're dreadfully bad. I started writing when I was twelve. From twelve to twenty-two, all that was bad writing. But if you love writing, it doesn't make any difference, it's a way of learning. And you don't mind; you can't see how bad you are, or you're glad you had enough brains to fall in love and do it at all.

How did you deal with early rejections?
You have to feel the editors are idiots or misconceived. We all do that. It's wrong, but it's a way of surviving. I try to teach young writers to say the same thing. You sit down at the typewriter again and do more work and try to get a body of work done so you can look at it and become your own teacher. If you do fifty-two short stories it's better than doing three, because you can't judge anything from three stories. It's very hard to write fifty-two stories in a row and have them all be bad. Almost impossible. The psychological benefits from my first sale, which I got no money for, had to last me for a year before I made my next sale. That year I sold two more stories and had a little extra residue of belief. But it wasn't until I was twenty-two I began to sell quite a few short stories, and most of those were at fifteen dollars apiece. When I was twenty-four I sold about forty short stories in one year to the various pulp magazines. I got thirty or forty dollars apiece, finally a halfway decent income. Must have made twelve hundred dollars that year. I thought I was rich.

When did you become financially secure?

In my early thirties. The day I got married I was twenty-seven and had around forty dollars in the bank. I gave ten dollars to the minister and he handed it back and said, "You're a writer, you need this more than I do." Then my wife worked for a couple of years and between us we made about seventy dollars a week. She got pregnant when I was twenty-nine and it scared the hell out of me. But God was watching. Went to New York that spring with eighty dollars and I sold *The Martian Chronicles* and *The Illustrated Man* to Doubleday for five hundred dollars apiece. Wow, a thousand bucks! I thought I was very rich. My income the next year went up to one hundred dollars a week.

Did you send many of your early novels around from publisher to publisher?

Sure. I wrote a children's book on how not to be afraid of the dark. See, I'd get it coming and going: I'd scare the hell out of them, then I'd write a book on how not to be afraid of the dark. It was called *Switch on the Night*. I sent it out for four years to anywhere from forty to seventy publishers. Nobody wanted it. Then around 1955 a big publisher wrote to me and said, "Hey, you don't happen to have a children's book somewhere, do you?" I got this thing out of my file and sent it to them and they published it. It's been in print ever since—it's been taught in schools, it's won prizes. So it's flukey and strange, children's books. Everything in the arts is crazy. You've got to get the right editor at the right time. And if that editor will go to bat for you and die for you, it gets published. Because a lot of horse trading goes on in a publishing company.

You've written that you lived a life from the age of three until thirty-three believing you were wrong about everything. What did you mean by that?

Doing everything that people told me not to do. Everyone told me not to do science fiction. People told me not to write in imitation of Edgar Allan Poe—who cares about horror stories? So I've had two ways of living in writing which everyone considered to be destructive for me, and I've proceeded to go on being wrong all that time. As a result, I have a reputation. So what I try to teach students is, for Christ's sake, be wrong, don't be right whatever you do. Because then you'll be following everyone else's wishes and molds for you and you'll wind up being an imitation of something that other people think is good for you. Other people can't help you. Actually, I had three ways of being wrong: poetry was one of them too. I wrote lousy poetry, really terrible, until I was forty-eight. Then it began to get good. I've done some poetry I'm very proud of, and I've done one or two that will be around a few years after I'm dead.

Which ones?

I think my poem "Remembrance," the first one in my book of poetry *When Elephants Last in the Dooryard Bloom*. Everyone I've talked to burst into tears when they finished that poem. I go back to my hometown and stand under a tree and I look up and remember when I was ten I used to climb up into that tree and leave notes in a squirrel's nest. So just for the hell of it, here I am, forty-eight years old, I climb up that tree and I find this note that I had put there when I was ten. I open it and it says: "I remember you, I remember you." Well, that's good stuff. It's the child remembering his old self.

Do you get accused of being a sentimentalist?

Oh sure, but people don't know what they mean by the word. Our society's afraid of emotion, which is a terrible thing. And I have to come in and undo all the bad work done by teachers and by fools who surround these people. Psychiatrists are in the world because of this sort of situation. If you don't know how to feel, how to live, then you need people either in some of the arts or directly, as friends or teachers like myself, to come and open you and lance the wound before it's too late. If you live the creative life, you never need a psychiatrist. I'm teaching people to cry. Men are so frozen. I've written a poem about crying in the shower. When my first daughter got married, I got into the shower that night and when the water hit me the tears just came flooding out. Wow, what a great thing—when you're done you're clean inside and out. But a lot of men don't know about this, so I've got to teach them. To touch, to laugh, to love one another, to kiss, to be real friends.

In an essay on "Machines & Storybooks," Saul Bellow wrote, "In the twentieth century writers are often educated men as well as creators, and in some the education prevails over the creation."
I don't believe anybody should ever go to college. What you get there is a bunch of professional intellectuals who are trying to impress you with how bright they are and what they've read and what they think about it, and other people's opinions are of no value. What's the use of learning what your professor read and why he read it? It's how you react to *War and Peace* or *Moby-Dick*.

When I got the job from John Huston to do the screenplay for *Moby Dick* in 1953, I arrived in Ireland and said, "What do you want? Are you a Freudian? A Jungian? Are you a Melville Society man?" He said, "I want Ray Bradbury's *Moby Dick*." I said, "Great, that's what you're going to get." Because I've got to feel the thing, I can't intellectualize about it. And immediately you're going to make all kinds of mistakes—it's all going to be wooden and artificial. You've got to get in there as Melville did. Melville fell in love with Shakespeare. I did a long poem about that: Shakespeare stood under his window one night and said, "O Lazarus, Herman Melville, truly come here forth," and he yanked Melville's soul right out of his body. And *Moby-Dick* was created on the spot, because Shakespeare was the midwife. No intellect. All the metaphors were automatic. Anytime Melville got self-conscious, he got wooden and it doesn't work. But where he's feeling, when he let Ahab and Shakespeare write for him—Shakespeare inside of Ahab—then, boy, you've got a big harpoon on the side of the whale and he's stabbing it and he's writing the novel on the side of the whale. Pure wonderful poetic emotion!

How many times have you read *Moby-Dick*?
That particular year I read it nine times, in order to get it into my bloodstream. Then, at the end of six months of reading the novel, I

got out of bed one morning in London and looked in the mirror and said, "I am Herman Melville." On that day I rewrote the last third of the script. It was pure emotion and it all came right.

Is *Moby Dick* your best-known screenplay?

I think so. When I finished it I was offered all kinds of screenplays to write. A lot I turned down because I just wanted to get back to my short stories and novels. I love films, there's no snobbery in me about it, but I knew I should build a career that would be stable in my first great loves. I was offered *War and Peace* by King Vidor, for the American production. But I've never been able to read it. I'm missing something, I know, but it's just not my taste.

What other movies have you written?

I did the screen story for *It Came From Outer Space,* which is still around. But that's awfully lightweight. It was my very first screen job. It was such a cliché: invaders from outer space. There's not much you can do with it. I did a thing called *The Picasso Summer* which the director tore up behind my back and shot a lot of ad lib through it. I'd gladly love to kill that man. I got him fired off the film. Got another director in to reshoot. But by that time they didn't have enough money left to do the job.

You're a big collector of comic books. Were they an early and ongoing influence on your imagination?

Yeah, and comic strips. *Buck Rogers* when I was nine, *Flash Gordon* when I was fourteen; *Prince Valiant* when I was seventeen. These are huge influences. They've helped me to become a very good writer, because I learned about plotting from them at a very young age, and seen a lot of movies, too. The two fields are almost identical and both grew up at the same time. Not enough comparisons have been made between the two.

What do you think of one critic's opinion, that you are "essentially a moralist who weaves fantastic fables as a commentary on modern man"?

This is where my kinship with Jules Verne shows. He was a writer of moral fables and he made you proud of mankind instead of shaming you. I think shame should be used very carefully and sparingly. Verne's ability was amazing: to challenge you, to say, "Hey, how about going around the world in 80 days? Why don't we try and see?" And you go around the world in 80 days and come out of the novel and the film, which is almost identical, with this wonderful feeling of, we did it! Or he says, "How'd you like to be a whole bunch of Robinson Crusoes? Go off to a mysterious island and survive?" "How'd you like to be Nemo and clear the seas of the armadas of the world? Teach people peace, quiet the blood on the waters?" Nemo is the other side of Ahab: Ahab's destructive, Nemo's constructive in his madness. I feel a huge kinship with the morality of that man, who did it without pontificating. He gave you examples, which is what Schweitzer was always talking about: no use talking if you don't provide an example.

What's your definition of science fiction?

Idea fiction. Almost all science fiction is the art of the obvious. It's nothing new at all. It's quite obvious during the last thirty years things like credit cards would come into our society and do what they've done. But nobody wanted to notice. It was obvious someday someone would invent a pill which would then shake and terrify the Catholic Church. So all we're doing—those of us who write on occasion in the field—is simply telling something that is already a cliché in our minds.

Science fiction is realistic fiction, always dealing with possible things; it's never impossible. Fantasy is the art of the impossible, where you walk people through walls or time travel. There's no way a man can jump out of a forty-story building without being killed. If he lands and stays alive, you're writing fantasy. Now, in a science-fiction story, you could have him jump out of a building and on his way down turn on his jet-propelled pack on his shoulders, which wasn't possible until the mid-sixties. We saw it in *Buck Rogers* when we were kids, but we didn't think we'd see it in our lifetime. Suddenly we've got the guys in their jet packs running about in the sky, defying gravity. The art of the obvious. Idea fiction.

If you go back in history and I'd been a teller of tales in the streets of Baghdad 2,000 years ago, I would have told an obvious thing: somewhere up ahead a man is going to invent a new science. What? The science of horsemanship, which did not exist in the world. And everyone would say, "Oh wow, that's not going to happen." Oh yes it is. "And what is he going to do with this art?" Well, the Persian horse is going to be developed with a rider on his back, and with this horse we will throw back the Roman Empire. And everyone will say, "Oh, that's never going to happen." And the science-fiction writer in the streets of Baghdad telling that tale would have been laughed at. He was the master of the obvious. The others were masters at ignoring the obvious. Nothing fantastic there at all; we saw it happen, the Persians pushed back the Roman Empire. That is science fiction.

It starts with Plato's *Republic,* in which you take an idea and squeeze it dry. What is a republic? How do you put it together? It doesn't exist right now, how do we build it? What are human beings? What is a man? A woman? A slave? What is money? Try to say what they are and how to use them better.

All philosophy is automatically science fiction: the science of thinking about things before they happen and trying to make them happen better. I predicted in 1950 if Bertrand Russell ever wrote stories they'd be science fiction; and that's exactly what he wrote. He turned out two books of short stories and they're all science fiction and fantasy. A philosopher can't stay away from us, because we're all in the same business.

So you're high on the future of the genre and its acceptance as literature?
It's going to dominate our fiction for the next tens of thousands of millions of years, because we're going to learn to respect it. It's going to move into the exact center of literature, where it belongs. Because there's nothing else to write about. That's been true for this century. Especially true since 1940, and fantastically true since the late sixties. Everything that happens in modern life has to do with the impact of some machine or device on changing our culture. Like I said, the

birth-control pill is a good example as a science-fiction device that didn't exist in 1965. Once it appeared though, it changed our culture, our art forms, the male-female relationship, politics, work habits, populations—my God! The changes of this one science-fictional device which, if you'd written about it in 1950, you couldn't have published it in the United States. The Catholic Church was that powerful here.

I sent stuff to science-fiction magazines in 1960 they wouldn't dream of printing. Stories about religion you couldn't publish if it in any way was innovative or dealt with any possible changes in religious thought.

How much prophecy is involved in science fiction?
That's never been my business. It's too easy, anyway. Anything that's too easy, I'm not interested in.

In one of your books there's a passage which says, "Science ran too far ahead of us . . . and the people got lost in a mechanical wilderness." Somewhere else you've written that science fiction is trying to relate man to the technical world he inhabits. That seems to be paradoxical.
It is. With our revolutionary background in every activity we've ever touched—electricity, communication, flying—we've revolutionized just about everything in the history of the world, and it's interesting to me that we Americans are not interested in paradox more, and in ideas. The literature we read up until the early sixties has been almost bankrupt of ideas. A man like Hemingway hardly had an idea in his life. It was always one idea: the male situation. It's good stuff, I love it, but he was not an idea man. Neither was Steinbeck or Faulkner. Fitzgerald came closer to being a kind of idea writer; he had wonderful insights into human personality and foibles, his notebooks are full of ideas.

Do you see yourself as a science-fiction writer?
I am a good part of the time. But then, I'm a magic realist. And I'm a disciple of Poe, which means I'm a horror fantasy writer. I'm inter-

ested in frightening myself on occasion, because part of life is very frightening. I get letters all the time from people who find solace in certain ways I have of approaching death. I did a story about my great-grandmother in *Dandelion Wine* who, one day when I was about two or three, decided just to go upstairs, go to bed, and die. She had had it with life. So I did a story about her, where she calls everyone in and says good-bye and then talks to me and says, "I'm not really dying because out under the car at this very minute part of me is fixing the engine, and down in the kitchen part of me is making a pie, and out on the tree part of me is climbing and picking apples—the extensions of myself, my grandchildren, are doing all these things. So how can you say I'm dying?"

That's a wonderful thing to read in the moment of your own death or in the death of others; or after a funeral, if you can give that to someone and say, "Hey, read this." At any service that's held for me, that'll be the story I'd want read to my friends to represent me: I left the theater at the right time.

What do you do to frighten yourself?
All of the stories in *October Country* were ways of scaring myself. The ideas don't happen quite as often now. When you're in your teens and early twenties you finally begin to understand death means you. I remember going to a doctor when I was twenty, I had a sore throat and he said, "Oh, there's nothing wrong in there, you've just never noticed before. It's just all the gristle and ligaments. You've got a lot of things in your body that you've never felt, like the ends of your elbows or knees or ankles, the way your skull is shaped." So I left feeling this and wrote a short story called "The Skeleton" about a guy who discovers he has hidden, way inside of his body, this symbol of gothic horror: a skeleton. Inside his body. It scared the hell out of him. I wrote a story about the competition between the symbol of death in him and the flesh and blood that surrounds the skeleton. It's a totally new story in the history of literature: nobody has ever written about a man terrified of his own skeleton. People are always saying there are no new ideas in the world: there are indeed, and I've found ways of

discovering them. You look in the mirror and see the skull behind the flesh.

How much of what you've written as fiction has become fact?
Nothing, because that's never been my way of approaching the subject. I'm interested in the psychological overtones that go with inventions. It's the obvious, you see. You write about the obvious ahead of time.

I wrote a short story once about a man and his wife in South America when the hydrogen bomb falls, and the whole world is destroyed except the part of South America they're in. They're in a small native village, and they're the only white people around. Then they have to wait on tables and be servants and shine shoes. And the story is whether or not they can do this and remain human and forget their past, be Christian servants. Christ would have taught them how to do it, but can they teach themselves? Then, what they see, is that when power shifts anywhere in the world, the people who get the power are not any better than the ones who gave it up. A liberal doesn't want to believe this—and a lot of conservatives don't want to believe it either. But I've always known it, and sense it, that because a person's black doesn't mean he's morally better than I am, or vice versa. We're both the same human beings and both of us reprehensible when we get too much power handed us too quickly.

So what has happened since I wrote that story back in 1951? Look at Africa, hmmm? People pulled out of the colonies too fast and what have you got? Jesus Christ! When you hand things over to ignorant people, what happens? All of a sudden you're getting the Indians driven out [of countries such as Uganda and Kenya]—and they were the shopkeepers, so there goes your whole shopkeeping class. All of your engines and technology's fallen into disrepair. In some countries you've got a better situation, which would indicate whoever was in control did a better job of educating before they pulled out. You've got to be careful how you talk about these things, because people think you're being some sort of reactionary and all you're doing is being a realist.

Would you agree with one critic's opinion of you, that you are "one of the world's most visionary reactionaries"?

No, that's not true. The word *reactionary* could mean a lot of things. If a thing's worth reacting against, like book burning, you're a reactionary, right? *Reactionary* is a loaded, pejorative term but it can apply to liberals as well as conservatives. The better thing is to say we're moving into a period of radical conservatism. Which is the best kind of radical to be. The energy crisis of the mid-seventies has shown us we must conserve in order to survive. Education is a combination of conservative-liberal tendencies in all of us; you must conserve knowledge in order to liberate yourself into new action.

The family is a conservative thing, but it can also provide the world with radical thinking, so that you can go and change things relative to the family and individuals. I love to provoke college students. I tell them, You know what you all are? You're radical conservatives—you're not liberals. You're afraid of these labels; they're all loaded one way or another. Angela Davis says what? "More power to the people." That is not a liberal slogan, it's conservative. The really great conservatives have always said it. So, she's a radical-conservative, saying, Give us back the power to use on a local level. She's in favor of states' rights, local rights, citizens' rights. That's conservative, not liberal. There's no answer—I've got 'em. And they haven't done enough reading to know whether I'm pulling their leg or not.

Speaking of liberals and conservatives, you're somewhat of a disappointed Democrat, aren't you?

We've had a run of bad presidents, starting with Truman. Truman had many good things. The Marshall Plan is terrific; his handling of a lot of things is all A's, but Korea is a minus. Everyone's forgotten— you go up to the average man in the street and ask, "Did President Truman have a chance to run to be president again?" The answer is yes, of course, and he stepped down. Everyone's forgotten, including the people in the Democratic party, that they had a loser for president who was forced to step down because the people didn't like his war. The night that Eisenhower on the radio said, "I will go to Korea," we all knew the election was lost.

Eisenhower is the least bad of all the presidents we've had since, because he was sort of a nice, genial, papa nonentity. He didn't commit us too much to too many things in too many places and destroy us. Kennedy comes along pretending to be a liberal and immediately involved us in an invasion of Cuba. Great liberal act? Come on. Big reactionary Republican. He was a Republican under the skin. Then he goes off and talks to de Gaulle, who says, "Don't go into Vietnam, for Christ's sake, we've got 100 years' experience there, you'll be sucked under and destroyed." So Kennedy comes home and commits troops to Vietnam, and then okays the assassination of Diem, which everyone's forgotten about; then three weeks later Kennedy is assassinated, and Madame Nhu says, "How does it feel?" And we didn't like her for rubbing our noses. But after all, assassination is assassination, isn't it? If you do it, don't be surprised if someone does it to you.

Then you had Johnson, who almost destroyed the country singlehandedly. The worst president, probably, in modern history. Because he brought the country closer to revolution than any other president I can think of. Then the irony is, Nixon comes along, a man that we all hate, and he stops the war. No one likes to talk about that. All they want to do is hate. But history will write it differently. History will say Nixon is the man who stopped the war, so all praise to him. Watergate will be forgotten, because there's nothing to remember. It's so minor. Believe me, I'm head of the list of hating Nixon; but I'm also an objective person in being fair. Hell, Mayor Daley did a worse thing: he got Kennedy the election by throwing the ballots into Lake Michigan.

Do you think Nixon would have been a better president than JFK in 1960?

I don't think he would have gotten into Vietnam. The Democrats seem to have the need to prove themselves—it's quite astounding. And I voted for every one of these Democratic presidents and I've been sorry.

Another area where you're not very liberal is modern art. You don't like it?

I like the grotesque. I like illustrators. I love art that I can look at and judge whether or not the person has any talent. I hate people who get up on ladders and drip paint, because I can do that—anyone can do that.

But you can't get $2 million for it.

Well, 100 years from now everyone is going to look back at this period and say it's the most bankrupt art period in the history of the world. We didn't do anything. We had a few people like Wyeth, who could really paint.

What do you think of the women's movement and how have their concerns affected your writing?

I've had letters from girls at Vassar asking me to rewrite *The Martian Chronicles*. And I write back and say, "Flake off. If I choose to do a certain kind of story, you must allow me to do it. I'm not out to please you or any other group. I'm out to find out about myself. If you don't like the story I write about women for some reason, go write your own." In the last ninety years in America there've been 50,000 women writers. What is this nonsense about women not being represented in American culture? Some of the greatest writers we've had—Willa Catha, Eudora Welty, Katherine Anne Porter, Jessamyn West—have taught me. I read their books and learn from them about life. The greatest mystery writer in the world is a woman: Agatha Christie. So what are they talking about?

Could you elaborate on what you once said about machines, that they are "amoral but they induce us to behave immorally?"

The paradox is very obvious: machines are both bad and good. They are amoral. The car induces you to behave immorally, because of the power and the speed, the new aesthetic which Huxley described for the first time. The automobile introduced a whole new aesthetic into the world: the aesthetic of speed. The only way you could get the sen-

sation of speed up until our time was by getting on a horse and gal-
loping. But nothing came comparable to getting in a car and going
even forty miles per hour. You could get a sensation of speed for five
seconds from jumping out of the tower of Pisa, or you could dive off
a cliff into an ocean. But these inventions which induce you to behave immorally are indeed with us and are beginning to destroy a lot
of countries and cause a hell of a lot of trouble in the cultures of the
world. The very countries that made fun of us are now going
through the traffic jams and the smog and the murder on the
highways.

**Once you make all these mistakes, can you go back and erase
them?**
Yeah, we're going to do it. I've written an article on the steps we have
to take to change, rebuild and rethink a lot of things. We're on our
way there. A lot of big corporations are interested in this, and we're
going to have corporate responsibility on many levels. We're going to
build a lot of small towns again, ones which work in new terms.
They'll be humanistic, technological small towns of the future which
will have all kinds of travel in it, ways of getting around without using cars. It will have so many textures that we need, or think we need,
as educated hedonists of the future. There are two or three now being
built, and when they work there will be hundreds, and then we'll get
people out of the big cities. The big cities will be partially blown up
and replotted into gardens, and they'll be made to work again.

**Didn't you write a story about cities and countries losing their
populations?**
I've done a poem, a play, and a story about the fact that sometime in
the next 200 years England, Ireland, and Scotland may very well be
empty because of the ability of people to borrow money from the future, through credit cards, and go off on long journeys and never
come back. It's already happened in Ireland. They lost four million
people through immigration. They used to have a population of eight
million: it's down to three million now. That's a big loss—more than

half the country's got the hell out. And the other people who are missing died in the potato famine.

The problem of many of the countries of Europe is one of immigration, keeping the young people home. They don't want to stay home. The weather's lousy there; the employment is lousy. America is the center of the world. We're still the greatest and most wonderful country in the world. Otherwise, why do 500,000 people a year want to come here? We're so negative about ourselves—and there's plenty to be negative about. I attack, but then I construct. I don't believe anyone has the right to criticize unless in the instant of destruction you construct. It's got to be fused.

Perhaps some of these immigrants will be heading one day into space. In *The Martian Chronicles* you wrote: "No matter how much we touch Mars, we'll never touch it." Also, "We Earthmen have a talent for ruining big, beautiful things."
I'd like to believe that the astronauts who eventually go there will have read *The Martian Chronicles* and that I may have a part in preventing that future that I worried about when I wrote the book. Space travel is a very self-conscious endeavor; when you've got three billion people concentrating on you, indeed, that's very intense, and it will be very moral as a result.

Do you still believe man's pioneering into space is a religious movement more than a technical or military one?
Absolutely. The technical stuff is a way of doing it. The military is an excuse. But the real thing is survival in the universe.

I've always thought it would be appropriate to put a poet on a space flight.
The only time they've done it is the night when one of the astronauts quoted from the Bible—and it touched everyone as a result. Sure, it was artificial in some ways, but nevertheless, damn lovely too. One of the craters on the moon is named for *Dandelion Wine*. I'm very proud of that. I think it was the Apollo 13 team that named the crater. I

don't know if those labels will stick over the years. I hope so. I would love to have my name on something like that.

Have you had any dealings with NASA?
NASA called recently and I said, "Where've you been? You've needed me all these years." Because they talk too many technical things and they don't talk poetry. They heard that I want to do an hour TV special on space travel. I said, Look, three years ago I gave you people all the articles I've done—from Stonehenge to Tranquility Base and Remembrance of Things Future—in which I put all my philosophy and poetry. So I expect to be meeting with some TV people and hope we can put together a program which will fly. Not just be a Cronkite sitting there with an astronaut telling you about trajectories and orbits and weights. That's all very interesting, but you can only do that for a while until someone's going to say, "Don't tell me the weights again, tell me why you're doing it. What does it mean to the human spirit?"

Didn't you also get in touch with Walt Disney to tell him how much he needed you, too?
I went out to see Uncle Walt some years ago. I heard he was going to rebuild Tomorrowland. I said, "Walt, why don't you call me in and let me help work on it with you?" He said, "Ray, it's no use. You're a genius and I'm a genius, we'd kill each other the second week." That's the nicest rejection I ever got.

Back to your *Martian Chronicles* for a moment. In that book you said that you were "out to prevent futures, not make them." Could you elaborate?
When you have polarities between all kinds of political and religious groups, old and young, everyone wants to burn some kind of books, don't they? The Arabs want to burn the Jewish books. Jews want to burn Arab books, the Irish have a list of books in Ireland you wouldn't believe. Then Women's Lib came along and they wanted all the books rewritten on their terms. You can't allow that. As soon as you allow one minority group to do that, then all the books have to

be burned. Because they'll be meaningless. *Little Black Sambo* can't be read anymore. I pointed all of this out in *Fahrenheit 451*. You've got to say to every minority group: Hands off! Get away with your rewritings. You're a danger to all of literature and all of culture. You have to prevent that future.

A question you asked in *The Martian Chronicles* is one I'd like to ask you: Do you think the civilizations of two planets can progress at the same rate and evolve in the same way?

In many ways. It's mind-boggling to consider the civilizations that must exist somewhere else in the universe, so incredibly different and even more humane than we are. It's hard to imagine a creature that doesn't look anything like us being a human being, but, of course, that's what they would be. Any creature born of a universe like ours with suns has got to be a sun creature, with fears of the dark. But there everything stops and you go on to try and imagine the shapes and sizes, and the best way to imagine it is to go into the jungle or to look into the ocean at the creatures there that are so totally different from us and yet have many characteristics like us. The dolphin, the whale. So you can imagine spiders that are human, that refuse death, that refuse murder, that are afraid of the dark. These are all things we would share in common. The choice between good and evil, free will—if that exists in the creature then you're looking at a human being on another world. It could be any size, shape, and color. It could be a mile wide and a half inch tall; it could be a long flat worm that runs on for ten miles. It could be anything, as long as it could communicate and refuse evil acts.

How did you feel when you saw the pictures of Saturn that Voyager sent back?

It was wonderful for the human spirit. It was something we could all share, something that united us in its beauty. It had nothing to do with sex, race, or country. It embodied no philosophy. It showed that we could do anything—rebuild our cities, clean our streams and end our energy problem while colonizing the moon at the same time. It has nothing to do with money. All we have to do is use our imagination.

What do you see as the future of man and space?
The future is endless. Once we make it, we'll live through all eternity. That's exciting. I'd like to come back once every 100 years for the next ten billion years and see what we're up to in the universe, because we're not going to stay here. We don't know anything, scientists don't know anything, we all live in ignorance.

When we discussed his creative process, Linus Pauling told me he often stores an idea away in his mind and lets his unconscious play with it, sometimes for years. What do you do to keep the ideas coming?
Same thing. You put all the information in there and let it percolate. Creativity in every field is almost identical. All great ideas, and much of the scientific ideas, come from percolation. Make sure you feed yourself all kinds of stuff from various fields, outrageous fields, every day.

Constantly picking up images?
Right, and hoping two of them will collide and make a new one. I like to imagine cross-country journeys with my favorite people, staying up all night on a train with people like Shaw, G. K. Chesterton, Gerald Heard, Aldous Huxley—it's like a traveling porch. When you were a kid you loved it when your parents and relatives talked on the front porch late at night, hoping it would never end because the talk was so good, talking about life and you hadn't lived it yet. What was it like in 1905 when your dad ran away from home and went West, when he was sixteen and had adventures and slept in jails, hit all the harvests and worked in the silver mines? God, that's great stuff.

That's one of the things missing from American writing: the philosopher is missing, the poet is missing. The poet and the philosopher who dare to do asides for you in their fiction. That's why I like what I'm doing because I'm doing what a lot of people are not. But it shouldn't be done self-consciously, it should be done with passion.

I wrote a short story about going through space with a George Bernard Shaw robot to talk to. I sit long hours and he tells me his prefaces and his theories of the life force. It's a delicious idea, being able to sit with a robot, because Mr. Shaw isn't around. I always wanted to meet him. Out of that frustration I've written a story which is a monument to my love. It's a long, philosophical aside, really, in which I'm able to let Mr. Shaw say a few things about himself.

You've also done that in your *Life* story about Hemingway.
Yeah. I gave him a decent burial, because I was so frustrated by his death. I felt sorry for the man. He should never have walked away from that second plane accident in Africa. He should have been killed that day. God was not good to him. The story says, if you're lucky may you die on the right day.

Back to my great-grandmother again: when you know it's over, get up and leave the theater. The trouble is, a lot of us want to stay on, even after it's over. Because we love life so. It's a hard thing to give up, to make that decision. Hemingway made the right decision finally, but it was about seven years too late; he went through a lot of agony with his body, which was tired.

You've already mentioned some of your personal heroes—Shaw, Chesterton, Heard, Huxley. Are there others who have influenced you?
I've never picked friends because their intelligence was less than mine. I've tried to pick friends who are better than myself, so that I would be forced to grow. So when I had a chance to meet Huxley and Heard and Bernard Berenson and Bertrand Russell—Jesus Christ, it was exciting! But half the time I was stunned, I didn't know what to say. I was just so glad to be with them, I was terrified. And then I gradually realized I was able to talk.

I know who influenced me in the past, and I'm grateful. I have borrowed and learned from people like John Collier, the English short story writer, Jessamyn West, Willa Cather, Edith Wharton, Katherine Anne Porter. I've assimilated and grown through their humanity and aesthetics. And people like Steinbeck and Kazantzakis. But now the more I look around, the more I realize the poets have influenced me so much, too. Shakespeare has constantly. Melville. And Shaw, Shaw, Shaw continually—I keep going back every week of my life. His ability was so amazing that he could write reviews of people you've never even heard of, some very obscure composers or obscure pieces, and make it as vivid as if it were happening today. That was his genius: to make you care about a thing that was long since dead.

You've stated that Edgar Rice Burroughs, the creator of Tarzan, "was and is the most influential writer, bar none, of our century." How many critics would agree with that?

They wouldn't agree at all, except they would misinterpret what I'm saying. I'm not saying he was a great stylist. He was a great romantic and he caused changes in children which were very important. The way the world changes and grows is through romance. The way you change the history of the world is to grab a ten-year-old child and pour this romance through that ear or eyeball and that child then says, "Oh God, life is great!"

I have talked to astronauts, biochemists, anthropologists, astronomers—they all say Edgar Rice Burroughs. We're not talking about literature, we're talking about reading. God, he was not a good writer, you can't go back to that stuff, but when you're ten he reads like gangbusters. And it's immediate, it goes right into your bloodstream—you act, you climb a tree and fall off. It doesn't matter what the intellects think, they're always wrong about these things.

I feel a blood relationship to that man who changed my life and helped me to grow. Then you get a little more sophisticated and pick up on people like Jules Verne, H. G. Wells, and Huxley. But they don't change your life the same way. We're on the moon because of Burroughs, not because of the scientists who came later. Those scientists were influenced by him.

Burroughs never made it to Africa, which is a continent of ghosts and spirits. You've written about ESP, astral traveling, and ghosts. Do you believe in them yourself?

I'd like to. Since we are sun energy, and since thought is electrical, just as everything else about us is, there's no reason this isn't possible. We see all kinds of things occurring with animals that can see and hear things we can't. I'd like to believe in ghosts because they're fun. It's a reincarnation of the spirit traveling in the world that's fun to think about.

I've done a wonderful science-fiction horror tale as a play about the last dead man in the world. He comes out of the earth and realizes he's the last representative of "The Monkey's Paw" and "The Cask of Amontillado" and "The Black Cat," what have you, because all the great writers of the world have been cleaned out by book burners and horror burners, and all the bodies have been shoved into the incinerator, and everything's gone up in smoke. As soon as you die in this culture of the future, they take you immediately to the incinerator and send you up the flue, so there are no bodies or graveyards in the world, no memories of death, it's all immediate sunlight and fire. So he doesn't like that. He goes to the libraries and discovers that no one knows who Poe is—this story predates *Fahrenheit 451* by five years—and he then sets off to blow up the incinerators and introduce death to the world, and the fun of ghosts, and horror, and what have you. So he's going to get dead bodies and use exorcism to raise them up and have an army of the dead. So he goes to the nearest morgue after he's destroyed the incinerators, and he makes the cabalistic signs and says the words, but the dead won't get up because they were raised in a culture that didn't believe. He then resigns himself and they come and wrap him in mummy cloth and shove him in the furnace and his last words are, "For the love of God, Montressor!"

In an article about horror movies you wrote, "I have raised my daughters to be the hunch on the back of that bellringer of Notre Dame." What does that mean?

We all love to go to horror films together. I've taught them it's okay. Society's always saying those are not important films. Well, they are. *The Exorcist* is a superior piece of work—it's a love story. Any time a mother is willing to kill herself to save her daughter, or any time a priest who's lost faith is willing to take the spirit of the devil into his body and then throw himself out a window to kill that spirit to save the girl, that's a love story. That's a great theme, I wish I'd thought of it.

The Exorcist was a best-seller as a book before it became a popular movie. Have you ever had a best-seller?
I've never had a best-seller in my life. All my books sell around 8,000 copies hardback. In paperback *The Martian Chronicles* sold on an average of 100,000 copies a year in a twenty-five-year period, but that's not a best-seller. One hundred thousand copies of a paperback is nothing. It's taken twenty-five years to sell two million copies. A best-seller is a thing that sells in two months or a year. The best I've ever had in hardcover is a book of short stories, incredibly enough, *I Sing the Body Electric*. Sold 25,000 copies the first year.

Do you resent not selling more books or do you take it in stride?
You learn, over the years, to be whatever Fate decides you are to be. There's no way of pushing or changing it. You go with your talent and the love of people who really love you. That love compensates for a lot. If one person comes up to you on the street and looks you right in the face with this glow and says, "You are the greatest thing that ever lived in the history of the world," boy, that's worth a thousand bucks right there. How often does that happen to Harold Robbins? Not very often. And he must make ten times my income every year. Life teaches you your values.

You're a strong defender of Los Angeles. You've called it the best place in America and "the stud bull of the future." What is it about L.A. that makes you into a visionary?

I grew up here, I've been here since 1934, I've seen everything, and we're God's natural creature. We're not intellectual, thank God for that, and that makes us better human beings. We use our intellect, but we use it more naturally than people do in New York City, with their hierarchies and pecking orders. We know how to live better.

Is fantasy absolutely necessary for survival?
Sure. We couldn't live any time without it. From the time we're thirteen and start to move into puberty, if you take a boy's fantasies away from him he'd go bats. Because he's got to get rid of his sexuality somehow; he's not making it with girls—and he doesn't until he's into his twenties. This is a whole thing women today don't want to talk about: the reality of the sexual male. Fantasy helps you to become and stay a human being, otherwise we'd have to kill all the villains we really hate.

What current fantasies do you harbor?
I want to find the ghost of Puccini and really write a grand opera, because I love the form. I'd like to do a science-fiction opera, there've been very few of those.

Do you see the role of writer as one of showman and entertainer?
The very best things have always been that way. The greatest plays have always been entertainments. The reason Shakespeare is still around today is because all his plots are absolute trash. All the great stories are trashy stories, but they're dressed up in beautiful clothing. We must be entertainers—carnival people, circus people, playwrights, poets, tellers of tales in the streets of Baghdad, we're all of the same family that exists throughout history to explain ourselves to one another; we need to tell each other everything's okay or it's not okay.

Aldous Huxley called you "One of the most visionary men now writing." Christopher Isherwood compared you to Poe. How do you see yourself?

Jesus, I don't know. Comparisons are so odd, you have to be careful. I know what I would like to be in my old age. I would like to follow the footsteps of George Bernard Shaw and Shakespeare, and wind up in their company. You have to set your goals high. If you can just live in their shadow. Even if I'm just a shadow within a shadow someday, I would like to stand there.

Time will tell. Capturing time is often a major problem for writers. Is it for you?
I've never really thought of it that much. I want to use time well. I want to drain it of its meaning and intensity as I pass through it, so that I come to the end of my life, as Shaw once put it, having completely wasted myself away; but good ways, so that you've never let a moment pass that hasn't been delicious.

Kazantzakis had Zorba say he wants to leave death a bag of bones.
Um-hum. Look back and see your fingerprints on everything. A billion fingerprints behind you. Writing is a contest with death anyway—especially when you put a new book in the mail: that's a triumph. Because you say, "Okay, Death, one up. I may be dead tonight, but that's out."

Why won't you drive a car or ride in an airplane?
I'm a coward. I know exactly where my fears are. The idea of being in a plane that fell is so terrifying to me. And I'm positive the day I go up is the day all the planes fall.

Is there anything that could ever get you into a plane?
Yes. If the Nobel Prize committee wired me tomorrow and wanted me in Stockholm forty-eight hours from now, I would get drunk and get on the plane.

J. P. DONLEAVY

I Have an Aversion
to Literature and Writing

IN THE 1950S, AFTER JOE MCCARTHY AND BEFORE SPUT-
nik, a few American writers took a look at the world we helped
create and saw the flaws. The Nazis had been destroyed, the
atomic bomb detonated, Stalin was not the kind of man you'd
want to invite for dinner, Nixon was the vice president and
scheming higher dreams. The time was ripe to put it all in perspective, and the writers who caught the absurdity and the seamy
underbelly of the American dream were dubbed black humorists.
They helped restore the American novel to relevance.

Among the leading practitioners of this perverse and twisted
take on their cold war times were Terry Southern (*Candy, The
Magic Christian*), William Gaddis (*The Recognitions*), Joseph Heller
(*Catch-22*), Thomas Pynchon (*V.*), William Burroughs (*Naked
Lunch, Nova Express*), John Barth (*The Floating Opera*), Kurt Vonnegut Jr. (*Cat's Cradle*), and J. P. Donleavy (*The Ginger Man*). They
helped change the course of American literature in the twentieth
century.

"As societies convulse, art turns emetic," Conrad Knicker-
bocker wrote in a *New York Times* essay on black humor in 1964.
"Whether the new humor ominously resembles the Latin satire
that flourished while the totalitarian power of the Empire grew,

or the glittering harpoons of Dr. Johnson's age that drew their aim on stupendous social arrogance, indifference and misery, depends on who has the last laugh. One thing is certain: the new humorists bear witness to convulsions."

In 1955, the only publisher who would touch *The Ginger Man* was the Olympia Press in Paris. Its bawdy prose and its highly original style made it an immediate classic (that green paperback first edition is now worth more than $500), but Donleavy was unsatisfied because it appeared in Olympia's pornographic Traveller's Companion series. This led to a twenty-year legal battle that resulted in Donleavy purchasing his first publisher in a curious and remarkable case of literary revenge, which he discusses in this interview (and which is detailed in John De St. Jorre's *Venus Bound: The Erotic Voyage of the Olympia Press and Its Writers*).

Known to his friends as "Mike," James Patrick Donleavy was born in Brooklyn on April 23, 1926, and was raised in the Bronx. He attended the U.S. Naval Academy and then left the United States to study at Trinity College in Dublin. Ireland had an effect on him: he dressed like a university lecturer, carried a walking stick, affected an accent and eventually, once his writing started to bring him a decent income, he adopted Ireland as his home. It was more a financial than a romantic move, as Ireland doesn't tax its writers. He lives in a large stone mansion on 180 acres of farmland in Westmeath county, an hour's drive west of Dublin. He raises cattle, swims in a thirty-foot indoor pool, and writes until midafternoon.

It was Bernard Wolfe, author of *Limbo, Trotsky's Dead, Come On Out, Daddy*, who turned me on to Donleavy. Wolfe taught a writing class at UCLA that wasn't a class at all but more along the lines of a mentor-student relationship. I'd met with Wolfe between 1965 and 1968 whenever I had written a sufficient number of pages, and we'd discuss them. Or we'd talk about what he was writing. Or about other writers. "Read *The Ginger Man*," he told me. I did, and the book exploded in my head in the way Joyce's *Portrait* and Eliot's "Prufrock" did earlier. We all have books that hit us at a certain time, when we're ready for them. It usually happens when we're young. For most of us, it begins with Dr. Seuss, Frank Baum, or Edgar Rice Burroughs, or a Hardy Boys or Nancy Drew mystery. As we approach puberty someone whispers Salinger and *The Catcher in the Rye* makes us appreciate that we're grown-up enough to enjoy something called literature. Then, the floodgates open. The world of books lies before us. We go off in different directions. We discover one or more of the writers in this collection, or Dostoevsky, Joyce, Kerouac, Vonnegut, Proust, Capote, Tom Robbins, Italo Calvino, Borges, Wole Soyinka, Amy Tan, T. C. Boyle, David Foster Wallace. There's always *that* writer, at *that* time, which sets bells ringing in one's head.

When I discovered *The Ginger Man,* I had my moment. Rarely have I ever read a book, put it down, then picked it up to read again. But Donleavy's way of weaving words, his use of first and third person in the same paragraph, his telegraphic sentences, his ribald humor, was just so fresh, so singular. Dorothy Parker called the novel a "rigadoon of rascality." *The Nation* said, "Donleavy's Irish eloquence and American drive make him a Don Juan among the eunuchs." *Time* wrote that in Sebastian Dangerfield, "Donleavy created one of the most outrageous scoundrels in contemporary fiction." I remember the first time around I came across the passage where Dangerfield sits on the toilet and his wife Marion begins shouting from downstairs. When you're used to American plumbing, you can't imagine the kind of scene that Donleavy creates. And you never forget it.

> . . . One morning there was sunshine and I was feeling great. Sitting in there grunting and groaning, looking over the news, and then reach up and pull the chain. Downstairs in the kitchen, Marion screamed.
>
> "I say, Marion, what is it?"

"For God's sake, stop it, stop it, Sebastian, you fool. What have you done?"

Moving with swift irritability down the narrow stairs, stumbling into the kitchen at the bottom. Perhaps things have gotten too much for Marion and she's gone mad.

"You idiot, Sebastian, look at me, look at the baby's things."

Marion trembling in the middle of the kitchen floor covered with strands of wet toilet paper and fecal matter. From a gaping patch in the ceiling poured water, plaster and excrement.

"God's miserable teeth."

"Oh damnable, damnable. Do something, you fool."

"For the love of Jesus."

Sebastian stalking away.

"How dare you walk away, you damnable rotter. This is horrible and I can't bear it any more."

Marion broke into sobs, slammed into silence with the front door.

When I finished the book for a second time I went on to *A Singular Man, The Beastly Beatitudes of Balthazar B,* the short stories *Meet My Maker the Mad Molecule,* and the novella *The Saddest Summer of Samuel S.* And after college and the Peace Corps, when I began writing for *Newsday*'s Sunday magazine in the mid-seventies and they came up with the idea of my interviewing "household names," I immediately suggested Donleavy, who had been compared with Evelyn Waugh, P. G. Wodehouse, Franz Kafka, Henry Miller, Nancy Mitford, and James Joyce. They weren't sure if he was "household" enough, but I went to Ireland anyway. By then he had written two other novels, *The Onion Eaters* and *A Fairy Tale of New York,* each of which were hailed as his best work, though none of his books (including six more novels, a novella, four works of nonfiction, five plays, and an autobiography, *The History of the Ginger Man*) have had the impact of *The Ginger Man.*

"Mike" Donleavy looked like the pictures that appeared on the back jackets of his books: salt-and-pepper hair and beard, a man of tweed and cane, his Russian wolfhounds by his side. He was very soft-spoken and somewhat shy, but there was a sparkle in his eyes that made you aware that he knew whatever score there was to know and that he had managed to pull off a lifestyle that most writers, even successful ones, would never know.

His living space was a surprise only in that it was more like a modern New York loft with its shiny wooden floors than the inside of a rock-solid estate where one expected cold drafts to blow through the rooms. After our conversation he showed me his large, comfortable upstairs office where he worked on a portable Hermes typewriter. And downstairs near the swimming pool was a Ping-Pong table. When I suggested a game his expression changed. He was no longer the shy and retiring author or the lord of the manor or the gentleman farmer—he was more the guy who got into brawls in Dublin bars as a youth, or the sailor who ran naked past military guards. He looked at me like I was fresh meat to devour and soon we were facing each other across the green table, slapping at the white ball with our paddles. He played a mean, tricky game, and while I thought I might have an advantage because I had a fast serve, I soon found out that *his* serve was his strength, a devilish curvy thing that made a return almost impossible. At least not until I had gotten used to it, and by then he had won a few games and felt refreshed enough to call it quits.

In the car back to Dublin I thought more about those games than all the questions I didn't have time to ask. And of

> *that sly*
> *mischievous serve*
> *Of the one*
> *and only*
> *Ginger Man.*

You once said that fame and fortune were the main reasons you wanted to write. Is that really true?

There's some degree there of truth, because they form very basic propelling instincts in everyone. Everybody's conscious of the importance of money even if they're not conscious of the importance of fame, but as that appears to go hand-in-hand with anybody who is making a lot of money, they're pretty basic ingredients for someone becoming an author. It's always been colored romantically in terms of American life, that if you are a writer you become famous and rich. Otherwise, you're not an author.

But did you have literary ambitions as a boy?
Yes, I always had, from a fairly early age. As one gets interested in things like music and so on, I obviously had interests in writing. But nothing formally, nothing that ever made me think of it in terms of career, which is an unacceptable career in the United States. It's like a kid deciding to tell his parents he's going to go and live on the Bowery for the rest of his days.

Did your parents encourage you to be a doctor or a lawyer and write on the side?
There was some tendency towards that, but then both my parents were immigrants to the United States, so they did have an unconscious European attitude. They didn't particularly force me to do anything.

George Simenon once said that "Writing is not a profession, but a vocation of unhappiness."
I would think so. I came across some work that Franz Kafka wrote about being a writer, that it somehow wrenched you out of the kind of contemporary world that people knew. You unpleasantly had to be torn from this human compatibility that other people enjoy. I think this is, regrettably, true. You can't live like other people. And I don't suppose that any author wants to admit that this is true, finally, because it makes him appear to be such a difficult thing, and people are *always* trying to appear pleasant and acceptable to the world. But I think this is the case whether one likes it or not. It's not a very happy

way of life, except that you don't seek other ways of life. I can't describe my life as being particularly unhappy, except that I am aware that this other part of it does exist; that you literally tend to isolate yourself, and you proceed in what appears to be a very unhappy existence. I'm aware that people who have office jobs, working with their associates, it's a pretty bloodcurdling, tough, harsh, debilitating way of life.

What were some of the jobs you had before you began earning your living as a writer?

I never had a job. I *did* have one job where I worked cutting grass in Woodlawn Cemetery. And I did have a newspaper route for a short period. But I've never worked at all in any job since. Probably one's experience in the navy would give one an idea what it would be like to work for a living. But I can remember even in the navy finding it absolutely impossible to get myself to accept doing a chore or work. I literally used to do almost *impossible* things, risking a general court-martial, to avoid work.

Was that when you used to break from your transfer unit during work detail, running like a madman to escape the security police?

Yeah. That was an appalling thing. Even to this day I am horrified to think that I would have dared to do such a thing. But I would do anything to get out of these working parties. One thing I knew, pretty much for certain, was that no one could catch me. Each day this entire unit of between 3,000 and 10,000 men would be waiting for me to break out. One morning, the security police were stationed everywhere, patrolling up and down with their billies. Finally, it was time for me to make my break. There was a hushed silence. I thought, I can't do this, it's insane. But such was my horror of having to work, I made a bolt for it. I then discovered that this lieutenant had the whole area covered with military police to catch me. The way I finally escaped was to run into one of the Quonset huts, and, as I did, I pulled off my jumper and undressed totally and came out the other end. Between the Quonset huts were these great big washstands, and I just plunged my clothes in and turned on the tap. Six MPs converged around every corner knowing that they had tracked me to this spot, and there I was scrubbing under this thing. It was a terrifying business. But that was my work history. I just couldn't stand working for a living.

Was it after the navy that you left the States to attend Trinity College in Dublin?

After the war I was interested in going abroad. When I was in the navy, it had come up that one could travel, but this meant risking your life, so when I got an appointment to the U.S. Naval Academy it meant that I could stay in the U.S. Europe had a kind of unconscious attraction for me. One imagined it was totally unlike the U.S., which indeed it is. So I wrote to Trinity. This, plus the fact that my grades were not all that good, and I was having trouble getting into an American university.

Your writing style, with its short staccato sentences, seems influenced by some of James Joyce. Was he an influence when you went to Ireland?

Unquestionably. Certainly his use of language would have made one conscious to how one could handle words. Joyce came up tremendously as one came to Dublin. Everybody was very conscious then of James Joyce. The way he lived and his dedication to writing became a symbol for writers. The other one among my contemporaries whom we were very conscious of was Henry Miller. Miller was on everyone's lips—mostly sensitive and intelligent people who had read him. But as a writer I became very much influenced by spoken language, the way people actually spoke and used language. I didn't tend to be awfully literary. My background wasn't that at all. It was in painting that I got my first taste of acceptance and my first feeling about being someone who's doing something. I escaped, to a large degree, being influenced. I was able to sit to my work and decide what is the most efficient and best way of using words and language.

There was a lot of exciting writing going on in the mid-fifties and early sixties: Heller's *Catch-22*, Kesey's *One Flew Over the Cuckoo's Nest*, Vonnegut's *Cat's Cradle*, your *Ginger Man*. The critics called you black humorists. Were you aware of what else was being written at the time?

I don't think so. I certainly wasn't aware of what was happening in America then. A lot of these writers were just working on their own, just as scientists suddenly discovered that they'd been pushing in the same direction as one another.

Is it true that you don't read your contemporaries?

Yes. It's not something I deliberately avoid. I'm not interested in it. But I'm a great, avid newspaper reader. I do a lot of nonfiction reading. Literature as such doesn't interest me. One might even say I have an aversion to literature and writing. Possibly because in the early days, the competitiveness of authors . . . contemporaries, like Brendan Behan, were, in some ways, enemies as well as audience.

Have you always been shy, as one may assume from reading your books?

Yes, that's very true. Because you're in the business of being an author, you're aware that it's important that people know of your existence, because this is frequently why people buy books. I find myself giving interviews and being publicized as a recluse, an inaccessible person. I'm not someone who likes to go out or be at parties. I find them very difficult. If nobody knows who you are, you're generally ignored. If someone knows who you are, you find yourself then confronting somebody who knows a great deal more about you then you care to be known, simply because one's books are highly personal. You then are put in a position where you tend to be shy.

You once noted that people often smile at you because they are thinking of that scene in *The Ginger Man* when Sebastian Dangerfield pulls the cord in the toilet and sends its contents down on his wife below.

Yes, I always imagine that, but I'm not sure whether that's the case. It varies from time to time, whether people recognize your face, on a lot of factors. Even though, say, you appear on television, people will only recognize you for two or three days afterwards, and then it fades away. But anyone who's read a book and seen a picture of me on a book generally will remember me better. When I was visiting London last, I tended to walk in pretty grim, out-of-the-way places. I don't know why I do it, but I walk for miles. And walking along one of these very anonymous places, totally out of where you'd expect to find an author, there was a man on the other side of the street who literally lost control of himself laughing. And clearly he was an Irishman who recognized me. The thing that interested me was the fact that he was so damn sure who it was. I mean, there was just no mistake. He never bothered looking a second or third time, he just started to roar with laughter as he walked down the road. It's a very strange business.

When you were writing *The Ginger Man*, did you see yourself as Sebastian Dangerfield?
It was based on contemporaries. I suppose it had a strong autobiographical basis. Everybody in the book with the possible exception of Dangerfield was very much based on real persons.

Have your feelings about *The Ginger Man* changed with the different receptions it's received?
I'm always concerned, with that book as with any subsequent book, whether, if one picks it up and does look at it, you can still read it with a certain amount of interest and attention. One is always pleased then, because it's one of the few times you ever get any pleasure out of a book. Because when you're working on a book you don't get any pleasure at all. It's very grueling writing it; not that it's an implacable grimness, but you're working at it, so you never get a chance to sit down and enjoy it. I actually find myself not referring to *The Ginger Man* all that much. Possibly because I have, over the years, had

to pay a lot of attention to it. One has had a lot of troubles about the book.

How did the troubles begin?
Its major complication is the fact of its first publication with the Olympia Press, which caused a great deal of trouble for me.

Because the publisher, Maurice Girodias, put it in their pornographic paperback series along with books with titles like *School for Sin, The Whip Angels, The Loins of Amon, The Sexual Life of Robinson Crusoe,* **and you took back the rights?**
Yeah. Then litigations ensued and indeed are conducted to this very day. But there were also censorship problems, which weren't ever as severe as the litigation problems, which required a great deal of money, and I didn't have much money. It was a kind of grim battle for many, many years to survive.

Have you made money from *The Ginger Man* **or has it been so wrapped up in litigation that . . . ?**
No, I've made a fair amount of money on it. It wasn't that someone else got the money. This was while I was being sued by the Olympia Press. They were trying to get the money out of me. A rare case, because most authors sue in the opposite direction. But my wife is now the owner of the Olympia Press, so one has that very curious satisfaction that few authors ever have: to own their original publishers.

Does she own it in your name?
She owns it in her name. And that has stopped the litigation. In effect, one owns both parts of the litigation. I'm in some ways suing myself. It's still complicated.

How did it wind up that your wife now owns it?
Well, in the course of all the litigations, the Olympia Press went bankrupt and was offered for sale by a liquidator in Paris. My Paris lawyers

told me of this, and my wife went over to Paris and, in what is thought to have been the most dramatic commercial auction in Paris history, bought it.

This was all your doing?
Oh yes. I had sent her with my then-secretary to Paris. She's a very able, quick-witted girl, and she went through the most unbelievable kind of things a day or two before the auction, because even to get permission to bid at a Paris auction as a foreigner is a very difficult and complicated thing. She managed to do all of this. But if she hadn't, someone would have spotted her and that would have prevented her getting it.

And do you have any involvement now with the Olympia Press?
It's not operated as an active publishing house at all. It might be one day, but at the present I have enough things to handle without getting involved with it.

Do you see what happened occurring in some future story?
It more or less is incorporated in *A Singular Man*. The whole life of litigation and how it affects somebody and the intimidations involved are part of the book. This is one of the reasons why I could understand precisely the similarities it has to Howard Hughes. Yet, I wasn't aware of the existence of Hughes when I was writing that book. What I was aware of was a man who is being sued and who has to lead a certain kind of life. This is precisely what happened to Hughes, how he got isolated and estranged. It's a natural thing that happens because to be successful in business you are fighting an enemy and the rest of the world is your battle and you have to be very careful as to how you proceed. Secrecy and that type of thing has a lot to do with it.

Fights figure into your books. Did you fight much when you were younger?
I was very adept with my fists. I used to have a lot of fights in Dublin. We visited an old friend of mine who lived in Dublin in those days

and my wife asked him what was my life like then, and he said that he'd never been present at a fight himself, but that he knew someone who had frequently been. His comment was as follows: "You never have to be frightened to go anywhere with Mike Donleavy in a Dublin pub or party, because if there's any trouble and there's a fight, the other guy just flakes out." In other words, suddenly the man is unconscious on the floor. So this picture of me as Bruce Lee suddenly came out. I would find myself involved with people just lying there unconscious on all sides. And everyone who had accosted me would meet this fate. There did come a time when people used to come into bars looking for me, and these would generally be challenges, guys who were pretty big and strong. People would come over to them and say: "There he is over at the bar." And they would say: "Christ, that little guy?" The refrain was then: "Well, that's what they all say, but there he is; everybody says that: there's that little guy." In this particular case there was some great, big tough guy who, in fact, declined to get involved with me, in spite of the absolutely inviting sight of this chap with the choir boy looks and the delicate hands.

I saw you on a talk show with Merv Griffin. It was a strange appearance. You almost immediately started talking about death.
I was mostly nonplussed by Griffin, simply because I can recall just turning when he asked me a question and looking at him, and instead of facing one of these bland cut-off kind of people, I found he was actually listening to what I was going to say—which so terribly threw me that I could hardly say a thing. This I found the most strange thing about him. You get so conditioned talking to people who don't listen to you or give a damn what you're going to say that I was very much off-put by Griffin, who clearly wanted to hear what I had to say. And our reaction instantly to this is you want to listen to him. You immediately sense an interest in the man. I was interviewed to go on the Johnny Carson show but was failed. The reason being that I couldn't talk. Also that one does tend to be a bit shy, and I don't make any efforts to project on television because it's totally

alien to me. On the other hand, it makes for good television, too. People see enough people projecting and glad-facing in public. It's almost an insult to people's intelligence.

You were there to talk about your book of manners, *The Unexpurgated Code*, which is a strong departure from your novels. It's as if you used a lot of extraneous details which could go into novels and made a collage of manners and morals. How did you come to write this? Were you tired of fiction?

No, no. It's always interested me as a subject. I've always been amused by it. I've always been conscious of this curious thing of European manners and, being an American, the whole contrast of this business. It's not thought unusual for an American to go to someone's icebox and open it up and take something out. But this would be unforgivable in Europe. You'd be ostracized. It's this basic thing that fascinated me to write about. I'm also interested in how one survives and what does this mean to a person. Throughout history people would build themselves great big houses and all kinds of manifestations of their importance, because clearly in life you can walk around looking scruffy, down-at-heel, and that's what you are. Unless somebody recognizes you and says, "Hey, I know that person, he's such and such and I know his pedigree." This is how life works. I'm very conscious how people present themselves and to what degree that presentation is then estimated to be representative of this man's position in the world. It's the most difficult book I ever tried to write, much more difficult than a novel.

Do you find writing easier now?

If you've had a very good writing day—which happens maybe once every six weeks—you think the next day is going to be fine, but the same difficulties, the same kind of problems gearing your brain to do the work, happen. The only basic thing to do in the writing game is just form your life and organize it so that you get up in the morning and your intentions are to go towards the desk and begin. You can't really make extremes in the working conditions; you've got to keep up fairly level without driving yourself *too* much. You're always attempting to be a gentleman author if you can. That can be one of my faults. You very rarely find yourself sitting around and enjoying yourself. For instance, if you take a walk in the rose garden out there, you sometimes catch yourself up a whiff of roses to your nostrils and suddenly you have to remind yourself that that's to be enjoyed. I also have to literally train like an athlete, just to keep myself alive. It's a very debilitating way of life, being an author. Just sitting there is very bad for the body.

Joyce once said he could do anything he wanted with words. Do you feel the same?
Not really. Words are tough to handle. Each day you're constantly restruggling. You wake up and you're trying to find new words. It's an unending business.

You believe that your style of writing resembles the way the brain thinks, don't you?
I do use language, or hope to use it, to get it as quickly as possible into the mind of the reader. But I can't even claim that that's always successful. Even when I read the proofs of *The Unexpurgated Code,* it was a highly complicated book if you're trying to read and see that there are no mistakes in this line. I found myself having to go back and reread lines three, four, five times. I thought to myself, O good lord now, is this incomprehensible? Yet, at the same time, I went back and read it at some speed and found that it did come out with all the flavor and intention that I had. It's a kind of worrying business.

Since the feminist movement, has your consciousness changed when you're writing about women?
No, no. In the *Code,* I was amazed as I read through it that it's so totally, totally male-oriented. Totally. One almost ignores women entirely, except as a foil. Changes have clearly come in women's relationships in the world, but I don't think the nature of the female or the male has changed.

You wanted to set the world on fire with *The Ginger Man*. Do you ever worry about burning out?

There's a very deep, basic feeling with an author that he can burn himself out with unrequited ambition. I'm conscious in America you'll hear someone saying about an author who has got a famous literary reputation, "Well, he's all washed up." I'm always astonished, because this is not the attitude in Europe. If you're an established author, you are simply that.

If you never wrote another book, could you live off your royalties?

Yes. I don't think I could live as I now do. I have a larger overhead than most authors. I employ five people and run a great big operation.

Is the way you're living what you wanted when you came to Ireland?

No, I really wanted to live in a suburban house with some land around me, because I'm very conscious of the practicalities of a working author. You are faced with the terrible dilemma of having a proper place to work. A place where you can sleep soundly at night. This is as important as anything in the world, being able to sleep. Where you're not conscious of the fact that somebody can interrupt your peace of mind. Fortunately for me, this farm pays for itself, and surprisingly, this may turn out to be the cheapest place I've ever lived.

Was your incentive to come here that it's tax-free?

Primarily. The only drawback about it is that if you're suddenly tax-free, then you try to go out and make a lot of money, but you find it impossible to make any money. This can happen. A lot of people smell your interest. Previously, I was always having to not accept money in terms of having to spread out income over a period of years. I'd sign a contract and say, "I'm sorry I can only take so much money now and the next will have to be on April 8th." Now I can say

I want everything you can pay me and as much as you can pay. And it's tougher getting money.

How much do you write each day?
I wouldn't think that I finish more than two or three hundred words a day. Work goes through various drafts—five, six, seven drafts. These get built up and practically edited like a filmstrip.

Have you ever considered allowing a film to be adapted from your novels?
Yes, it's come up. Nothing's ever been made of any of my things. I thought I was so stubborn and difficult that I wouldn't agree to anything, but that's not true. I did sell the film rights to *Balthazar B,* but it didn't get made because the option ran out. So I'm aware that I will actually come to some agreement. I even toyed with the idea of making films myself, but that's unsatisfactory as a novelist. I don't think there's a Hollywood director who's ever lived who hasn't wanted to direct *The Ginger Man.* When I look into my pile of correspondence going back twenty years, I find every name cropping up at one time or another. But it's a difficult business. It involves a lot of people. I have sound respect for producers, who are reviled, because they're businessmen, and that's what I am. As a businessman, nothing worse can happen than you put out a picture and you lose a lot of money. And this could happen with *The Ginger Man.* You could lose your shirt with it. It's dangerous, my stuff. It looks good, but it's dangerous to handle. Again, it could make a good film. I'm conscious, too, that we had a production in London of my play of *The Ginger Man,* and the director nearly went out of his mind. He said, "Good God," watching the audience come in. They were all eighteen, nineteen, twenty years old, all cinemagoers. It began to impress him what, in fact, *The Ginger Man* did mean—how many people would come to that kiosk to put their money down. And he'd start screaming at me why I didn't do something. But I think what's going to happen is my heirs will be very rich when I depart this world.

JAMES ELLROY

There's Never Been Anybody Like Me in American Letters

JAMES ELLROY LIKES TO PERFORM. IN PERSON. ON THE page. He likes to pepper his conversation with growls and barks. He likes to say outrageous things and to promote himself. He likes to write about violence in violent ways. The characters in his novels get thrown out of buildings, get fed shotgun shells and have their lips glued shut, have their hands submerged in boiling oil. People's faces get blown off, famous real-life politicians and mob associates mingle with his made-up people, and oftentimes characters carry over from one book to another.

Ellroy's background uniquely qualifies him to write about the underside of life. In 1958, when he was ten, his mother was brutally murdered in L.A. and her killer was never found (he wrote about this in *My Dark Places*). When he was seventeen he was thrown out of high school, his father died, and he began a life of crime. He became addicted to drugs and booze, got caught stealing on numerous occasions, and spent more time in jail than he'd like to remember. Only when his brain was almost fried and he couldn't remember anything did he decide to take charge of his life and start to write. His first novel, *Brown's Requiem*, was published when he was in his early thirties. Five others followed (*Clandestine, Blood on the Moon, Because the Night, Suicide Hill, Killer on the Road*) before he published his breakthrough book in 1987, *The Black Dahlia,* a novel about another unsolved L.A. murder. Said Elmore Leonard of that one: "Ellroy's got more energy in his writing than anybody going today. There should be a warning on his *Black Dahlia* that it should not be read aloud or you're liable to shatter your wine glasses."

That was the first of what Ellroy calls his L.A. Quartet; the next three only enhanced his reputation: *The Big Nowhere, L.A. Confidential* (the basis for the Oscar-nominated film), and *White Jazz.* One of his friends, L.A. police detective Dennis Payne, says, "I don't know anyone who has better insight into what L.A. was like in some very bad years in the '30s, '40s, and '50s."

Hollywood Nocturnes appeared before his new trilogy, *Underworld USA,* began. The first of those novels, *American Tabloid,* was met with great critical and popular success in 1995.

"It's time to demythologize an era and build a new myth from the gutter to the stars," Ellroy declared at the beginning of this novel. "It's time to embrace bad men and the price they paid to secretly define their time."

Time magazine called *American Tabloid* "a big, boisterous, rude and shameless reminder of why reading can be so engrossing and so much fun." It's Ellroy's take on five years of American history, from 1958 to 1963, years when Howard Hughes, Teamster boss Jimmy Hoffa, Jack and Robert Kennedy and their father Joseph, Fidel Castro, the Mafia, the CIA, the FBI and its boss J. Edgar Hoover were all involved in various political shenanigans and corruptions that would lead to the disastrous Bay of Pigs and the assassination of President Kennedy. Loss of American innocence? Not according to Ellroy, who believes there never was an innocence to lose. America was always corrupt.

> The real Trinity of Camelot was Look Good, Kick Ass, Get Laid. Jack Kennedy was the mythological front man for a particularly juicy slice of our history. He talked a slick line and wore a world-class haircut. He was Bill Clinton minus pervasive media scrutiny and a few rolls of flab.

Jack got whacked at the optimum moment to assure his sainthood. Lies continue to swirl around his eternal flame. It's time to dislodge his urn and cast light on a few men who attended his ascent and facilitated his fall.

"Ellroy's style is so hard-boiled it scorches the pot," noted *New York* magazine. "There's so much violence in his work that it proves that books can still out-gore movies by incredible margins." *American Tabloid* has been described as so over the top and cartoonish that it can't be taken seriously, and yet Ellroy has been compared to Don DeLillo, Thomas Pynchon, and Robert Coover—"madcap, conspiracy-minded postmodernists who reimagine American history."

His muscular, pungent prose has been compared to jazz great Charlie Parker—peppery and unpredictable, racing the edgy rhythm of a bebop groove. Futuristic novelist Steve Erickson says, "Ellroy has put terror back into American crime fiction—not the Stephen King kind of terror, but the terror that arises from ordinary urban disease."

Ellroy's editors, not surprisingly, agree. His first publisher, Otto Penzler of the Mystery Press, has said, "He has the ability and the courage to be perhaps the great crime novelist of our time." Sonny Mehta, his current editor at Knopf (who paid Ellroy $1.1 million for three books), says his books "represent the best of crime writing in that they stand above the plot and address the issues of justice and motivation and history."

Ellroy himself trumpets the ego of a Muhammed Ali. The fifty-three-year-old writer has set himself up for critical attack by proclaiming: "I want to burn crime fiction to the fucking ground. I want to destroy every last bit of niceness and cheap empathy in the American crime novel. All other crime novels are tepid compared to mine. I want to be known as the greatest crime novelist who ever lived! I want to be the American Tolstoy."

What more appropriate place to begin when we spoke in 1998?

You've been known to say you want to be the Tolstoy of American crime. The greatest crime writer who ever lived. Did

you learn from Mailer and Muhammed Ali how to draw attention to yourself?

No, because other than *The Naked and the Dead* I've never read anything that Norman Mailer has written. And although I'm a huge boxing fan I was never a big Ali fan. I always rooted for Joe Frazier.

Still, Mailer did write *Advertisements for Myself,* which you seem to have taken to heart. At least the title. Writers like Mailer and Truman Capote were able to get into our consciousness even if one hadn't read their work. You seem to be inheriting that mantle.

I like to go out and sell books. I like to talk in front of a crowd and I'm good at it. That's it right there.

Where does all the violence in your work come from?

It comes from this awe that I feel for American history. It's a great dark and bloody journey enacted on a dark and bloody ground and anyone who wants to write great, popular fiction has to embrace the language of violence.

How do you feel you've been critically received?

My critical reputation has snowballed. *American Tabloid* was *Time* magazine's novel of the year in 1995; *My Dark Places* was a *Time* best book of the year and a *New York Times* notable book for '96. There's never been anybody like me in American letters, and I think I've divorced myself from the crime genre very handsomely.

Do you remember mostly the negative reviews?

Oh sure, and I still get 'em. I've been called a racist, a fascist, an anti-Semite, a homophobe, a misogynist, an anti-Mexican, anti-Communist. And there have been people who have just rejected the books on aesthetic grounds as well as political grounds. It's all okay. I get pissed off, grrrrrr, and I forget about it.

Most of those names you've been called appeared in one *New York Times* review of *The Big Nowhere.*

Yeah, they gave the book to a radical lesbian feminist separatist.
When I saw that I just howled. What can you do?

Other critics say you have reinvented the genre of the noir mystery. Think you have?
I hate the word mystery, it's a dismissive term. And I don't really
know what noir fiction is. I write big, historical novels that deal with
crime, take place in the film noir era—the mid-1940s to the early
1960s—a lot of them in L.A., the film noir epicenter. I guess that's
why I get the noir tag, and it's a tag I can live with.

Your novel *L.A. Confidential* has achieved critical acclaim as a noir film. Did you ever think such a good movie could be made from so complex a book?
No. I figured that with all the film options that I've had that they
would lay some money on me for nothing, which they did, and they'd
never make the fucking movie. And if they did it would be fucked up
past redemption. So the amazing thing for me is that Curtis Hanson
and Brian Helgeland, the director and coscreenwriters, did such a
fucking good job containing, compressing, cutting plot lines, adding
some characters of their own, and generally condensing this monster
book of mine.

Did you have anything to do with the movie?
No. I had heard that Hanson was involved throughout the process
and was impressed with the fact that he didn't contact me. When he
and Brian Helgeland had gone through seven drafts of the script they
let me read what they had. I found it interesting and compelling and
a good job of retaining the essential narrative integrity of my book,
i.e., the dramatic lives of the three main characters. From that point
on Hanson and I became friendly and I became an informal consul-
tant. Chiefly, Curtis would call me up and ask me questions pertain-
ing to L.A. in the fifties and the police corps then. "Do you turn left
off the rotunda at City Hall to get to the detective bureau in 1953?"
Things like that.

What did you think of the cast—did they bring your characters to life?

None of the characters in the film physically resembled the characters in the book. They were markedly different. They became something else. I was very impressed with the film. Hanson flew my wife and I out to Tacoma, Washington, to view a test-market screening. Here was a story with characters and a milieu that only I could have created and an overall worldview that is entirely mine that had assumed a compatible yet completely unimaginable form. So I was quite startled with it. Here was dialogue that I had written, spoken with inflections that differed from the voices I already had in my head.

Kim Basinger won an Oscar for her performance, what do you think of her?

She's very gracious. What's interesting about her performance specifically, and it flabbergasted me, is she's essentially older than Russell Crowe. She's forty-three or forty-four and Crowe's thirty-two or thirty-three, there's a decade between them. It shows. Here is a policeman whose mother was murdered, he viewed the crime, and remained in the room with the decomposing corpse, who is now being mothered by a substantially older woman who happens to be a prostitute. I don't know how much of that was conscious on Curtis Hanson's part, but it certainly hit home with me.

***Cop*, an earlier attempt to adapt one of your books, *Blood on the Moon*, to the screen didn't work as well, did it?**

I don't talk about *Cop* for attribution. What I say is "No comment."

Do you think more of your work will now be more accessible for adaptation?

You can't predict that because a large world of dysfunction exists in Hollywood. Although they just finished shooting a low-budget $1.2 million adaptation of my first novel, *Brown's Requiem*.

Nick Nolte wants to do *White Jazz*. Anything happening there?
I adapted *White Jazz* for Nick Nolte and Fine Line Pictures. Nothing's happening that I know of. I talk to Nolte's partner regularly. If they ever make it, which they state is their intention, it will be wonderful. It's completely uncompromised Ellroy in a way that *L.A. Confidential* isn't.

Anybody considering turning *American Tabloid* into a movie?
It's been optioned by HBO.

What kind of movies do you like?
I go to very few movies. I only like crime movies. I collect film noirs from 1940 to 1960.

What are your five favorite film noirs?
The Prowler, a Joseph Losey film. *711 Ocean Drive,* the Joseph H. Newman film. *Johnny Cool,* the William Asher film. *The Lineup,* the Don Siegel film. And *Sunset Boulevard.*

Novelist and ex-cop Joe Wambaugh said that he suspects you wouldn't be saddened if you found out you couldn't write anymore but could be a major movie star.
That's horseshit. Wambaugh, by the way, is my greatest teacher. The guy's been in decline for many years as a writer, but his early work is very moving and powerful.

Are cops generally as corrupt as criminals? Especially in L.A.?
No, that's a cliché.

What did you think about how detective Mark Fuhrman affected the outcome of the O. J. Simpson trial?
He didn't do most of what he said he did. Ninety-nine percent of it he couldn't have got away with it. He just shot his mouth off to impress that woman screenwriter. But he did a good job of deep-sixing the LAPD case.

In your world it's been pointed out that the system isn't corrupt; corruption *is* the system. Fair?

Yeah. Keep in mind that the books I write, I write about life in extremis and the hermetically sealed inner world of hepcat jazz musicians, desperate homosexual informants, corrupt D.A.s, and bent cops. These books don't purport to be overviews of the total police experience.

Would you agree with the Boston writer who wrote that if L.A. is the city of dreams, then you are the keeper of its nightmares?

Sure, sounds good.

How do you feel about L.A. today?

I don't know anything about it. I only go out there to do business and media. It's incomprehensible to me. I prefer the L.A. that's in my head.

Do you still have a fear in L.A. that you don't have anywhere else?

It actually, over the past several years, has abated. Whenever I go to L.A. I like to go through the old neighborhoods where I've lived and feel the weight of time.

That said, you seem to have left L.A. behind with *American Tabloid*. Was it also your intention to leave crime fiction behind as well?

Yeah. *American Tabloid* includes the Cuban exiles, Bay of Pigs, Castro coming to power, J. Edgar Hoover—known to many as "Gay" Edgar Hoover—Howard Hughes, the Kennedy brothers, Bobby's war on organized crime, the McClellan Senate Rackets Committee, Jimmy Hoffa and the Teamsters, JFK's death, all kinds of mob intrigue. When I wrote that book I made a conscious decision to get out of L.A. and to write a book that could no way be characterized as a mystery, thriller, or crime novel. It's the first book of my *Underworld U.S.A.*

trilogy. I'm writing the second book now. The overall design of the trilogy is three books, fifteen years of American history broken down into five-year increments. *Tabloid* covers '58 to '63, the next book '63 to '68, and the third '68 to '73. The private nightmare of public policy, that's the overall theme of these books.

You've called what you've done a tabloid sewer crawl through the private nightmare of public policy. How well do you feel you succeeded?
Brilliantly. I've rewritten American history in *American Tabloid* to my own specifications.

Did John F. Kennedy deserve to die?
By the laws he lived by, absolutely. He betrayed the mob, he betrayed the Cuban exiles with the Bay of Pigs, he fought with people he shouldn't have fucked with and he paid with his life. If *Tabloid* wasn't anything else, it's really the story of Bobby Kennedy's Oedipal dialogue. Bobby Kennedy had a very strong moral center. He was the only one of the brothers who saw through the Kennedy family mystique. He was the only one of the brothers who sided with Rose Kennedy emotionally. His going after the mob is really the act of going after his father, and his brother paid the price.

How did you decide that Marilyn Monroe never slept with the Kennedy boys?
Fred Otash told me. He was the private eye to the stars. Otash was a big, big self-promoter and self-aggrandizer, but there were certain things he said and certain things he didn't say. He was documentively all over Marilyn Monroe in the last days of her life and her death. He was the one who went in to wipe the place down when Peter Lawford called him. Bobby was just trying to get her off Jack's back. By the way, Marilyn and Jack were about an eight-night stand over the course of eight years. They'd meet once a year and fuck for half an hour, that's all that was.

Among the major real characters in *Tabloid*—Howard Hughes, J. Edgar Hoover, the Kennedys, Hoffa, Castro—who's your favorite villain?

"Gay" Edgar Hoover is absolutely the premier villain of the American twentieth century. There's nothing good you can say about this guy. Parenthetically, he no more went outside in drag than I can flap my arms and fly from Kansas to St. Louis. He was much too discrete to do something like that. I don't think he was an active homosexual. I think he and his roommate Clyde were some sort of Victorian homosexual couple who never had sex.

Who was the most powerful man in America at that time?

J. Edgar Hoover is a good call.

Would you place Howard Hughes second?

Hughes was a germaphobic racist, far right-wing, dope-addicted fuckhead, lucid only about half the time. In *American Tabloid* I played Hughes for some real laughs, and he returns in the next book. I've got him shooting codeine into his dick.

What do you make of Castro?

The Beard? The Bushy Bearded Beatnik Bard of Bilious Bamboozlement? History has exposed him for what he is, a tyrant. He has staying power, however. He's been around since 1955.

What about today? Who's the most powerful man in America?

It's got to be the P, Bill Clinton, who looks more and more slitty-eyed and porcine the older he gets. I hate the cocksucker. I think he was doing Monica Lewinsky, I think he suborned perjury, and I loathe the American people for not wanting his hide. But apparently the American economy is good and people are feeling fat and sassy, so let Bill Clinton get some head from some stupid girl whose life he's effectively wrecked in the sense that nobody will ever take her seriously. She may get a trillion-dollar book deal and go on to have a life on some level, but people will just snigger and snigger at her because Bill Clinton, the Pig, had to get some head.

Is your intention to recreate the entire history of twentieth-century America?

That's the grand design for the rest of my career. As many books as I can squeeze into my lifetime without sacrificing quality.

How long does it take you to write a book?

Two years. The new book, the sequel to *American Tabloid*, is my magnum opus. It will be a 750-page hardcover.

The plot was so thick you apparently wrote a 250-page outline first. Is this typical of how you work?

I'm extremely meticulous and diligent. I have to know where the story's going, down to the most minute detail, before I write the first word of the text. If you want a big, dense, complex, and well-layered book you'd better outline it first.

How convoluted do your plots become—even for you?

I can fully comprehend them, and my outlines are so detailed that I have them to the right of my desk blotter as I write the text, so it's just a matter of consulting it.

Is the writing easy because of the outline?

It's not easy because I rewrite and rewrite until I think I have it perfectly. Nat Sobel, my agent, has been the chief editor of my books going back fifteen years. He goes over my outlines with me in detail.

Is it true that you print your first drafts?

I print all my drafts. Sooner or later I send them to my typist. I don't know how to type, don't work on a computer.

What did you think of Oliver Stone's film *JFK*?

Brilliant filmmaking but a preposterous statement. Jim Garrison was a whacked-out psychopath on some kind of weird antigay pogrom. He was popped for hawking young boys at the YMCA in New Orleans sometime in the late fifties. He used to run into the poor sonofabitch Clay Shaw. I think Clay Shaw's only crime was fucking the wrong kid in the wrong bathhouse at the wrong fucking time. The movie is full of shit. Very well turned out until Donald Sutherland opens his mouth and the plot takes in the entire world.

What about Don DeLillo's novel *Libra*?
Libra is in every way the inspiration for my novel *American Tabloid*. I credit it every chance I get. After I finished the book I wrote DeLillo a letter saying, "Thanks, daddy-o, you inspired me." I was never interested in the JFK hit before, even though I was fifteen at the time that happened. I realized when I read *Libra* that this is so good that I could never write a book specifically about the JFK hit. But I thought I could write a much larger book wherein the JFK hit was just one of a series of politically motivated killings.

Have you read DeLillo's *Underworld*?
No. I don't read much. I avoid popular culture. I like to spend time with my wife, brood, exercise. Rarely go to movies, rarely read.

Did you look at Norman Mailer's *Oswald*?
No. *American Tabloid* came out before that one did.

And what about Seymour Hersh's *The Dark Side of Camelot*?
I read that, it had absolutely no revelations in it for me. I'd been hearing all those rumors for years. I was astonished that that book was controversial. If you want a racier version of the Kennedy presidency, read my book.

***Kirkus Reviews* called you the comic-book Dos Passos of our time.**
I never read Dos Passos. Kirkus can suck my dick. Fuck them up the ass with a faggot pit bull with an 18-inch dick and shoot a big load of syphilitic jism up Kirkus's ass.

With that said, let's go to the era you're working on now. What's your take on the Vietnam war?

Futile, ugly, preposterous, American imperialistic expansionism at its absolute worst. It shouldn't have happened. A dark blotch on American history. I'm astonished that we haven't completely revised our opinion of it. I was appalled when Bill Clinton—an appalling human being to be sure—ran for president in 1992 that he actually had to defend his not wanting to go to Vietnam.

What about the assassinations of Martin Luther King Jr. and Robert Kennedy, did they deserve to die?
It was preordained by the rules they lived by.

Watergate?
Watergate put me to sleep. Snoresville U.S.A. I may bypass it or only mention it tangentially in the concluding volume of the trilogy. Also, most of the principles are still alive, which means I wouldn't be able to use them as characters. Nixon will be in the third book, he's dead, I can use him.

How corrupt is America? And when did the country lose its innocence?
America never had innocence, that's bullshit. Look at the prologue of *American Tabloid:* We popped our cherry on the boat over and looked back with no regrets. How corrupt is it? I don't know. And I'm not being disingenuous. I don't follow current events. I live and work in a vacuum. I isolate myself in the periods of time that I write about.

New York **magazine wrote that you use murder the way other writers use paragraph breaks, as a pacing device.**
No, that's not true. That makes it sound like these murders are never morally justified, never adequately couched with psychic weight, and that's just typical bullshit slash journalism.

One murder that had more psychic weight on you than any other was your mother's. You wrote a book, *My Dark Places*, and then

spoke frequently about it to promote it. Was it at all difficult to do that?

No, I'm an exhibitionist by nature, by inclination. I've made a conscious decision to honor my mother by attempting to find the man who killed her by taking the story public. It wasn't painful to write that book. It was self-revelatory about my mother and more than anything else it was exhilarating.

You wrote that you hated your mother at the time of her murder. You were just ten—did you really hate her?

I did hate her and knew it at the time.

Did you hate her because she slapped you when you said you wanted to live with your father and not her?

Yeah, I was very much in the thrall of my father. He systematically played into my mind against her. Yeah, she did hit me on the occasion of my tenth birthday. At the time of her death my greatest wish was to live with my father exclusively. And that wish came true.

How difficult was it to write so coldly about your parents? Your mother, you wrote, "majored in booze and minored in men." You said you called her a drunk and a whore. Your father called her a lush and a tramp. She called him a weakling and a parasite. This is pretty rough stuff for the ears and mouth of a ten-year-old.

Yes, it is.

How did you react when you came home from junior high to find your sixth-grade teacher in bed with your father?

I looked. The dog was on the bed with them. He was curled up on some sheets at the foot of the bed trying to get some shut-eye, dodging these flailing legs. It was funny. More than anything else, I was just curious about the physical aspect.

Did you ever talk to your father about it?

No. He didn't know that I was watching.

**You said you forced some tears when you heard of her murder
and have never cried since. Is that true?**
Right.

How cathartic was it to write *My Dark Places*?
It was cathartic, but closure is bullshit. My mother and I will continue, the book is very much about my journey of recognition and
reconciliation with her, and she's very much a part of my mental and
spiritual life now.

**Did you believe you might discover who her killer was when you
began researching the book?**
I knew it was an extreme long shot going in. And that proved to be
the case.

Are you still hopeful some new lead will turn up?
The book continues to get a great deal of publicity; it's possible, but
it's not probable.

Do you still have an 800 number for anyone to call with possible tips?
Yes, we get occasional calls but nothing substantive.

**When you wrote *Clandestine*, you fictionalized your mother's
murder and gave the killer some aspects of your father. You were
with him when she was killed, but somehow do you blame him
for it?**
No.

**You wrote that you have never understood your motive for doing
this—could it have been psychological? Had they not split up, she
might still be alive?**
No, the character that I created in the outline process resembled
my father; he was the most powerful potential character in the book
to assume the role of killer. Since it was fiction I could do what
I wanted.

Do you still have nightmares?
No.

Are you still afraid of the dark?
No.

Was it an emotional experience, to look at the pictures of your dead mother?
It wasn't as shocking as you might think it would be. The pictures aren't terribly graphic. It was more shocking just to live in this world of concentration with her for the fifteen months of the actual investigation and the seven months I spent writing the book and the many months that I spent touring for the book here and abroad in hardcover and paperback.

After writing the book, did you reach new conclusions about your mother and yourself?
Yes, but it would take an hour to discuss them.

Would you say you're more like her or your father?
More like her.

What did her death teach you?
Self-sufficiency by negative example. Her death engendered in me a tremendous curiosity for all things criminal, specifically, L.A. and its criminal history of the 1950s. And I turned her death into something useful very early on. Her death gave me something useful, that's something that a lot of people find odd to hear or don't want to hear. The truth is, my bereavement was complex and ambiguous.

How different a writer might you have been had your mother not have been murdered?
I never think hypothetically. It's one of those things: this is the way the die was cast and that's it.

Seven years after her murder you were kicked out of high school. Was it for obscenity?
Yeah, I went to Fairfax High School and got kicked out not for obscenity but for creating disturbances.

Was this after you once unzipped your pants and chased a girl from your school?
No, this was much later. I was a wild kid.

Did you ever receive your high school diploma?
No, I did not.

What did you do after you left school?
Joined the army. I was seventeen.

It didn't last long. How'd you manage to get discharged before you were inducted?
I was inducted.

I thought you ran naked through the reception station and they kicked you out.
The induction station was in downtown L.A. The reception station was in Fort Polk, Louisiana. That's where I was sent for basic training. My father had yet another stroke at that time and in order to capitalize on it and get out of the army I faked a nervous breakdown and enacted a stutter. Getting naked was just icing on the cake.

You made it back to be with your father when he died. His last words offer any relief?
He said, "Son, try to pick up every waitress who serves you." A legacy I have fulfilled at moments in my life.

Did you shed any tears when he died?
I forced myself to shed a few.

Did you feel alone, isolated, or liberated after both your parents were gone when you were seventeen?
Liberated.

When did you get interested in books?
When I was six years old. I started to read when I was three-and-a-half.

When did writing become a secret passion?
I always wanted it but I didn't start writing until I was thirty-one.

Seventeen to twenty-nine were your dark years. How long did you live on the streets?
On and off, and mostly on, from 1968 to 1975. Mostly in L.A., though I spent a few months in San Francisco.

Which was your larger vice, drugs or booze?
Booze was more constant because it was more available.

You were shooting Benzedrine and taking uppers and downers?
No, I wasn't shooting anything. I swallowed the cotton wads out of Benzedrex inhalers. You have to dismantle the inhalers. I met a freak named Harvey, a hippie I got into a conversation with at the Hollywood Public Library, and he told me about it.

What kind of high was it?
An amphetamine high.

Did you steal this from doctor's offices?
No, I stole from drugstores. It was sold over-the-counter.

Did you ever get caught stealing?
Oh yeah, a half dozen times. Petty theft with a prior one, with a prior two.

So you were not a very careful thief?

I was as careful as I could be. I shoplifted during my career on hundreds of occasions and got arrested seven or eight times.

How shocked were you when seven cops with shotguns burst through a door and arrested you for burglary?
I was shocked. That was November 30, '68. I was just sleeping there, I wasn't stealing anything, there was nothing to burgle. It was one of those typical LAPD overkills. Here I was, a punk drug-addicted wino kid and they came in with shotguns.

How many times did you have to do jail time?
I saw a partial rap sheet on me once and that had about eighteen arrests. There were ones that weren't on there that I recall. My guess is about thirty times.

You often sound proud to have been a thief, to have a jail record. Is that to help sell books, or do you look back to that time as being most alive?
To me it's just preposterous. I was not a tough guy or a violent criminal or any kind of a hard case. To me it's tremendously amusing given the life I have today.

It wasn't so amusing, though, when your behavior forced you to attack a Doberman Pinscher with a two by four, was it?
That's right. I killed him too. It was horrible, because I love dogs. I shoplifted and was being chased, so I hopped a fence into a lumberyard. I was provoking the dog, he'd have been within his rights to kill me. He got to my legs, I've still got the scars on my left leg.

Was that as terrifying as anything in your life?
Terrifying in the moment, sure. Not as terrifying as the brain syndrome thing I went through.

Is that when you were diagnosed at twenty-seven with alcohol brain syndrome?

Yeah. It just meant that I had a psychotic brain rupture when I was coming off of alcohol. It was a brain malfunction where I couldn't think of stuff I wanted to conjure. I snapped out of it.

And did you join Alcoholics Anonymous soon after?
I got sober two years later in '75. But I continued using drugs for a few years.

Was this a turning point for you?
Oh yeah.

How close to madness would you say you came?
I was physiologically insane at the moment I had that brain episode.

Elmore Leonard described alcoholic withdrawal as like having a sunburned nervous system.
Yeah, that's good.

During your rehabilitation you worked as a caddy at private golf clubs. What insights did you get into celebrities you caddied for?
The several that I met impressed me on a case-by-case basis. A couple of them were gracious, some were alcoholic blowhards and stoops. It's a kick that wears off fast: you're out there in the sun, it's hot, it's cold, your feet are getting wet from the sprinkler system, you want to go home and choke your chicken or read a book or write a book or get laid, you're thinking of the next pizza you're going to eat, and you're carrying a bag for some movie star who doesn't care if you live or die.

Did you golf yourself?
No.

After growing up hungry and now having made it, do you agree with your wife that your life resembles F. Scott Fitzgerald's Gatsby?

Well, I've got a lot of shirts just like Gatsby. And a lot of cashmere sweaters.

I thought you were into Hawaiian shirts?
I gave that up for a more restrained look.

You've been described as looking like Hitler and like an Ivy League professor. Which is more accurate?
Neither one. I'm too tall for Hitler. I've been losing my hair at a rapid clip for the past several years. I don't think I look like either one now.

You've been married twice. What went wrong with your first marriage?
I don't talk about my marriages. That's the one thing I keep private.

Are you happily married?
Very happy.

Are you surprised you've got a large readership, considering how difficult some of your books are?
No, in a lot of ways quality outs, especially if it's quality hooked up to great, great interesting stories that people want to read.

Is it fair to say that the violence you describe has been matched by the violence you do to the English language?
It's constructive violence. With that as a qualifier, sure.

Your former publisher, Otto Penzler, says the flaw in your books is that there are no sympathetic characters, that your vision is too dark.
Otto's mistaken. I find my characters tremendously sympathetic. Otto's very much a hard-core mystery guy. Got to have sympathetic characters to create attention or your readers won't care about what happens. I disagree completely.

Have you ever questioned your own vision?
I've consciously addressed each of my books from the standpoint of how can I get better and better and better and better. And I've been trying to do that for many years. I've a covenant of consciousness with myself, God, my readers, my wife, and my dog that I'm about to get. I have taken great risks as a writer. Every book of mine is written in a different style or a narrative variation that's suited to the story that I'm telling. I want to keep taking the risks and get better, better, better, and better.

Novelist Katherine Dunn has said that you're driving yourself to genius. What do you think of that remark?
I think I had genius to begin with, but the older and more experienced I get the more meticulous and diligent I become and the more aware I become of what I'm doing.

You don't agree that your view of the world is dour or depressive, do you?
No, it's passionate. I'm actually very happy. And very square—I live in Kansas City.

Why do you live there?
It's quiet, peaceful, there's no discernable culture, no media here, and it's physically beautiful.

One of the things that disturbs your peace is rock 'n' roll music. Why do you hate it?
It's institutionalized rebelliousness. Just bad immature Mickey Mouse straight up-and-down ugly stupid raucous music. Nothing's more pathetic than middle-aged rock and rollers or middle-aged people who take that shit seriously.

There are still a lot of people who take writers seriously. You've said you hardly read fiction anymore, but let's see what writers have impressed you. We've already touched on Wambaugh and

DeLillo. What about the writer that so influenced Elmore Leonard: George Higgins?

Loved his early books, but after a while his style got the better of him. I don't have much feeling for East Coast white ethics.

Ed McBain?

Loved him when I was a kid. The greatest young adult writer of all time.

Charles Willeford?

Read one of the Hoke Mosely books, there's one amusing bit in *New Hope for the Dead* where Mosely needs to find a place to stay and the woman informs him she'll rent him this house if he jacks off the dog. That was great.

Thomas Harris?

He's the greatest pure thriller writer who ever lived. Especially *Red Dragon*. As absurd a character as Hannibal Lechter is—real-life serial killers don't rip wires out of their teeth and escape from high-security jail cells in spectacular fashion—he is so good that he can make you believe it.

Are you familiar with any Japanese writers? Oë? Mishima? Kawabata? Tanizaki? Murakami?

No.

Have you ever been to Japan?

No, but I'd go if my publisher brings me over. I only like to travel on book tours. The idea of sightseeing for its own sake bores me.

How many languages are your books published in?

All the European ones, Japan, the Orient.

What countries provide the most royalties outside the U.S.?

I could make a very nice living from England and France.

Four publishers wanted you, some offered more than the $1.1 million of Knopf; why'd you go with them?
Because Knopf is the greatest publisher in the history of the world and I wanted to be there. They also put out the most beautiful books on earth.

Is there a Nobel Prize in the future for the kind of work you do?
No. I'll never receive a major literary award because my books are too genre driven. It's the same reason as John Le Carré, another great genre-drived writer who has never received a National Book Award, Booker Prize, National Book Critic Circle Award or anything like that. Will never happen.

Long before any such talk of prizes, you wrote a book called *L.A. Death Trip* which was rejected seventeen times before being published as *Blood on the Moon*. How did you deal with rejection?
I denied the validity of the rejection for the course of those seventeen rejection slips, realized I had to rewrite the book, and fired my existing agent and hooked up with Nat Sobel.

What happened to the book you were working on called *The Confessions of Bugsy Siegel*?
It was a deeply flawed partial manuscript of mine from years ago and I'm never going to finish it.

Is it true that for years when you couldn't sleep you would reenact Hemingway's suicide scene in your head?
Yeah. I read his books bombed out of my mind. I just happened to know he put the butt end of a double-barreled shotgun to his forehead and went off into the big sleep. There were times when my mind was racing so hard that that sounded like a good thing.

You still think about it?
Not any more.

ALLEN GINSBERG

The Breaking of Taboos

ALLEN GINSBERG WANTED TO BE KNOWN AS THE MOST brilliant man in America. He wanted to be God. He said so in his poems. He said a lot of things in his poems—and a lot of what he said was controversial and unique and had never been said before, which is what we expected from the poet who, along with his friends Jack Kerouac, Gary Snyder, Gregory Corso, and William Burroughs, defined the Beat Generation in the fifties. They were cool, hip, free-spirited word anarchists who invoked the visions of Blake and Poe, who romanticized the road, who turned nonconformists into goateed, finger-snapping beatniks and established rebel havens in San Francisco's North Beach, New York's Greenwich Village, and Venice beach in Southern California. In the sixties it was Ginsberg still leading the way, walking the streets of Haight-Ashbury, coining the phrase "flower power."

Ginsberg was always in the forefront of youthful rebellion, ever since he told us in his groundbreaking poem "Howl" that he had seen the best minds of his generation destroyed by madness. He had seen, for sure, his mother destroyed by madness—by family spies and visions of Hitler's mustache in her sink, by electric shock therapy—and wrote "Kaddish," his other great, confessional poem, for her.

"Take me home," his mother Naomi would beg when thirteen-year-old Allen visited her at Greystone, the mental hospital in New Jersey.

"No, you're crazy Mama," Allen would say. "Trust the doctors."

Her last words to her son came in a letter delivered two days after her death. "Get married," she told him. "Don't take drugs."

But she was crazy, so how could he listen to her? How could he abandon the lifestyle that was the source and catalyst for so much of his poetry—the love of other men? The visions gained from peyote, mescaline, methadrine, pot, LSD?

Although he wrote nearly two dozen books of poetry, if he never wrote anything other than "Howl" and "Kaddish," Ginsberg would remain in the pantheon of American visionaries. "Howl" was just that, a four-part rhythmic scream that Richard Eberhart described in the *New York Times* as "a howl against everything in our mechanistic civilization which kills the spirit, assuming that the louder you shout the more likely you are to be heard. It lays bare the nerves of suffering and spiritual struggle. Its positive force and energy come from a redemptive quality of love, although it destructively catalogues evils of our time from physical deprivation to madness." The minds that Ginsberg saw destroyed were people he knew, "who were expelled from the academies for crazy," "who ate fire in paint hotels," "who chained themselves to subways," "who vanished into nowhere." The evil was Moloch, "Moloch the loveless! Mental Moloch! . . . Moloch whose mind is pure machinery! Moloch whose blood is running money." And redemption was in the Holy. "The world is holy! The soul is holy! . . . Everything is holy! . . . Everywhere is holy!"

"Kaddish" was more personal, as Ginsberg told his biographer Barry Miles: "I realized that I hadn't gone back and told the whole secret family-self tale—my own one-and-only eternal child-youth memories which no one else could know—in all its eccentric detail." The detail was what made the poem so memorable because it included, as Ginsberg told Miles, "embarrassing scenes I'd half amnesiaized. . . . Images that were central to my own existence such as the mass of scars on my mother's plump belly." The poem begins with his mother's death: "Strange now to think of you, gone without corsets & eyes, while I walk on/the sunny pavement of Greenwich Village," and then traces back her tragic life and descent into madness: "All the accumulations of life, that wear us out—clocks, bodies, consciousness,/shoes, breasts—begotten sons—your Communism—'Paranoia' into/hospitals." The poem's power is in its raw nervous energy, and in its agonizing detail that turns into metaphors for all who have troubled families ("Everybody has crazy cousins and aunts and brothers," Ginsberg later said).

"His voice is on the land," his friend and fellow poet Lawrence Ferlinghetti wrote on hearing of Ginsberg's death by stroke after being diagnosed with liver cancer in April, 1997. (Ferlinghetti published "Howl," which landed him in court on distributing obscene materials in 1957—he was acquitted in a landmark decision.) Ginsberg's demise at seventy-one was reported on the front page of newspapers around the world, his words quoted in coffeehouses, on radio shows, and on the evening news. Ginsberg was a giant among poets: he walked in the shadow of William Blake and Walt Whitman, he edited Burroughs's *Naked Lunch,* he championed Kerouac long before *On the Road,* he was unafraid—challenging war, censorship, the CIA, government intrusion—spreading his vision of a Buddhist convert, singing out on the page and in song in favor of human love and free speech and happy highs.

Phil Ochs wrote the song "The War Is Over" after seeing the bearded Ginsberg wearing an Uncle Sam hat and Hindu chanting against the Vietnam war. Bob Dylan got turned on when he heard a recording of Ginsberg reciting "Kaddish," and later recorded songs with the poet. The Beatles came to hang out with him; John Lennon introduced him to macrobiotic food. During the antiwar movement, Ginsberg was among the leaders of marches at the Pentagon, along with Norman Mailer and Robert Lowell. In 1965 he was crowned May King and paraded through the streets of Prague. In 1970 he was at a dinner with CIA chief Richard Helms, who denied any CIA involvement with opium traffickers in Laos. Ginsberg bet Helms there was such a relationship and proffered the scandalizing information to C. L. Sulzberger at the *New York Times*. Sulzberger scoffed at the idea, but eight years later he wrote Ginsberg an apology, saying, "I have been reading a succession of pieces about CIA involvement in the dope trade in Southeast Asia and I remember when you first suggested I look into this I thought you were full of beans. Indeed you were right. . . . "

A lot of people who didn't get him, who perhaps felt threatened by the poet who was always writing about death and skeletons as well as light and sunflowers, felt he was "full of beans." If anything, Ginsberg was full of sunshine; he was an enlightened being. He was also an innocent.

In 1985 I went down to Laguna Beach in Southern California to do a cable television interview at a bookstore with Ginsberg. To me, Allen Ginsberg was *always* the image of the Poet—sandaled, bearded, speaking his mind in rolling cadences, bringing joy and insight and righteousness in his wake. We had hired a limousine to pick him up and I'll never forget his boyish enthusiasm when he got inside. "I've never been in a limousine before," he said, marveling at the liquor cabinet and crystal glasses, at the telephone and stereo speakers. He bounced on the cushioned seats and beamed beatifically until we got to the bookstore and he saw that behind the seat that awaited him was a shelf of books without any of his showing. "This isn't good," he said, grabbing handfuls of books from the shelf. "Where are *my* books, they should be in the camera shot." The shelf was rearranged under his astute supervision.

For the next three hours we talked about everything that mattered to him, about his youth, his sexuality, his mother's mental illness, the incestuous feelings he had for his father, his love of Kerouac and Burroughs, Peter Orlovsky and Neal Cassady, his days at Columbia University, the whole Beat movement that began in San Francisco in the early fifties, and the politics of America, including his deep-felt belief of CIA conspiracies, the Kennedy assassination, Cuba, J. Edgar Hoover, Vietnam, Nixon, Reagan, the numbing influence of television, and Truman Capote's putdown of Kerouac's prose (and Ginsberg's by extension) as not writing but typewriting.

When we began to wind down I brought up the subject of death, a subject Ginsberg had given much thought to, and I wondered, did the spirit world continue or did it end when we did?

Ginsberg gave this a few moment's thought before he bent to pick up his harmonium, a small accordianlike instrument, put it between his legs, and began to play and sing.

> *Born in this world, you got to suffer,*
> *everything changes, you got no soul—you got no soul;*
> *Touch whom you touch—touch whom you touch*
> *Think what you think—think what you think*
> *Let go, let it go slow*
> *Earth Heaven and Hell—Earth Heaven and Hell*
>
> *Die when you die; Die when you die*
> *Die when you die; Die when you die*
> *Lie down, you lie down*
> *Lie down you lie down*
> *And you die . . . when you . . .*
> *. . . d i e.*

By the time he had reached the refrains "Die when you die" his whole body was in motion, his knees were bouncing, his shoulders shaking, his head bobbing, it was the image of the mad poet, not in the sense of crazy, but inspired, singing out to the world at large through the medium of television that what you are and what you do is all there is and you had better make the most of it. It was a magical, mystical, spiritual moment, sitting across from Allen Ginsberg as he played out his vision of life, death, and the

Great Unknown in an Orange County bookstore near the Pacific Ocean.

When the interview was over, we got back into the limo for the drive to the airport where, before a dozen strangers who stared at him as we passed through the electronic doors to the ticket counter, Allen Ginsberg did something no man had ever done to me in that way before: he kissed me on the lips. Then he thanked me for the conversation and the ride and waved good-bye as I stood there. I'd like to think that I was smiling.

Norman Mailer once wrote an ode to you saying, in part: "I sometimes think/that little Jew bastard/that queer ugly kike/ is the bravest man/ in America." What did you think when you read that?
I like Norman, he's got all this generosity and spirit, and he's very kind, but that was a bit hysterical. Why did he think I was brave? Did he have something in him that he was afraid to bring out? To be one with yourself, with your own body and feelings, is not such a big deal. It's easier than being split in half and being a schizophrenic. From the point of view of repression, it may look like bravery.

It also seems brave to be a full-time poet. Did it take a psychiatrist in San Francisco to release you from any guilt feelings about not working a conventional job?
It was a little more complicated. He asked me what I wanted to do in 1954 and I said I'd like to move in with Peter and quit my job and just write. He said, "Why don't you do it?" I said, "What will happen when I'm an old man and I got pee stains on my underwear and no-body loves me? What happens if I cut myself off from normal life?" And he said, "Oh, you'll be all right. You should do what you want." I said, "What would the American Psychoanalytic Association say?" He said, "There's no party line." And that made sense: There was no party line. We're free to choose and make up our own lives with some judiciousness and intelligence, to do what you think is right rather

than take the authority of a psychoanalytic association, pope, president, general, captain of industry, even artists or gurus—you still have to do what you think is correct.

Still, it obviously wasn't an easy path for you. One of your early poems begins: "Now that I've wasted five years in Manhattan . . ."
"Life decaying/ Talent a blank . . ." That was the five years that I was working in market research. It wasn't really wasted. I learned the meaning of American brainwashing, which is what market research is. You go into somebody's brain by free verbal associations, get their clichés or habit patterns, find out what attracts and propels them, and then you feed it back to them in the form of a product. It's sort of like going to Nicaragua and having anthropologists study the Indians there and then with all that information setting the CIA on them.

While working as a market researcher, did you suggest that the company would be smarter to replace you with a computer?
They would have been smarter. And that's what happened: I put everything I was doing on a computer and then I was able to get fired and collect unemployment insurance.

And now you're part of an historical literary movement.
That's what they say.

And what do you say?
It's like Rudolph the Red-Nosed Reindeer.

Let me rephrase it then: How do you see your place in American letters and culture?
I fit into a lineage of the development of an American measure, which is what William Carlos Williams called it. There is a tradition of open-form verse that began long ago. In America it started with Walt Whitman. There are elements of it in Emily Dickinson and in the prose of Melville, but it comes to an acme in Whitman with his open

biblical form. Then in the early twentieth century Ezra Pound, Williams, Marianne Moore, and many other poets worked on the problem: How do you arrange the verse form on the page when you're no longer counting the accents, or stress, so that there's some kind of order and regularity? Everybody had different solutions to this problem. The reactionaries like Robert Frost said, "Oh no, you can't play tennis without a net, you've got to measure." And Williams, who was my teacher, said, "You listen to your own voice, hear the cadences, hear the rhythms, and put them down on the page." Like bebop, in a sense. There's a shift in the ear which could include the length of the vowel, or units of mind or mouth phrasing. You hear the syllables which might not fit in the regular meters, but they are rhythmical and they can be heard and imitated on the page. Every time you open your mouth you speak in rhythm, so it's a question of listening to the actual rhythm that one is uttering all the time, becoming mindful of that and making use of those shapes on the page. That's the big shift. That was what Williams began to accomplish, Kerouac continued to accomplish, and I consolidated.

So, it's a bit more than Rudolph the Red-Nosed Reindeer.
It's historically important for having developed the oratory or vocalization of American poetry in the American rather than the English language, with rhythms appropriate to New Jersey speech like William Carlos Williams on a large scale, making it possible to speak poetry in public with the same weight as any businessman speaking real serious turkey, or any president talking out his poetic fantasies about world evils, or with the same seriousness as a secretary of defense giving forth his particular daydreams about Star Wars. Only here what we have is somebody not indulging in super fantasy but talking straight turkey—personal; what actually goes on in his mind, rather than the fantasy he has of trying to manipulate other people. That is the problem with public speech in America: most of it is paid, commercial, manipulative, hypnotic in trying to con. Hype is the whole point of television and almost all media. It's a commercial operation. The non-commercial situation of poetry is the one area where you can really

tell the truth about what you're thinking, because you're not running for president, and you're not trying to peddle anything, other than books. And if you're peddling little pamphlets of poetry you don't have to worry too much about that perverting your motive.

The movement you're associated with, of course, is the Beat movement. Looking back, how do you access the Beat generation?
Well, looking *forward,* it seems that unless people come back to certain values that we proposed, everybody is going to be quite unhappy for a long time. The values are, specifically, some kind of spiritual surge or accomplishment, consisting of awareness of the pain of existence, the transitory nature of existence, and the fact that there is no permanent soul, self, ego. To quote Rimbaud, "The spiritual battle is as tough as the battle of mankind, or as tough as the battle of men, but the vision of justice is the pleasure of God alone."

So the Beat creed would be . . . ?
That reason is a necessary quality of human mercy. That generosity, charm, and majesty are our original nature, rather than dog-eat-dog competition and rivalry. That beauty has permanent value for the young. That sexuality is open. That art is a hopeful way of being lyrical in the springtime. That politicians should learn to practice meditation in order to ground themselves and be in good relation to their own fantasies. That the sacred heart makes sense, although the pope might be a bastard or even Satan, as Blake said.

What do you think of words like *beatnik, hipster, hippie, yuppie*?
They're media words. It is the media that are all these things, which they then project on other people.

Are such labels useful in any way?
In the long run they confuse more than help. Given the fact that everybody wants to simplify to slogans like that, then the best attitude is to try and make something like the word *beatnik* honorific, by honoring the word rather than resenting it. The word itself was in-

vented by a gossip columnist, Herb Caen, in the San Francisco *Chronicle* at the time of Sputnik. His angle was *beat* and *Sputnik* = *beatnik*, out of this world. It was from a guy who lived in a world of dreams, society gossip, and perversions of his own by laying a trip on people who had less money, calling them beatniks.

Another remark that became famous was when Truman Capote criticized Jack Kerouac's work, saying "That's not writing, that's typewriting." Did that offend you?

It was a witticism that he pronounced on television. I heard from a faggot friend that I slept with, who used to have some gay luncheons with Truman Capote and Andy Warhol, that Capote actually liked Kerouac's prose and was a little ashamed of becoming famous for that remark. Although, like Kerouac, Capote drank so much and downed so many pills and was such a hysteric, it was probably hard for him to reverse it publicly. Though I've heard other people say in private conversation that he rejected not only Kerouac but Burroughs and Mailer and everybody else, probably Jean Genet, too. It was a cheap shot. Kerouac was a more important writer and a greater prose artist than Capote. Capote is still a nineteenth-century naiveté and Kerouac is twentieth-century open forum post-Pound post-scriptured Stein, post-Joyce. Capote as a stylist wasn't as advanced as that. He didn't have any idea why Kerouac was writing spontaneous rhapsody and he didn't have any grasp of the Zen Japanese Buddhist Tibetan Chinese origins of that kind of style. This is an ancient style spitting forth intelligence, like the yogi poet's book, *The Hundred Thousand Songs of Milarepa,* which were spontaneous songs taken down by Milarepa's disciples. That's the background for Kerouac's spontaneous prose. So Capote's remark is relatively shallow. But it was funny, nobody can deny its humor.

What did Kerouac feel about that remark?

Kerouac liked Capote's prose but he saw him as an insignificant little faggot twit for saying a thing like that, and I did too. I thought that was really beneath Capote's dignity to be attacking another writer like that. It was an undeserved attack. There's an alcohol downer in that remark. It's a slob's remark.

What about Norman Mailer's remarks from *Advertisements for Myself,* that Kerouac lacked discipline, intelligence, honesty . . . that "his rhythms are erratic, his sense of character is nil, and he is as pretentious as a rich whore. . . . To judge his worth it is better to forget about him as a novelist and see him instead as an action painter or a bard"?
That's slightly different. Mailer has this boxer's contentious amusement. It doesn't have the poison that Capote had in his remark.

Was it Jack Kerouac who inspired you to take yourself seriously as a poet?
Yes, in the sense of taking my feelings seriously, as being allowable. He was constantly on my back trying to get me to improvise and open up, stop being so formal and stuck in my father's kind of lyrics.

And yet didn't he also accuse you of stealing ideas from him?
Oh sure. That's what poets do all the time. I'm surprised he was such a monopolist. But he stole ideas from me, too. Phrasing. I owe most of my ideas about reading and a lot of my ear to Kerouac. He was completely my teacher. Anything I have I've learned from him, so his accusation is quite correct.

You were seventeen or eighteen when you first met Jack Kerouac. What was your initial impression?
I met him through a friend in St. Louis who told me that there was a guy who was a writer and a sailor. I was curious and went to see him in his apartment. We made friends when we acknowledged that we were both mortal. He helped me move out of my rooms at the Union Theological Seminary. As I left the room I said, "Good-bye door, good-bye room, good-bye hallway, good-bye step one, good-bye step two . . ." all the way down seven flights. And he said, "Oh, do you do that too?" I answered, "Yeah, I think like that all the time." He said,

"Saying good-bye is like dying. Saying hello is like saying good-bye." I said, "Yeah." So we realized that we had the same sense of mortal transitory phantomlike mind, that we were all ghosts still talking. Or we were of the nature of being ghosts, though our weak existence was quite real. We were both struck by that. That moment seemed more poignant than when we were not aware of such dreams.

By this time you already knew William Burroughs, didn't you?
The same friend who introduced me to Kerouac brought me downtown to Greenwich Village to see Burroughs.

Was he on junk then?
No, he never had any. He had just come from Chicago, where he worked as an exterminator and was living on Morton Street. I remember him reacting to an anecdote—someone had described a fight with a lesbian in a lesbian bar and Burroughs quoted Shakespeare; he said, "Too starved an argument for my sword." That was the first time I ever heard Shakespeare quoted so wittily.

Diana Trilling, recalling your college days, said you made life too messy.
I don't know what she means. I don't know what her idea of messy is—I didn't give birth to my mother exactly. It may be that I had met Burroughs and Kerouac and was going to visit her husband, my professor, Lionel Trilling, and telling him about the culture that I shared with them and about their writing, and maybe even describing my experiences with marijuana in the mid-forties. Maybe she felt that was messy, but actually I was just talking about reality that I experienced and was going to an older person to check it out.

How significant was Burroughs to your development?
Burroughs psychoanalyzed me when I was eighteen. I had a conversation with him from when I was seventeen to the present. He was a constant mentor and teacher who looked at my poetry and told me what he liked. We spent almost a week together at the Naropa Insti-

tute on his seventy-first year at a Burroughs festival, there were a lot of Buddhists, Gregory Corso was there, Anne Waldman, his biographer Ted Morgan. It was a celebration of the wisdom, brilliance, and genius of Burroughs.

The great inspiration in Kerouac's life seems to have been Neal Cassady, whom he called the most intelligent man he ever knew. Did you feel that way about him?

He was very intelligent in terms of moment-by-moment awareness of his thought processes and the considerations and thoughts and empathies of the people in the room at the time. He was very attentive to the present space. He was willing to open up and consider the needs of everybody that he was with, to sacrifice his own comfort to ease the pain of other people, to ease them out of their paranoia of loneliness.

Do you think that Kerouac captured his vitality in *On the Road*?

Very much so, especially in the sequel to *On the Road*, which is *Visions of Cody*, which I think is Kerouac's greatest prose work as an experimental open explosion of a new consciousness and a new prose.

Cassady wrote a 40,000-word letter to Kerouac, which was the inspiration for *On the Road*. Kerouac apparently thought it was the greatest piece of writing he'd ever seen.

It was.

Then you borrowed it. What happened next?

I lent it, along with a copy of my own poems and Kerouac's *Visions of Cody*, to a group of literary people, Fritz Stern and others, who were living on boats in Marin County. It was all brought back except for Neal's letter, which was missing. I never could find it.

Did you feel guilty about the loss of that letter?

No, no, there was nothing I could do about it. I didn't want to accuse the people I had loaned it to because I didn't want to make them feel guilty. It'll turn up sooner or later. Part of it is printed in a book by

Neal Cassady published by City Lights called *The First Third*. About five pages.

T. S. Eliot had Ezra Pound to help him shape some of his most famous poems. Have you had anyone like that in your life?
Yes. I had Basil Bunting, who was a contemporary of Pound and Yeats. William Carlos Williams, who actually went through my first book and separated out what he thought were bad, inert poems from the ones that he thought were active. Once he pointed it out, it was obvious and clarified my own awareness. It really isn't a subjective matter: it's, does the poem have some concrete evidence of the external world, or just abstractions from your head? He took about a hundred pages of poetry and boiled them down to forty. Then I had Kerouac and Burroughs and Gregory Corso, who actually cuts up my poetry and revises it as I do with his. I also show a lot of my work to Robert Creeley. There's a community of poets, we all work together.

When "Howl" first appeared, did this community of poets immediately recognize it as the classic it became?
The local literary people and people of discrimination and judgment thought it was a great poem and told me. Kenneth Rexroth said, "You're going to be famous from bridge to bridge." I said, "Maybe in San Francisco." He said, "No, bridge to bridge." And then I sent it to William Carlos Williams, who appreciated it.

Not everyone, of course, appreciated it.
There was quite a bit of opposition from the police—the vice squads and customs. It was first printed in England in 1955 and five hundred copies were seized by customs when it was sent over. We had a lot of legal trouble. The ACLU intervened and the customs gave it back. Then it was seized by a local juvenile vice cop in San Francisco. They arrested Lawrence Ferlinghetti and Shigeyoshi Murao, the manager of City Lights bookstore. Shigeyoshi got out because they couldn't prove that he had read the book. And Ferlinghetti didn't sell it, Shigeyoshi did. But the poem was declared legal, protected by the

Constitution's freedom of speech because it contained relevant social commentary, so that was the end of any real attempts at censorship, though there was some opposition from Catholics and from what are now known as Moral Majority types.

How concerned were you about the censorship battles in the fifties?

Most people don't remember but there was total censorship with certain books and magazines like *Playboy,* and then by 1958 there were a series of legal cases that broke the back of censorship and liberated the word. "Howl" was one of the early cases in 1957. Following that was Henry Miller's *Tropic of Cancer,* and Frank Harris's *Autobiography.* There was the racy nineteenth-century novel *Fanny Hill,* and Jean Genet's *Our Lady of the Flowers.* The original case of the late fifties was the classic *Lady Chatterley's Lover* by D. H. Lawrence. Ezra Pound had said of *Tropic of Cancer,* "At last a dirty book that's fit to read." Even T. S. Eliot liked it. Incidentally, Eliot, the acme of respectability, was writing this fantastic obscene poem called "King Bolo," which he only sent to friends in letters. It has never been published, but it was full of Jew boys, assholes, kikes, pricks, and cunts. Probably Eliot's greatest work.

What's your opinion of Eliot as a poet?

Oh, he's a very great second-rate poet. He's a poor guy, though. He suffered so much. He had a terrible marriage. His wife covered herself with ether and took morphine and bled all the time. She had some terrible menstrual problems. And he was always a little rocky, or shaky sexually. It was the last thing he needed. She was mad, and her family and he finally put her in a mental hospital. He didn't come into a good relationship with a woman until he was about sixty-five. He married his secretary and transformed completely, had a happy ending. Wouldn't stop smoking though. He liked those strong French cigarettes and had constant bronchial problems. Very little of that is reflected in his poetry. He kept complaining of a writer's block, but he wrote the same way everybody else writes: you put it down, piddle around with it, go over it and over it and over it.

Getting back to "Howl," how did your father react to your coming out so publicly about private things?

That was very difficult. That was the big barrier, because when I wrote "Howl" I wasn't intending to publish it. I didn't write it as a poem, just as a piece of writing for my own pleasure. I wanted to write something where I could say what I really was thinking, rather than poetry. From that point of view I thought I couldn't publish this. I didn't want to shove my ass in my father's face: "Who got fucked in the ass by handsome sailors and screamed with joy." I didn't want him to read that, because given our relationship that would be quite embarrassing. We never talked about sex seriously and certainly there was some subliminal erotic thing going on between us, which I shouldn't touch on lightly. Very strongly so. Without him knowing it. So it really would have disturbed him a great deal. So while I had no intention of publishing it I sent the original manuscript to Kerouac who put a title on it and he sent it to John Clellon Holmes. Two months later Kenneth Rexroth, the resident elder poet in San Francisco in 1955, asked me if I could help organize a reading at the Six Gallery and gave me Gary Snyder's name. So I went to visit Snyder in Berkeley and found that he had also worked with William Carlos Williams and wrote in that kind of open form like Williams and Pound. He said he had his friend Philip Whalen coming down from Portland and Kerouac was coming in to San Francisco, so we all met. And I had just met Michael McClure, who was living in San Francisco. And I had known Philip Lamantia since the late forties from the Village and he was there. So we all got together to give a reading at the Six Gallery where a bunch of interesting, later to be famous artists showed their paintings. It was actually an old garage on Fillmore Street. That's where I read the first part of "Howl." I was 3,000 miles away from my father. And it was great. Then I realized that this piece of writing was a poem and people thought it was good and actually said something, so I thought my father will just have to put up with it.

And did he?

He said, when he saw it, it shows a lot of energy and invention and ex-

plosiveness and youthful feelings. He didn't like the language, the
dirty words, didn't think they were necessary, but he recognized that
the whole thing had a flow and a power that maybe the language was
a part of, and so within a decade we were giving readings together at
his poetry club, the Poetry Society of America. So he got over it, and I
got over it.

**What about your mother, where was she when she first read
"Howl"?**
I sent her "Howl" at Pilgrim State Hospital, where she was in her last
months before her stroke. She hadn't recognized me about a half year
before when I visited. She thought I was a spy, actually. It was very
disturbing—I wept. It seemed like the farthest limit of dehumanization and illness and madness, that she couldn't remember me.
"Howl" was actually written with her in mind. "Carl Solomon! I'm
With You in Rockland" really is my mother and **"I'm with you in Pilgrim State Hospital,"** in the sense of a release of feeling, an acknowledgment and release of maternal tenderness, which though thwarted
still exists intact with me, or in anyone, probably. Tenderness toward
mother, the only mother I have after all, whatever condition she was
in. So "Howl" was actually an emotional reunion with my mother.
And so I sent it to her thinking it would be way beyond the pale as far
as understanding was concerned. And then I got a telegram from my
brother that she had died. And then a day after that I got a letter
from my mother, mailed before she died, saying that she read the
poem and that I should watch out and take care of myself and not
take drugs and get married and have children.

What's your earliest childhood memory of your mother?
Lying in bed with a nurse after coming home from Bloomingdale
Mental Hospital Sanitarium. She had brought back a wicker basket
that she had woven and I was in my child clothes with those kind of
night suits that button up around the feet and all the way up. And I
didn't have my shoes on. I was three or four. So I lit a match and
dropped it into the wicker basket and the next thing I knew the fire-

men were there and I was being blamed. It was a big deal. I don't remember what happened in between except lighting the match and the firemen, but I couldn't put it out because I didn't have shoes on, just these funny night-suit cloth feet.

Would you say your childhood was cut short by your mother's mental illness?

Yes, I think so. I didn't get mother love, and that's always been a kind of grief. It's been a dominant motif in whatever I've done. I had to take care of my mother basically, and so I got sick of taking care of women. It was just too much trouble, too horrifying a task at that time. Probably alienated me from women's bodies and smells and situations and blood.

Why didn't your father take care of her?

My father was away at school teaching, making a living. And my mother's paranoia was directed at my father, so that kept him deliberately distant. My brother also went through the same initiation I did, but I had a closer relation with my mother.

In "Kaddish" you wrote that when your mother returned after many years away she said to you, "Don't be afraid of me, I'm your mother."

I don't think I was that afraid of her. I was sort of longing for some kind of physical warmth and recognition from her, but her reaction was "Don't be afraid, I'm your mother." It was a little scary.

How difficult was it between your parents when your mother was home?

Her belief was that he had given his money to my grandmother, his mother, and my mother thought that his mother was alienating his affection from her. And my grandmother was one of those little Jewish matriarchs, very strong.

And your relationship with her?

Oh, I dug my grandmother, she was great. She took care of me when my mother was in the mental hospital. So it was a very mixed-up situation. Lots of conflict.

Were you ever able to defend your grandmother to your mother?
No, no, it would be too difficult. No, my mother was really mad. She was in mental hospitals just for things like that. She thought people were walking up and down the apartment lobby with poison gas to spray at her. Some people were hanging around the bus station across the street spying on her. And my grandmother was climbing up on the fire escape with old clothes on to spray poisons on her. It was really very difficult.

At what age did you start having an understanding of madness?
Oh, very early. The understanding was that if everybody disagreed with me all at once, then I would know that I better check out my reference points to reality.

And how close did your mother's illness bring you to your father?
Quite close.

Did you talk to him about your mother?
Yeah, we talked quite a bit. But I was never sure who was right and who was wrong, as in any family dispute.

How did you eventually feel when your father remarried?
It was a relief. Because he was very lonely.

You would go on to give poetry readings with your father . . . what was that like?
Well, we had to get used to each other's styles and learn a certain amount of peaceful coexistence.

Did you ever turn him on?
Yes, I did once, in Big Sur. We sat out on the beach and I pulled out a

big joint and my mother took a toke or two and my father took a toke. He had quit smoking by then, but he did it to be companionable, to compromise himself and join me in my criminal behavior.

You joke, but while you were a student at Columbia you managed to get your picture on the front page of the *Daily News* as a criminal mastermind . . .

That made my father very scared. The difficulty there was the people I was involved with, Herbert Huncke, Burroughs, Kerouac. I was the wayward student who he considered had fallen in with evil companions. He thought if I didn't cut myself off from them I would end up in jail or the bughouse. It caused a social conflict of painful intensity.

And you did wind up in a mental institution, didn't you?

With the help of Lionel Trilling and a few other professors I had myself put into the New York State Psychiatric Institute to get away from being indicted for burglary.

Once there, did you begin to feel you were crazy?

Oh yeah. The amazing thing was that I doubted my own senses, I doubted my own heart. I felt that I was supposed to renounce my affection for Herbert Huncke, which was a very chaste affection, but I admired him and he was a writer. And I felt I shouldn't see Kerouac or Burroughs for a while. That was my madness section. The other thing was that I had had some kind of visionary experience relating to William Blake and hearing his voice, having some kind of illuminative vision of the vastness of space and sky and rooftops in New York. I wasn't sure whether that was real or if the wall of the state hospital was real.

What was it like in the state hospital?

Fun. At that time it was an elite place. It was for the children of the rich to get away from going to jail. It was an experimental place, too, they were doing prefrontal lobotomies and shock treatments, but I didn't get involved with that.

Didn't your mother go through shock treatments?
Yes, many. Both insulin shock, Metrazol, and electroshock, thirty or forty each. She had a lobotomy.

So it's really no mystery figuring out what you meant when you once wrote that between you and oblivion an unknown woman stands. You asked yourself then why you feared the one hole that repelled you.
Well, I'm talking about my mother's vagina. Since I had to take care of her, as I said before, it was a repellent situation.

Still, you've said that you've had wet dreams about everybody in your family.
That's probably common, don't you think?

Not really.
Maybe not all people remember such dreams.

Of having incest with all members of one's family?
Sure: fathers, mothers, sisters, brothers, aunts, uncles . . . trucks, grasses, earth. When I was about eight I had a dream about rubbing up against the hood of a large truck and having some sort of orgasmic reaction. I did. The imagination knows no limits. That's the essential nature of our humanity, that it's unlimited imagination and dreams. The world of dreams is notorious for adventuring into areas which are forbidden the conscious life, including incest and all other taboos. That's where we experience the breaking of taboos. I doubt that I'm very different than anybody else, though I haven't done any statistical survey. I just remember my dreams. This is my nature and I can't quite apologize for that. I gather from your question that you're surprised?

I guess I just don't remember wanting to make love with my father.
Not wanting, actually *doing* it! Actually doing it is not wanting.

In your mind?

No, in dreams, dreams, dreams, actual 3-D dreams! I think almost
everybody has this, but I'm not sure. Maybe not so pronounced as the
homosexual incest, but certainly heterosexual incest is common.
Making it with your mother. It might be that heterosexual incest is
more common than homosexual, but I'll bet it's universal. According
to Freud it's between five and ten when you probably have more
erotic dreams.

**As a student of Freud, you must have some interesting thoughts
on Jack Kerouac's relationship with his mother.**

It was interesting. They would get drunk together and speak the most
foul language I've ever heard between them. She didn't like any of his
friends. She particularly didn't like bearded Jews, but she also didn't
like Burroughs, or Jack's wife, or his girlfriends. Jack was close with a
painter, a strong, good woman, and his mother once pulled him aside
and said, "I don't trust her, she's a witch, I saw her sharpening knives
against the candles." She didn't like it that I was gay. At one time Jack
said his mother was absolutely crazy like mine, but that he didn't
want to throw her to the dogs of eternity, as he said I had. So he put
up with shocking things. I still remember it, great phrase: dogs of
eternity. But he paid the price of his own life by staying with her.

**Have you paid a price for your lifestyle? You've said that
homosexuality has been like a *koan*—a Zen riddle—for you.**

Well, it must have been, otherwise I wouldn't have said it. You're
asking me what do I mean by that? That it sort of set me aside from
a majority of people and made me question my own identity and
wonder who I am, which is a famous *koan*. A *koan* is a mind-
personality-ego riddle that makes you explore the nature of consciousness itself.

**How much courage did it take to be public about your
homosexuality?**

None at all. It seems to me it took a lot of courage to keep it secret.
It's like constantly going around lying. It'll make you a nervous

wreck. Once I had told Kerouac I was gay when I was eighteen, it just seemed no problem.

How did Kerouac react to your telling him you were gay?
He groaned and knew there was trouble. Kerouac and Burroughs liked me and I liked them. Kerouac was a little disturbed and uneasy about it because I loved him and we finally wound up in bed together a few times. He was very ambivalent about it and basically heterosexual. He didn't want to be troubled by my needs, but on the other hand, he was very compassionate. So, given the closeness that we all felt as writers, the outer world where everybody was in a closet seemed like a maniacal rat race and disturbed. I didn't feel disturbed because that was my nature, but certainly there was a repressive situation where people had a "love that dare not speak its name." There was something wrong with that, something really sick. But I felt firmly grounded. Especially after reading Walt Whitman, who had the same feelings I had.

You begin your poem "Many Loves": "Neal Cassady was my animal: he brought me to my knees/and taught me the love of his cock and the secrets of his mind." Then you describe an arousing night you spent with Neal Cassady back in 1946.
I'm glad you were aroused.

He wanted to please you and you made a mistake. What was the mistake?
You're taking it out of context, which only sensationalizes it. Not that it's not sensational anyway, it's just that you're isolating only one moment of the poem. Let me read the end of the poem:

> *I raised my thighs and stripped down my shorts to my knees, and bent to*
> *   push them off*
> *and he raised me up from his chest, and pulled down his pants the same,*
> *humble and meek and obedient to his mood our silence,*
> *and naked at long last with angel & greek & athlete & hero and brother*
> *   and boy of my dreams*

I lay with my hair intermixed with his, he asking me, 'What shall we do
   now?'
—And confessed, years later, he thinking I was not a queer at first to please
   me & serve me, to blow me and make me come, maybe or if I were queer,
   that's what I'd likely want of a dumb bastard like him.
But I made my first mistake, and made him then and there my master, and
   bowed my head, and holding his buttock
Took up his hard-on and held it, feeling it throb and pressing my own at his
   knee & breathing showed him I needed him, cock, for my dreams of
   insatiety & lone love.
—And I lie here naked in the dark, dreaming

You ask what the mistake was? The mistake was to spell out very
clearly, instead of playing some kind of game trying to get him to
blow me, I went and blew him instead, and so from then on our roles
were set.

**In a 1947 letter to Cassady you wrote: "I will always be afraid, I
will always be worthless, I will always be alone till I die & I will be
tormented long after you leave me."**
It's true. Totally true. That probably applies to everybody, but I'll take
the cross on myself if nobody else will.

Do you feel that you've always been alone?
Sure, don't you? Doesn't everybody? We are alone. We die alone. On
our deathbed, do you think we go with our girlfriends and boyfriends
and Hollywood producers and lawyers? We're on our deathbed all the
time.

Does this mean you have a lonely life?
Oh, I don't know what it means anymore. How would I know at this
point when everything's so mixed up with *Playboy* and the mass media, Khrushchev, Ronald Reagan, Joseph Stalin, Mao Zedong, China,
and the Tibetan lamas—it's all so mixed up, how can I tell whether
I'm lonely or not?

Do you feel badly that you don't have any children? That perhaps it would have made you less alone?
Sometimes, yes. Certainly. But I'm not sure that I have the desire to have everything that goes with having children. It would be very difficult. I'd have to get myself a house, a wife, there's a lot of work involved.

You once wanted to write a long poem about everybody you ever fucked or slept with. How long would it be?
I've forgotten all the people now, so I can't do it anymore.

How many lays of a lifetime have there been?
I don't know. I think about it sometimes and I can't remember. I have written a good deal of that poem, it's just that with living people I wouldn't want to expose them to my own gossip, it's too kiss-and-tell. It's an aesthetic matter. Also, I somehow have an affection for straight men and have had some romances, which makes it a bit more difficult to be frank than it would, say, with Peter Orlovsky.

Can a man who has homosexual affairs be considered straight?
Yeah, straight in the sense that he won't prefer mostly gay experiences. People who prefer mostly straight experiences are straight. There's infinite variety in between. According to Kinsey, almost everybody's done everything at one time or another. He said that the majority of men have had one orgasm or more with men and the majority of women have had one orgasm with women and that the number of people who are consistently pleased by their own sex is five or ten percent and the number of people who are consistently pleased only with the opposite sex is only ten or twenty percent. It's a minority of people who have never had any homosexual experience of any kind.

You haven't led an exclusively homosexual life, there have been women you've made love to. . . .
Well, they made love to me. I've been in love with women, yes. And slept with them.

You've said that you could make love to "blonde furry fucky dolls." How does that sound to you today?

It sounds pretty attractive.

How promiscuous were you after you achieved fame as a poet?

More. More promiscuous. People knew who I was and what my loves were and sometimes empathized and sometimes made it easier to talk straightforwardly because they expected it. If I fancied some young fellow I could openly talk to him and declare my crush and take my chances.

You've been rather articulate, even eloquent, on the pleasures of anal intercourse.

I spoke about it in a *Playboy* interview because I thought it was about time that some kind of exploration of that area was given openly, because it's the one area of greatest machismo fear and anxiety. It's also the least horrific and least frightening situation.

Is it possible to achieve an anal orgasm?

I'm not able to. Not that I haven't tried, but everybody has a different physiological balance. Some people when they have an orgasm stiffen up and some people relax. Burroughs has said that he's seen God in his asshole in the flashbulb of orgasm. That's the symbolism of the hanging scenes in *Naked Lunch,* the involuntary orgasm: look, no hands.

Have your sex habits changed since AIDS became such a widespread disease?

It hasn't changed mine very much because I've been sleeping mostly with straight men. I hear from friends that it's changed the homosexual lifestyle considerably. There's more fidelity and monogamy and less orgiastic wildness.

Do you have any feeling about finding a cure for AIDS?

My instinct is not to bullshit, how does anybody know? If AIDS were invented by the CIA, as it may well have been since it only hits Jews, junkies, and blacks, then maybe some Southern Jesse Helms stringer of the CIA, some stringer goofing around like stringers used to do spraying germs in the subways, experimenting for the CIA or giving people LSD without telling them, you never can tell, but if there is someone out there, then presumably somebody's got the key to how to unlock that. I suppose they'll cure it sooner or later. They can split the atom, I'm sure they can figure out a virus.

The man you've called your wife is Peter Orlovsky. Can you talk about your relationship with him?
At the moment he's in a Buddhist retreat center and he's asked me not to talk about him.

Did you fall in love with a painting of him?
Yeah, love at first sight. It was a painting by a Seattle artist, Robert Levine, who was a neglected painter. The painting world is a con world, like the gallery world is a con world, like the world of big-seller books is, and the Mafia-controlled distribution for magazines or hit records are. Not that the art world is Mafia controlled, but it's another kind of heavy thing.

It's quite a segue from Peter to politics, but since you've made it, and since you often write about it, how corrupt is America?
America's completely polluted. The whole thing's a mess. Just think of how many species of animals we've killed. The first thing we did when we landed on this continent was spread small pox and venereal disease and kill the natives. They started with the American Indians, they're still doing it in the Amazon with the Amazon Indians. Then you bring in the priests to convince them that their native consciousness is not appropriate and that they should worship some kind of deus ex machina from outside. The Catholic priests act as fronts for the bandits and murderers who kill everybody and take their land

and make treaties, then break the treaties for the next hundred years. They say to the Indian, you can have this land, but they take it away a hundred years later after oil is discovered on it. All of us immigrants who came here don't have any ownership of the land, yet we grabbed it, and we're treating it with neither courtesy nor discretion. It's really a shame that we're polluting the entire planet.

You believe that the only thing that can save the world is the reclaiming of the awareness of the world, don't you?
You've got to realize that if you dump shit in your own well, you're going to get dysentery. You can't poison your own nest, you can't piss in your own bed. You get shit in your mother's face—Mother Nature—and then it requires bribes to get people to forget that you're shitting in your mother's face in terms of toxic waste. Those people didn't pour that toxic waste in Love Canal without bribing somebody first. They were perfectly conscious of what they were doing. Everybody now knows that the more plutonium they make, the less chance there'll be of ever getting rid of it. It cost $480 million in public relations money in 1978 for the nuclear industry to make itself appear halfway respectable. It didn't even succeed. Almost half a billion dollars, as reported in the *New York Times*, for the nuclear industry to try and convince people that they were not shitting in their mother's face. The point I'm making is that they spent a lot of money to make people unconscious about the nuclear industry. All that dumping was in the hands of the Mafia, for the most part: landfill, trucking, garbage—that's always been the province of organized crime. So the nuclear waste industry dumping, as well as other industrial poisonous chemical dumping, was always in the hands of shysters and criminals. And that took a lot of manipulation. The public was lulled to sleep. Eisenhower even told the Atomic Energy Commission to lie to the public about the difference between the atom bomb and the hydrogen bomb—that came out in the *New York Times* in '78 when the records of the Atomic Energy Commission were released. When all the sheep in Utah got wiped out, that was Eisenhower's big fib. He told the nuclear energy commission to "confuse the public."

You also feel the public has been lulled to sleep regarding President Kennedy's assassination, don't you?
I think the CIA bumped off Kennedy. Actually, I think a stringer with the CIA working with the Mafia did it. The major political scandal of my lifetime has been the fact that criminals and secret police could bump off the president when he was trying to make peace. That's the great canker and cancer of politics in our time. That's the way Nixon got in and the whole of our American politics has developed through such assassination—JFK, Robert Kennedy, Martin Luther King, Malcolm X—sheltered and bypassed by the FBI. The republic is rotten to the core.

Your outspokenness brought you to the attention of the FBI, which kept a dossier on you. Do you know when that first began?
I never had a dossier until I got on a television program with Norman Mailer in 1960 speaking about the laws against marijuana. I suggested decriminalization, which threatened their corrupt bureaucracy. So merely by opening my mouth and saying we should change the laws, the government began building a dossier on me.

And in the years since, do you think we're any closer to decriminalizing marijuana?
It's been much decriminalized since that 1960 opening on national television. It's like asking, "Do you think we'll blow up with the atom bomb?" If we don't blow up with nuclear bombs we'll probably decriminalize marijuana. And since I don't think there will be a nuclear disaster, I'd say it might take another hundred years for marijuana to be decriminalized. Remember, the change in the way you measured the line of poetry on the page was introduced in 1907 and it took until 1970 for people to begin to understand that.

Are there any drugs which you felt positive about once but have changed your mind since?
No. I always had a moderate position about drugs and my own use. I was interested in getting the government off our backs and getting

corruption out of the drug business. Like William Buckley and Ronald Reagan proposed, I'm for a free market: put junk in the hands of doctors instead of corrupt police and organized crime. Let junkies go to doctors for an illness like in England, where there is no big junk problem or crime problems from junk. Simple as that. Marijuana should serve as a useful cash crop for small-scale agriculture. Family farms are all going bankrupt, so they need a cash crop, and that would be the ideal thing to save the good old American Norman Rockwell tradition of the family farm. Acid should be given to the priests, rabbis, swamis, doctors, and psychiatrists. Amphetamines are a drag—you use them once and sleep for a week and never repeat it. I always thought that that was invented by Hitler, who was an amphetamine head in the last year of World War II. Peyote belongs to the earth, nobody needs to interfere with that, and nobody has. I had some Ecstasy once, which I think is misnamed: it should be called Empathy. Ecstasy is too overdramatic—somebody with a very bad sense of poetry and an inaccurate sense of psychology must have named it. It would be useful for the secretary of state and his Russian equivalent to get together on a little bit of Empathy drug so they could empathize with each other instead of paranoidize. That would be really interesting. I took some of it and had a very strange experience with an old school friend—Norman Podhoretz. I've always had him in the back of my mind as a sort of funny opponent, diametrically opposite in temperament. And I realized, "Gee, how nice of Norman Podhoretz to have been on earth all these years to be a foil for my anger, my jealousy, and my irritability."

When did Podhoretz make you angry and irritable?
I was at the party where Norman Mailer stabbed his wife, but I wasn't there at that hour because I had gone out with C. Wright Mills and a few other people after I had gotten into a verbal battle with Norman Podhoretz. He had said, "Listen, Ginsberg, you're a good writer, what are you doing hanging around with these no-account people like Kerouac and Burroughs, who can't write? You can have a career in New York if you just get rid of them." And like an idiot I got mad at him. I

saw the scene like a grade-B movie with him as the villain: you can tempt the upper classes with your villainous demitasses, but Heaven will protect the working girl. I said to him, "You dumb mother-fucker! You stupid asshole!" Mailer rushed up and said, "Don't hit him." And I said, "Don't hit me!" Mailer has this enormous lust for power and violence, so I guess he was projecting his own psyche on me as he did on Kerouac. He thought Kerouac was a violent juvenile delinquent.

Are you often irritable?
Yes, lots of times. I'm trying to come into a relation with it so I can diffuse it, or make it workable, you know, extract the wisdom of it.

Do you chant much to contain your irritability?
No, for that I do sitting practice at meditation: classical Zen and Tibetan Buddhist style quieting of the mind and being aware of the space around. I'm a student of the Whispered Transmission School of Crazy Wisdom and Meditation, founded in the ninth century by an eccentric yogi in India and continued through the centuries by a series of monks called the Karmapa lamas. It's not chanting but silent meditation on the breath. I read a lot of the old books about this in the fifties: the *Tibetan Book of the Dead, Tibetan Yoga and Secret Practices,* the life of Milarepa, the eleventh-century poet yogi singer. And then when Tibet was invaded in 1958 by the Chinese there was a diaspora and many lamas came to the west. In 1963 I was in India and met Gyalwa Karmapa and many other lamas versed in the school of meditation. In 1970 in the U.S. I met one of the more eloquent practitioners, Chogyam Trungpa, who founded the Naropa Institute in Boulder, Colorado. I've been working with him as my meditation teacher since 1972.

Has meditation helped with your poetry?
When you pay attention to your breath going out into the air and dissolving and then not pay attention to the in-breath, you'll find that your mind wanders and that your attention strays into memory,

fantasy, planning for the future. The traditional practice is to acknowledge your thoughts and then bring your attention back to the breath until it dissolves. This is a method of writing poetry also. By observing the rising and flowering and dissolution of thought forms, you actually see poems rise in your head and dissolve. Simply a beginning, middle, and end. All it requires is to copy down what you thought. It's like a big bubble that dissolves.

So you must always keep a notebook handy?
Yes, always. By meditating you develop the habit of being aware of your mind. It isn't that one sits and tries to think of something to write. No, it's just the opposite. You sit to sit. That sharpens the awareness of what's going on in your mind.

What is the state of poetry today? Is it as important as it seemed to be in the fifties and sixties?
That's a double question. First of all, there is more poetry than ever. There are more people listening to poetry since poetry affected the entire Rock and Roll, New Wave world, Punk. And before that you had Robert Johnson, Skip James, Leadbelly, Bessie Smith, B.B. King, Dylan. Everybody listens to it without calling it poetry. It's lyrics. So everyone is very much in touch with oral poetry, which is the basic medium for poetry: the oral form. Academic people aren't aware of it as poetry but the blues lyrics of the early twentieth century are the supreme poetic form of the United States. When anthologies are made a hundred years from now they'll include early blues verse like "Where the yellow dog meets the Southern Cross," or "Empty Bed Blues," or "Give me a pig foot and a bottle of beer." "I'll give you sugar for sugar, you'll get salt for salt, baby you don't love me, won't get nothing at all." Or, "Sometimes I think you're too sweet to die, other times I think you ought to be buried alive." That's Richard Robert Brown, New Orleans, 1929. It's a great poetic tradition. Everybody is listening to it now without knowing it. Then there's a literary poetry.

The other aspect is that almost everything spoken in public is subjective language made up by the people who speak it, or ghost writers.

That's all pure theater. It might be a prosaic poetry that a president speaks on television, like Reagan, someone writes him a speech and he's an actor, he delivers it.

Speaking of pure theater, could you talk about the time you and Ken Kesey and the Merry Pranksters tried to keep the Hell's Angels from attacking anti-Vietnam war demonstrators?
Around Berkeley in 1965 there were increasing masses of students and intelligentsia who didn't like the Vietnam war, thought it was crude and unnecessary, which it was. It was founded on the wrong basis: trying to contain China; which is the opposite of what we want now, which is to be friends with China. So the students formed a march through Berkeley and into Oakland. As we approached the Oakland border we found a line of both police and Hell's Angels. One Angel stepped forward and cut the electric wires connected to the speakers of the sound truck for the rally. The Hell's Angels had announced that they would attack the march. Then provocateur finks and agents inside the Berkeley antiwar Vietnam committee, agents from the government, said we should take chains and fight the Hell's Angels, since they were just like the brownshirts in Germany. It was the Reagan–John Wayne macho line. So I issued a little poem saying we should make the march a piece of theater: there should be masses of flowers and grandmothers and children, floats of the Hell's Angels, and a corps of trained fairies to go on ahead and blow the Angels before they could get to the line. Make theater of it, because it's all theater—the march, the politics. Before the march took place Ken Kesey and his bus and Neal Cassady and I went to visit the Angels' leader, Sonny Barger. We all dropped acid, the Angels all dropped acid. I didn't because by then I was getting bum trips. But we found out that the Angels were being advised by some kind of a John Birch right-wing group towards violence, and were also being backed by the Oakland police. So, everybody got high and Cassady was very cheerful and Kesey was very diplomatic. Then somebody had this lightning bolt idea and pulled out my harmonium which I'd brought along for the occasion. I began chanting the highest perfect wisdom sutra, the

ultimate statement of Buddhist reality. Pretty soon the Hell's Angels joined in and we were all making a good sound together and the division was resolved. The Hell's Angels said they wouldn't attack the march but would send a letter to President Johnson volunteering for service as guerillas in Vietnam. So the next march went on with me and Gary Snyder mantra chanting from a sound truck to downtown Oakland. Of course, nothing happened . . . the war went on.

What would this country be like if Allen Ginsberg were president?
I wouldn't get anywhere near that. It would be like winding up in vadra hell. Anybody who wants that power is doomed. Also, I have been advised by my meditation teacher to avoid that situation. That's his phrase: you'll wind up in vadra hell. The contradictions and neurosis of my own making. I hardly have time to answer letters as it is, forget trying to do it from the chair in the Oval Office. Imagine trying to get laid there? Sneak boys into the White House. That would be fun though. It's about time. That would be the only temptation.

What about policies?
If I were president I would start a large-scale person-to-person exchange so that we get to know the Russians and Chinese and whoever it is we're supposed to be enemies of. Send a million college kids down to Nicaragua to exchange information and do a little work, instead of arming the Contras to create a giant battlefield, wrecking the land mass of Central America. I'd do the same with Russia: take the cost of a couple of battleships or bombs and use it to send a million American girls and boys over there to hang around in Siberia, get high with the Russian kids, exchange information. I'd have people-to-people communication rather than the way it is now, with our politicians who haven't mastered their own aggression or paranoia.

So instead of politicians we should elect poets?
There have been poets who have run things. Abraham Lincoln was a good writer, John Adams and John Quincy Adams were extraordinarily learned and artistic, as was Jefferson. Mao Zedong was a poet.

Most of the Chinese emperors were poets, that was part of their training. Throughout history there have been great poets and musicians among the kings and ministers. A statesman who doesn't know how to write poetry or play music is the curse of the twentieth century. Today it's reached a point of human degradation that people admire aggression rather than intelligence and sensitivity.

Is that why poets often die such tragic deaths?
Well, they're no different from insurance brokers who commit suicide or drink themselves to death. Though I think the health and life expectancy of poets in my generation has been better than the average American businessman. It's a middle-class myth that the neurosis and madness and suicide falls on the bohemians rather than on the middle class. Philip Whalen is a Zen priest, Gary Snyder is quite healthy chopping wood in the forest, William Burroughs is going on seventy-two, I'll be sixty in 1986, Peter Orlovsky is in his fifties and ready to get married and have a kid. Kerouac, Neal Cassady, Lou Welch are dead, but for the most part our generation is quite healthy. Robert Duncan, Michael McClure, Philip Lamantia—all poets from the San Francisco renaissance are still hail and healthy. Frank O'Hara died in New York. Kenneth Koch and John Ashbery are making it into their late maturities. If you take a survey of the poets who were breakthrough artists in the fifties, you'll find that most of them are stronger than before. I don't know if you could say that about our secretary of defense, who jumped out of a mental hospital window thinking the Russians were after him.

Does a writer's power diminish with age?
I don't think anybody ever thought that until Jerry Rubin said don't trust anybody over forty. Traditionally, writers are supposed to grow in power, like the late Shakespeare, the late Burroughs. Look at Beethoven, Michelangelo, Titian, most artists improve and get sharper with age. Maybe not Wordsworth.

What about your own work?

It's kind of steady. Youth, time, lyricism is best reflected in "Howl."
Maturity, middle age is best reflected in "Kaddish." Older age in
"Don't Grow Old" or "White Shroud" or recent poems appropriate to
the times.

**Has fame been the downfall of writers like Hemingway,
Fitzgerald, Kerouac, Capote?**
Every single one of the people you named had a tendency to drink.
Fortunately, I don't drink.

Do you smoke?
Irregularly. Just when somebody has a joint, because I don't carry it
around. I'm too wary and paranoid from years of dealing with the
narcotics bureau trying to set me up for a bust.

How often have you been set up?
I know of three or four situations where they tried. I never got busted.
Usually the people they tried to use to set me up came and told me
and then I would fight it.

Wasn't one of those friends Herbert Huncke?
Yes. They busted Huncke and threatened to throw the book at him
unless he brought marijuana to my house. So he told my brother, who
is a lawyer. But there were much more sinister situations than that.
There was an Inspector Imp who used to beat people up, chaining
them to radiators in the Lower East Side. He and this other detective
went to a jazz musician named Jack Martin and threatened to throw
the book at him unless he set me up for a bust. So Martin and some
filmmakers hired the Broadway Central Hotel and gave a public an-
nouncement of this before a large crowd. Six guys in Hawaiian shirts
climbed on the stage and dragged them down. They resisted, thinking
they were goons of some kind. It turned out to be Inspector Imp and
his narc buddies who didn't show their badges. It went to trial for resisting arrest and Martin and these filmmakers lost because the law
says that you can't resist arrest, even if you don't see any badges.

Isn't that when you compared our police to the police state in Prague?

Yes, that got into the *New York Times* and *Life* magazine. It went all the way to my congressman's office and through Robert Kennedy's office, back through the Treasury Department.

How many times have you actually been arrested?

Never for drugs, but about a dozen times for protest.

In 1965 you were thrown out of Cuba. Why?

For criticizing Castro's persecution of gay minorities. Just before I got there in January he'd given a speech at the university denouncing homosexuals. He broke up the theater school and sent a lot of gay people to labor camps. I complained about that in private to my hosts, Casa de las Americas: I was there officially as a judge for an inter-American literary contest. I also complained to some Cuban newspeople and got caught in a fight between the bohemian literary organization and the relatively militaristic police-state immigration authorities, who appeared at my room two days before I was to leave with the rest of the judges and put me under arrest. They cut me off from any communication. I said, "Have you told this to Haydee Santamaria?" She was one of the twelve members of the ruling council and the head of Casa de las Americas. They said, "No, she'll hear about it later." I was taken in a car to an airfield. "Why are you doing this?" I asked. The head of immigration said, "For breaking the laws of Cuba." "What laws did I break?" "You'll have to ask yourself that," he said.

And so you boarded a Czechoslovakian airplane and wound up in Prague, where you wound up being crowned King of the May and getting thrown out of that country as well!

That was an accident. I was in Prague for a month. Some of my poetry was really well known there and the students at the Engineering School of the Polytechnic had nominated this novelist Josef Skvorecky for May King, but he had a cold and asked me to go in his place. I asked if it was political, because I didn't want to get mixed up.

He said no, it's just the student demonstration, they haven't had one of these since the Nazis came in. So some students came and put a crown on my head and took me in an open flatbed truck through Prague. We gathered a big crowd and went to this park. It turned out that instead of 10,000 people at a student festival, all of Prague came out, 100,000 people! People gave speeches, but I didn't speak Czech so I sang a song using finger cymbals. I got elected the King of Majalis by a voice vote and show of hands. Then the minister of culture and the minister of education got together in the park—they were aghast that an American beatnik dope fiend fairy capitalist had gotten elected, so they had a strongarm goon squad come and lift me physically off the stage and declared that the election was null and void. In the next morning newspaper they had my picture as King of Majalis in the first edition, then somebody else's picture in the second edition. The duty of the King of May is to sleep with anybody he wants in Prague—it's a fertility festival for May Day—so I went around playing spin-the-bottle. I was relatively chaste, except for two adventures in the outskirts. Then a couple of cops picked me up and said, "You lost a notebook, somebody turned it in to the police station, come down and sign for it and we'll give it to you." So I went down with a friend and when we got there they told my friend he couldn't come in. They suddenly got very serious and took me upstairs. I signed for it and they put me under arrest. I asked what for? They said, "For writing statements against the state." I said, "This is my private notebook, I didn't publish anything." The cop said, "It's illegal to write it down." The statement I had written was: "All Communist lies about capitalism are true, and all capitalist lies about communism are true." That's what they got me for. So they isolated me and then they sent me on a plane to England. I landed the day Bob Dylan landed and the next day I was acting in the opening scene of his *Don't Look Back*. And two days later I was in a room with him and all the Beatles . . . but that's another story.

When did you first meet Dylan?
Nineteen sixty-three. Peter and I had gone around the world and I

was living in the Village, upstairs from the Eighth Street Bookshop, which was run by a guy named Ted Wilentz, who had put out one of my little books of early poems [*Empty Mirror*]. He threw a party for me and Peter on our return from India, after being away from New York from 1961 to 1963, during the height of all the beatnik noise that was being laid on by the media. Al Aronowitz, a journalist for the *New York Post*, brought Dylan to the Welcome Home party. Dylan had been given this civil rights award for "Blowing in the Wind" from the Emergency Civil Liberties Committee, but he had declared his independence of politics because he didn't want to be a political puppet or feel obligated to take a stand all the time. He was above and beyond politics in an interesting way. I had heard his music on the way back from India and I wept when I heard "A Hard Rain's A-Gonna Fall." It seemed like such a miracle that somebody with such a youthful consciousness could say it all. It seemed like an answering call or response to the kind of American prophecy that Kerouac had continued from Walt Whitman. Dylan seemed right in that line of illuminated genius. So I knew who he was, but I didn't know how young and fragile he looked. I hadn't any idea that he had any awareness of the writing that had gone before him from Kerouac and myself. But years later he told me that what had turned him on to poetry was Kerouac's *Mexico City Blues*. He said, "It blew my mind." It was the first poetry to talk to him.

Did Dylan know your work?
Yeah. He liked "Kaddish" particularly. He heard a recording of "Kaddish" on Atlantic Records back in the mid-sixties and he liked that a lot. He thought it was a high peak of my work. In his *Renaldo and Clara* film I read the beginning of the poem to a bunch of old ladies at a mahjong convention in a motel in Rhode Island. He was interested in how these sixty- and seventy-year-old Jewish ladies would take it, since they'd been around, knew about menopause and death.

Dylan also sang on your *First Blues* album, didn't he?
Yeah, Dylan, David Amram. It was a double album of tapes that I had

made which John Hammond put out many years later, which was distributed by Columbia.

How many records have you recorded?
About a dozen. Back in the sixties I recorded with Ed Sanders and the Fugs. Then I put out a set of albums. One was Blake's *Songs of Innocence and Experience.*

None of these, I assume, have made you much in royalties. What does money mean to you?
Oh, the same to me as anybody else: to buy sex, dope, books, houses, Empire State Buildings.

Didn't you recently sign a lucrative publishing contract?
Not at all, that's purely mythological.

Wasn't it for $160,000 for four books of poetry?
Six books over seven years, so what's that, about half a high school teacher's annual salary?

Still, you're known to give money away whenever you can.
Yeah, I've set up little foundations to give away money to artists and other poets who are in trouble. I have lots of artist friends who are not as fortunate as I am in making money, so I give them money sometimes.

Do you pay taxes?
Very little, because my expenses are so high. Most of my money goes into maintaining archives and secretarial fees, telephone bills, photographic film and prints, Xeroxing. This year it's cost me $800 a month just getting photographic prints made. So I live on a very penurious level in an inexpensive apartment on the Lower East Side.

You also donate when you can to the Jack Kerouac School of Disembodied Poetics, which you helped to found.

That started at the end of the summer of 1974 when Chogyam Trungpa asked me and Anne Waldman to organize a permanent school of poetics. Anne suggested "Disembodied" because Jack was dead. The idea was to teach the Buddhist's Golden Mouth, to introduce that element of stability that comes from meditation, tranquility, wisdom, equanimity, majesty, straight back instead of paranoid slump, to poets who were plagued by dope, sex, revolution, indiscipline, wildness, and traditional energy. It was to be an exchange between American aesthetics and Oriental aesthetics, American consciousness and Himalayan consciousness. I was always interested in Tibetan Buddhism, so it seemed like a great marriage of East and West, the background of Zen masters, Tibetan lamas, classic tradition from the Orient, wedding the western classic tradition of Kerouac and Burroughs. I go there every summer for a jamboree.

Can one ever obtain complete consciousness on this earth?
No, of course not. You can, however, follow the path of accumulation and by means of examination in one's own passion and aggression and ignorance come to a state of openness that might widen the area of consciousness to sympathetic receptivity to almost any situation.

A lot of your writing calls out to God, or some form of God. Do you believe in God?
No. Because of the Blake vision that I had, and a misunderstanding of it, I kept assigning divine—or God—value to it, using Western terminology. It was a mistake until probably the mid-sixties. The monotheistic or theistic notion reference point is a major mistake that America is hooked into. So is Russia and China with their monotheistic vision of communism. Here it's of In God We Trust. That's a relatively primitive notion of reality and my early poems have that built into them. Although there's always an ambivalent use of that kind of Western divine terminology, because I didn't really experience that. I experienced something more direct, which was simply just open space, which anybody can experience.

So when it comes to death you . . .
[*Sings*] "Die when you die."

Have you ever had a vision of your own death?
Oh all sorts: dying, screaming and shooting, in a hospital bed of cancer; the asp; or car crash; or falling out of an airplane; or drowning in an ocean of shit; or dying peacefully in a bed in the Sierra Mountains, three thousand feet up in the western slope in a rustic, meditative cabin; or maybe with some Tibetan lamas reciting the instructions from the *Tibetan Book of the Dead*. I've had all sorts of fantasies.

Does it frighten you?
Sure, sometimes.

Have you written an epitaph?
Nope. Never got around to do it. "Every third thought shall be my grave"—Shakespeare, *The Tempest*.

We haven't really touched on the Bard's influence on you.
Actually, I'm getting tired. Aren't you? I'm getting a slight headache. I don't mean to be difficult, but I didn't know we were going to go on so long.

Okay, let's call it quits.
Are you sure? Did you have any more material you wanted to cover? Got enough?

You've got a headache.
Yeah.

Thank you, Allen.
You're welcome.

Andrew Greeley

What It's Like to Be God

Andrew Greeley has been called arrogant, cantankerous, pugnacious, irascible, tenacious, a smart-ass, and his own worst enemy. He is outspoken, controversial, celibate, and prolific. He's a priest, a professor, a sociologist, a researcher, a writer. He has written shelves of books, from the nonfiction works *God in Popular Culture, Angry Catholic Women,* and *The Catholic Myth* to best-selling novels with lurid covers and titles such as *The Cardinal Sins, Ascent into Hell, Patience of a Saint,* and *Fall from Grace.* He is an Irish Catholic diehard Chicagoan who spends part of each year in Tucson, Arizona. He is convinced God is female, and he hasn't lost his faith in the Chicago Cubs. He's given away millions of dollars for religious causes, and has had a pledge for $1 million—to help inner-city schools in Chicago—that was rejected by the city's cardinal because, he speculates, the Vatican wouldn't approve of the archdiocese taking money from a priest who writes "salacious" novels. At the age of fifty-seven he took up windsurfing.

Born in 1928, he looks on his life as a series of adventures that he wouldn't trade with anyone else. If a movie was made about him, he'd be happy with Martin Sheen or Robert De Niro cast as the central character ("I don't think Robert Redford is quite up to it," he says, "and Bing Crosby's dead").

"Call me Andy," Greeley said in 1993 when he opened the door to his Tucson house, which is outside the city, with a view of the mountains and the saguaro cacti. There's a swimming pool and a Jacuzzi, which he uses daily before sunrise whenever he's writing, which is most of the time. During our conversation he was interrupted by two phone calls: one from a *New York Times* reporter doing a survey, and the other from a woman who lost a relative and needed consoling. Greeley is a man who wears many hats, and all of them seem to fit his brainy Irish head.

You seem to be your own best—or worst—critic: one chapter in your autobiography lists the most common complaints about you: one, that you write too much and have never had an unpublished thought; two, that you're the richest priest in America; three, that you have serious psychosexual problems; four, that you write pornographic trash; five, that your novels are puerile potboilers that sell because of the novelty of a priest writing about sex; six, that you're brokenhearted that you were not made a bishop.
Yeah, that's a pretty good list.

So where do you want to begin?
Well, as for writing to make money, I've given most of the money away. The serious psychosexual problems was said by Eugene Kennedy, a former priest, psychologist, and also a novelist. I don't know anybody who doesn't have sexual problems, it goes with being human. But I don't think mine are either serious or incapacitating. The same Dr. Kennedy said I wrote trash, but the academic scholars who have worked on my stuff don't think they're trash. And they're not pornography, they are less erotic that the *Song of Songs* in the scriptures. These are hard things to refute, because how do you defend yourself against them? Potboilers that sell because I'm a priest— that's not true. People like them because they're good stories. One of the great put-downs of my work is to say that I'm no Graham Greene, to which I say, "I suppose that's true, but why need I be? Why is that

the criteria? I'm not James Joyce or James Michener either." Am I brokenhearted that I'm not a bishop? The day I set the first word on paper I concluded any chances of becoming a bishop and I knew what I was doing.

Is it an ambition of most priests to continue up the hierarchy, hoping to become a bishop, then a cardinal?

It certainly wasn't my ambition. I don't think most priests think of it as even a possibility. We have 40,000 priests and a couple hundred bishops. The odds are so heavily against it. And if you start to write, forget it!

Was it when you were in the second grade that you decided to become a priest?

That's certainly when the thought first occurred to me. I never really wanted to be anything else.

Your father knew a number of priests and they weren't all of sterling character. Did your wanting to join them disturb him at all?

My father had taken care of a number of alcoholic priests at the Knights of Columbus, and given the fact that there were alcoholics all over our family, he was very concerned that I be clear in my head about this.

So your image of a priest was not necessarily that of a good man, but of a troubled man?

Yes, but I knew all kinds of good men, too, and some of the troubled men were good men when they were sober. But it was a realistic image.

When did you come to accept God's existence?

I always have.

Never doubted?

Not more than a couple times a day.

You've said your most powerful childhood memories are that of silence. Why silence?

Silence when my father's business was wiped out by the Great Depression. We remember the grimness and the pessimism of that era.

Interesting that out of that silence came such an outpouring from you. In analytical terms, would you say your prolificacy is like a scream in answer to your parents silence?

That's a very interesting analysis, and seems to me to be a very reasonable interpretation.

Your father died of a stroke when you were nineteen; how did his death affect you?

Life is never the same. I still dream about my father and my mother. A door shuts in this world; it's a really savage blow to the system.

Did your weekly nightmares begin before or after his death?

I've had them as far back as I know.

How horrifying are your nightmares?

Scary, like Stephen King novels, or like a well-done horror movie. They're not paralyzing frightening, but in addition to being scary, they're kind of fun. You're out there fighting off things.

Among the things you must wrestle with is the image of the priesthood, which has been taking its knocks of late. You've written that "the good of the church is ill-served when psychopaths, sociopaths, antisocial personalities, pederasts, crooks, alcoholics, and incompetents are routinely appointed to the American dioceses." You paint a bleak picture.

It is a bleak picture. It's bleaker now than when I wrote that. What has happened to the detriment of the priesthood is that we have tried to make priests more than human and in the process we have created an image of somebody that's less than human.

Does the problem start at the top, at the Vatican?
The Vatican has established an ever greater distance between themselves and the laypeople, which is a very serious and dangerous thing. The leadership of the Church has lost its nerve. For the last thirty years the Vatican, bishops, priests have done everything we can to drive the Catholic laypeople out of the Church—but they won't go.

You're not a big fan of the current pope, John Paul II, are you?
Well, I wouldn't call John Paul II the worst pope, but I think he's a tragic pope because he is a man of enormous talents who has been unable to understand the Western world, and because of that he's been a failure as a pope, and that's a real tragedy. A man of extraordinary gifts—a poet, a playwright, a singer, a skier, a swimmer, university professor—but he grew up in a country under siege and he views the Church as under siege in the world, where it really isn't. The Reformation is over.

You've written that Pope John Paul II is "a pessimistic man who expects world disaster."
He seems to, certainly. The pilgrimages of his are ceremony, they no longer capture the imagination of people because they're just not listening to him, they don't dislike him, but they're not listening.

Who has been your favorite pope?
In my lifetime certainly John XXIII, who had a sense of the way the wave of history was going and he climbed aboard and went with it. And unlike the two men that came after him, he was utterly secure. He was not worried that openness and change would be a threat to Catholicism.

You've described the present Church leadership as morally, intellectually, and religiously bankrupt. Is that still your opinion?
Yeah. They can't cope. They can't cope with the pedophile crisis, they can't cope with their loss of credibility, with the decline of vocations,

with the decline in contributions, with women and women's demands for equal treatment in the Church. I'm hard put to think of anything they're doing right.

If you led the Vatican, that is, if you were pope, what would you do?
Resign. [*Laughs*] That's a felicitous answer. It's a serious question. The first thing I'd try to do is set up channels of communication, so I'd know what's going on in the minds of the laypeople and the parish priests. I would try to listen. It seems to me to be the abiding failure of Church leaders and maybe of all leaders: they don't listen. And the Church leaders seem to think they have the monopoly on the Holy Spirit and that God speaks only to them and that She doesn't communicate through ordinary folk, and that's just crazy.

So the main problems of the Church today are . . . ?
They are twofold. There's no means of upward communication. The Vatican doesn't ask because it knows all the answers. The bishop doesn't ask because he knows all the answers. Secondly is the equation of religion with sexual morality, to the exclusion of all else.

That morality deals with the volatile issues of birth control, abortion, homosexuality in the priesthood, molestation, and child abuse. Where do you stand on these issues?
On birth control, Catholics don't believe it, they don't accept it, neither do most priests. The Vatican should reappraise its position. On abortion, I'm not sure when human life begins. I disapprove of abortion but I don't think that we can enforce our position by law. I don't think you can really force women to carry pregnancies to term. It just won't work.

What do you think of the prolifer who murdered a doctor outside his clinic because he performed abortions?
I don't think it's fair to judge any movement by the crazies in it. You can be opposed to abortion and still be horrified by what happened.

Having said that I do think that the rhetoric of some of the prolife people creates an atmosphere in which all kinds of things can be done. The violent demonstrations create that atmosphere. I find myself put off by the rhetoric of both sides of the debate and, in fact, all the data show that most Americans are in-between. They are neither prolife nor prochoice.

What are your feelings about homosexuality in the priesthood?
There surely have been gay priests, gay bishops, gay popes, and gay saints, but one would not want the whole priesthood to be gay because this would mark it off rather strikingly from the rest of humankind. As long as one or two or even five percent of the priesthood are gay, I have no problem with it, particularly if they don't flaunt affectual orientation in the face of the laity. Once the proportion of priests who are gay becomes higher than that, then the priesthood gets marked as a gay profession in people's minds and it will lose its attraction for heterosexual young men.

What is the Church's position on child abuse?
The Church's official position on child abuse is that it's a terrible evil. In practice, we're not prepared to do enough to stop it within the priesthood. The increase in the number of pedophiliacs and practitioners of the gay lifestyle is a threat to the whole priesthood. And it is a threat that is still denied! It's profoundly alarming.

Is there a solution?
The solution is to tell the truth, which church leaders find very difficult to do. Also, priests must tell the truth to themselves. They must acknowledge the existence of the problem, their responsibility for it, and their obligation to police themselves.

Pederasty is something you dealt with in your novel, *Fall from Grace*. But some critics have criticized you for not going deeper into the subject.
That's fair, but it's less a novel about actual victimization than it is

about the Church's response to it. Moreover, the kind of sexual abuse
of kids is such an ugly thing, I don't want to try and portray it. I
don't want to get inside the head of a sexual abuser. I would much
prefer keeping it offstage. I don't describe a scene in which a priest
begins to molest a kid. I don't think you have to go that far. Even if
the ultimate ugliness is not portrayed, it's still a terribly ugly subject.
I have written on the pedophile problem since 1986 and have been
warning and warning about what's going to happen, and now it's
happened. And the priesthood is in disarray because it's covered up
these things, it still denies that they happen.

**You've written that the seminary in the 1950s was a "terrible way
to prepare men for the priesthood." How terrible was it?**
Even worse than I portray it in my novels. It was an awful place. It
kept us in immaturity; it deprived us of the ability to make decisions,
to think for ourselves, and didn't even offer us the recompense of serious intellectual challenge. So we came out of the seminary unpre-
pared for our work. It was a very, very bad place.

So why did you and others stay?
I wanted to be a priest in Chicago. So I set about to educate myself.

**Your first parish, at Christ the King, was also your last. You were
there ten years. Were they fruitful years?**
They were decisive for me as a priest, a sociologist, and as a novelist.
It was very clear to me early on at Christ the King that this parish was
the wave of the future. As a sociologist, I found myself doing much of
my work on the acculturation process of the third- and fourth-
generation immigrants. What they left behind and what they didn't
leave behind. As a storyteller, all my stories are about those same people. Blackie Ryan, my priest detective, grew up in the parish.

**Your stories are an exercise of your imagination. Why is it that
the Church remains so unimaginative that they can't conceive of
women being priests?**

The argument is: because they have never been priests. And people don't want to share power. If you make women priests you're going to have to share power, and change the way you do business. It's terribly unjust.

Why is that such an issue with the Church?
The ordination of women would break up the male clerical monopoly and notably change its culture and orientation.

Are you uneasy around nuns?
Yeah. I was very uneasy around them in the parish and I'm uneasy with them now. Nuns don't like priests.

Why not?
Because priests have all the fun. They have good reason for not liking them. We've treated them like cheap help in the Church for ages and ages. They have a lot to be angry about. And there are not very many doing it anymore. It's hopelessly unfair.

Is celibacy also unjust and unfair? It seems that the problems many priests have would be reduced if they were allowed to live a more normal life.
The celibate witness is important because it points to a world beyond this one, and it does mean that there are some men in this world who can care about women very strongly without jumping into bed with them.

That seems a bit lame, Father. The fact is, priests are so troubled by this vow of celibacy that they're breaking it all the time. Archbishop Sanchez of Santa Fe was charged with sexual misconduct. Isn't it too high a price to pay?
Certainly too high for some people. Bob Sanchez is not the first archbishop to have these problems. In past ages it would have been more typical for archbishops to have concubines than not, so the notion that this is something new or startling I find odd. For much of

Catholic history celibacy was only a rule in theory. My friend tells me that a third of the population of Iceland are the descendants of the last Catholic archbishop [*smiles*]. I've been doing some work on the peasant religion in the Middle Ages and your typical priest had a woman, he just couldn't survive by himself. So celibacy as a norm really only became typical after the Council of Trent, for the last four hundred years. If Catholic layfolk have been totally trusting of priests' emotional and sexual maturity in the past, that's a real bad mistake and they're not going to make that mistake again. On the other hand, when the celibate priest comes into the parish, he sets up a certain benign kind of sexual tension. The women tend to trust him far more than they would trust any other man, and the men may find themselves uneasy about the intimacy, in the psychological sense, between their women and the priest. But the tension is a benign and positive tension.

I have two feelings about these issues: one is that celibacy ought to continue, and that secondly, we ought to ordain women. I'm the only one I know who holds both those positions. I also have a third one: people should be able to leave the priesthood after a limited term of service.

What you call a priest corps?
Yes, like the Peace Corps. But I can't get anybody to take it seriously. Until very recently, until the end of the last century, you were a priest for ten years and then you died. Now you're a priest for fifty years. If you're burned out at forty, you can't stand teenagers, you don't like the work, you want to start a family—volunteer for ten years and then go forth with dignity and gratitude. It would solve all our vocational shortage problems. Ordain women and ordain people for limited terms of service. But the Vatican now resists any change because it's afraid of losing celibacy.

What's puzzling is that in spite of your liberalism on most things, you still believe in celibacy, even after shows like "60 Minutes"

and "Prime Time Live" bring us tales of priests gone bad because of it.

You hear everywhere now that if the priesthood wasn't celibate there wouldn't be all this sexual abuse of children. Well, the Lutherans and the Episcopalians and Jews have that problem, as do people in education and Boy Scouts and Little League. It's by no means a Catholic monopoly. Moreover, most pedophiles are married men. I think there's an assault on celibacy that's not fair.

A priest from the Boston archdiocese administered a battery of psychological tests on personal satisfaction, life satisfaction, job satisfaction with priests and with a control group of married, well-educated, successful laymen, and the priests won at every measure. I said, "What you are saying is that priests are the happiest people in America." And he said, "Yes, that's basically it. Priests are happier than their counterparts in the lay world, on the average." So what happens when the celibacy thing is discussed on shows like "Prime Time Live" is that you get the malcontents, the people who are unhappy.

But you yourself have said that most priests suffer from low self-esteem.

Do they?

That's what you wrote.

Sometimes they do. Part of it is we fail so often. It's a job, like being a high school principal or a psychiatrist; you lose a lot more than you win. And even when you're moderately successful and you're trying to console the bereaved, for example, well, you do a little bit toward easing their pain, but you don't do much. You're dealing with an impossible problem: to ease the pain of loss. You fail at the things that are important. The other thing is that in our seminary training, self-esteem was thought to be pride, and if you really had respect and esteem for yourself and your work, you were guilty of the sin of pride and that was the sin of Satan.

Still, you're a proud man . . . and proud of it, aren't you?
I find it hard to say yes to that because of the training that that was a bad word. Now, the right answer is yes.

Wasn't your giving $1.25 million to the University of Chicago after they denied you tenure a classic example of one-upsmanship? You must have been very proud!
[*Laughs*] It was to build a bridge between the university and the Church, that's really why I did it. But I also enjoyed the one-upsmanship.

Did the denial of tenure in 1972 come as a surprise to you?
It did, because I knew I'd done the work and I thought the university would be fair. I didn't know who my allies were in the sociology department. And who my enemies were. And, God forgive me, I had some people pegged as enemies who were not, they were strong allies. I don't understand what happened. I know now who the guys were who politicked against me, but I don't understand why. One of them said I was a student of his and had a second-class mind, but I was never one of his students. He had me confused with someone else.

You've worked as an academic, a journalist, and a priest: Which are the most envious?
I have to choose? Envy is part of the human condition and each of those professions are shot through with envy. The priesthood is the worst, because the reward system is so small, and because envy is such a disgrace to what the priesthood is supposed to be.

Within those three professions, who are your most severe critics?
They are mostly priests. I'm part of the brotherhood of priests and when the brotherhood goes after me, it hurts me very deeply.

What about book reviewers?
As criticism is practiced today by book reviewers, there's very little to learn from them. They are usually personal attacks.

Yet in spite of these attacks you consider yourself an "incorrigible romantic" and believe God is one, too. What makes you a romantic?

To be a real romantic I would define as to believe in happy endings. I believe in happy endings.

As does God?

She'd better believe.

Even with all the pain and suffering we see in the world?

Well, certainly there aren't going to be happy endings in this life for everybody, or for anybody, since we all die. We have to see God as a parent who suffers when we suffer, suffers with every Muslim woman who's raped by a Serb, suffers with the families of those who died in the World Trade Center blast. If you yield to the absurdity of evil, then you still have the problem of life itself—of love, of the sunshine, of the moon coming up at night.

But if God can create, can She also change?

It would appear that in the short run there are some things that God can't change. Now why that would be so, I don't know. But beyond that there's the question of why is there anything at all? We live sort of suspended between why is there evil and why is there anything at all.

I know you define God as an Irish female comedienne. Was that a revelation or just wishful thinking?

The most fascinating people that I've met in my life are strong and funny and tender Irish women; therefore I think they are a tremendous force for God, and so that's how I define it.

Is God really as sexy as Jessica Lange?

She'd better be. Or as Audrey Hepburn.

Since we're speaking of personalities, who among the celebrated has impressed you?

I met Mother Theresa once, she impressed me. Dorothy Day impressed me. [Senator] Pat Moynihan is certainly larger than life, as is Mario Cuomo, who could have been president.

You mean you're not impressed with Clinton?
Oh, he's an improvement over his predecessor, but he lacks courage. For example, the gays in the military—he shouldn't have brought that up in the beginning of his administration. Once he made that decision he shouldn't have let Sam Nunn, who thinks he ought to be president, and Colin Powell stop it. Go ahead with it! And cutting the budget: he's afraid of Benson in Texas if he cuts the superglider and the space station. And he's afraid of Nunn and Powell if he brings the troops home from Europe and Asia like Moynihan wants him to do. So his tragic flaw is that he doesn't have the courage to do the tough things. I'd like to see Hillary as president instead of this guy. She has a lot more courage.

What's the most courageous thing you've done as a writer?
The greatest risk was to turn from nonfiction to fiction. It took me a while because I wondered if I was able to do it. It was a risky business—not because I was going to put some eroticism in my books, I'm unself-conscious there, sexual attraction is part of the human condition, you can't write a story without it—I just felt telling stories was a risk.

It's certainly in the tradition of your religion, beginning with Jesus. If he were here today would he be a novelist, a screenwriter, or a rap singer?
He would certainly tell stories, because that's what he was more than anything else. And that's why the people followed him around, to hear his stories. So he would probably do all three.

You've said that writing novels has made you know more about how it feels to be God. Isn't that a bit audacious?
Well, you see, God creates us and, for reasons perhaps in poor taste,

falls in love with us, and then can't control what we do. And that's what happens to the storyteller. You create these people and you fall in love with them and you can't quite make them act right. So yeah, I think the storyteller has some sense of what it's like to be God.

With all your novels, do you think you might affect any change in the thinking of the Church hierarchy?
I don't think so, because they don't read them. They know what's in them without reading them.

What would you say is a main theme that runs through your books?
Second chances. That we keep getting second chances.

Would Chicago always be a subtheme?
Somebody once said, "Why don't you take your novels out of Chicago, it's not the center of the world." And I say, "Yeah, it is." Faulkner was comfortable in Mississippi; I'm not Faulkner, but I write about Chicago.

Is there any other religious thinker who is writing novels like yourself?
Who wrote *My Name Is Asher Lev*?

Chaim Potok.
I think he and I are doing parallel things. We are struggling with what happens in the acculturation of the second- and third-generation immigrants.

Didn't you once accuse Stephen King of writing religious stories?
To his face. And he said I'm right. I hate to admit it, but I have not read many of his books. They're just too long. It's similar with Tom Clancy. He's a good storyteller, deserves every dollar he makes, which is a lot, but they're too long, too long.

If you could write like anybody else, who might that be?

It would be a woman, certainly, because they are much better novelists than men. It's their marvelous feel for texture, the rich detail of a situation. Somebody whose work I admire enormously is Louise Erdrich, who writes about the Chippewa Indians in Minnesota and North Dakota.

What percentage of your readership do you suspect is not Catholic?

Twenty-five percent. I don't suspect. We did research.

You've been a professional researcher, connected with the National Opinion Research Center, for more than thirty years. What does the NORC do?

It's a general research center. Most of their work are huge government contracts, following cohorts of people through life-cycle experiences. Get people in high school and follow them until they're thirty, see what happens to their occupational choices and decisions; health studies. Within the framework there's also a number of us who do more academic research, questions like the effect of Catholic schools, or the effect of prayer. One of the most interesting things we do is since 1972 we interview 1,500 Americans and we ask the same questions every year. This gives us some measures of social change and social continuity in America. How people's attitudes have changed on extramarital sex—it hasn't. How they've changed on homosexuality— surprisingly, they haven't changed on that either. What about their attitudes on premarital sex? A real revolution in those attitudes. It is that survey that I've principally worked with. And I fund part of it. I give them some money so they can ask a battery of religious questions, about images of God.

And what have you found?

About 35 percent of Americans think of God as equally mother and father, or more mother than father. Which means the notion of the womanliness of God is out there in the population. And we who are the elites are just beginning to discover it.

Bottom line: What significance is such research?
What is the significance of anything that most people do? Most scholars do? Not much. My work in sociology and religion may help us understand a lot better what religion is and what it is not. My work on American Catholics has presented challenges which the Church is going to have to face. One is that Catholics are no longer paying any attention to what the official Church says; the other is that they're still Catholic. Those are findings which have some importance for the Church.

Haven't you also done studies regarding sex with singles and married couples and those over sixty?
I did two articles for the *Jesuit Magazine of America* and one of the findings was that Catholics have sex more often than other people. Flies in the face of all conventional wisdom. And another study found that while sex does decline with age, an awful lot of people over sixty were still very active sexually. About a third of them, men about the same as women, had sex at least once a week or more. And they were the most likely to say their spouse was a good lover and that the spouse was physically attractive. That surprised me. It delighted me. That somebody who may not look particularly beautiful to someone else still looks beautiful to the beloved.

You've admitted regret to never having married or having children. How deep is that regret?
Not very great. It would have been nice, but I wouldn't trade the life I've lived for the other one.

Yet you also cheerfully admit that you've always had women's bodies on your mind. Are you just trying to be outrageous when you say that?

I'm a heterosexual male member of the human species, of course women's bodies are on my mind.

Are these the kind of bodies that appear in swimsuits on the cover of *Sports Illustrated* or in the buff in *Playboy*?
I don't think *Playboy*'s very good at eroticism. And every year when that *Sports Illustrated* issue comes out there are outraged cries from feminists. Where the magazine makes their mistake is that they don't have models that are much older, because they would be much more erotic. An attractive forty-year-old woman in a swimsuit, even if it covers more, is far more attractive to anybody that's got any taste at all than a nineteen-year-old.

While we're on the subject of women, why do men like Norman Mailer, James Michener, and Marlon Brando believe that most men have a hatred of women?
Fear too. The reason for the fear is that they have so much power over us. They can in the strict sense of the word *unman* us, they can so attract us that all else slips out of our minds. Then, having attracted us and let us perhaps make fools of ourselves, they can dismiss us.

Which is why man feels the need to dominate?
Yeah, and that's finally no good. The only effective way for a man to deal with a woman is with tenderness and gentleness and respect.

Do you think you could ever deal with the Chicago White Sox like that?
No. I don't understand why anybody could be a Sox fan. I'm an Irish Catholic Democrat Cub Fan from the West Side of Chicago. That's my identity. And it has nothing to do with whether the Cubs win pennants or not. It would be nice if they would, but the last time was 1945, so we're under no illusions.

Speaking of illusions, you've done research into mysticism and psychic phenomena. What conclusions have you come to?

That they are widespread and generally benign and that paranormal is normal and ecstasy is good for you. As far as ESP goes, it seems to me these things do happen, that people do become aware of events happening a long distance away, and that they do indeed have experiences of contact with the dead. Mystical experiences have been recorded since humans have been reporting things. It's silly to say they don't exist or to try to write them off as being schizophrenics or to try to explain them in terms of brain chemicals. I think they happen. And near-death experiences happen too. What they are and what they mean is another matter.

For that we'll have to ask Woody Allen.
Woody Allen in his films argues with what life means. There's a marvelous line: It's not that he doesn't believe in God, but he thinks God is an underachiever.

Do you know Lenny Bruce's line: If you live in New York, you're Jewish. It doesn't matter if you're Catholic, if you live in New York, you're Jewish.
That's wonderful. Wonderful. And if you live in Chicago, you're Irish.

On a more serious note, is it your belief that anti-Semitism in America has diminished?
I don't know. If I were Jewish I would still be very wary of anti-Semitism and very eager to fight it wherever it raises its head. It's out there, it's an historic given, prejudice is part of the human condition and Jews and blacks and Irish are favorite targets. Now it's dead white men, which I find as offensive as any other kind of prejudice.

Dead white men?
Dante, Plato, all those other folks who shouldn't be in the curriculum.

What dead white men would you like to bring back to life for a special dinner party?

Leaving aside religious leaders, Thomas Jefferson, Abraham Lincoln, G. K. Chesterson, and Mr. and Mrs. James Joyce.

Your own death, how do you envision it?
I hope I'm well enough to die with a smile.

And still with the epitaph: Nothing but a loud-mouthed Irish priest?
It wouldn't be a bad epitaph.

ALEX HALEY

Brothers in the Same Ultimate Boat

OF THE MULTITUDE OF WRITERS WHO CAN START A SEN-
tence this way—"After some 20 years of having crossed my fingers
every time I mailed to editors something I had written"—only one
could finish it like this: "now *Roots,* which represented 12 of those
years of work, had already sold close to 1,000,000 hardcover
copies, and the television miniseries had collectively attracted the
largest audience in the history of the medium."

After Alex Haley's death at seventy in 1992, Benjamin Hooks,
executive director of the NAACP, said of *Roots,* which won the
Pulitzer Prize in 1977 and was reprinted in thirty-seven languages, "It was the story of our people. It was the story of how we
came from Africa." An editorial in the *Los Angeles Times* concluded: "*Roots* permanently revised the collective myth of a nation's origins. Few writers have ever attempted, much less accomplished, so much."

After its enormous success, Haley would write articles for
Reader's Digest and *Playboy* about what *Roots* meant to him and
whether or not it was personally worth it. Considering that he
subsequently never wrote anything of such consequence, the author of *Roots* and of *The Autobiography of Malcolm X* may have felt
the burden of best-sellerdom. Yet those two books alone made
Alex Haley a world-renowned writer, the subject of hundreds of

articles, the object of lawsuits, the recipient of thirty-seven honorary degrees.

He was born in Ithaca, New York, and grew up in the small town of Henning, Tennessee. His parents were well educated, but he got his gift for storytelling from his grandmother and aunts, who would sit on the front porch of their home talking about "the African," Kunta Kinte, who was brought to America in chains from Gambia, and whose children and grandchildren had names like Chicken George, Miss Kizzy, and, eventually, Alex Haley—but he never knew this was the story he was born to tell. After disappointing his father with poor grades, he decided to leave college early and join the Coast Guard, where he spent the next twenty years roaming the seas, honing his writing skills by penning love letters for fellow sailors. When he left the Coast Guard at thirty-seven, he used his skills to freelance for magazines. In 1962, his conversation with Miles Davis became the first *Playboy* Interview. He followed that with interviews with Malcolm X, Cassius Clay, Dr. Martin Luther King Jr., Melvin Belli, George Lincoln Rockwell, Sammy Davis Jr., and Johnny Carson.

The magazine work subsided, however, as his idea to trace the history of his family up from slavery to modern times grew to an obsession. The payoff was enormous, but so were the legal battles, the accusations of plagiarism, and his own frustrations about not having the luxury of time to develop other stories. There was one more book, *A Different Kind of Christmas,* published in 1988, and a posthumous work, *Queen,* which was finished by another writer.

I admired Haley for his *Playboy* interviews, all of which I had studied before I began writing for that magazine. So when we finally met in 1985 we had that in common. I had also spent three years in the Peace Corps in Ghana, West Africa, and had visited the dungeons in Elmina and Cape Coast where captured Africans were kept before sailing into slavery. Haley was a soft-spoken, gentle man who was proud of what he had accomplished and willing to share his rags-to-riches story. As Murray Fisher, his

Playboy and *Roots* editor, said of him, "I consider him the finest and most decent man I've ever known." Many people who knew Alex Haley echoed that sentiment.

Your interview with Miles Davis was the first *Playboy* Interview, a feature that has become almost as much of an institution as the centerfold. How did that come about?

I had written mostly for *Reader's Digest* at the time and wasn't very well known. *Playboy* wanted to do a piece on Miles Davis. I was excited at the opportunity because *Playboy* was the most exciting magazine in the world of periodical writers. It was adventuresome; it was reaching for new directions. I didn't know at the time that Miles and I were very, very different. I was as square as a block. I came out of Tennessee, was twenty years in the service, what did I know about jazz and his world? I tried every way I knew to get to Miles but I just couldn't. He would not talk to me. His lawyer told me that not only was I not going to get to talk with Miles, he didn't like the press. I was so desperate to get this story that when he told me where Miles trained as an amateur boxer when he was in New York, I bought some gym gear and went to Wiley's Uptown Gym on 135th Street in Harlem and enrolled for six months. Sure enough, when Miles was in town he'd turn up, and I was there. Miles was beautiful to watch in the gym. He had this compact body with rippling muscles. He put on this powder-blue sweatsuit and be almost like a dancer doing his exercises and training. He knew I was there and one day he came up to me with his hands on his hips and jerked his head toward the ring. The invitation was clear: get in the ring with him or forget any hope of an interview. So I got in the ring and it didn't last all that long. He didn't really hurt me—I taught him a whole lot about clinching [*laughs*]. Afterwards we went to the showers. There's something about two guys under adjacent showerheads that's not terribly formal and he began to talk. He asked me about my "gig." He was curious about me as a writer. It just happened that when we went downstairs there was a newsstand and I had a piece in *True* magazine about a ship revolt, and another piece in *Reader's Digest*. I bought both copies and showed them to him. Then we got into his Lamborghini and drove to his home on West 77th Street. He introduced me to his wife, Frances, and then he began to take me around to his night activities. Wherever he appeared, the people at the door just evaporated. He was the king of jazz. He was called the Prince of Darkness. He'd walk into a club and these musical living legends would embrace him. I met and observed the world around him, especially the women. I was always taking notes because *Playboy* had given me six weeks to write a 6,000-word article. After five weeks I realized I had fascinating things about his night life, but I didn't have enough quotes from Miles. So I took a gamble: I wrote 3,000 words about the nightlife of the king of jazz, and then for the other 3,000 words I went through every quote I could find, made up questions to fit, and that was how the *Playboy* Interview took form.

Your next interview for *Playboy*, with Malcolm X, became the basis for your first book. Was he as difficult to figure out as Miles was?

Malcolm X had a fearsome image, tough guy, articulate but hard. For the first several sessions he just would not talk about himself. This was after the *Playboy* interview, when we were working on his book. I was uptight because I hadn't been able to get through to him. I was ready to go to the publisher and suggest they try another writer. Malcolm kept going on about the Nation of Islam and his leader, Mr. Elijah Muhammed, and I just asked him to tell me something about his mother. At the time he was up walking—almost stalking, the way he would walk—and he stopped as if someone had jerked a string to him. He looked at me and I knew that I had touched some button within him. He began to talk again, but more slowly. And when he spoke his voice was up a notch. "It's funny you'd ask me that," he said. "I can remember the kind of dresses she used to wear. They were always faded and gray." He walked a little more. "And I remember she was always bent over the stove, trying to stretch what little we had." It was 11:30 at night and that man walked that floor until daybreak and spilling out of him came the first chapter of *The Autobiography of Mal-*

colm X. It was the memory of a little seven-year-old boy of his mother beginning to have great strain trying to hold together her brood of seven children whose father, her husband, had recently been murdered. He'd been thrown under a moving streetcar. And after that night Malcolm was never, ever reluctant to talk.

Malcolm X felt the white man didn't want to lose somebody to be supreme over. Do you feel that's still true?
It has a good element of truth in a subliminal way. We're talking about white and black, but if you look at the women's movement, you see the same white male's resistance and phrases applied to women as to blacks. "It's okay if they stay in their place; they can work and receive less money for the same job."

Malcolm X believed the black man survived by fooling the white man. Is this still the way it is?
It's a tactic, but so do white people survive by fooling the boss. Practically everybody does it to some degree. It's not just a black-white thing, it's a human nature thing.

How did you feel personally when Malcolm X would say to you that "Thoughtful white people *know* they are inferior to black people"?
That's what he said, and what he thought. My job was to quote him. My own personal reaction to that is I am not big on saying anybody is better than somebody else. White, brown, yellow, polka dot: we are brothers in the same ultimate boat.

Do you feel, as Marlon Brando does, that Malcolm X was a great man?
Sure. The fact that you and virtually every interviewer I meet ask about him says that better than I ever could. He affected the thinking of a society. What is obscured is that he really was saying what had been taught to him by Mr. Elijah Muhammed, the leader of the Nation of Islam, or the Black Muslims locally. It's one of those vicissi-

tudes of history that Malcolm is the one talked about, and not his teacher.

That has something to do with you as well, don't you think?
Yeah, it does.

You followed Malcolm with one of his disciples, the boxer then known as Cassius Clay.
Who had a tremendous amount of mother wit. He had a capacity for putting you on, but underneath he was very cunning. He would do things to put you off as an interviewer. I'd ask him a question and he'd appear to be asleep. This was very disconcerting. Then he would open his eyes and answer. So you didn't know when he was listening or not listening to you. He told me how, when he was in Kentucky, he missed the school bus and he knew if he went home his mother was going to whup up. Because he was afraid of his mother he ran after the bus and he saw how the kids on the bus were watching and enjoying him running. Up to that time he was just another kid in the playground, nobody paid him any particular attention. But after that day he began to be pointed out as the kid who ran behind the bus and that taught him something: always perform—do whatever you do to make people watch you. And that is what he used in and out of the ring.

You interviewed another great black athlete, Jim Brown, who once harbored fantasies of going in the ring against Muhammad Ali, didn't he?
There was talk about a mythical fight between these two and it was not without interest to Jim Brown. He took me to a restaurant on Crenshaw Avenue and Ali was there. They met each other and then they stepped outside and took off their coats and began to shadow box. Not a finger was laid on either of them but it was a blur of movements. Afterwards Jim Brown and I were at the Continental Hotel on Sunset and he verbally played the fight out, saying, "I'd win, because what Ali doesn't know is how fast I am." I laughed, because earlier

when I was interviewing Ali and had asked him about fighting Jim Brown, Ali had said, "I would have to win because Jim Brown thinks I don't know how fast he is."

Ali is often ranked as the greatest fighter of all time, but do you think he could have beaten Joe Louis in his prime?

I don't know. But one of my most moving experiences was meeting Joe Louis. After *Roots* had come out, I was speaking to a communications group in Las Vegas and David Wolper, the executive producer of the *Roots* miniseries, said he had a request for me. Joe Louis wanted to know if I would take the time to see him. Well, I felt like dropping to my knees because when I was a boy Joe Louis was the biggest thing in our world. When he would fight the black community in Henning would gather together to listen on the radio. We little kids would grab each other and say, "I'm Joe Louis." It was said that Joe Louis was the only black man in America who could legally knock a white man down and get away with it. When his fight would be over and Joe Louis had knocked out his opponent the place would go into pandemonium. Joe Louis was our god. Now here was this god asking me to come and see him. I went to his home and he had a copy of *Roots* and asked if I would sign it. My eyes were just grinning with tears. I never will forget what a thrill that was.

Was it also a thrill to interview Martin Luther King Jr.?

He was a very pivotal figure, an artist who comes along only once every so often. But I never felt that I knew Dr. King.

How different and how similar were King and Malcolm X?

They were very, very different. They had the same objectives but their approach was very different. I've often played in my head how easily either of them might have been the other, given the other's background. If a Malcolm X had been sent to the best high school in Atlanta for blacks, if his father overlooked shepherding his son as Daddy King had, and if Malcolm X could have gone to Morehouse College in Atlanta and then to Boston College School of Theology as did Dr. King, think what a minister Malcolm would have made. Conversely, take a young Martin Luther King and put him in the streets of Roxbury, Massachusetts, selling marijuana, shining shoes, and making the rags pop so people would give him a little more money, and then to go get his graduate degree in the streets of Harlem, what a hustler he would have become!

Did each of them influence the other?

I don't think a whole lot. Both of them were very self-sufficient forces in their own way. When I was writing *The Autobiography of Malcolm X*, *Playboy* asked me to interview Dr. King. So periodically I would go down to see him in Atlanta. Dr. King knew I was writing a book about Malcolm and he was cool about it. He would answer a half dozen questions, then he would say, "By the way, what's Brother Malcolm saying about me these days?" Then I'd get back to New York and Malcolm was much more impatient. His number one thing: "What did he say?" So though these two men were presented as adversaries, they were very much aware of each other and had a great admiration for each other under the surface.

How did King and Malcolm X affect your own life and thinking?

Not a whole lot. I say that not meaning any disrespect or lack of reverence for either of them, but by the time I met them I had already been twenty years in the U.S. Coast Guard and been to a fair number of places and had formed my own philosophy and way of life. Also, coming from a little town called Henning in Tennessee and growing up with small-town values, you will be a pretty solid person if you retain that. I was lucky I had educated parents. My father was a college professor, my mother taught school, and they made me aware of blackness early on. My fourth birthday present was a thick slice of a tree. My grandfather owned a lumber company. Through his connections he had gotten a slice of a redwood, eighteen inches thick. On my birthday they swung open the garage door and there was this slice of tree leaning against the wall with little white markers in different places. My father took a pointer and explained to me what those markers were, how every year there was a new growth ring. He said these markers are where this tree was in size when some particular thing happened. That was the first time I ever heard the words *Emancipation proclamation*. The other things were like the birth of Chicken George and the founding of the college where my parents had met, and so forth. It was my first acquaintance with black history. In later years, when I was grown, my father explained to me that they had spent lots of hours trying to think how they could introduce me to blackness without making it black versus white. And I have in my mind gone back to that tree slice, because that early influence had something great to do with my deep interest in history and obvious interest in things black. *The Autobiography of Malcolm X* and *Roots* are among the most important books having to do with black things in this country. So I had my own distinct sense of blackness before I met these people. I had not had the kind of hustling in the street experience that Malcolm X had, but I don't know that I had been any less black. I was just somewhere else black.

Of the seven in-depth interviews you did for *Playboy,* which are you most proud of?
In a clinical sense I would say the one with the Nazi leader, George Lincoln Rockwell. Because I learned most about how an interviewer needs to be detached from the subject and even be hospitable to what the subject may say and feel, because your job is to communicate to the reader what that person feels. The magazine was looking for controversial and exciting people to interview. They told me they would like to interview the head of the Ku Klux Klan and the head of the American Nazi Party. I selected the Nazi Party leader because he had more education. It wasn't that the other man didn't have any, but he didn't have anything like the background of Rockwell, who was a graduate of Brown University. He had become a lieutenant commander in the navy. He'd been a jet pilot and commanding officer of a pursuit squad. No matter what you thought, you couldn't be stupid if you'd done those things. I was living in upstate New York at the time and he was in Alexandria, Virginia. He wasn't sure he wanted to do

this interview but felt he could use the exposure. He called to ask me a personal question: "Are you a Jew?" I quickly said, "No, sir." Well, when I turned up there was a very shocked set of Nazi people! [*laughs*] It just never occurred to them that I was black. They were so upset. There were six gentlemen standing on the porch with swastikas, belts, and side arms. He was not there. They put me in a station wagon, two in the front, two behind me, I was in the middle seat, and drove me down the highway into the woods. There was a clearing with a white farmhouse and a big pole with swastikas flying. They frisked me before I entered the house. As I went up the steps I felt very, very uncertain about the whole thing. He came to the door—a darkly handsome, angry man. Very angry. Had on a white shirt with dark trousers. He flung his fingers right in my face, almost on my nose, his face mottled with anger. "I'm going to tell you right now," he said, "we call your kind niggers and we think you should all be shipped to Africa." Somehow a calm descended on me, right at that moment, and I said to him, "I've been called nigger before and this time I'm being paid very well for it, so now you go ahead and tell me whatever you've got against us." And that was how the interview began.

How long did you talk to him?
It took about a week. He had become a prisoner of his own philosophy. He was a quite intelligent man, but he had become a salesman of hate. After he got to feel less apprehensive about me he would show me selective letters that came daily, things like: "Dear Commander Rockwell, We are on social security, we do not have much, but here's our two dollars to please keep America pure," or "keep America white," or "Christian." He was a man who felt himself trapped. He was one of three whom I interviewed for *Playboy* who predicted he would die violently, and every one of them was right. In his case he said, "It isn't that I feel some of the enemy will kill me, it will be some of my own people." And it was one of his lieutenants who shot him to death one morning in a laundromat. Why I say this was a special interview was that, though I hardly agreed with a syllable the man uttered, I learned that an interviewer must be like a surgeon with a pa-

tient on the table. You may disagree violently with what that patient believes philosophically, but your job at that moment is to perform surgery the best you can.

What is it that you have basically learned from interviewing others?
That most people would like to be better understood.

And that is why they would open up to you?
Yes, because we all feel that we are not understood.

It's really more than that though, Alex. Wouldn't you say that to be a good interviewer you must exhibit a chameleonlike personality, be fully prepared, and have self-confidence?
I think so. Those three things would be the things you really do have to be.

What else have you learned?
Not to look for any particular answer or quote, because you'll never find it. It will be something that you will happen upon. I often remember not the specific questions but the area of questioning which tended to open up different people. I have had psychiatrists tell me that they had studied *The Autobiography of Malcolm X* during their training focusing on certain questions I had asked that opened him up. I understand what they're talking about, because you learn while interviewing people that it generally is a question you may ask without awareness that will open up a person.

For instance?
I interviewed Johnny Carson—a very collected, cool person, difficult to reach. We were at the Bel Air Hotel and he was giving his conventional responses, but then we got to talking about his having left Nebraska and that got him to open up. He was in school there and was peripherally running a little radio station—he was everything from general manager to janitor. He told me how he used to spin records

and how he would think about wanting to do television shows. He said one day he was writing out a sketch for a show he thought might work on TV and a great revelation came to him—that what he wanted to do was not in Nebraska. Once he realized that, within two weeks he left Nebraska and started to California with his wife and children. As he was telling me this he became nostalgic. He began dragging his words, remembering. Then Johnny Carson stood up and walked to the window and looked out on Sunset Boulevard as if he was almost seeing a mirage and said, "We drove right down there on Sunset." He was playing it back to that time. And then he told me about his big break, where he landed a job as an assistant to Red Skelton who, during a rehearsal for his TV show, went through a breakaway door that didn't break. Skelton was knocked out and Carson had to go on in his place and that was the beginning of the big road in front of him.

Who was the most disappointing person you've ever interviewed?
The late Bishop Pike. To say he was articulate is to understate—the man could talk like a faucet turned on. And he kept you engrossed with what he was saying. But when the stuff was transcribed I realized that he never answered a single question. He had just talked in circles. So they never ran the interview. I actually enjoyed him, he was a very warm fellow.

Who would you especially not like to interview?
Henry Kissinger. He's a very impressive personality and I've had occasion to meet with him. He and I belong to the Moroccan Royal Academy and I meet him in Morocco once a year. His knowledge is overwhelming. He's a genuine world figure and an important man, but I would hate to interview him because of the way he speaks in oblique ways. He won't come right out and answer something, because of the innate political strategist that he is.

Were *Playboy*'s writers privy to Hefner's celebrated parties when he was still in Chicago?
In 1969, Hugh Hefner bought this hotel back of the Playboy building

in Chicago. He gave a party inviting everybody who had helped his dream become a reality, about 160 people. There were eighty-four of the best writers in the country, and not one of us among those who wasn't proud to be there. Journalists and academic people came distributing questionnaires and asking questions to find out what made all these writers tick. The two things I have always remembered about their findings were that of these eighty-four top periodical writers, only four had finished college. And the other thing was that more than half of us were from the South. What we southern writers came up with is that we, more than the others, had grown up in a culture, in a region of the country where families gathered together after the evening meal and the elders would tell stories and the children would listen. It was really oral history which influenced us toward becoming professional storytellers.

Okay, truthfully—you're at a *Playboy* party during its swinging heyday: Are writers really talking to other writers?
I know people may not believe it, but at that party, and at the Playboy mansion in the early hours of the morning when the girls they called bunnies would come in from work, after the clubs had closed, these unbelievable-looking women with their hair done up, in their robes, the place exploding with activity—the photographers were gathered together talking about F-stops, and the interviewers were asking each other about the perfect question.

And did you come up with one?
The one question I got out of that was if you were talking to a married couple, ask each of them if they remember the first time they ever set eyes on the other. It always evokes a response. Seventy-five percent of the husbands remember, wives almost instantly remember. That would make a lovely book: the fascinating stories of how people met who later became married.

What about the moment when a couple knew the marriage was over? You've had two ex-wives . . . do you remember that time?

I remember when my first marriage ended with Nan, who was a sweet lady from Beauford, North Carolina. She and I had married just before I went overseas in the Coast Guard. We had two children and she was with me when I got this writing mania. By the time I came back from overseas, I was hooked as a writer. When you really desperately want to write it's like a habit. I was stationed in New York's Third Coast Guard district headquarters. When I'd get off at five o'clock, instead of going home, I'd stay at the office an extra three hours trying to write for magazines, because you cannot write with two children around. I'd get home at eight, and then I'd stretch it and write until ten-thirty, then midnight. This went on for about two years and she was getting angrier and angrier. Then one Sunday afternoon we were in the kitchen and she just banged her pretty little fist on the table and said, "Look, it's either me or that typewriter." I never will forget it. The flash went through my head, I didn't say it, but I thought, "Honey, I wish you hadn't played it just like that." There was no explosion, we remained good friends. She told me later that she knew when she said it what was going to happen, but she couldn't help saying it. And I understood that.

You were in the Coast Guard for twenty years. Do you look upon that time as your apprenticeship as a writer?
Most of the truly important things in my life have occurred as a seeming accident. I was seventeen when I went into the Coast Guard—I went in because I had flunked French during my sophomore year in college and Dad thought that was too much for the family to bear. That was the summer he took me aside and talked to me about how much he had enjoyed the army in World War I. He felt what I needed to do was tour, then come back and finish school, get my doctorate, become a professor, and be as decent as he was. He was not prepared for me to fall in love with the sea. But becoming a sailor was like a red carpet to me. Adventure, marvelous people, friends, shipmates I never knew the likes of. I was so excited that I would write letters to everybody I knew describing my adventures. Because I got so many letters in response, I quickly became the most prolific

letter writer on the ship. Then we went to sea in the southwest Pacific—Australia, New Zealand. And in the world of sailors, the topmost priority is girls. When we'd go ashore, guys would meet girls, and when we'd ship out, all the talk was about those girls. Somehow a few sailors would ask me if I would help them write a letter to a girl they had met. I was a cook at this time, and I'd cook all day and set up shop in the evening at a mess table with a stack of three-by-five index cards. My clients would line up and I'd interview them about the girl. Then I'd take these profile cards and write a letter which the sailor would copy in his own handwriting. I'd come up with things like, "Your hair is like the moonlight reflected on the rippling waves." And every night there'd be a bunch of guys carefully copying all this stuff. Other ships would come by, pick up the mail and take it ashore. And I will never forget one night in Brisbane, Australia, after we had been at sea for seven weeks, during which time three batches of mail had been taken off our ship. By midnight, all those who had liberty to go ashore came wobbling back to the ship except my clients. They came back later, smiling a full thirty-two teeth, and one after another they'd testify before astonished, awed sailors how those letters I had written for them had met fantastic results. In the world of sailors that made me heroic. And that was how it began. They began to pay me a dollar a letter and within a few weeks I was making more money writing letters than I was being a cook. And that was how I got the first idea of trying to write for magazines. I got hundreds of rejection slips, but by the time I got out of the service I was selling about as much as I was earning as a sailor.

Your phenomenal success as a magazine writer led to your moving on to spend a dozen years researching and writing *Roots*. But it wasn't an easy path for you, was it? Did you actually contemplate suicide before finishing the book that would make you famous throughout the world?

Oh yeah. That was the toughest time. I had finished the nine years of research, still writing some magazine articles to get enough money to make the next trip. I had gathered an unprecedented compendium of

information about the institution of slavery but I wasn't sure how to
tell that story effectively. Had I been more scholarly oriented I could
easily have written a six-volume set of the Afro-American experience
from 1750 on. But the most effective book that came out of the
whole Third Reich was *The Diary of Anne Frank*, so I thought, how can
I tell about what happened to millions of Africans? Let me strip it
down to one, Kunta Kinte, this little boy that my grandmother had
told me about. Let me let him be born on page one, so the reader can
watch him come into the world, and then deal with him day after day
after day. So I wrote the first third of *Roots*—from the birth of Kunta
to his capture—on a Norwegian freighter called the *Villanger*. It went
from Long Beach, California, around South America and back. Kunta
became like my little brother—I could sit in my room on the ship and
talk to him. That's what I love about going to sea, you're isolated, you
can talk to people by yourself. But then I was faced with this nice
young fellow who had to be dropped in the hole of this stinking slave
ship. I tried writing this section from an apartment in San Francisco
but it was atrocious. I kept throwing the pages out. I felt I had to do
something physically to help me better understand what he was going through. So I went to Africa and found a ship called *The African
Star*, sailing from Monrovia, Liberia, to Jacksonville, Florida. I got on
that ship as a passenger and found that they had cargo with one
hatch that wasn't sealed off. It was only half filled with bales of raw
rubber, and after dinner I would slip down in that hatch undetected.
It was dark, eerie, dank, and I took off my clothing to my underwear
and just laid down on my back on these big planks, trying to imagine
that I was Kunta on the slave ship. I did this for two nights and
caught a good, rousing cold. On the third night I couldn't make myself go down into that hole. Instead, I walked like a zombie to the
stern of the ship and stood there. I had my foot up on the bottom
rail, hands on the top rail. It was dark, but you could see the irides-
cence that happens behind a ship. And all my troubles came in on me
standing there by myself. All my debts. It seemed I owed everybody I
could think of. And I knew that almost everybody I knew was beginning to laugh at me about the book, that I'd never finish it. The pub-

lisher wasn't happy. I wasn't. It was just such a low point in my life. Then a simple thought came to me: all I had to do was step through that rail and drop in the sea and it would be over. I wasn't alarmed, it came almost as a sense of relief. Then I had an experience that I've never had since: I heard people talking who I knew were behind me somewhere, and they were saying things like, "No, don't do that, you must go on and finish." And I knew exactly who they were: my grandmother, Chicken George, my great-grandfather, Miss Kizzy, her father—the African. They were all the people that I had been writing about. And I had a wrenching sense that I had to get away from the stern of that ship. I turned myself around and went scuttling over the hatch like a crab because I didn't want to go near the rail on either side. I got back to my little room and pitched down headfirst on my narrow bunk and I cried. I don't think I cried like that since I was a baby. It was a purging. Then I got up, about midnight, and went down the hole and laid back down again in my underwear and began to feel, for the first time, not guilty. I made notes like crazy and wrote out what I had scribbled the next morning. And that's how I wrote the section of *Roots* where Kunta is in the slave ship.

With all your research, what disturbed you the most about slavery?
Mankind's capacity for cruelty to his fellow man. Slavery was terrible, but so was ten other forms of oppression. All of us clearly share the same destiny, and yet we persist in the idiocy of spending every kind of energy trying to amplify how "different" we are from one another, as opposed to how together we are in our common peril.

Was *Roots* always called *Roots*?
Oh no, no. For a long time I was calling it *Before This Anger*. It was conceived in the 1960s when there were lots of civil rights struggles, and I thought of my book as one that would give readers some perception of what had preceded this anger. Many, many white people were saying, "I don't understand why they're unhappy." A lot of whites were bewildered, so I thought I'd give a historical perspective

to this. To know about anger you had to know about slavery and about Reconstruction.

How do you assess the impact of *Roots*?
It caused people to have a better perception of the black experience historically. Until *Roots,* the biggest single image maker, worldwide, of the history and culture of Africa had been Tarzan. Also, it gave a better perception of what the world *slavery* had meant. Prior to *Roots,* and some other books which didn't have the fortune to become as widespread as *Roots,* slaves had been portrayed as anonymous, faceless masses in the cotton fields in the South. The first black ever recognized as an individual on a mass basis was Uncle Tom in *Uncle Tom's Cabin.* Now *Roots* came along with other people: Chicken George, who was my great-great-grandfather; the Fiddler; Miss Kizzy; Kunta Kinte—and they gave a sense of characterization to people who were slaves. Then it had a genealogical effect. Genealogy was, for a long time, a snob appeal thing, linked with people who could trace themselves back to royalty. When *Roots* came along, black people, who had been characterized as being at the bottom of the pecking order, began thinking about their roots. Now there's a virtual wave of interest in family searching among people who previously never thought about it.

And yet, your mother was embarrassed when your grandmother spoke of the African, Kunta Kinte, wasn't she?
Yes. My mother was the first generation in the family to be college educated. My grandmother had finished sixth grade. My mother felt she was much too sophisticated to be talking about slaves. The only time I remember them having a falling out was when my mother would say, "Ma, I'm sick of hearing you talk about all that old slavery stuff." Then my grandmother would get very indignant and say, "You don't care where you come from. I do." I was very close to my grandmother who told me these stories; if I ever had to hear them from my mother, I would never have heard them. In this way my mother and grandmother were like millions of families who came on immigrant ships

from Europe. When they got here, the older members fought to clutch on the security of the old culture; the younger ones couldn't wait to become "Americans" and they rejected everything they could of the old ways. There's a saying in Africa that every time a very old person dies, it is as if a library has burned to the ground.

At the time of its publication *Roots* was hailed as one of the most important books of the century, as well as the most important civil rights event since the 1965 march on Selma. Do you hold it in such esteem?

I never would have said that in the first place. I have a much more basic view of myself. I feel myself as a conduit. *Roots* got born on the front porch of a pretty big house in Henning, Tennessee, where I came from. It was my grandmother's porch. After my grandfather died, my grandma invited her sisters to spend the next summer with her. I was six that summer, and after supper we would gather on the front porch, thick with honeysuckle vines, and the women would all start rocking in their rocking chairs. Then they'd run their hands down into the pocket of their aprons and come up with a can of sweet carrot snuff. They'd load their lower lips and just start talking about their family. They'd talk about their parents, about their daddy's daddy, this harum-scarum individual always fighting chickens, people called him Chicken George. Then they would talk about his mother, Miss Kizzy. All of this went on night after night, and that's where I first began to hear the story and why I think of myself as a conduit.

Some have called *Roots* a novel, but you prefer another word, don't you?

Faction. I saw that word in a book in London. It means a mixture of fact and fiction. Most books are. Nobody can say with absolute accuracy what happened 150 years ago. Get six books about the battle of Gettysburg and you'd think it was six different battles. The best any of us can do is do the best research we can and then try to create around that. With *Roots,* I worked my head off to research everything and still a lot of the book is fiction. How do I know what Chicken George said over a hundred years ago? I made it up.

Along with its phenomenal success came the inevitable lawsuits, including a few which claimed you plagiarized their work. Did you?
The best way I can respond to that is to say that it's almost impossible for anyone to write a book like *Roots* where people don't bring a suit. I was at a function where twenty-four authors sat at two long tables, and every one of us had great big books. We were asked to raise our hands if we've never been involved in a lawsuit. One hand went up. Twenty-three of us were involved in lawsuits. That's why I think the greatest thing written in our time was Hemingway's *The Old Man and the Sea.* For the metaphor. This old man spent all his life learning the fish the best he knew how. One day he put his hood down and felt the bite—he knew it was a big fish and he waited until the time was right. Finally he began to fight the fish, and when it surfaced he saw it was bigger than any fish he'd ever dreamed. Then it went back down and it fought the old man. Finally, the frail old man beat the fish, and in time he was able to lash it alongside his little skip. He put up his homemade sail and started home with his prize. Then came the sharks, one after another, taking chunks of the fish until what remained was the skeleton. The metaphor that relates to being sued is that if you do a book that has the fortune to get like *Roots,* if you catch that big fish, you can rest assured that on your way home the sharks will come. And in the literary world, they take the form of people who bring lawsuits.

Did you make a financial settlement with Harold Courlander, the author of *The African,* which preceded *Roots?*
Yes, and the reason I did was simply the timing. We were getting ready to film *Roots 2,* which is my own life story, and I had the option, after all those weeks in court, to spend at least another six weeks at yet another trial or to say, "Let's settle and let me go back and be

where my life is being filmed." That was the option I took. The only thing I regret is that I didn't do it earlier.

What was the problem, exactly? Were certain sections accidentally lifted? Did some of your researchers include material from that book which you mistook for original research?
It was said that several paragraphs in *Roots* came from *The African.* That's not true. There were two lines, as I recall, and the only thing I could come up with is that I employed sixteen different people who helped me, and I would use material they sent me relative to slavery. In the course of dealing with these bushels of material, you do not remember the source of every piece.

A London reporter went to Gambia and wrote that the people there had put you on—the *griot* oral storyteller told you what you wanted to know. That report shook you, didn't it?
Of course. It was the first thing that challenged the authenticity of *Roots.* This reporter never talked to me at all. He had been on some press junket in Gambia and he went to the village I wrote about and somebody there said to him that the people had put me on. So he told this story. Because *Roots* was so famous the story flashed into this country, but it was nothing but his allegation that they had put me on. I don't know if they did. If they did, they did a very good job of it.

Was the enormous success of *Roots* harmful to you as a writer?
Boy, you sure go to the heart of it. Yeah, it was. I've talked to three other writers who've had big successful books and we've all said that we fear we would never again write as well. It goes back to that bugaboo, Mr. Time. It used to not matter if I took eight weeks to do an article. Who cared? Now, if I go to do a new book, it's a formal setting where publisher and agent come together, we have a big dinner in a fancy restaurant, the shrimp look like lobsters, and what is about to happen is a seven-figure contract is going to be drawn up, and I

haven't even written a word of the book yet. There will be clauses saying that the book is to be finished by X time, and if it's not, some
portion of the money is going to be extracted. So you become almost
mechanized. I find myself writing with more sense of urgency than of
simply love of the craft. I don't write with the same romantic idealism
I used to.

**After the success of *Roots* you went from asking the questions to
being the subject of interviews. Which side do you prefer?**
Lots of times I wish it was possible to buy some of the way it used to
be. After an experience such as *Roots,* it really does change your life beyond your own control. I wish I had the kind of time I used to have,
clear, free. But time becomes an entirely different factor. The fact that
you are sought out for interviews, that people pay you to do things, is
all very flattering, but only then do you really begin to realize that after life and health, the most valuable thing in the world is your time
and what you do with it. So when you ask which side I would rather
be on, it's a mixed blessing. Of course I love the way it is now for lots
of reasons, including that there are ways I can be helpful to people in
different situations. I've had experiences where, with a phone call, I
can help get somebody into college. That's very touching to me. Or I
bought a farm in Tennessee where I can wake up to the sounds of
birds, walk out and there are squirrels scampering up trees. I had a
pond built and it's been stocked and every day between six and six-
thirty the fish are fed. Those things I find are much more enriching
than anything I could do in Beverly Hills.

**We've talked about the book, but what did you think of the
miniseries made from *Roots?***
I thought it was fabulous. Television is the most exciting medium
among us. I would love to see it be more socially positive. To me, the
most powerful scene in the miniseries was when Lou Gossett as the
old slave Fiddler burst into tears after Kunta Kinte was beaten and
forced to say his name was Toby. There were no tears written in the
script, but when Kunta was cut down and slumped into the Fiddler's

lap, Gossett said, "What difference it make what they call you? You
knows who you is. You is Kunta." Then there was a beat and this vet-
eran actor clutched Kunta and burst into tears and said, "There's
gone be a better day." It moves me very much to think that on both
the slave ships and the immigrant ships that came to this country,
what was uppermost in the hearts and minds of the people on either
ship was that phrase, "There's gone be a better day." Not for them,
their die was cast and they knew it, but they had to hope it for their
children and their children's children. *We* are the better day. Every
one of us manifest the dream of our ancestors who came on either
the immigrant or slave ship.

**Did your better day start after the eighth and last episode of *Roots*
was aired?**
I didn't know how to react after that. I was almost numb. I saw the
last episode in a New York hotel with Warren Beatty. He had a big
suite and I had gotten to know Warren through my manager, who is
a good friend of his. At the end of the last episode I came on the
screen and talked about the book. I forgot how many millions of people were watching, but it set the record that still stands for a miniseries. The next morning I got out of the taxi at Kennedy airport and
this black skycap did a double take and shouted my name. And man,
I was just mobbed for the first time in my life. I felt a hand go down
the back of my collar and felt the button go, and somebody grabbed
my coat. An American Airlines guy appeared and said, "Stay very
close to me." He maneuvered his way through this mob to a private
room, and he said to me, "You're going to have to be preboarded.
Your life probably won't be the same from now on." That was my first
exposure to how the public reacts towards somebody who has, like,
been popped out of a bottle.

**Americans don't label our artists National Treasures, as they do
in Japan, but you've come pretty close with having your
birthplace turned into a historical landmark. How has that
affected you?**

I don't know exactly how you get to be what is called a "world-class writer," but I'm glad I am. The governor of Tennessee was talking about this honor of making my home a state landmark and I said that I'd be happy to sell the home to the state for one dollar. They agreed and it became the property of the Tennessee Historical Commission, to be maintained by the state. I feel blessed to see, in my lifetime, the home where I was raised put into that context. I travel a lot and if I find myself near the home of some famous writer, I never lose the opportunity to go visit. It's like visiting a shrine. I went to Mark Twain's home in Elmira and stood in a little gazebo where he wrote *Tom Sawyer* and I felt as if I was on holy ground. I went to Oxford, Mississippi, and poured a little bourbon on William Faulkner's grave. I went to the home of Paul Lawrence Dunbar, the great black poet, in Ohio. So I guess if I could have a dream, it would be that one day people might go to Henning after I'm gone and feel something of what I felt going to the homes of these other writers.

JOSEPH HELLER

Competing with the Past

WHEN I WAS SIXTEEN MY FATHER THOUGHT IT WAS TIME
for me to spend my summer working rather than drinking malt-
eds at Sandy's or hanging out at Colony up near Jericho Turnpike
in the Birchwood Park, Long Island, development where I spent
my teen years. Since he was in the pharmaceutical business, he
had connections to land me a job at the Interstate Drug Exchange, a few towns down from Jericho, where we lived. It wasn't
an easy job: I would fill orders from pharmacies—finding cough
medicine or poison ivy lotion or contraceptives on the warehouse
shelves and placing them in boxes going down a long, curving
conveyor belt; or load and unload trucks, which was backbreak-
ing work. My fellow workers were driving in from the city, many
from Harlem, and they treated me like the kid I was. They teased
me about the condom orders; they called my name whenever a
truck came in so they could throw me the biggest, heaviest boxes,
which I'd have to catch and stack; and when I was on the conveyor line they'd throw X-acto knives into wooden posts near my
head to get my attention. I considered this job a Long Island version of Dante's Hell. We had a half-hour lunch break at noon,
and a fifteen-minute coffee break at 3:15. What saved me that
summer was Joseph Heller's *Catch-22*.

It's a book I will never forget, because it took me out of the misery of manual labor during those forty-five minutes when I could

go off by myself to chew a sandwich, sip an iced coffee, and laugh out loud at Yossarian's dilemma. Over the years since, I have recommended that book to dozens of people, and have found that every guy I've ever known got it, and most women didn't. I never saw a book that could divide the sexes as this one did. When the Vietnam war brought the draft to our doors, those of us who read *Catch-22* understood that if we wound up in the military our chances of survival would not be good. If the military was anything like the book, and one suspected it was, then Heller's novel served as a warning to us all: stay the hell out of the army, the navy, the marines, the air force. As Herbert Gold noted, "Joe Heller . . . wrote the novel which, in its fantasy about wars and bureaucratic foolishness, summed up the experience of a generation of draftees." It also served as a sort of antiwar bible for those of us who shouted "Hell No, We Won't Go!"

Catch-22 appeared in 1961, a long time after Heller established himself as a writer of promise while he was an undergraduate at NYU, getting his stories published in such magazines as *Esquire* and the *Atlantic Monthly*. He went to college after serving in the Army Air Corps, where he flew sixty combat missions in a B-25 over Italy and France during World War II. He received an M.A. in American literature at Columbia and studied English literature on a Fulbright scholarship at Oxford. In 1954, the first chapter of *Catch-22* was published in "New World Writing." Heller was by then working in an advertising agency; then he went to work at Time, Inc. and at *McCall's*.

When Heller's next book, *Something Happened,* was published thirteen years after *Catch-22,* I eagerly awaited what he had written as an encore. At first, I was thrown by how different in setting, mood, tone, and structure it was from *Catch-22*. As the *New York Times* noted, Heller had "turned his back on expansive comedy and tried his hand at claustrophobic tragedy, composing an anguished novel of suburban manners and morals." I got into it the way one went from the folk Bob Dylan to the rock Dylan, or from the early James Joyce to the advanced Joyce. Heller had found another voice for this book, he was telling the story of a family and of corporate life, and he seemed to capture it magically. It was another stunning work. The main character, Robert Slocum, is named, but not the rest of his family (other than his retarded son). Slocum thinks of leaving his wife, is constantly competing to one-up his fifteen-and-a-half-year-old daughter, and constantly reassuring his other, nine-year-old, son. Everyone portrayed has some kind of neurosis, and Slocum finds himself wondering: Is this it? Is this all there is? (And answering himself: Yes.) Kurt Vonnegut wrote, "As far as I know, Joseph Heller is the first major American writer to deal with unrelieved misery at novel length."

In 1977, *Writer's Digest* asked me to talk with Heller over lunch at the Beverly Hills Hotel while he was promoting his new book. Between ordering and eating, there's really not enough time to conduct an extensive interview, but I was happy to have the opportunity to meet a writer I so admired. Especially considering he had only published two novels and was just beginning *Good as Gold*. The other three novels (*God Knows*, *Picture This*, *Closing Time*), the nonfiction collaboration with Speed Vogel (*No Laughing Matter*), about the neurological disease, Guillain-Barre syndrome, which left him in near-total paralysis for three years in the mid-1980s, and his memoir, *Now and Then*, were still ahead of him. Yet he had assured himself a place in America's pantheon of influential writers with his first two books. With *Catch-22*, as James Michener noted, he introduced a new phrase into the English language. Not many writers have done that.

Joseph Heller was seventy-six when he died on December 12, 1999. Six months later, his novel *Portrait of an Artist, as an Old Man* was published. It is the story of a writer who—like Heller, J. P. Donleavy, Alex Haley, and Norman Mailer—gained fame early and was never able to equal or surpass what brought him such great public acclaim and attention. As Heller writes: "This is a book about a well-known, aging author trying to close out his career with a crowning achievement, with a laudable bang that would embellish his reputation rather than with a fainthearted whimper that would bring him only condescension and insult." For writers, that is perhaps a universal wish. "Where," Heller's alter ego Eugene Pota wonders, "had ingenuity gone? He could guess some answers, for himself and for so many of his contemporaries, and for renowned others of similar occupation who now were long gone. In earlier days of youthful mental vigor and stronger drive the dependable literary thoughts and inspirations that vaulted out of nowhere into mind whenever he beckoned for them had seemed inexhaustible. Now he had to ponder and wait. . . . He craved almost desperately for the flicker of a vibrant and usable idea to come gliding into his attention from somewhere in an illuminating flash of revelation. . . . "

The usable idea for this novel is a collage of all the unusable ideas he had attempted to turn into a sustainable work of literature. But *Catch-22* hung like an albatross around Heller's stature: ". . . early success leads invariably to greater, grandiose expectations and also, sooner or later, to lesser success, to decreased popularity, to more exacting scrutiny and exacting criticism . . . and to feelings of failure, even when the new accomplishments are recognized."

When his publisher questions why he's so determined to keep on writing when he doesn't have to, Heller's alter ego confesses, "I have nothing else to do. The phone isn't ringing much anymore with calls I don't want to receive. There are no faxes coming in with requests for interviews I don't want to give, no invitations from people I don't want to see for parties I don't want to go to. Damn it, I miss those interruptions! . . . Writing is about the only way I can define myself."

Heller, of course, wasn't alone. It seems to be the fate of all good writers. In this last book, Heller highlights this by bringing Tom Sawyer to life, making him a character in search of his creator, and when this fails, he travels the country and crosses the ocean to try and see the other great (yet miserable) writers of his time to get some answers about the writing trade. Jack London, Bret Harte, Ambrose Bierce, Frank Norris, Henry James, Stephen

Crane, Joseph Conrad, Emily Dickinson—one after another turn out not to be enjoying the fruits of their success. So he calls up the sad memories of Nathaniel Hawthorne, who "had struggled all his life to earn enough from his serious writing to sustain himself and his family," who "had lived his last years in wretched solitude and with declining creative powers, suffering psychotic deteriorations"; Edgar Allan Poe, "penniless, alcoholic, paranoid, perhaps drug addicted"; and Herman Melville, who "had spent his last years in poverty and obscurity, without a public and without a publisher. As with others whose best novels had brought demoralizing failure and a decline in reputation, Melville's final best efforts led to the ruination of his career as a writer and to his despair as a man." Heller's Tom Sawyer came to the conclusion that the writing life was no life at all and that his ambition to find his creator and collaborate on a novel was the wrong direction for him—better to become a railroad engineer: "his literary ambition had waned, his curiosity was sated with discoveries about the lives of literary celebrities that were cumulatively appalling. His travels through the literary hall of fame of America had steered him into a mortuary of a museum with the failed lives and careers of suffering heroes who were only human. These were not the heroes of the ancient Greeks and Trojans like Achilles, Hector, Zeus, and Hera. These were only driven human beings of high intentions who wished to be writers and who, in most other respects, seemed more than normally touchy, neurotic, mixed-up, and unhappy."

Heller's novel is a poignant testimony to what he calls the "literature of despair." The writers he illuminates had made a major mark on American literature, and yet they were often unappreciated, unwanted, and unloved. Heller was following one of the primary dictums of his trade: to write about what he knew. "I find it just about impossible to think of another occupational group with the same incidence of severe unhappiness and distress among the most famed and accomplished figures," he wrote in *Portrait*.

« «   » »

My visit with Heller was still early in his career, when thoughts of Nobel prizes still danced in his head. I had heard that *Catch-22* had been rejected by fourteen publishers before Simon and Schuster bought it. At the time, the book was called *Catch-18*, but Leon Uris's *Mila-18* had come out first, so the title was changed. I asked Heller about the title change and the rejections when I gave him the book to sign. He wrote: "This novel was accepted for publication, as *Catch-18*, three years before it was completed, and was never rejected."

As a way of showing my appreciation of his work, I told Heller that I once wrote a parody of *Catch-22* for my college humor magazine and offered to send it to him.

Heller hesitated for a frozen moment, holding the Polo Lounge lunch menu between his hands, then lowered the menu, looked me in the eye, and said softly, "Don't."

Do you have an audience in mind when you're writing?
Yes, somebody who has a taste like my own. It's true of *Catch-22* and it's true of *Something Happened*. Each book is the kind of book I'd enjoy reading if somebody else had written it. The books are vastly different from each other. *Catch-22* was read and enjoyed by people who were much younger than I was, with less education, less interest in literature than I have. The people who buy my books are interested in serious reading, even though the works themselves are humorous and funny. Not for a reader who's interested in plot or erotic literature. There's a lot of sex in both books, but the erotic element is played down.

The style of both books is very different. Is it true you were surprised when people found *Catch-22* to be funny?
I *was* surprised. I thought I was being humorous, I didn't know I was being that funny, or wasn't sure I could be that funny. You get surprised as a writer; it's nice. I was surprised at the reaction to *Something Happened*. Things I would not have anticipated—that women would

identify with Bob Slocum as well as with women in the book and that younger people say they identify with every character—there's a thought-recognition factor; I would not have predicted that.

What is your method of writing? Do you rewrite much?
My method of work is to get a very good idea of what I want to cover—assign a time percentage—and I will rewrite each page, then each few pages, moving ahead very slowly with the handwritten page. When I finish a whole section I go back and type what I've rewritten. That is an extensive rewriting process—largely with language; usually it will be taking out much and then getting new ideas to put in. Then I'll read it again and pencil it and give it to a typist to type.

Do you write every day?
I try to. It's not compulsively. The past four years when I was working on *Something Happened* I was teaching at City College, so there were certain days when I'd have to do preparations or read manuscripts and I wouldn't have time to write. To me, writing is largely a matter of memorizing. I will have in mind what I want to write, often to the extent of language, phrases and sentence structure. I walk from where I live to where I write, and by the time I get there I know most of what I'm going to do in the next two hours. And when I finish I'll have a very good idea of what I want to do the next work session.

Do you have periods of anxiety when you're unable to work?
No. I'm able to write in airports, on airplanes, between appointments.

You have claimed to write your books around the opening line. You begin *Something Happened:* "In the office in which I work, there are five people of whom I am afraid. Each of these five is afraid of four people." How did this ignite the novel?
The first line of *Something Happened* was not the original opening line, but the opening line of the second section. Those lines bring with it the type of company—the fact it's a large company; that there's only five people of whom he's afraid means he's got a pretty high executive

position, because if you're low down there'd be 3,500 you'd be afraid of, and if he's an executive, then he's old enough to be married and have children. So that line brings to it a suggestion of other possibilities. It's not easy. I can get forty or fifty first lines and still not get an idea for a book.

Was the company Time, Inc.?
Time, in a beneficial way, contributed most of the atmosphere and the personality of the company in *Something Happened*. I say beneficial because the company is not a particularly harsh enterprise, if anything, it's benevolent. It's tolerant, it pays well, it has long vacations, great sick leave policies, major medical plans, and nobody in the company really contributes to Slocum's anxiety. The man he works for is kind of neurotic, but any of the dissatisfaction or anxiety in which the book begins is something he brings with him. In the entire book he's not really threatened. He *feels* threatened, but the company itself is passive, almost paternal.

In the book, Slocum's wife, son, and daughter are not named. Why is that?
There are several reasons. I felt it would be effective, don't ask me why. Secondly, Americans, when they think about their wives or children, even when they talk about them, rarely use their names. I talk about "my wife." The typical way is to talk about "*The* wife"; "*The* wife and kids." And since this is a first-person book, he would not refer to them by names.

Another reason is that the people he doesn't name are the ones who are very, very close to him—so close they're in positions to cause each other pain. The other son that he does give a name is handicapped (brain damage) and it's almost a wish to separate the self from that son by giving him a name. He wishes he didn't have that son.

There seems almost a Kafkaesque quality to the novel.
Like *Catch-22*, the narrative sequences are subordinate. There is a chronological sequence to *Something Happened*, which I can lay out

very simply: the first chapter he's offered a chance for a bigger job. As the book progresses he's told he's going to get the job. At the end of the book he's got the job. There's a chronology in relation to his wife, or what he thinks about his wife. And the little boy, certainly. It begins at the start of the school term and he's got those fears and anxieties that many children get at the start of a school term. As the term progresses he overcomes every one of the anxieties he has. The daughter is fifteen-and-a-half in the beginning and wants to use the car. At the end of the book she has a driver's license and her own car. It's very simple. *Catch-22* follows a sequence that has to do with the increase of missions, but they are subordinate.

Time is often a difficult thing for a writer to capture, but you seem to do it incredibly well in *Something Happened*.
The same thing in certain areas of *Catch-22*, particularly the death of Snowden. That episode took place months before the time of the first chapter, and my effort was to have him die all through the book.

You also make heavy use of parenthetical phrases in the new book.
That didn't come to me until I started writing in 1964. When I got the idea for the book in '62 the use of parentheses wasn't in the plan. It was a nice surprise: despite the vast amount of outlining and thinking I do, when it comes to writing there's always new inspiration.

How much outlining do you do?
There was less of it in *Something Happened* than in *Catch-22*, because it was easier to keep most of what I had in mind in my mind. Whereas with *Catch-22*, with its forty-four named characters and time span and the vast number of episodes, it became necessary to put things down in order. At that time, I had a desk blotter which I ruled into parallel columns and horizontal boxes, putting a character and the name at the top of each column. In the left I had a series of events. I tried to keep from having anachronisms from occurring, and to make sure where each character was.

There seems to be a parallel between your work and James Joyce: both of you started with short stories, both of you have one play, and each book can be seen as a true artistic progression. Would you agree?

Joyce was very conscious of himself as an artist and as a developing artist. I have not mapped that out for myself—I just feel very lucky to get an idea for a novel. I'd say the parallel might be closer to Faulkner. I think that Faulkner wrote the best novel he could at the time he was ready to start another novel. His more complex and most successful novels, like *Absalom, Absalom!* and *The Sound and the Fury* came in what might be called his middle period, and then his later books were all superb, not as ambitious. Whereas in Joyce you have each successive work more ambitious and taking on a larger challenge. I'm not doing that.

What writers have influenced you technically?

There are sections in *Catch-22* that reminded me of Joyce. Mainly mood. The walk through Rome had a Joycean coloration, a Dostoevskian content. In *Something Happened* there were many times I was reminded of *Finnegans Wake*. But they're circumstantial—they fit that particular section or page. The structural model I had in mind would be William Faulkner, particularly *Absalom, Absalom!* I was also influenced in *Catch-22* by Celine: his rather random and free use of coincidences, his use of street language as part of the author's vocabulary, the flippancy, the impertinence that you find in *Journey to the End of Night*. I don't think I could have got the idea for *Catch-22* if I had not read Celine's work. And, to a lesser extent, Nabokov's *Laughter in the Dark* and Evelyn Waugh.

Like Salinger's *The Catcher in the Rye*, *Catch-22* was the novel of a generation . . .

I'm aware of three books that have had what I think of as an amazing longevity: Vonnegut's *Cat's Cradle*, Ken Kesey's *One Flew Over the Cuckoo's Nest*, and *Catch-22*.

How do you see your contemporaries?

There are an awful lot of very good American novelists, more than I can name. Many of them working in forms of fiction so different from each other, as different, say, as fiction is from poetry or theater. There are some writers that I like better because what they write coincides with what I'm going to write. There are at least fifty American novelists who are writing superbly.

Do you feel yourself in competition with any of them?

No. You can't avoid being conscious of comparisons, like E. L. Doctorow's paperback sale of *Ragtime* and *Something Happened* [*Ragtime* went for $1.8 million; *Something Happened* for $650,000]. You're not competing for attention or publicity, and certainly not for the same readers. Competition in terms of trying to do a novel that's better than what other novelists are doing—that's not the motivation on my part. When it's done I hope that somebody will say that this is one of the best novels of the year or the decade, but that type of competition is not with other writers—you're competing with the past. I suppose it may be what a golfer does. A golfer wants to play his best game every time he goes out, and I feel I want to do something as least as good as what I've done before. Or, if not as good, even if it fails, at least it's a respectable failure.

How sensitive are you to criticism?

Once a book is out I'm sensitive to it. If there's to be praise, I want it. It's very much like Slocum in *Something Happened*. He's not particularly ambitious—in the early part of the book he's apathetic, content to remain in his present job until he's old enough to retire or die—it's when that opportunity is presented to him he finds himself wanting it more and more . . . and still does not do anything that's unethical. It's like the National Book Awards, which I've never liked. I don't even like the idea of its existence. I was a judge once and I didn't like it, and the prize is not worth much in terms of publicity, though occasionally, I suppose, in Philip Roth's or Bernard Malamud's case, it helped give a reputation to a new writer; but most of the time it has not done that. Still, I wanted it very much for *Something Happened.* Had a feeling I wouldn't get it, and when I didn't I was angry. I wanted it.

Speaking of prizes, do you ever think about the Nobel Prize?
Of course. And if I do two more novels and they're well received, then maybe some day. . . .

Are you sorry you haven't written more?
No, I don't think I could have. I couldn't have written a novel before *Catch-22;* I wasn't ready. I didn't have enough knowledge of literature. I have no belief at all in superstition or anything spiritual, but it seems to me these books *chose* a time in which they could be written. I could not have written a novel five years before *Catch-22* about my war experience—it would have been a realistic novel. I needed the distance, the education, I had to read Celine and Waugh and get a feeling that other writers were getting at the same time without even being in touch with each other. A new style was coming out. It hadn't been called black comedy or absurdist literature, but the nonrealistic type of literature. And while I was writing, so were Kurt Vonnegut, Thomas Pynchon, Kesey, Kerouac, John Hawkes, and J. P. Donleavy.

Pynchon, Salinger, and Donleavy . . .
Three of my favorites.

When Pynchon's *Gravity's Rainbow* came out it was hailed as the next step after Joyce's *Ulysses*. It's a difficult book to read . . .
But when *Ulysses* first came out you would have had real difficulty reading it, too. Pynchon is a gigantic talent—it's formidable, almost immeasurable. *Gravity's Rainbow* came out at a time when I was in the last section of *Something Happened,* so I read it for content, and want to go back and read it for depth. When you deal with someone like Pynchon or Salinger or Joyce or Barth, the question of enjoying it or not enjoying it, good or not so good, becomes almost irrelevant.

You're dealing with creative, original artists with enormous abilities, and I don't even like to use the word *read,* I prefer the word *study.* Pynchon is someone to be studied, as is Salinger. You don't just read them easily or quickly. Faulkner is a very difficult writer. Many of my favorite writers are difficult: Melville, Henry James, Thomas Mann, Dostoevsky, even Tolstoy—they're not what reviewers call "a good or easy read." *Catch-22,* to my surprise (though not the first year) has become a very enjoyable read.

Has success affected your writing?

No, nor has it affected my life. Same marriage; same apartment. [*Ten years after we spoke, Heller would divorce and marry the nurse who cared for him after he suffered from Guillain-Barre syndrome.*] I'm one of those very rare people who's doing what he wants to do and enjoys doing it. And who's been rewarded in virtually every way by it. The fame part is nice; the celebrity is nice; the income is nice; the critical praise is nice; I'd be bullshitting you if I pretended I didn't enjoy it.

You wrote a piece for *Holiday* called "Catch-22 Revisited." You don't do much magazine journalism, do you?

I don't write articles easily, I'm not good at it. They're only good if they can evolve out of the personal experience. I'm not good as a reporter, as a factual writer. "Catch-22 Revisited" was for shit, I could have taken it out of the Encyclopedia Britannica. I'm very lucky that I've been able to write two books I've wanted to write. Neither book, you'd think, would have a really big chance of being mass sellers. *Catch-22* was entertaining, but there's a lot of depth, and a lot of pessimism; *Something Happened* is much slower and has less entertainment. I don't think I have the talent to write a potboiler, just as I don't think I could write a realistic book as well as the people who do them. I'm not good at details, I don't see things, there's very little visual description in my books. I can't handle sequences comfortably. But I've been able to earn enough money from my two books so I can write the next one. When *Catch-22* sold to the movies in 1962 I was able to resign my job. I was making good money when it came out

($19,000 a year from *McCall's* plus $2,000 in expenses), and then the income from the movie was spread out over a four-year period. The biggest expense we had was associated with the children and college.

How did your family react to *Something Happened*, since it seemed so personal?
I had much concern, because in order for it to succeed it would have to be very convincing; it would have to sound like an autobiography. I don't think there's a neurotic symptom or anxiety any member of the family has which isn't right out of a textbook. A lot of it came from my own experience—the discussion with the daughter at the dinner table arguing over money; a trip out of town—I was afraid there might be some embarrassment caused, but there wasn't. It would have made them unhappy if the book had not been well-received.

How much of it was painful to write?
None. The only thing painful to write is when you're writing and you're feeling it's not good. My emotional response to writing has nothing to do with the content. I'll give you an example; the death of Snowden in *Catch-22*. When I wrote that I knew it was good. I just sat back and wanted to laugh. What makes me unhappy is when I'm writing poorly.

If you had the books to write over again, could you make them better?
In the novel there's much room for error; one can overwrite or under-write. I don't think the success of a novel is going to be affected by details. If I had cut *Something Happened,* taken out much of the repetition, speeded up the pace, it would have lost its most valuable quality, which is the emotional closeness it was able to establish with the reader. Many of the best novels, or Michelangelo's sculptures, or Beethoven's symphonies are imperfect, unfinished.

What's your next project?
Another book, which is going really fast. I'm managing a chapter a

week—the fastest I've ever written. It's a book in which the narrative line will be predominant. It will move swiftly, more like *Catch-22* than *Something Happened.* It will be using humor and satire very consciously, much of it of a political nature.

I've read that you don't care if there's a God or not.
I don't.

And you look upon death the same way you do root-canal work?
Exactly. People get through it, how difficult can it be?

ELMORE LEONARD

Embalming with Perma-Glo

ELMORE LEONARD THINKS HE'S SHRINKING. HE USED TO be 5' 9", he says, but not anymore. As the money from his thirty-seven books makes his bank account grow, his body seems to re-act differently, as if it's telling him he isn't worthy of such ac-claim and riches. He figures it comes with growing older—he's now in his mid-seventies—and not getting enough exercise. Sit-ting at his desk knocking off a novel a year is not going to stretch his spine, he figures; and jogging, as far as he's concerned, is a criminal activity. He tried it but quit. Unless you're running from the law he doesn't think anyone should have to run more than forty or fifty feet at a time.

I tell him about this guy who conned his friends: he'd invite them out to dinner, then show up late because he'd first rob their houses, knowing they wouldn't be there. We're sitting in his comfortable house in Bloomfield Village, Michigan, a neigh-borhood that is with enough upscale pretentions to have changed its name from Birmingham to Bloomfield Hills to Bloomfield Village. Leonard's in the process of redecorating it, and because of the nature of the books he writes—about crimi-nals who like to rob people who live in houses like his—you can't help wondering if he's ever been tempted to put to use all his ex-pertise about lock picking and making C-4 plastique bombs from local hardware store materials. He's mild-mannered enough to easily slip undetected into someone else's hotel room and make off with a bag of jewels.

Nah, he tells me. He fumbles with the keys to his own hotel rooms when he's on the road; he'd never be able to pick a lock, even though he's read plenty of books and pamphlets on the subject. The surest way, he says, is to get a fire key that opens all the doors in a building. That's how hotel burglars often do it, according to what a cop once told him.

"Come on," I say, "surely with all you know you've been tempted. It's like if you worked for a bank, you'd at least *think* about getting away with something. In your business, that's *all* you think about—or at least all your characters think about. What about hitting your neighborhood? There are lots of wealthy doctors, lawyers, pro basketball players."

"I can't imagine committing a burglary, because it's so scary," the Dutchman says. "Especially if you know somebody's there. Although most burglars go in during the day or at night if no one's home."

"How well do you know your neighbors?" I ask.

"I'm more at home with you than with any of my neighbors," he says. "We have more in common, more to talk about. The fellow next door is a cancer specialist who deals only with terminal cases. We were at their house for dinner one night and his wife asked me, 'Why do you write what you do? You live in this nice house, this nice neighborhood, how can you write what you do about these people?'"

"There you go," I goad. "*Critical neighbors*—the perfect couple to hit. So, how would you do it?"

Leonard looks at me like I'm crazy, but then, hell, he decides to humor me. If he was the type of guy who was willing to risk his life in pursuit of criminal behavior, he'd go in brashly, not try to sneak around in a dark house.

"I lean toward the desperado idea," he says. He looks not quite like a professor, but rather an aging teaching assistant who will never finish his doctorate; or like an ornithologist who spends a lot of time looking at stuffed birds at the local natural history museum. Certainly not like a guy whose fantasy life consists of creating outlaws who can do the unthinkable without a tinge of guilt—but then Jeffrey Dahmer didn't look like a guy who ate people. "Going in with a gun, sticking 'em up, getting the money. Robbing the stagecoach, you know?"

Now he's into it. Let's forget stagecoaches, I say. Let's rob the cancer doctor. How would you do it? "I'd wait for a party," he says, "where you see the cars lined up and you have a couple of guys and you go in with guns, put everybody on the floor, take all their money, then somebody runs up to the bedroom and gets the jewels and get out."

I look at him with disappointment. His books are so original, his bad guys so imaginative. They'd surely frown on this amateurish approach to burglary. The doctor and his wife have nothing to worry about. This is a guy who's gone from a $1,250 advance for his 1961 western, *Hombre,* to a three-book $4.5 million deal after *Newsweek* did a cover story about him in 1985, where they dubbed him "the best American writer of crime fiction alive, possibly the best we've ever had."

Those three books (*Bandits, Freaky Deaky, Killshot*) in addition to *Rum Punch,* which appeared after *Maximum Bob* but before *Pronto* and *Riding the Rap* (the man is *very* prolific) have all been optioned by Miramax because *Pulp Fiction*'s writer–director Quentin Tarantino said Leonard's the guy who most influenced him and that he'd like to write and direct *Killshot* and oversee the other three. That was all Miramax had to hear, and Leonard's happy to go along for the ride. He's been "discovered" before, and he'll be "discovered" again, but as long as those checks don't bounce, he's not complaining.

"I love Elmore Leonard," Tarantino told Charlie Rose. "*True Romance* is like an Elmore Leonard movie."

Why Leonard thinks Tarantino might be able to successfully translate him from book to film is because "he specializes in set pieces. In *Pulp Fiction* these two guys are going to kill somebody and they're talking about what you call a quarter-pounder in Europe. A royale with cheese. And that's what I do. He lets his scenes play, his people talk. You keep waiting, what are they talking about? It's so interesting, so natural, so human."

Tarantino admits to "owing a big debt to figuring out my style to Elmore Leonard. He was the first writer I'd ever read who let mundane conversations inform the characters. And then all of a sudden, *woof!* you're into whatever story you're telling."

After Leonard saw Tarantino's first film, *Reservoir Dogs,* he recognized a kindred spirit. "People say how violent it was. I didn't think so. It's the expectation of violence. As Tarantino says, he has violence hovering over his story all the time, and you never know when it's going to land on you. If you get twenty minutes into a movie and you know what's going to happen, that's not telling a story. You tell a story, you make up stuff as you go along. What has happened with my stuff is that it's always been cut down to keep the scene moving with action, using just enough dialogue to impart information. But Tarantino's the guy who can draw the names: everybody wants to work for him. So maybe he'll get it right. He was asked if he'd do *Reservoir Dogs* again the same way, and he said exactly the same, although instead of doing it for $1.3 million he'd do it for $3 million. But it would still be a little picture. I see my books as little, low-budget pictures."

No one's more savvy to the wheels and deals of Hollywood than Leonard, whose *Get Shorty* is about just that: a producer who's squandered up-front money, a loan shark seeking to get it back, the uneasy partnership they form to get a movie made. Movies about the movies seem a little incestuous, but this one attracted John Travolta, Danny DeVito, Gene Hackman, and Renee Russo and became the first film of a Leonard novel that actually captured the sense and sensibility of the writer.

While he looks at Hollywood with a jaundiced eye, Leonard is a champion of the blue-collar worker. He describes men who are as handy with a thirty-five-pound impact wrench as with a hammer and saw. Like he writes of one of his heroes, the photographer and ex-Secret Service man Joe La Brava, Leonard has felt himself attracted to street life. *"It was a strange feeling, he was at home, knew the people; saw more outcast faces and attitudes than he would ever be able to record, people who showed him their essence behind all kinds of poses."*

He writes knowingly of towing barges and building skyscrapers, of wiring explosives to cars and how many incisions are needed to embalm a body. His books detail his fascination with guns, comparing Belgian FN-FALs to AK-47s, or discussing how to convert an AR-15 Colt into an M-16. His good guys often walk the edge between ambivalence and temptation; and his bad guys are not without ambition: some want to con millions from their employers, others want to rob a bank in every state of the union except Alaska.

Sitting in his workroom after a day's work, Leonard turns on the television and is captivated by the ramblings of fight promoter Don King. Leonard is smiling as King extols the virtues of black fighters, the prejudiced way the press treats him, and the miracle of America that a man like King could rise so far and be so rich. It isn't what King is saying that makes Leonard happy, it's the *way* he says it. "Man, listen to the rhythm of those words."

It's the sound that impresses him. Just as it's the sound that impresses critics and fans such as Tarantino or Joyce Carol Oates, who extol the virtues of his books. The sound of Elmore Leonard is the sound of the street, the sound of the hustler and con man, the drinker and the drunkard, the cop and the killer. His is the sound of people talking and dealing in Detroit, New Orleans, and south Florida, where, he feels, "there's got to be more greed than anywhere—and that's what crime is all about." Listen as Leonard describes the lower end of Miami Beach:

> . . . the neighborhood taken over by junkies, muggers, cutthroats, queers . . . Cubans off the boat-lift, Haitians who had swum ashore when their boats broke to pieces, old-time New York Jews once the backbone, eyeing each other with nothing remotely in common, not even the English language. The vampires came out

at night and the old people triple-locked their doors and waited for morning. Ass-end of Miami Beach down here.

And what do these vampires talk about? "Shooting a woman and understanding a woman are two entirely different things," says one of his bad guys in *Killshot*. "If I notched my gunbutt you'd get splinters running your hand on it, you dink," says another in *Gold Coast*.

One might think that a man who writes about such things grew up in tough neighborhoods, had a father who was either a cop or a hood, fought his way through school, and probably spent some time behind bars where he picked up the lingo he uses with such a sure hand. By his own standards, though, Leonard's not that tough. He never did brutish work as a boy, never got into fights, never carried a sap or gun into dark places (though he did chase rats with a stick down Detroit alleys). It wasn't like that at all for Elmore Leonard, who was born in New Orleans on October 11, 1925.

His father worked for General Motors scouting locations for car dealerships, and the family moved through Texas, Oklahoma, Michigan, and Tennessee six times in nine years, until finally settling in Detroit in 1934, when Elmore was nine. Leonard was an avid moviegoer and a good, obedient child who was taught by nuns in elementary school and by Jesuits in high school, where he took four years of Latin and two of Greek, and played center in football and first base in baseball. About the worst thing he can remember of his youth was once stealing a baseball glove—but he gave the glove to another kid on his team who didn't have one.

During his sophomore year in high school, a boy sitting near him told him "Elmore" was no kind of name for a kid and dubbed him "Dutch," after the knuckleball pitcher for the then Washington Senators. The nickname stuck.

In 1942, during his senior year, his father was transferred to Washington, but Leonard chose to live with his football coach and graduate from the University of Detroit High School. With the world at war, Leonard tried to enlist in the marines at seventeen, but was rejected because of a bad eye. A year later he entered the navy and spent most of his time maintaining an airstrip in and around New Guinea, drinking beer and watching Humphrey Bogart and Lauren Bacall movies. He lost his virginity to a Philippine whore for five bucks and had his nickname tattooed onto his arm for a dollar.

When he returned from the navy he enrolled at the University of Detroit and, in 1949, married his college girlfriend, Beverly Cline. Within a year they had their first child, and by 1965 they had their fifth. Leonard's first job out of college was as an office boy for the Campbell-Ewald advertising firm. Eventually he moved up to copy writer and worked on car and truck promotions. For two hours before he left for work he wrote stories about the west—a place he had never been, but a genre that was popular among the many pulp magazines. He sold his first story, "Trail of the Apache," to *Argosy* and was encouraged to write others. He liked the Apaches because of the way they dressed, their love of mule and dog, their dislike of fish and turkey, and because James Warner Bellow had already made them popular in his stories. His first novel, *The Bounty Hunters*, was published in 1953. The following year he wrote *The Law at Randado*, then *Escape from Five Shadows* in 1956 (first editions of these early books go for up to $4,000 today). In 1957, two of his short stories, "The Tall T" and "3:10 to Yuma" were made into films. His novel *Last Stand at Saber River* appeared in 1959, and *Hombre* in 1961. *Hombre* has been ranked among the twenty-five best westerns ever written by the Western Writers of America, but it was the last book Leonard would publish for eight years. The western market had dried up and Leonard decided to leave his job in advertising to freelance.

At first he got work writing short films for the *Encyclopedia Britannica*, then he continued writing ads on his own. In 1965, *Hombre* was sold to the movies for $10,000 and Leonard thought he could devote himself to his writing. When his first agent, Marguerite Harper, died, he found H. N. Swanson in Los Angeles to represent him. Swanson read Leonard's next novel, *The Big Bounce*, and vowed to make him rich. Instead, he met with eighty-four rejections. Neither Leonard nor Swanson got discouraged, and eventually the story was sold to the movies for $50,000. *The Big Bounce* came out as a paperback original in 1969, the same year Leonard wrote *The Moonshine War.* Between 1970 and 1972 he wrote his last two westerns: *Valdez Is Coming* and *Forty Lashes Less One.* He also wrote two scripts that became movies: *The Moonshine War* for MGM (starring Alan Alda and Richard Widmark) and *Joe Kidd* for Universal (starring Clint Eastwood).

Then came Leonard's switch to crime. *Mr. Majestyk* appeared in 1974 and became a Charles Bronson movie. *Fifty-Two Pickup* (1974) was made into a film starring Roy Scheider and Ann-Margret in 1986. Over the next ten years he wrote ten more novels: *Swag, The Hunted, Unknown Man No. 89* (which Alfred Hitchcock wanted to turn into a movie before he died), *The Switch, Gunsights, City Primeval, Gold Coast, Split Images, Cat Chaser,* and *Stick.* Both *Cat Chaser* and *Stick* were made into not very good movies, the former released in England, the latter starring and directed by Burt Reynolds. *La Brava,* considered by many to be Leonard's finest novel, appeared in 1983 and came close to being a Dustin Hoffman film. It won the Edgar Allan Poe Award from the Mystery Writers of America, edging out John le Carré's *Little Drummer Girl* and Umberto Eco's *The Name of the Rose* as the Best Mystery Novel of the year. *Glitz,* in 1985, was the so-called breakthrough book, which stayed on the best-seller list for sixteen weeks. After that, Leonard became a multimillion-dollar writer.

Another novel, *The Touch,* about an innocent stigmatist, was sold to Bantam in 1977 for $30,000, but when the publication got stalled Leonard bought back the rights and resold it to Arbor House ten years later for $300,000 and to the movies for a hefty sum as well. That year Leonard wrote the screenplay for William Kienzle's *The Rosary Murders;* and for Universal-TV he wrote his second television movie, *Desperado.* (His first was *High Noon Part II: The Return of Will Kane* in 1980.) He followed *Get Shorty* in 1990 with *Maximum Bob,* about a hated, tough-sentencing chauvinist Florida judge, some bad guys who'd like to kill him, and a female parole officer who must deal with both sides of the law. (Donald Westlake wrote the script for a four-hour TV miniseries.) His next novel, *Rum Punch,* brought back his bad guys from *The Switch.* Then came *Pronto* in 1994, *Riding the Rap* in '95, *Out of Sight* in '96, *Cuba Libre* in '98, *Be Cool* in '99, and *Pagan Babies* in 2000 as Leonard demonstrated his dexterity interweaving dialogue, characters, and storylines at a dazzling pace.

A prolific writer who writes in longhand and never uses a computer, Leonard's novels have been translated into sixteen languages including Czech, Greek, and Hebrew. All of his books are still in print, and most of them have been bought by Hollywood. He was recently honored in New York with the Edgar Grand Master Award.

The biggest luxury his success has brought him is being able to afford a full-time researcher, whom he pays $40 an hour. His worst vice is smoking, which he does, he says, *because* he's a writer. Leonard, a former heavy drinker and a member of Alcoholics Anonymous, says that his personal battle with alcohol led to the disintegration of his first marriage after twenty-seven years. In 1977 he took his last drink and in 1979 married for the second time, to Joan Shepard.

Leonard's experience with the bottle brought out some of his sharpest, most descriptive writing. In *Freaky Deaky* he describes the ritual upchucking the morning after: ". . . being sick was part of waking up . . . cleaning up a bathroom looked like somebody'd been killing chickens in it." Then, once the mess was cleaned, came the day's first drink: "Vodka sitting on the toilet tank while you took a shower, something to hold you till the bars opened at seven."

Part of the enjoyment of reading Leonard is catching his one-liners: "If the man was any dumber you'd have to water him twice a week," or "He was like something stuck to the bottom of your shoe you couldn't get rid of, like chewing gum." Here's vintage

Leonard describing a woman by her sex: "He told her she had centerfold breasts. Actually she had heavy white peasant breasts with
big brown nipples. She had a round belly and the trace of a
Florida tan line below the navel. He was horny all right. Her pubic hair grew wild and scraggly and reminded him of Che Gue-
vara's beard."

After Joan's sudden death from cancer in early 1993, Leonard
took an interest in his gardener, Christine, and wound up marrying her six months later. Though still somewhat bewildered by all
the attention that has come his way, he is a man at peace with
himself, who knows what he can and cannot do, and who's proud
of his accomplishments. As critic Jonathan Yardley said in the
Washington Post, Leonard has raised "the hard-boiled suspense
novel beyond the limits of genre and into social commentary."

After spending a week talking with him at his home in December 1990 and seeing him for another few days in Los Angeles during a visit west in 1998, I continued to wonder how such a gentle,
gracious man knew so much about the dark side; but that's part
of Leonard's magic. When we finally parted, he left me with two
pieces of advice: write for as much money as the market will bear;
and if a limo is ever offered to take me to any business meeting,
refuse it, "because you may want to walk out of the meeting and
you won't have any transportation."

**Writers are often ambitious people. They watch the best-seller
lists just like any rock musician follows the music charts. Your
success was a long time in coming. When it finally came, did you
feel you were finally where you belonged?**
I'm surprised I am where I am. I'm very surprised that I've been recognized the way I have been. I'm surprised to be doing this interview. I
don't have anything profound to say. I'm not even that sure of where
I stand on different issues. At this Literary Lions luncheon at the
New York Public Library I was surprised at the people who recognized me—names in American literature—and commented on my

work: Norman Mailer, William Manchester, a woman biographer of Virginia Woolf who teaches at Wellesley and uses my work in teaching dialogue.

Does it affect you when a Pulitzer–Prizewinning writer like J. Anthony Lucas calls you America's finest suspense writer?
It does affect me. I have to tell myself this is not something you have to live up to. Because who says so? It's unimportant. But some of the notoriety has created some amount of pressure, yeah. Notoriety has nothing to do with doing the work.

So you try to ignore being "the Dickens from Detroit," as *Time* magazine dubbed you?
It's alliteration, that's all. It was the *Newsweek* quote that was getting me a lot of trouble: "The best crime writer living, perhaps we've ever had." But then there was the writer with the *Sun-Sentinel* who called me the most overrated writer in America, not in the same league with G. K. Chesterton. How do you compare me to him? I don't see how you can compare writers, to begin with.

That *Newsweek* cover story came out in '85 with the publication of *Glitz*. Was that book that different from your others?
When *Glitz* hit, it wasn't because of *Glitz,* it was because my time had come. It could have been *La Brava,* it could have been the next one. In the last ten years I have finally come to realize this is what I do for a living. I write books. It isn't a temporary occupation. And it's a very good feeling. I don't see any reason to become dramatic about it and think of it as difficult. If it's difficult then I shouldn't be writing it.

There are an awful lot of crime and mystery writers in America. How do you account for your popularity?
I think it's based on the fact that my books are entertaining. It must be that simple. My readers like the references to what's going on in the world, to television and movies, they feel a rapport with these people. It might be just the dialogue, that the story moves very, very

quickly. They like it that you can get on an airplane in the east and finish the book before you're in L.A. Maybe that's it.

Though you question how writers can be compared, you are constantly being compared to Dashiell Hammett and Raymond Chandler. Does that bother you?

I've always been reviewed well, but I was always thrown into that Hammett-Chandler school, either by the publisher or the reviewer, because they like to label you, it's easier. This tells the reader what you do, and I always resented it because I didn't come out of that school. I was never influenced by Chandler or Hammett. I barely read Hammett. Chandler, I've read maybe three of his books. I've never done a private eye, I've never written in first person. My ideas come from out of my head, from real life, from the way I see what's going on with people who are walking the line, who want to get away with something, who get into a hustle. These are the people who intrigue me—some guy who has been in prison and has come out, what is he going to do now when he looks around? So I'm doing something different and the publishers and the reviewers don't know what I'm doing. That's why I've gone from publisher to publisher. At Delacorte in '74, '75, they came out with a half-page ad: "Move over Phillip Marlowe, here comes Frank Ryan." It was Jack Ryan, they got the name wrong. But they had to bring in Phillip Marlowe, they have to bring in Chandler.

Is there anything you think you have in common with them?

Of course. They're talky, and this is the way I do it. Early on I got a good idea of what I could do and what I couldn't. Based on that, I try to move the story with as much dialogue as possible and concentrate on the characters. I don't write effectively in the traditional manner of narrative writing, in telling a story with language, with my words. I don't have enough words to do that, so in lieu of that I approach it from the standpoint of the characters. I'm not sure of my ability to describe what's going on; to me it's more interesting to let the characters do it—that way, you not only find out what's going on, but you also learn something about the character. You're doing two things at once. I'm not good at imagery, similies, and metaphors. If they're not good they're very, very distracting. I said that to Joyce Carol Oates once and she said, "Well, so much for Shakespeare." But Chandler's tarantula on a piece of angel food cake—that kind of metaphor distracts you from the story. You're picturing the metaphor and you are away from the story.

You're not considered a mainstream writer, but rather a genre writer. Do you see any difference?

Sure I see a difference. Of course. In the genre writing you are telling more of a story. I'm not going to presume to label myself. I write what I want to write. I don't really worry about the reader. I'm the one I have to please, that's the beauty of this. But I don't want to be called a mystery writer. I'm in that section of the bookstore, but I certainly don't write mysteries. I don't *read* mysteries. I don't even read that much crime. I seem to be a little bit different, so that attracts readers on both sides of whatever separates genre from mainstream. I'm not solidly on one side or the other. Crime readers are disappointed that I don't have as much action and shooting in my books as I used to. Although I feel more secure in having a gun in the piece. If there's a gun I know I can pick it up any time in that book and shoot somebody. And that's going to keep the reader reading. I don't know what I'd write if I just wrote about some guy who's got a job in an ad agency and is having problems at home, or has been asked to take a job in L.A. and he wants to stay in Detroit.

In other words, you avoid the autobiographical and prefer to stick with the bad guys.

They're more fun, sure. I like those dumb guys because you can never count on what they're going to do. In most crime novels, the bad guys wear black hats, they wear big signs on them, you know? "I'm bad." But they're not like that.

How do you find out what they're like? Do you hang out with hoods, thieves, con men?

Not at all. I don't know any hoods. Oh, I've talked to a dope dealer once, I've talked to convicts in prison, but didn't get much. When I was researching *Bandits* I went to Angola [to visit the Louisiana State Penitentiary] and a couple of deputies introduced me to this black convict who's the editor of their monthly magazine. We sat down to talk and I asked, "What do you call the guards here?" He said, "Oh, we call them Sir." I knew then that I wasn't going to get much at all. I asked him, What time do lights go off? He said, "At ten P.M., but the television can stay on till midnight." Then I asked, Who selects the programs? He didn't have to answer because I knew I had a scene, a reference I could use in the back story. Of course he said, "The hogs. If the hogs want to watch Bugs Bunny, that's what you're going to watch." And then he did open up a bit about knifings and things like that.

Do you have any problem walking in to talk to cops or convicts?
I used to walk in cold, but now I have a researcher, a big guy named Gregg Sutter, who does all the preliminary stuff. He's good at making the cold calls that I'm kind of timid about. By the time I get there they know who I am and they've read my books, so it's perfect. Like when I went to the Miami Beach Police Department to find out what's going on around there, the guy I wanted to talk to had been briefed about me and he was dying to talk. He wanted to tell me all his stories. And that's how I become familiar with that world.

For instance?
When I was researching *Bandits* in New Orleans a cop at police head-quarters told us a story about a robbery of a Brinks warehouse in Memphis that was pulled off by a group that included two or three New Orleans cops. They all brought the money back to New Orleans and one guy put it in a hole he'd cut in a wall. He would take the packets of money out, take the straps off and throw them in the wastebasket. When they apprehended them they found all the bank straps. I'll use things like that as back story for one of my characters.

Do you also get expressions and dialogue this way?

Once this homicide sergeant was taking the statement of a murderer, a guy who had strangled a woman to death behind a bar. He said, "Earlier we were sitting there playing around, we had some sex right there on the steps. Then I went over to the car and she come over and she starts playing with my puppy." The cop looks at me and I look at him. Like, this is a new expression, you know? So the cop says, "She's playing with your puppy, huh?" And he says, "Yeah, I had my dog in the car."

Funny story. As a fiction writer, do you turn that into something more?

I get dialogue from what I remember. From the years I was in the service as an enlisted man, from the construction summers I've worked when I was in my early twenties, from growing up with kids from blue-collar families.

You also draw scenes from morgues, which can be a chilling place to do research. How often do you go to look at dead bodies, and what's it like?

It isn't like what I thought it would be. I remember the first time walking in and turning a corner, waiting for an attendant. I felt my back was against something and I turned and there was a woman lying on one of those tray tables, nude, decomposing. She had been found in her bathtub several days after she'd died. She was an old black woman who was turning white in patches where her skin seemed to be peeling off. That was the first close shot of a dead person I've ever had. Then scattered around the main room were people lying on tray tables in the way they died. Some were rigid. There was one young black woman whose hands were in the same position as when she had held a shotgun and put it under her jaw and blew her face off. Her face was gone, the buckshot had gone up right through the inside of her face. My impression was that they didn't look like people anymore, they were more like store mannequins.

Did any of this make you squeamish?

I thought I might get sick but I didn't. I heard the electric saw going as we walked into the autopsy room. They were cutting into the skull of a young woman to get some brain tissue and had taken the scalp and folded it down over her face. I made a note of that and used it in *Unknown Man No. 89,* when they pull the face up and he sees it for the first time, it was like pulling a mask on. They sawed the woman open and took the rib slabs and just put them aside, then they took the whole organs out and cut samples from them, then they put all the organs in a bag and put it all back into her and replaced the section of ribs and then stitched it up with what looked like very heavy cord. Sewed her head back up. Then they showed me a cold room where there were probably thirty naked bodies lying there together, a paper sack between the legs of each one with their clothes and personal effects in it. Then when I was researching *Bandits* I called a friend who's a mortician and spent the day with him. We picked up the body of a woman who had committed suicide. I went through the embalming process. When I saw that the embalming fluid was called Perma-Glo and that the little machine that pumps it in was called a Porta-Boy, I thought, they're playing right into my hands.

What's the most gruesome thing you've ever seen?

The most gruesome happened in Memphis when I was about eight. A horse that had been pulling a wagon had broken its leg and was lying on the side of the road when a cop shot it in the head. Its brains came out and it looked like red Cream of Wheat. I can still picture it vividly.

Did it give you nightmares?

No, my dreams are very obvious. I used to dream about falling down very narrow stairs all the time, waiting to hit, but it wouldn't happen. Till I started making a lot of money, then I didn't have that dream any more.

How much money is *a lot* of money?

Before I went to Delacorte I was offered a four-book deal for $5 million from Arbor House. I told my agent I didn't want to *have* to write four books. He asked me how many I wanted to write. I said three. So he got me $4.5 million for three books. After those, I went to Delacorte for the same deal.

What's the largest single check you've ever received?
I sold the screen rights to *Out of Sight* for $2.5 million.

And what does money mean to you? Is it a way of keeping score?
More than anything, yeah. Because there isn't really anything that I want. Your serenity has to be inside of yourself. You can't say I'm only going to be happy in Palm Beach, or I *have* to have a Mercedes. We have a house in Palm Beach, I *had* a Mercedes. But you don't need them.

Having been on both sides, do you find that the rich are different?
Yeah. For the most part they are less aware of what's going on in the world, or they have a narrower Republican view of what's going on, and a fairly simple answer to it. I can't say that blue-collar people have a wider scope, but they are in the midst of it more and the people that I deal with who are on the fringe of crime or are into it, it's happening to them. They've got to deal with it directly. It's not something that they read about.

For most of your life you've had to deal with life directly; now you're signing four-million-dollar contracts, has . . .
Four and a *half.*

Right. Excuse me. Has writing changed for you over the years? Ross Thomas, for example, said that he liked the writing process when he first started but not as much now because it's too familiar. Can you identify with that?
Sure, that's why I only write three pages a day, when I used to do five

or six. Because you don't want to repeat yourself. You don't want to shoot people the same way.

Three pages is still prolific, considering the number of books you already have out there. No problem with writer's block?
I don't believe in writer's block, so why have it? And I don't understand why it takes writers so long to write books.

Truman Capote used to agonize over getting down to write. He'd sharpen fifty pencils every morning just to delay the agony.
Yeah, Steinbeck describes that in *Sweet Thursday*. Getting all the pencils ready . . . putting it off, putting it off. I try and get right into it, become part of it. I have trouble expressing what I do, because I don't know what I do. I haven't outlined the book, I don't know what's going to happen next. I just have a sketchy idea. The reader knows as much as I do. I have trouble beginning a book. I will think, Oh my God, have I lost it? I can't get into the rhythm of this thing. I'm trying too hard to write. Then before I know it I feel the flow of it and it's working.

So when hopeful writers ask you how you do it, you tell them to just plunge in and go with the flow?
I would tell them to read. That's the best way to learn how to write. I get manuscripts sent to me at times and I return them stating that I'm not an editor, that reading manuscripts is work and not something I would choose to do even if I had the time. And a reply came back from this one writer saying: I would have thought that a letter from a professional writer would have been more artfully crafted. I held back the urge to write back that you crafted artfully when you've got a contract.

Well, if he can't sell his manuscript, maybe he can sell your initial letter and get something for his efforts.
I was signing books in Los Angeles five years ago and a guy comes up and says, "A letter of yours was auctioned at a library fund raising and I bought it for $500." I said, "You paid $500 for a letter? Give me

your address, I'll *write* you a letter." And I did, then wrote him another letter, thinking he deserved more, and I included a typescript of
whatever book I was working on at the time. A few months later at a
bookseller's convention I found out that he sold the two letters and
the typescript for $1,250.

**Once this gets out, you'll probably be inundated with letters from
people hoping to cash in on your replies. Or do you already get a
lot of mail from readers?**

Quite a bit. I got a letter from a reader who brings up my grammati-
cal mistakes. I say I'm not going to use the right word or the right
construction for the sake of grammar if it gets in the way of a flow of
the narrative. [*Reaches into a drawer, takes out a file of letters, obviously delighted*] Here's a letter from a woman who feels that the dust jacket
photo of one of my books explains its raunchiness: "You look a lot
like some of your characters. You look like a street bum, a wino. Why
do you stupid writers put pictures like this on the back of your
books? Wouldn't being a classy-looking man, like, say, Gregory Mc-
Donald, increase your market? Oh well, what does it matter? It's the
last book of yours I'll read anyway."

Did you write her back?

There was no return address, otherwise I might have written to tell
her I'd wear bib overalls in the photo if I could write narrative like Jim
Harrison, or I'd wear a dress if it would help me write in as many
voices as Joyce Carol Oates.

**That's quite a file of letters you've got, what are some of your
other favorites?**

Here's a good one: "I just finished reading *Bandits* and the ending was
so goofy, it made me furious. What a stupid ending. Roy gets a bullet
and a murderous Indian and a spaced-out rich girl walk off with all
the dough. Please, no more stupid books. P.S. The ending of *Stick* was
almost as goofy and unsatisfying. You're a weird guy, dude."

Well, at least he's still reading.

Here's one from Frederick Forrest, the actor, after I wrote him back. "I framed your letter. You are now alongside my only other autographs, Doke Walker and Jack Dempsey. Jackie Bissett autographed a book of mine once but that doesn't count, she's not in the same league with you and the Doker and Jack, but she sure ain't bad." And from a woman: "I have never written anyone a fan letter in my life. My husband is getting tired of me spending more time in the sack with a Leonard book than with him, so I told him, 'Get my attention.'"

Ever hear from prisoners who might read you for inspiration?

I've got this one from a convict: "I thought you might be interested in a report on your growing popularity among this prison's hardcore readers. While Harold Robbins, Sidney Sheldon, and Lawrence Sanders remain the most generally popular authors here, more and more of our hardcore are discovering you. This group includes a few college-educated whites, quite a few American-born blacks, Italians, and pre-Mariol Cubans. Some of your most recent converts are Charlie, twenty-four, a heroin seller out of 143rd St., Harlem; Stanley, thirty-five, a heroin seller out of the Kennelworth Projects in D.C.; and Mike, a heroin seller and user from Pittsburgh. Your books don't seem to have attracted the cocaine and crack people yet, they are younger, wilder, and less educated. The Italians like you but they prefer Judith Krantz and Sidney Sheldon, anything about the lush life in New York City. Jamaicans read westerns, Africans read nonfiction, Indians and Pakistanis read the *Wall Street Journal*."

That one should be framed on your wall.

It's wonderful, isn't it? Here's my favorite letter: "I just finished your book entitled *Split Images* and it is dull, uninteresting, and most of all it uses such foul language that is very unnecessary. Why did I buy it? Sounded like a good mystery with good statements from the *Chicago Tribune,* the *Detroit News,* and others. How much did you have to bribe them to say such nice things about your book? Maybe they're as low-down as you are. I didn't even finish it, I threw it in the trash so no one can read it, even my husband. Since foul language is all you understand, you are a fucking, shitty, half-assed person to write such trash! How anyone can stand you is beyond me. Hell, I'm not a prude, but goddamn! a good book can be written interestingly without your kind of foul language. Too bad you don't try it. I will certainly never recommend your books to anyone."

That letter alone should bring you a whole new readership! How receptive are you to criticism?
Some criticism has helped me. The smart-aleck criticism I don't go for at all. I've never written to a critic to tell him he's full of shit, but I've been tempted to.

Like to the one who wrote that the characters in *Bandits* were etched in cardboard and that your writing was repetitious and full of clichés?
Yeah. I don't know why a reviewer would pick on that particular one. It seems to me that those characters are as real as any of my other books. One other critic in Ft. Lauderdale opened his review of that book with: "I think Elmore Leonard is the most overrated writer in the country." He criticized a character who's been in prison twenty-seven years and when he comes out he knows all about the latest security measures that banks take in protecting their money. How would he know that? Well, that's what you *learn* in prison! You learn all that stuff. It's school.

You've also been criticized for your sexual attitudes, haven't you?
There was a *Detroit Free Press* reviewer who's a friend of mine who said that my attitude about women was on a par with Mickey Spillane. I started to concentrate a little bit after that on developing the female characters. But you have to remember that the reviewers are writers. Who think they can write. [*Laughs*]

When did *you* first think that you could write?
The first writing I did was a play in fifth grade. I had just read *All*

Quiet on the Western Front and the play was about the war. There was one black kid in my class and I made him a German because I'd just come up from the South the year before. The only audience was the Mother Superior in Blessed Sacrament Grade School. Then, in college, I wrote two short stories. The first was entered in this contest and it placed in the top ten; the second, during my senior year, placed second. I graduated in '50 and got a job as an office boy at an ad agency. I decided then that if I was going to write I should go about it in a professional way; pick a genre to learn *how* to write. So I chose westerns because of movies like *Stagecoach, The Plainsman, My Darling Clementine, Red River.*

What was it about some of those movies that got to you?
Well, *The Plainsman* was just all action, done on a grand scale. The Indians were mean-looking and it was okay to shoot Indians then in the movies. *My Darling Clementine* was because of that black-and-white look of it, the realism. Henry Fonda with his hair plastered down, sitting in front of the jail, leaning back in his Douglas chair with his feet up and somebody came walking out and sniffs and said, "What is that I smell?" And it's his hair tonic.

So it was the movies that were your original source of inspiration?
Yeah, because westerns were so popular in the fifties, and because western stories were in all the better magazines—*Saturday Evening Post, Colliers*—and the pulps were still alive. There must have been a dozen or more, and the better ones were *Dime Western* and *Zane Grey Western*. Before I did the research I wrote a couple of westerns and sent them to the *Saturday Evening Post,* but they were rejected because they were too relentless, too gray. I didn't have any comic relief, no blue sky. I then began to research the Apaches, cavalry, cowboys, the Southwest. I subscribed to *Arizona Highways* magazine, which gave me illustrations. If I needed a canyon, I'd go through the magazine and find one and describe it. It was better than being there.

You're already married at this time, aren't you?

I got married in '49. Our first child, Jane, was born in '50, before I started writing. My son Peter was born in '51, then Chris in '54, and Bill in '57, then Katy in '65. So when I first started writing I'd get up at five A.M. to have time to write, because I was always busy with them. From five to seven I'd do two pages. I made a rule for myself. I had to start writing before I could put the water on for coffee.

And when did you find acceptance?
I wrote a short story and sent it to *Argosy*. They passed it on to one of their pulp magazines and asked if I had anything else. I sat down and immediately wrote a 10,000-word novelette, *Trail of the Apache*. They bought it for $1,000 and it was published in December of '51. So that was the place to learn. In the fifties I sold about thirty short stories, wrote five books, and two of the stories were sold to Hollywood: "The Tall T" with Randolph Scott, Richard Boone, and Maureen O'Sullivan, and "3:10 to Yuma." So that was very encouraging.

But not encouraging enough to give up your job at the ad agency?
Right, but I didn't like it at all. I was a writer on a Chevrolet account. The copy had to be sprightly and smart, cute and alliterative. The good stuff never got published. I was good at doing truck ads. I went out in the field and got testimonial material from truck owners. That was fun.

So while you're working on car and truck ads in Detroit, you're thinking about cowboys and Indians out West. Yet you've said that you didn't like the western period in America. Is that true?
When I think of the nineteenth century, it has no appeal to me at all. I hadn't even read many westerns. When I picked up Zane Grey I couldn't believe it was so bad.

But when you picked up Hemingway, particularly *For Whom The Bell Tolls*, you discovered a way to write westerns. How'd you make the connection?
That book was a western, in a way. They're out in the mountains with

horses, with people speaking Spanish, it could be a border story, could be in Mexico. I noticed the way Hemingway used his senses, he had everything going at once. He made it look easy, because on so many of his pages there was a lot of white space; very often his dialogue went straight down the page and it wasn't more than a couple inches wide. You didn't see dialogue anywhere else—the serious novelists seemed reluctant to use dialogue. And yet he used it so effectively, and he said so much, there was more there than the words themselves. So I began to study him very closely in construction, in his describing a person, what he described and what he didn't. In contrast to writers who describe someone's face in such detail—the wide-set eyes, narrow chin—things that you immediately forget. I started to put him on my typewriter to see what it looked like. Do a paragraph of Hemingway as it appears and then write the next paragraph myself.

And what did you discover when you studied him this closely?
That he was so serious. I realized that I didn't share Hemingway's attitudes at all about himself or myself, about life. So then I began to read people like Mark Harris, who wrote *Bang the Drum Slowly*. And Kurt Vonnegut, Richard Bissell, to see that you didn't have to be that serious, you could have a little more fun with it. But I didn't begin to have fun with the westerns until I wrote *Valdez Is Coming*.

The western you're best known for is *Hombre*. Why is that the only book you've written in the first person?
Because you're too limited, you can't move around, you're stuck with one point of view.

By the time *Hombre* came out in 1961, you made the decision to leave advertising and just freelance. It wasn't exactly the best of times for western writers, was it?
It was very risky. I was scared to death, but I knew I had to do it. I had only got a $1,250 advance for *Hombre* after I'd gotten $4,000 for the one before. But a friend of mine was producing some films for Encyclopedia Britannica and he offered me a thousand dollars for each

twenty-seven-minute script I could write. So I made more money immediately freelancing than I did at the ad agency. Though I used to
have a dream where it was the first day back at the ad agency where I
spent ten years and they were showing me my new office and one of
my friends there came walking by real fast and I said, "Chuck, Chuck,
I'm back." And he'd say, "I'll catch you later, I'm in a hurry." And he'd
be gone. And my office was lined with shelves of canned goods and in
the middle was a school desk. That was my desk. I was going to be in
there forever.

**Was it that kind of insecurity that kept you from publishing
another novel for eight years?**
Well, after I had quit my job I was doing freelancing for at least four
and a half years, those Britannica films, industrial movies, all kinds of
advertising stuff, everything but cocktail napkins. Then I switched
from westerns into crime, because television dried up the western
market. At the height of their popularity there were more than thirty
westerns on prime time during the week. And people stopped buying
the pulps. And the market for crime was there. Everyone's interested
in crime for some reason that I've never thought about.

Did the change of genres also change your thinking process?
In doing the westerns you had to think of an idea, a plot. You didn't
see little scenes in everyday life that you could apply to the western.
Now, you see all kinds of things going on and you think, I could use
that, that could be a scene, or somebody's back story. That just didn't
work for westerns. Now I see ideas all the time.

**Was it the sale of *Hombre* to the movies for $10,000 in 1965 that
enabled you to concentrate on your next novel, *The Big Bounce*,
which your new agent, H. N. Swanson, was convinced he could sell?**
Yeah, my first agent was very ill and so she sent it to Swanie, who
called me up and asked, "Did you write this book?" I said, of course.
He said, "Well, kiddo, I'm going to make you rich." Then he got
eighty-four rejections on the book—a dozen in New York, the rest in

Hollywood. The editors all said it was a downer, there was nobody to like. So I rewrote it. And Swanie sold it to the movies for like $50,000.

The movie, with Ryan O'Neal, came out the same time the book was published as a paperback original. What did you think of the film when you went to see it?
I was in New York and got in late. The woman in front of me said to her husband, "This is the worst picture I ever saw." And the three of us left. I still haven't seen the whole thing. It comes on television once in a while and I'd watch a few minutes then switch to something else. It's the second-worst movie ever made.

What's the worst?
I don't know, but there's got to be one.

Soon after that experience you began writing scripts, beginning with *The Moonshine War* in 1970, then *Joe Kidd* in '72, and *Mr. Majestyk* in '74. What made you think you could be a screenwriter?
I liked movies too much and I believed that I could be good at it.

The money wasn't bad, either, was it?
When I was going out to Hollywood to write the revisions for *The Moonshine War,* Swanie said, "How much do you want a week?" I said, I didn't know, so he suggested $2,500. I said, why not $3,500? He called back in twenty minutes and said, "You're getting $3,500." I just pulled it out of the air. Now the producer had a $3,500-a-week writer instead of a $2,500 writer.

Alan Alda, Richard Widmark, and Patrick McGoohan starred in that; what did you think of the result?
I thought the casting was all wrong. McGoohan walked off the set and came up to me and said, "What's it like to stand there and hear all your lines fucked up?" I didn't know what to say to him.

You were just getting your feet wet; Hollywood would be fucking up a lot more of your work after that. How have you handled the mangling of so many of your creations?

It seems to be the nature of the business. In the first meeting they say, "Oh God, what a book! We know that you're going to write the ass off that script and it's going to be terrific." Then you assume that because they like the book they want the script to resemble the book, so the first draft is the book. You bring the 400 pages down to 110 and a lot of the good stuff's gone, you're down to plot, and plot doesn't interest me that much. But I'm willing to go along with whatever someone I respect wants to do. In my experience, even the ones that I've written, even the ones that have never been produced, I listened too much to people who were having ideas off the top of their heads. I've never seen a business that's so full of amateurs or people that I suspect aren't even that fond of movies. That's what gets me. It's just a product, just something to sell. You see Disney's Michael Eisner; every time you see him on television Mickey's walking by. What has this got to do with movies? It's all about money. That's why I took Chandler's advice on working in Hollywood, which was to wear your second-best suit, artistically speaking, and keep your mouth shut. Don't become cynical, because it won't do any good. So I always wore my navy blue suit, buttoned up, and said Please and Thank You, and got the first plane home.

There's never been a time when you were seduced by Hollywood, to move out, live the lifestyle?

Never, because then I would be consumed by the business; talk about movies, get calls from producers. It wasn't seductive at all, it was all work. On *Joe Kidd* I stayed at the Universal Sheraton and looked out the window at all the people at the swimming pool. I was sitting there in the room staring at the desk writing, working.

Did you have to do a lot of rewriting for Clint Eastwood?

Yeah. I would rewrite pages and hand them to the producer, who would get out his pen and rewrite my dialogue. Then I'd take the pages back to my office and cross out all his lines and retype it. I probably should have left his lines in! Then Eastwood and the director, John Sturges, would come into my office every evening and I'd hand them the pages. Eastwood would read them, and in one scene, he thought when he's threatening four armed bad guys that he should have his gun out. I didn't think it was necessary. And Sturges agreed. When Eastwood asked why, Sturges said, "Well, the audience has seen all your other pictures." But when it was shot, he had his gun out.

Wasn't *Mr. Majestyk* also originally written for Eastwood?
Right. Eastwood asked me for something like *Dirty Harry* only different. That always inspires me, I don't know why. So I came up with an idea that evening and called him in Carmel. He said to work it up. So I wrote a twenty-three-page outline and went to see him. But by that time he had acquired *High Plains Drifter,* so he passed on mine. My agent gave it to producer Walter Mirisch, who sold it to United Artists, and they got Charles Bronson involved.

So what did you think of those two films?
I didn't think they were that good, though *Mr. Majestyk* is still making money. They were 1970s movies, that had that look.

Along with Eastwood and Bronson, you also got to work with Steve McQueen for a while, didn't you?
That was for a project called *American Flag,* about the little guy against the big mining company. It was another of those twenty-page outlines which McQueen liked and optioned. When I first met him I was very hungover and hoping he would offer me a beer. McQueen had an accident riding his dirt bike out in the desert the day before, and he slipped his pants down to show me this huge strawberry, a big scrape on his hip that he bandaged while we were talking about the movie. He was going with Ali McGraw then and he wanted her in the picture. But nothing ever happened to it.

Did you at least get your beer?
Yeah. He first offered me soda or some iced tea.

Those years, you were pretty heavy into the sauce, weren't you?
Yeah. Once after I returned from California I started throwing up blood and went into the emergency hospital. They thought it was some kind of an ulcer condition. They tried to stop the bleeding and they couldn't. The doctor said, "The only other thing it could be is gastritis, but we usually only see that in Skid Row bums. After the surgery he said, "It's acute gastritis." I was in the hospital a few days, and when I came out I eased back into drinking again.

Didn't that scare you?
It scared everybody else, but it didn't scare me, no. Because I didn't feel near death.

Didn't you also have a couple of drunk driving arrests around that time as well?
Right. In Malibu I was driving too carefully and ended up in the Malibu jail. In the morning they brought me a couple of fried eggs, which I complained about. I remember saying, "You know it's just as easy to fix them the right way; they don't have to be stiff and cold." Probably still a bit smashed. Two years later, in Michigan, it happened again. The charge was driving while visibly impaired, and they took my license for a while.

Symptoms of a problem, wouldn't you say?
Right, right. Definitely. I got into drinking because I was shy, somewhat introverted, self-conscious, and it brought me out, it was the macho thing to do. I drank from the time I was sixteen until I quit in '77 when I was fifty-two. More than thirty-five years. And I had more fun when I was drinking than any other time.

Did you begin as a social drinker?

You start out saying you're a social drinker. Not admitting that you have to have it, that you don't go anywhere where you can't have it. With my wife and friends we were always meeting, having parties, drinking, having fun. We'd have either a drink or a couple of beers every day, go home and have a drink before dinner, then we'd go out. It didn't cost a lot of money then to get smashed. I didn't get drunk every night, but I always drank, every day.

And how did it affect your first marriage?
We had quite a good marriage, but I certainly drank far more than she did, and we'd get into arguments about it. When I was in the bag I'd bring up things that would antagonize her. Typical drunk. She'd want to go home from a party and I'd want to stay until all the bottles were empty. Or she'd want to drive and I would insist on driving. I also built up resentments that I didn't talk about earlier. For example, when I quit my job in '61, I had enough money to live on for six months or so. But immediately she saw a house that she wanted, so we moved into a bigger, more expensive house. And I didn't feel that she was very supportive of what I was doing, that if I didn't sell something she'd say, "Well, you're going to have to get a job." Never, ever suggesting that she might get a job. I didn't harp on things like that, but that was part of the resentment.

In *Unknown Man No. 89* you write: "His wife had told him once his problem was he didn't count his drinks." Did your wife tell you that?
I'm sure she did. Then the smart reply: Yeah, I counted them, I had fifteen.

Weren't you hiding liquor in your desk for a while?
Yeah, but I hid it from myself. I was the only one in the office. I'd open the drawer very, very quietly, take the bottle out, take a big swig and put it back. This was at the very end, where I would have to have a drink in the morning as well. And there were times when I'd drink anything if it was there.

What is a drunk's idea of normal?
A glow. The best time was to have a glow and to be making good conversation. There was nothing better than drinking and talking. And I
thought I was funny. Man. I was relaxed and having fun and I loved
the world.

And what's the best excuse to keep on drinking?
I suppose first of all not to admit you're alcoholic, that you're only a
social drinker and that it doesn't hurt anyone but yourself, and you
have a free will and if I choose to hurt myself in some way then I have
a right to. But you're always hurting others. I remember once on the
Donahue show, I was on with Grace Slick, Shecky Greene, Gail Storm,
and Donahue asked, "Why did you drink so much when you went
out?" I said, "I was afraid that at a party, being with a lot of businessmen, they would be boring." And Grace Slick said, "They are."

What finally got you to join A.A.?
A friend of mine who had been in the program said he thought it
would be a good idea. He was suggesting that I had a problem, but it
never occurred to me that I did. I drank for the fun of it. But eventually it becomes a physiological problem that your system requires. I
heard stories at that first meeting that were so familiar to me. When
my turn came to talk, I said, for the first time, "My name is Dutch
and I'm an alcoholic." I'm not sure I really believed it then, but I said
it. I saw that I would have no problem at all getting into this program
and, with my Catholic education, accepting the tenets, the idea of a
higher power. But admitting you're alcoholic is not necessarily accepting that fact. That comes next, and that's a big step. I thought,
okay, I'm alcoholic, but I can still have a drink now and then and get
away with it. So that's what I tried, every three or four months I'd get
smashed and then feel ill the next day. And I'd have to have another
drink to get myself back up, to feel better. Lines that I used in *Unknown Man No. 89* are out of real life. Someone saying: "You enjoy getting down there on the floor making love to that toilet bowl, huh?"
See, I didn't substitute for the booze a different attitude.

An attitude of acceptance?

Once you accept that you're alcoholic, if you have any sense at all you realize that you can't drink. It's that simple. That you're going to die or you're going to have mental problems if you continue. A change took place after I got in A.A. I realized that you have to take this problem and hand it over to a higher power and forget about it. That really changed my outlook. You're not simply abstaining, you're taking on a completely different attitude about yourself. You quit taking yourself so seriously. If you believe it, whether the higher power exists or not, it's going to work.

You've described withdrawal as like having a sunburned nervous system. How painful did it get for you?

Bad. It's really bad. Your skin is sensitive, you don't want anybody to touch you. And the least little thing makes you jump. I never had the shakes, though I've seen people with the shakes, couldn't pick up a glass. I joined A.A. in '74 and finally that day arrived on January 24, 1977, when I had a ginger ale and a Scotch and that was it. 9:30 in the morning had that drink, and that was the last one.

What about drugs—have you dabbled?

I've tried grass. Then I had a great idea and wrote it down. I found that I wrote very small, you could barely see it. You'd think you'd write big.

Was the idea any good?

Of course not. When I went to Israel to develop *52 Pick-Up* for Menachem Golam—a picture that was released as *The Ambassador* with Robert Mitchum, but had no resemblance to my book—I was smoking hash with an Israeli couple at their house. We were watching a Busby Berkley movie with the banana number. That was the funniest thing I've ever seen in my life. We were rolling around laughing, tears. That's still funny.

Since you've cleaned up your act, would you say you're more confident and less self-conscious now?

Much. I'm not self-conscious anywhere near the degree I was before. Now I can give talks and I don't feel that those people out there are looking for ways to criticize me or looking for some dumb thing I might say. I don't have to put on any kind of an act, I can just be myself and that's it. My purpose isn't to write books or movies, it's just to be. And to not be specific about what I want or what I need. Every morning I think about that before I get out of bed. This is my purpose: to get out of myself, to be available to others, to listen, to care. It relaxes me. I don't need anything. That's the key to it. You don't need anything. I'm happy to be with myself. And I'm never going back, ever. I don't have any desire. Which is the best part.

Now I can better understand your acceptance of how Hollywood had mistreated your novels. Nevertheless, getting back to that, do you ever wonder why before *Get Shorty*, none of your books were turned into a memorable motion picture?
I think a good movie could be made, but I don't think it would make any money if you stuck to the book. I was invited to London, they were going to put on all the movies that I've been associated with, then I was to get up on the stage and talk about them. I told the guy, "You're crazy. You think I'm going to show up for that?"

Where does Hollywood go wrong with regard to your material?
I'm interested in good movies with good actors. Before *Get Shorty*, the ones that had been made tended to become too theatrical. I would like to see the studios interested more in good stories, adult stories, and forget about the star vehicles and the kiddie movies that have been coming out since Spielberg. Just look at what works today: *Look Who's Talking, Ghost, Home Alone, The Mask, Stargate, Forrest Gump*. I like movies that I don't know what they're about, what's going to happen. I like foreign films for that reason. Like *L'Avventura* of Antonioni. You don't know what's going to happen in that picture. I liked the characters, I wonder what they're up to and who's going to end up with who. *The Passenger,* another Antonioni, you wonder what the hell's going to happen. It's not the least bit predictable. In some of my books

I have a guy who walks the line, you don't know if he's good or bad, which way he's going to go. That's a problem in adapting for the screen, no question about it. When you bring it down, all the good stuff's gone.

Yet you continue to take meetings, you option all your books, you still have hope, don't you?
Donald Westlake wrote me a letter and asked: "Why do you keep hoping to see a good movie made? The books are ours, everything else is virgins thrown in the volcano. Be happy if the check is good."

Why do you?
I'm optimistic by nature.

You weren't too optimistic with what Burt Reynolds did when he directed and starred in *Stick*, were you?
Well, *Stick* became a revenge movie, but it certainly wasn't a revenge book. The departure of the script didn't bother me, you know that that's likely to happen. But if you're going to do my book, let's try and get the sound of my book, the feeling. Let's try and get actors who you don't see acting. When Reynolds was on "Good Morning America" he was told that I didn't think too highly of the movie and he said, "I don't know what happened to him, I thought he was a beautiful guy and then he turned on me."

Didn't you write him a four-page memo detailing your objections after you'd seen the picture?
Yeah, and I never heard from him. I thought he'd be fine for the part, but he needed a director. After I saw a first cut, I told an interviewer that I thought it was awful. It got around, and they sent Reynolds back to Florida with new scenes and a couple million dollars to shoot them. Sid Sheinberg called me and said, "We want you to see the new version." Lew Wasserman said, "God, what an improvement, it's great now." So they fly us out and the limo picks us up and takes us to the

studio and we see the picture and it's no better. Now it's got machine guns and scorpions in it.

I've got a friend who asked Reynolds to sign his copy of *Stick*. Reynolds wrote: "It could have been a very special film, but Universal and Dutch Leonard himself sold out. It was a sad and bitter film that they finally released. Great writer, not a good man."
How could he blame me, for godsakes? He had it rewritten and *he* directed it! He inscribed my book? He's got no business doing that. It's really sad. He looks awful.

Did you see him in *Boogie Nights*?
I thought he was being Mr. Reynolds. It was a good performance, but I didn't see anything exceptional about it. It was restrained. But this is the kind of guy he is, he's been making porno movies in the movies for years and years, what's there to get excited about? I was disappointed with the picture.

You had even worse luck with *La Brava* and Dustin Hoffman though—that one didn't even get made.
Walter Mirisch sent *La Brava* to Hoffman in '84 and Hoffman said he liked it a lot. So we met with him at a Cuban restaurant in New York, then went to his apartment on Central Park West and discussed it. He told us how he had already made out three-by-five cards describing scenes and how they might work together. He said, "I'd like this one to be my next project." Then he went away and when he came back, he changed his mind. He decided that when you cut to the bad guys it became a B movie. Then Dustin called me and said, let's meet again. So we met. Dustin sounded like he really wanted to do it but he had to be sure of how the story developed. He felt that it would play better if he were in love with a younger girl than with the character in the book, a fifty-year-old movie star. Where were you going to get a good-looking fifty-year-old woman? I said Faye Dunaway, but the feeling

was she's too obvious . . . you would suspect her once the plot developed. A month later I came back with a new set of fifty pages and Dustin said, "I can fall in love with the older woman. I met Anouk Aimee over the weekend. She looks great." Then the phone rings and it's Anouk calling from Paris. He says to me, "Come on, get on the phone, say hello to her." I said, "What am I going to say to Anouk Aimee? That I love her picture, *A Man and a Woman,* twenty years ago?" He said, "Just listen to her voice, it's great." So I got on the phone, "Hi, Anouk." At the end of the meeting he called her number in Paris and we each had to get on and listen to her message voice in French. He dialed it each time for each one of us who were there. Then, during our third meeting with Dustin, he said right in the middle of it, "Oh, I forgot, I promised my daughter I'd take her to the movies." And he leaves. Walter Mirisch has come 3,000 miles, I've come 600, and we're sitting there looking at each other. The next day Dustin comes in and says, "Geez, God, it was a beautiful day yesterday, what'd you do, go to the park?" Go to the park?! I could have stayed home in my backyard. Then he left on personal business and we were stuck again. Then, the next meeting, Martin Scorsese was there. Now we're pretty close to something and Walter's trying to get these guys to agree so he can go make a deal with a studio. And Dustin said, "No, we want to be absolutely sure of the story and how it works all the way through." I remember I said, "Well, it's okay for you guys to say that, I'm doing all the work, and I'm out here past the point of no return. I've got to keep going, and I'm doing all this on spec." And Hoffman said, "Don't worry about it, you'll be paid retroactively." I told my agent that, he thought it was about the funniest thing he'd ever heard. He'd told me from the beginning: "It's not going to work, he's not going to make the picture, don't you know that?" The *next* meeting was just Scorsese and I. He's a real pro, no bullshit, he knows what he's doing. And that was the last meeting. Scorsese left to do *The Color of Money.* Hal Ashby was brought in by Dustin, then Dustin quit.

Didn't Hoffman drop out because Cannon Films, at the time, started taking out huge ads announcing his involvement?

Yeah. Dustin was to get $6.75 million plus a big chunk of the gross, and Cannon took out these spreads in the trades: "Welcome to the Cannon family, Dustin Hoffman. Soon to appear in *La Brava*." And Dustin resented that. As anyone would, being welcomed into that family.

But that wasn't the end of *La Brava*, was it?
No. They gave the script to Al Pacino. Walter called and said, "Al sees some problems with the plot." I said, "The plot? Wait till I get my pen, we can fix the plot. Does he like the *characters?*" So I went to New York and met with Pacino and he asked, "Why am I in love with this woman?" I thought, Oh my God. I could see he didn't want to do it.

Of all your books, has this one had the most movie history to it?
Well, more people have had *Swag*. And *Touch* was optioned long before the book came out. David Soul was the first one to option it, then Norman Lear had it for a while. Then Bruce Willis.

In your Hollywood novel, *Get Shorty*, you get a chance to write about what you've had to deal with over the years. You write of actors who get lucky, hit it big, their price goes into the millions, yet they're the same schmucks who made it on their tight pants and capped teeth, only suddenly they know everything there is to know about making movies. Who are the schmucks who come to mind?
Probably all of them. That would seem to be most actors who, soon as their price goes up, they're writing new dialogue. Actors are ad libbing all the time. They don't like to see the writer on the set.

***Get Shorty*, why did this one work?**
Because the emphasis was on the humor, but the characters played it straight. I could hear it. The words were mine for the most part. Scott Frank adapted it and did quite a good job. The ending's different. And the look is Barry Soddenfeld's. Because it has a comedy look to it. But the sound is mine.

What's more important, the sound or the look?
For me, the sound.

Did you have any approval on the production?
No. I was there for four days when they were shooting and Barry would come over twice and ask me what I thought and if I had any suggestions. Now that's got to be the first time in the history of Hollywood that the novelist was ever asked that. Most directors probably don't even know who the novelist is. But I wouldn't presume to have any suggestions.

My books haven't been easy to shoot because they've been shot with the wrong attitude, they've been taken too seriously. *Get Shorty* wasn't taken seriously, the way it was handled. It was taken seriously in the way the characters respond to one another. Two years before it went into production I was talking to Barry Sonnenfeld and I said, "I hope that you'll allow the actors to deliver the lines without cutting to another actor to get his reaction to it, a grin or a wink or a laugh." What happened when Bruce Willis sent me the script of *Bandits,* one character says to the other, "Do you know that every sixteen seconds in the U.S. a woman is physically abused?" And the guy shakes his head and says, "You wouldn't think that many get out of line." In the script he grins and winks. I explained to Bruce Willis that this is this guy's mentality, he's not being funny. Well, that's the way all the lines are in all my books.

Is it true when you were on the set, John Travolta was very respectful?
Yeah, he called me Mr. Leonard. And I let him.

For how long?
Just the first day. He got over that.

Did you get to know any of the other actors?
I met Hackman only at the premiere in New York. Renee Russo was easy to talk to and nice. DeVito, he's an easy guy, he's like a friend

now. In the new one, *Be Cool,* I gave him one scene where he comes back as Martin Weir, the actor, and he comes into Elaine Levin's office while Chile is showing her a home movie of Linda and her band, which looks like an MTV video. He comes in and says, "What? You're watching dailies and you didn't tell me? You're making a picture?" And he says, "You know, I've been thinking. We didn't use amnesia enough in *Get Lost.*" And Elaine says, "I think we may have a part for you in the one coming up. There's a gay Samoan body guard." And he likes the idea. See, I want to make fun of sequels while doing a sequel.

To understand the music business for *Be Cool,* did you meet a lot of the music people?

Oh yeah. I met [record producer] Don Was last summer and Richie Sambora was recording. I sat in the recording booth with the two of them while they went through one of Richie's songs, editing different tracks. I'll have a scene in *Be Cool* like that. Then I want another scene at the end of the evening at a venue when you settle up, a settlement meeting, because I hear that can be pretty interesting, that there have been times when a gun has been put on a table. I've met Arrowsmith's tour accountant and he said I could call him when I get to that point. I met Anthony Kiedis of the Red Hot Chili Peppers. He was at the premiere of *Jackie Brown.* I saw him the summer before, when they were rehearsing to go to Japan. I sat in a room no bigger than a garage with them. His arm was all smashed up, he had it in a box. Flea was there bouncing around, he's very important in the business. And David Navarro. Both Flea and Navarro I've seen since with another band.

Was there any pressure on you to write the sequel a certain way, based on how *Get Shorty* was received?

No, not after forty-five years. The way I look at it, either it will work or it won't. So what? I'll go ahead and write another book. The main thing that I learned in the mid-eighties: don't take it too seriously. Hitchcock said to Ernest Lehman, who was stewing over *North by Northwest,* "Ernie, it's only a movie."

How much credit do you give to Quentin Tarantino for the interest of Hollywood in your work now?

It helped enormously, sure. Actors want to work with him, he's the hot kid. Sure. I don't know him that well. I haven't been out with him socially. I hung around with him twice on the set of *Jackie Brown*. We talked about movies. He knows a lot about my work. He'll refer to things that I'll remember but that I haven't really thought of. He wants to write and appear in *Killshot* as Richie Mix, one of the bad guys, opposite De Niro as the blackbird. And he wants Tony Scott to direct. That's his plan. It almost came about at one time. But they all have companies and they all get involved and that's how it becomes a $50 million picture before you set up the lights.

Did you have anything to say to Tarantino about adapting your work?

No, because I figure he knows what he's doing. I was surprised at some of the pictures that he likes, his favorites, like *Blow Out* and Howard Hawks's *Rio Bravo*. He's so aware of what the director is doing, even if it's not a very good picture. He called me up a couple of weeks before he went into production with *Jackie Brown* and said, "I've been afraid to call you for the last year." And I said, "Why? Because you've changed the title [from *Rum Punch*], changed the location, and you're starring a black woman in the lead?" And he said, "Yeah." I said, "I think Pam Grier is a good idea. And you're the filmmaker, you've got to do what you want, your mark's gonna be all over it." I'm not concerned how closely the adaptation is. It's whether it's a good movie or not.

And was it?

The story's the same. I thought Samuel Jackson was great. He dominated the picture. Pam Grier is a little different from the girl in the book, though she was tough in the book. De Niro played it a little more aloft, kind of a sleepwalker. Well, he gets stoned all the time. And I like him a lot. In the book he's not quite that vague. Although he's not nearly the guy he was in *The Switch*. But this happens. He was in *Swag* and then in *Stick*, and he's a lot slicker guy than he was in

Swag. Not as slick as he was in the movie, but it seems the seven years he was in prison he gained an education.

Have you ever been in awe of any star?

No. And it's funny, because my wife and I would go to a restaurant and sit and look around for movie stars, when I'd been with some movie star all day. Once, in a Beverly Hills men's shop, we saw Paul Newman walking in. We sort of hung around to see what he was going to buy. My wife, Joan, said, "Go over and tell him that you wrote *Hombre.*" I said, "What if he didn't like it?" We watched him try on a jacket but we didn't hang around, we didn't want to be so obvious that we were watching him. But I've always been fascinated by movie stars. They're fun. I used to read movie magazines. The closest star friend I have would be Charles Durning. Brian Dennehy I thought was a really good guy, I'd like to get to know him better.

Who's your favorite actor?

Harry Dean Stanton. He doesn't act. The director Ulu Grossbart said he comes on the set and you don't have the feeling that he's an actor at all, but God, the guy never misses his mark, never messes up, he knows his lines. I'd like to get him in one of my movies.

Who else besides Stanton?

Duvall, De Niro, Pacino, Harvey Keitel, Christopher Walken, Keith Carradine, Matthew Modine, Michelle Pfeiffer—everybody likes her, huh? Walken was in *Touch.* He was funny. I liked that movie a lot and it didn't go anywhere. It wasn't given any kind of promotion. I thought it might catch on more with younger people. But it was a $5 million picture. The people who did *Leaving Las Vegas,* Lumiere, put up the money. After the first week they decided they weren't going to put any promotional money into it. So that was it.

It was never clear in *Get Shorty* who Shorty was. You mention Pacino on the last page—was he who you had in mind?

It's almost any star, they're all short. It always surprises me—the ones

I have seen seem so diminutive. And writers, too. I'm surprised at the number of short writers that I've met, like John Irving.

Irving wrestles, Mailer boxes—is there anything you do to unwind when you're not writing?

I hate exercise. I play tennis. I tried jogging twice. The first time I ran a mile and came home and threw up. The next time I tried I said, I'm going to run a mile every day for twenty days and if I don't like it by then, I'm not going to do it. I thought I would be able to think, get lost in some idea. It didn't work, it was boring. On the twentieth day I ran up two blocks and said, The hell with it, turned around, and haven't run since.

Unless you're running from somebody like Sam Peckinpah, who wanted to make a movie from *City Primeval*. You and Peckinpah seemed a dream team. What happened?

Well, this is when the movie was being called *Hang Tough*. I wasn't that happy about Peckinpah as a director because I didn't think he was the right one. At the first meeting, Peckinpah was talking about the story and he said that somebody should be taking notes. I couldn't imagine what there was to write down, since nothing made any sense to me. Peckinpah wasn't very specific about how he saw this picture. It was more abstract, almost philosophical. I was never sure of what he was talking about. We didn't share the same sense of humor—his was quite broad, mine is subtle. His idea of humor is James Caan and Robert Duvall: Caan spends a night with a girl and Duvall doesn't tell him until the next morning in the car that she's got gonorrhea. He thinks that's the funniest thing in the world and he's howling, laughing, got tears in his eyes. I don't think that's so funny.

Didn't he come here to see you?

Yeah, I showed him around a little, but we couldn't talk about the story because the Writer's Guild was on strike. I thought he would, but he didn't. Then he and another guy did a draft, but they moved the location to Texas and it was no longer an eastern–western, it was a western–western.

When you wrote *City Primeval,* which your publisher subtitled "High Noon in Detroit," did you think you were creating a new genre, with your eastern–western idea?
Not a new one, it's probably been done. It's an urban version of the classic movie western where the two guys stand face-to-face and confront each other and draw. Only it doesn't happen, because it didn't happen in the west, either. It only happened in movies and on television. So in mine, I have the face-off at the very end, where there are two guns on the table and one guy says, "Reach for the gun." The other says, "You're crazy," and goes into the kitchen to get a beer. When he comes back he reaches to get the opener out of his belt and the cop shoots him.

You write a lot about cops; what do you think of them in general?
Cops on the street I really don't know that well. Some of them certainly are very heavy-handed, beating up black guys, that kind of thing. You see it in documentaries, in news reports, on "60 Minutes." *Killshot*'s the only book I haven't treated law enforcement with great respect. Now I'm the Salman Rushdie of the marshal service in Cape Gerardo. But detective investigators—I have not met one I didn't respect. All the cops I know are homicide cops, and who's going to pay them off? I've been impressed by homicide cops and major crime cops who have all seemed to me to have been good at what they do, they have a sense of humor and apply themselves very industriously investigating crimes. I certainly don't see them becoming emotional the way they act in the movies or on the cop shows. They remind me of career, noncommissioned officers in the navy or the army, old pros.

Do different city police forces investigate murders differently?
I don't think so. Procedures are different, some forms are more efficient than others, but homicides, for the most part, someone tells them who did it. Or they know who did it. In the mom-and-pop mur-

der or the barroom brawl shooting or knifing, very seldom do they get the classic whodunnit. That's very, very rare. They might find a body at the airport in a trunk, yeah. But they still have a good idea of who did it from the way it was done.

Do you think actors who play cops have influenced the behavior of real cops who watch these films and TV shows?
Well, if you take something like *Lethal Weapon,* it was a little too frantic; I've never seen a cop who had that death wish. And TV and movie cops all wear shoulder holsters. You never see shoulder holsters in a police headquarters, they're too uncomfortable. But then life does imitate the movies at times. I heard a Detroit cop referring to when something was "going down." I said, I never heard that expression before from real cops, did you get that from TV? And he didn't know. Everybody was saying "Going down." Or then anytime a black character walked into the frame, almost the first thing he'd say was, "Say what?"

You've been pretty hard on blacks and on Detroit in some of your books. In *City Primeval* a character describes Detroit as one big niggerville with a few whites sprinkled in. Ever get any flak from blacks about what you write?
Yeah, I heard from one of the black groups who accused me of being a racist. But I'm sure they hadn't read the book.

Do you consider Detroit basically a lawless frontier?
Just in the neighborhoods with the drug dealers shooting each other. No more so than L.A.

You live in a peaceful, wealthy suburb outside of Detroit. How often do you enter the city?
We'll go in for dinner once every couple of months. There's nothing going on. Downtown is dead at night. I make the point in *SWAG* that you could drive a golf ball down the street at night and not hit anything. There's only one street downtown, in Greek Town, where there's any life at all. But even that popularity is beginning to dimin-

ish because of the street gangs that walk through there and shove people around. And it's only a block from police headquarters.

Is there any hope for the city's revival?

I can't imagine how it would happen. In major cities that I visit on book tours I see the new buildings downtown, it looks great. But here all the new buildings were put up outside, in Southfield or over in Troy. What I remember from earlier days, when I was a kid, taking streetcars downtown, playing with my friends, that was different. We lived in an apartment–hotel for four years and we'd go rat hunting in the alley with sticks with nails coming out to spear the rats. Then I'd walk a mile-and-a-half to school, kicking a rock all the way. But what does Detroit mean to me now? Not very much at all. I walk out in my backyard, there's a tennis court and a swimming pool, what does it matter where we are? We could be in Beverly Hills.

You also spend a lot of time in Florida, which you often use as background for your stories. What is it about Florida that attracts you?

I know it. And luckily there is a lot going on there. I like the high contrast from Palm Beach in south Florida to into the Keys. The mixture of people—from the very wealthy in Palm Beach, the retired, Midwestern people, down through Pompano and Del Rey and Lauderdale, then into Miami, where you've got all the Cubans and the boat lifters, the Marielito people, the Haitians, the Jamaicans—it's got everything going on there. There's got to be more greed in Miami than anywhere—and that's what crime is all about. I've been going to Florida every year since 1950.

How much has the lower end of Miami Beach deteriorated over the years?

By the end of the seventies it has certainly become a low-rent district. A lot of retirees from the garment district in New York had little apartments in those hotels and they sat out in the sun in their line of metal chairs. Then with the influx of the Cubans and the boat people there was a swarm of people who changed the neighborhood. It became a very active drug center, you could go out on the pier and buy anything you wanted. But I think South Beach will come back. It's too good for it not to.

Is there anything you've noticed that con men, killers, or burglars have in common?

The first thing I think of is they're lazy. They don't want to work, they don't want to do it the hard way. They don't want to have to learn how to do anything. It's like being a drunk: if you devoted all this effort that you do to drinking to some worthwhile effort, it could be worth money.

When you write about crime, you demonstrate an authoritative knowledge of guns and explosives. Did you get most of your education from Dale Johnston, the Detroit police firearms expert?

The first time I sought him out I asked him what gun a certain character would use for a murder he was planning. I remember standing at the counter in the firearms and explosives office and behind him was a glass case loaded with handguns, like a store. He picked out this high standard, long barrel .22 and said, "This is a very popular model with the organized crime shooters." Then I asked him what an Uzi with a suppressor on it would go for. He picked up the phone and talked for a while and then said, "Nine hundred bucks in Detroit, a thousand in New York, fifteen hundred in Miami. And the suppressor would cost you $400." Then when I want to know things like, Do you need to alter the muzzle of a gun to fit a silencer on it? I ask my researcher or look through books.

Do you need to alter the muzzle?

Not on a Beretta, that has the little nub sticking out. All you've got to do is cut the screw. You see silencers on revolvers in movies and that doesn't work at all, it doesn't silence anything, you still have the sound coming out of the chambers.

Do you own a gun?
No, I'm not interested in guns.

Even though they play such an important role in the security of your books?
"In the security of your books." That's good. No question about it. And I like the names of guns: Hard Ball, Colt Python—they've got good names. I was corresponding with a guy who used to work for Colt Arms. He told me that the guys in the field would rather have the AK-47s than their M-16s. And my researcher gave me a film on firing automatic weapons. I learned the best assault guns are the H & K MP 5 and the cut-down version, a Steirog 223 thirty-two-round magazine. And that the German light machine gun, the MG-42, is better than the M-60 American version.

Did your Detroit police contact also help you understand explosives?
When I did *Freaky Deaky* I asked him how to make a bomb and he handed me the *Anarchist Cookbook*. It came out in the late sixties. It's full of drawings and diagrams of how to put together bombs, booby traps, pipe bombs. I liked that a lot. I thought, hey, let's bring back the counterculturists, the bomb makers, the ones who blew up government facilities then, the Weatherman types. Bring them back now bombing for profit, having joined the Establishment. But I didn't understand any of the book's diagrams. When I came to the end of the book I called up my friend and said, "I want to open a drawer and set off a bomb." He told me real quickly how to do it. I said, "Wait, step by step." And he described it to me. Also, I sent away for a booklet that tells you how to make C-4 plastique using materials that are easily accessible at the hardware store.

There are booklets on this?
Sure. I've got a book on lock picking and where to send away to get tools for picking locks. It's all in there. In *Bandits* I found out from the cops about a hotel burglar who got hold of this fire key that'll

open up any room in a hotel. Then I got hold of this pamphlet, *Locks and Lockpicking.*

Where'd you get the idea for *Maximum Bob,* about a hard-sentencing judge, a sympathetic probation officer, and your usual cast of bad guys?

I had been corresponding for six years with this County Circuit Court judge, Marvin Mounts, and finally met him when I was giving a talk in Palm Beach. I went to his house and we sat on his patio and he brought out his box of photographs and legal materials. He'd tell me about different cases. Here's a guy who was arrested for beastiality—he raped a chicken. And there's a photograph of the chicken. I said, "How do they know he did it?" He said, "He had chicken feathers on his pubic hairs." Then there's a guy with a butcher knife in his head. And here are pictures of a guy who had murdered his wife and dug a hole big enough to hold the car and drove the car down into the hole and covered it up. Someone discovered the car and they pulled it out and found the body, which was so decomposed, the odor was so offensive, that the medical examiner did the autopsy at the airport with a small plane parked in front of them with the propeller blowing the odor away. So he's telling me these stories, see? And I thought, Gee, there's something here. Why don't I do a judge? What kind of judge? Well, a crooked judge or a hard-sentencing judge. A judge who has made a lot of enemies and somebody wants to kill him and attempts are made on his life . . . and that's how it started. Then I thought the main character should be a probation officer, a woman, so I talked to some of them. The judge, Robert Potter, who gave Jim Bakker forty-five years, is called Maximum Bob and I thought, that's a title. Of course my judge resents this guy being called that.

What are some of your own favorite titles?

Titles are hard. It has to come either before or while you're writing the book or you're in trouble. I like *Freaky Deaky, Get Shorty, Maximum Bob, Killshot, Glitz.*

**In *Freaky Deaky* you paint a cynical picture of the sixties. A
character says, "That whole show back then was a put-on. You
gonna tell me we were trying to change the world? We were
kicking ass and having fun." Was it all a put-on?**

A lot of it was, no question. In the fifties everyone seemed to be more
alike; everyone dressed alike and did pretty much the same thing. The
sixties were great, I think about the sixties a lot. But what amazes me
is that now that period doesn't seem to have made any difference.
We've kind of come back to what we were before. I didn't think there
would ever be any conservative people in the world after the sixties,
but there certainly are.

**The sixties seemed more spiritual, more inward-looking. You're a
religious man—what does God mean to you?**

I don't know. Until my forties I went to either mass or communion
every morning. What I missed in the formal practice of religion, listening to that relentless sermon, it's all . . . where's the gimmick? Who
is this priest and what is he doing for us outside of delivering this
canned speech every Sunday? You baptize the babies, you preside at
different functions, but what are you? They didn't seem to be talking
about love at all. It was always open your heart. What does that mean?
I came to feel that formal religion was really an impediment. In earlier
years I was taken with the Jesuits, they used their minds, they had the
proofs for the existence of God. They could present the Aristotelian
philosophy, they could argue all sorts of beliefs and truths.

**Now you wrestle with your beliefs and truths on the page, yet
you've said that you don't take your writing seriously.**

Right. I'm serious about it, but I know what it is. I'm a serious writer,
but I don't *take* it seriously, if that makes any sense. I don't stew over
it, I try and relax and swing with it.

**When critics discuss you, they point more to your "sound" than
to your style. What is the Leonard sound?**

It's the absence of a writing sound, of a prose sound; of keeping myself out of it, maintaining the sound of the characters. It's the attitude that determines your style, your sound. I have a fairly mild attitude in that I accept people. I accept my characters. I have an affection for them. Doesn't mean that I like them. Like the guy in *Glitz*, what the hell's his name? who murdered women. He's a bad guy. Then you see him with his mother and you start to understand a little bit about the guy. The more I think about these characters the more I work with them, they come to life for me, they take on individual characteristics and they become real people. I think bank robbers wake up in the morning and wonder: "What am I going to wear today when I rob that bank? What am I going to have for breakfast?" That's what I think about. And I picture most of my characters as children. I see them as they were at a certain age. Teddy Magyk in *Glitz* was kind of a loner and never got along with anybody. Kids picked on him. Probably picked his nose and ate it and everybody said, "Oh God, Teddy, Jesus!" He was just a weird kid. And as they grow up, they're still children. Some are childish and some are childlike.

You open *Glitz* with a memorable first line: "The night Vincent was shot he saw it coming . . . "
That might be my favorite opening. You want somebody to read your book? Hook 'em right away. I don't like books that open with the weather; with the wind blowing and the leaves falling, mood stuff like that.

You don't like: "It was a dark and stormy night . . . "?
Right. Yeah. I like to start with people. I've been thinking for the last week or so how to open the next book and I picked up *Fat City* just to see what it sounded like now. *"He lived in the Hotel Coma . . ."* I thought, yeah, that's the sound I want. What's Leonard Gardner doing since *Fat City?* I've often wondered about that.

He's done some journalism lately. Something you don't do very much of, do you?

I admire writers who can write in any area—journalism, poetry, prose—because I'm very limited in what I can write. I'm often asked to write something for the *New York Times Sunday Magazine*, for *Vanity Fair*, and I turn it down for two reasons. One, it's work, and I don't need the work anymore. And two, I'm not that good at it. The writing would be mediocre at best.

So you don't feel as diversified as someone like Norman Mailer?
Norman Mailer can write anything. When I met Mailer he said he wanted to do the movie of *La Brava*, but he said, "I would take your script and rewrite it." I said, "Of course you'd do that, that's the first thing anybody would do." Then I asked him, "You've made movies, how do you know where to put the camera?" He said, "You ask the cameraman."

Who are the writers you like to read, and who are the ones who influenced you?
Of crime writers that I like I start off with Pete Dexter, but nobody'd call him a crime writer. Then Ed McBain, Ross Thomas, Tony Hillerman, Robert Parker. William Goldman, John D. MacDonald. [James M.] Cain influenced me some. When I was very young I liked Sherlock Holmes a lot; Conan Doyle. Graham Greene is one of my favorite authors. Don DeLillo's *Libra* was a beauty. I've been reading your Huston book for the last three weeks.

What about John Updike?
I like him, but I'm more comfortable with someone like Bobbie Ann Mason, Raymond Carver, Charles Willeford. I felt that Willeford and I had pretty much the same attitude in the way we write. Before he died I tried to get him to loosen up more. He'd submit a book like *Kiss Your Ass Goodbye* and the publisher says, You've got to change the title. And he says, No, I won't do it. And walks off. Years pass before someone finally publishes the book. And it wasn't that good.

Ever read Agatha Christie?

Agatha Christie to me is on a par with Zane Grey as a western writer.
Kind of archaic.

How about Thomas Harris's serial killer novels?
The Silence of the Lambs I couldn't put down. I skipped dinner on a
book tour to go back to the hotel and read it. That doesn't happen
very often. The book that *really* grabbed me was Ira Levin's *Rosemary's
Baby*. Not knowing what it was about, I couldn't believe it. At writer's
conferences I say, Just break down and outline *Rosemary's Baby* and
that's how you write a book.

**Your opinion of two other best-selling writers: Scott Turow and
Tom Clancy?**
Turow's an old-fashioned writer. His books sound like they were written in the fifties. With Clancy, the *Times* asked me to review one of his
and I said, "I can barely change a lightbulb and you want me to review this high-tech book?" I always ask how many pages is this, first.
If it's over 300 I know I'm not going to read it.

Are you fond of James Ellroy?
Ellroy has got more energy in his writing probably than anybody going today. It's not the kind of fiction I normally read. I blurbed his
Black Dahlia and said that there should be a warning on the book,
that this should not be read aloud or you're liable to shatter your
wine glasses.

Who's the best pure writer of sentences today?
Oh boy. Calvin Trillin's funny; he writes pure prose. I like Walker
Percy a lot, too. And Jim Harrison.

**Wasn't it George Higgins's *The Friends of Eddie Coyle* that affected
your own work?**
Yeah. I think it's the best crime book there is, though he doesn't call
his books crime books. It loosened me up. I decided to be freer with
the language, use more obscenities, get into scenes quicker without

setting the scene. I noticed how he opened scenes with people talking before you knew where you were or even before you knew *who* they are. I liked the way that worked. That happens all the time in movies, that you open the scene after the beginning and you get out before it ends. You've got a little suspense before the cut.

Will you continue to turn your novels into scripts?
I'm definitely not going to adapt any more of mine. It's too much work, you're dealing with too many people who haven't left Beverly Hills in twenty years, telling you how the people in the world talk. If I wasn't making money now it wouldn't be work to me. Now screenwriting is just work. You write a book, you write whatever you want.

Why is the punctuation in scripts always so bad?
Because they don't pay attention in English courses. They're not writers, they're screenwriters. They're not writing. What's writing in a screenplay, outside of the dialogue? I don't think of it as writing.

What are your own favorite books?
Maybe *La Brava,* since enough people have told me that they like that one. But I like *Freaky Deaky,* too. I like 'em all. There seems to be a feeling that *Bandits* is the weakest, and I don't know why.

Where do you place *Rum Punch*?
I had a very good time with *Rum Punch* right from its opening, a white supremacy rally in Palm Beach, the neo-Nazis and the Klansmen marching down Worth Avenue, which I happened to have on videotape. Then I worked it into the plot.

It's actually a very skillfully written, complex novel. How would you describe it in a few sentences?
You think it was complex? I tried to intercut between the good guys and the bad guys, but I always do that. That's the advantage of writing from so many points of view—you can cut away to something else. That way you've always got something fresh going on. I don't begin

with a theme or an idea—none of my books can you describe in a sentence or two.

Try.

There's this forty-two-year-old flight attendant who is picked up for bringing money into the U.S. She's working for a guy who sells machine guns in the Caribbean. It looks like she might go away but she meets a bail bondsman who falls in love with her and helps her out. I don't know. You can't describe it.

What's the title mean?

It's a title title. It sounds like a good title. Then you find a place for it in the book. It's that kind of a title. Like *Pronto*. My wife Joan and I were in Italy and we were trying to think of a title, as I was getting a vague idea of what this book might be about. When we got back home I called my publisher in Milan and she answered the phone and said, "Pronto." And I said, "That's it!" She said, "What?" I said, "That's the title." And she didn't think much of it, naturally. But Delacorte thought it was great. You can look at it either way—it has an Italian sound, and two-thirds of the book is set in Italy, in Rapallo, where Ezra Pound lived for twenty years. Or you can think of it as *pronto,* right now, the Spanish meaning.

Joan's death in January, 1993, came as a shock to you, didn't it?

I couldn't believe it. We both thought that we were going to last forever. Her mother died at ninety-five, mine at ninety-four. My dad was fifty-six, but God, I'm way passed him now. I decided I must take after my mother. Joan was sixty-four. In the late fall of '92 she was getting tired when we played tennis. Then she had trouble breathing. By December she was having chest X rays, which didn't show anything. Before Christmas she went to the hospital and they diagnosed it as lung cancer. She had cancer in her lymph nodes and chest cavity. Chemotherapy made her worse. In early January she went back to the hospital, taking oxygen all the time, and died January 13. It was really sad. She would say to me, "If I go first, you're going to get married again to a younger woman." I'd say, "Never."

Seems she knew you better than you knew yourself.
So much has happened to me since Joan. I just coasted along, I certainly didn't have any plans. I didn't think I'd ever get married again, although I certainly was interested in seeing women, taking them out, although I hadn't "dated" in forty years. But when I met Christine, it just happened so fast. She's a master gardener; she ran a crew that came here to take care of the flower beds and stuff. So she would come once a week starting at the end of April. I started talking to her outside about movies and books. After a couple of months I asked her if she wanted to come in after work for a glass of wine. She's in her mid-forties, twenty-three years younger than I am. She's contemporary with a couple of my kids. She was married twice, one daughter, twenty-two. Then the second time we went out for dinner, not an official date. Then June 19th we had our first official date—we had dinner out and then went back to her apartment to look at a cassette of a picture that was coming out that Dick Berg, a producer, wanted me to see to check out the director, who he was considering for *Pronto*. We saw the movie and it was dumb, *The Wrong Man*, with Roseanne Arquette and John Lithgow. We were laughing at it, having a good time, and I've seen her every day since.

We got married August 19th, because my book tour was coming up that would take me to London, and I wanted her to go with me. So we decided to get married, and that was it. After that tour we went to Australia and New Zealand for some literary festivals. Then I began another book and we started to redecorate the house, put a new roof on because it had been leaking right over me for the last five years. So we're having a great time. It's fun. I think I need to be married.

How often do you and Christine go to the movies?
We go in spurts, we'll go see three movies, like *Titanic, Wag the Dog, Boogie Nights,* then we won't go for a few weeks. We'll get videos of the

ones we missed. I like the movies. I was talking to my publisher, who said, "You liked *Titanic*? What about that love story?" I said, "It worked. It worked. I wanted them to get together. So what if it's been done a thousand times?"

My favorite movie of the last few years is *Last of the Mohicans*. I love that movie. Daniel Day-Lewis and Madeline Stowe. It's a terrific love story. They never go to bed, but the way they look at each other, and touch each other. And the action, geez. With a good fall guy. Just a wonderful story.

A lot of your readers probably think you're married to your work, since you're so prolific. Do you think your readership is still growing?
I sell 150,000 hardcover and a million-one or -two in paperback, that's about it. I probably reached my peak unless I come up with a real good idea, a story that is just so smashing that everyone will have to read it. Something that hasn't been done. But I'm the most happy right now than I've ever been. I haven't compromised much. I've stayed with what I wanted to do. And I try to make each book better, though they don't always get better.

So, given the choice, there's no one else you'd rather be?
For forty-eight hours I would like to have been Doctor Julius Irving. God, he had a lot of color. And he's a good-looking guy, dresses well. Or a real screaming rock star.

Like Mick Jagger? Bruce Springsteen?
Oh no, more like Axl Rose from Guns 'n Roses.

NORMAN MAILER

Stupidity Brings Out Violence in Me

WHAT CAN ONE SAY ABOUT NORMAN MAILER THAT HE hasn't already said about himself? I grew up on Mailer. His great journalism in *Esquire;* his incredible gift of metaphor; his sure-handedness when it comes to writing about taboos, superstitions, and excrement; his knuckleheaded foray into the brave new world of women's lib; and his supreme self-confidence, focusing so superbly on himself in a book he audaciously and precisely titled *Advertisements for Myself* and later in *Pieces and Pontifications*. And, of course, his fiction—which until recently (and even still . . .) he always believed would earn him a Nobel Prize—those purely Mailer novels beginning with *The Naked and the Dead* when he was just twenty-five, then *Barbary Shore, The Deer Park, An American Dream, Why Are We in Vietnam?, The Executioner's Song* (history as novel), *Ancient Evenings, Tough Guys Don't Dance, Harlot's Ghost, The Gospel According to the Son*.

I had prepared many more questions than I had time to ask when we met in 1983, and he insisted that a portion of our talk concentrate on the novel he then had wanted to promote, *Ancient Evenings*. That wasn't a problem for me, I enjoyed that long, daring novel, and admired how he managed to get so many Maileresque themes into the narrative.

The Brooklyn-born, Harvard-educated National Book Award and Pulitzer Prize–winning larger-than-life father of eight and cofounder of the *Village Voice* is currently living in Province Town, Maine, with his sixth wife, Norris. At seventy-eight, he has survived five previous marriages, two hip replacements, public feuds with Gore Vidal, William Styron, and leaders of the Women's Movement, two New York mayoral campaigns, and a Mike Tyson–like battle with Rip Torn, biting open a piece of the actor's ear during the making of Mailer's movie *Maidstone,* which he wrote and directed. He's been at the forefront of antiwar demonstrations, he's covered such icons as John F. Kennedy, Marilyn Monroe, Pablo Picasso, Muhammad Ali, and Madonna, has poked his nose into the mysterious lives of Lee Harvey Oswald and Jesus Christ, and spent seventeen days under observation in Bellevue for stabbing his second wife at a party.

Mailer has been described as both a radical and a puritan; as pugnacious and gentle; as antiestablishment and part of the establishment. His early success led to his alienation, which he has called a twentieth-century condition. He believed from the very start that a writer of the largest dimension can alter the nerves and marrow of a nation, and he was determined to be that kind of writer. He's also called himself one of the most wicked spirits in American life. As far back as 1954, he claimed that marijuana was more important to him than any love affair he ever had. He called drugs a "spiritual form of gambling," experimented with LSD and said he tasted the essence of his own death, and wrote that a man must drink until he locates the truth. As for sex, he believes that masturbation cripples and leads to insanity, considers fellatio a weakness, raises the orgasm to the ultimate act of self-realization, defines great sex as that which makes you more religious, and gives the nod to William Burroughs for changing the course of American literature with one sentence: "I see God in my asshole in the flashbulb of orgasm." Civilization will enter Hell, he's suggested, when no more good novels are written.

At his bar mitzvah he said he hoped to follow in the footsteps of great Jews like Moses Maimonides and Karl Marx. There are those among us who would say, sixty-five years later, that he has succeeded.

**Whenever there's a brief introduction about you, what's usually
included is that you ran for mayor of New York twice, stabbed
your wife, and won two Pulitzer Prizes.**

That's because there was a worm of a publisher with a hard-on who
put out an ad in the *New York Times* listing my achievements and stuck
wife stabber in the middle of 'em. Since then it's been open season.

How would you prefer to be introduced?

The inimitable Norman Mailer [*chuckles*].

**You've said that you don't consider yourself moral at all, but as a
man who lives in an embattled relationship to morality. What do
you mean by that?**

Morality is always on my mind. I'm always saying to myself: Am I doing the right thing or the wrong thing? I may often decide on the latter and still go ahead and do it. But there are people who are free of
morality, they just never question their acts—they're animals.

Are you usually aware when you're doing wrong?

No. Wrong is often a matter of context. As that great remarker Sherwood Anderson said, "There is the truth of passion, the truth of virginity, the truth of violence, the truth of gentleness . . ." He goes on
to list all the truths there are. There's a moment in one's life when
it's right to be one thing or another. But you have to get into the nature of authenticity, which is a complex philosophical matter.
There's no way to go near these questions without diving deep into
philosophy.

**Another thing you've said is that you're so rarely true to your own
code that it's hard to maintain self-respect. What is that code?**

My code years ago used to be, never take any crap from anyone. My
god, I'd get into eighty fights a day if I were to take no crap at all. So
you finally decide that there are probably worse things in the world
than taking a little unintentional bullshit from time to time. If it
comes your way without truly ill intention, then ignore it. That's just
one aspect of the code. I used to have much more of a macho code

than I do now. I would take every dare that came my way. But you get to the point where finally, every time you've made a moral decision—that you mustn't stand up when "The Star-Spangled Banner" is being played because we're at war in Vietnam and it's an immoral war—you recognize after a while that you're not going to go to any public place where there's a chance they'll play "The Star-Spangled Banner" because it takes too much out of you sitting down when 3,000 people are standing up. So it's a terribly demanding code. It doesn't mean you think the code is wrong, you just decide the code is more of a man than you are.

When you say it's hard to maintain your self-respect, do you find that you often don't respect yourself because of that?
Most of us have an ongoing professional life where we're not looking to walk around with a vast amount of self-respect; I just want to walk around with enough so I'm not truly depressed. Once you get too down on yourself it's hard to do anything, it's hard to get out of it, and there's a pit in depression. So you try to keep enough self-respect so you're viable.

Have you fulfilled your own idea of yourself?
Half. That half's enough to keep you going.

José Torres said that you have the kind of immense ego of a fighter, that you don't like people to be too comfortable when you're around. Why?
I love to keep complacent people off balance. I can't bear their complacency. Stupidity brings out violence in me, because I consider stupidity a choice. There's a great difference between people who are stupid and people who are dumb. People who are dumb have been injured and there's something soft and tender about their brain. If it's permanent, it's touching, it's pathetic. People who are stupid made one wise decision in their lives, because if you're stupid and you remain stupid, people have to come to you, have to deal with you, you're the center of a great many energy transactions that you haven't

earned. If you can take the abuse, it's a way of life. But it's a way of life that poisons everything around you. So stupid people bring out my most unpleasant reactions and emotions. I will needle stupid people to the best of my ability.

Are there a lot of stupid writers?

Most writers are stupid at their level. You can be one of the world's greatest writers and still be stupid in that you're not as good as you want to be. I'm sure Dostoevsky thought himself stupid because he wasn't able to write the Life of the Great Sinner. And that probably was an act of cowardice.

Do you, then, like to needle writers?

Less than I used to, because when I was younger it was a great deal of fun giving them a hard time. But I've recognized over the years that we may be an endangered species, so I'm a little gentler with other writers now.

How old were you when you started writing?

Seven or eight. Two short stories. Then I wrote a really short novel about going to the moon, or Mars, when I was eleven. I had a genial, mad scientist on this spaceship called Dr. Hoor. It was a takeoff on Buck Rogers, Dr. Huer. I didn't write again until I got to Harvard.

Did your mother save those early writings?

Yeah, yeah. It's a wonder my mother didn't save my fingernails.

What kind of woman is your mother? There are those who say that the foundation of your ego is really based upon your mother. Someone made a comment that of all your wives, the real Mrs. Mailer is your mother.

The person who made that comment is an ex-wife, and she was looking to make a rotten remark. No, I never wanted to be married to my mother. She's fine as a mother, but I wouldn't have wanted her as a wife because she's a very opinionated woman. Strong minded and narrow minded. We've had many arguments over the years. I got one thing from her that not everybody gets from their mothers: I had an undivided, uncritical loyalty. It kept on, looking back on it, to almost comical proportions. To this day, if I were to shoot up some housing development with a tommy gun and slaughter twenty people and they came to my mother with this news, she would say: "What could they have possibly done to Norman to make him act that way?" In that sense there was this unquestioning loyalty, and it does give you an ego source. It's a mother-fed ego, which produces all kinds of problems when you get out in the world and start knocking around. Half the Jewish men on earth suffer and are benefited by that kind of ego that they get from their mothers.

And what did you get from your father?
He was a classy gent and a bit of a gambler. He was a dapper fellow with marvelous manners. He had trouble with jobs because he was a dreamer. He was a bit, not much, of a writer. When he'd write me a letter he'd spend eight pages of a twelve-page letter telling me about his difficulty in writing to his son who was a writer. That sort of thing. Terribly courtly man. Exact opposite of my mother.

You didn't enjoy high school and felt deprived for thirty years afterwards. Why was high school so bad for you?
High school's that place, that country, where you get laid for the first time; you have marvelous memories and you go around with a girl, you go to the prom, dance with her. I went to a boy's high school, there were no girls there. I was a year-and-a-half ahead of my class, as far as age went. I graduated when I was sixteen-and-a-half. So I didn't have a high school life and I think it is a form of deprivation. If I'd had a happier high school life I might not have been a writer, so you take what you get.

Were you competitive as a teenager?
Moderately competitive, not highly. I wasn't that good in anything. I

never sunk to Marty's level—us dogs must stick together—but I was always looking for some girl to say, "You're fantastic, you're wonderful, you're marvelous." They never did.

When did girls start telling you that?
Not until I was in college and writing. And it wasn't that dramatic. Probably after *The Naked and the Dead* came out is when it started.

You achieved huge success at twenty-five with that novel. Did you mishandle it?
Yeah, but I don't brood on it. There's no way in the world I ever could have handled it well. If you were to be made manager of a big league baseball team tomorrow, you wouldn't expect to do that well for a while, would you? It would be almost impossible, you'd have to make huge errors. I went from obscurity into being a well-known author overnight. I wasn't even an average twenty-five-year-old when it happened.

In describing how you came to know the officers you wrote about in *The Naked and the Dead*, you said you generally operate on hate, which is the best aid to analysis. That still hold?
We can get into that, but it's tricky. If you feel the kind of hate that just burns a red haze in front of your eyes, you'll do anything. If you've got a quiet anger—that is, without getting pious or pompous, a righteous anger—you feel that something is unjust in the scheme of things, that can fuel a lot of very good writing. In fact, most good writing is done with a critical edge. There are many more good critics around than there are good fiction writers. The reason is that a critic can get into something he doesn't like and what someone else is doing, and he can do it with a firm sense of self-righteousness. Which is why critics are keeping literary standards alive. And they can write well, so anger definitely is a tool, it's that grindstone that just sharpens the cutting edge of your instrument. But too much anger just wipes you out. Since you can't really control it, to keep

that nice balance, a lot of it is luck. When you get in a period of your life where you're full of energy and you've got an anger that's usable, then you can write well. I was very angry at the army when I got out. And that anger was immensely useful for writing *The Naked and the Dead,* because it wasn't just a crazy anger. It was a true anger. The book is true and was kind of funny as a result. It had its separation from what was going on. I also had the good literary instinct to pick on officers even though I hated officers. There couldn't have been a simpler enlisted man than I was. I just hated all officers when I was in the army. But by the time I got out I had enough sense to pick an officer who was halfway sympathetic, and that kept the book from being a parody. You can never do good work in writing if the hate takes over, it's gotta be balanced by irony, at least. Or detachment.

After that initial success, did you feel that the critics were going to be out to get you for the next few books, or do you feel the criticism of those books were deserved?

I've always been an optimist. I had no idea that they were waiting for the second book. I used to joke about it, "Well, I guess the reviews won't be as good as *The Naked and the Dead,*" shifting uncomfortably as I just did. It gave me a huge reputation I didn't know what to do with. It was only three years later when I began to realize what it is to lose your reputation—not to be taken seriously. I began to sense that people were saying, "Poor Norman, he wrote one book, *The Naked and the Dead,* and he'll never write another like it." Then my true anger began to come out.

Did that anger stay with you throughout your next novel, *The Deer Park,* or did it last until your next big success, which was with nonfiction?

That anger stayed with me for many years. It was all uphill after the first book. I wrote *The Deer Park,* which was a damn good book, one of my two or three best novels, and that got slaughtered. There were

eighteen major reviews at that time, seven were favorable, eleven unfa-
vorable—that's enough so you don't forget.

Did all that early criticism propel you to write more and more?
I wasn't prolific in those years. My powers to be prolific are in direct
response to needing money. Balzac was immensely prolific. Zola was.
Dickens. They earned their living. It helps if you have to earn your living from your pen; you discover that you can push yourself. It's analogous to what athletes do very often, where they'll go through
hideous procedures, they'll eat steroids in order to get more strength
in their muscles; they're into all sorts of things that are, ultimately,
damaging, not only to their bodies but to their souls. But they'll do it
in order to set records, because they've gotten into a set where they
truly want to break that old record, whether it's theirs or someone
else's. We do the same thing as writers. You can force yourself to write
much more than you want to write. And yet the writing will not necessarily deteriorate. People think you're going to end up a bad writer
if you do that. You won't end up a bad writer, you may end up with a
bad liver, or with a shortened life, but you go for transcendence too.
Sometimes working much harder than one wants to work can liberate energy. It doesn't always defeat it.

Many critics consider you a better nonfiction than fiction writer.
They could be right, they could be wrong. I couldn't care less. I think
that I'm good at fiction, but there's no reason they have to share my
opinion. The only important piece of nonfiction that I wrote was *The
Armies of the Night*. *Miami and the Siege of Chicago* is a good piece of re-
portage. *Of a Fire on the Moon* is a very good book. *Marilyn* is a good biography, but tainted to a degree. Where's all the great nonfiction?
Muhammad Ali is interesting. The novels are much better. The critics
very often have these opinions, but they don't stop and make a count.
You need a body count on books.

Which of your books do you think you'll be remembered for?

I can go through them in order. *The Naked and the Dead, The Deer Park, An American Dream, The Armies of the Night, Marilyn, Why Are We in Vietnam?, The Executioner's Song,* and *Ancient Evenings.* Those will probably be the ones.

Is it true you need to make $350,000 a year just to break even?
That's right, yes. With inflation the figure's gone from $200,000 to $350,000 over the last ten years.

Do you consider yourself a rich man?
No, I'm certainly not. I live on a reasonable scale. I own my own apartment and a car, but that's all. I don't have houses. Money's always a problem, we really live from month to month.

In the past, you looked forward to writing about the inner states of men like Hitler and Napoleon, Lenin and Castro. Yet you wound up with Marilyn Monroe, Muhammad Ali, Gary Gilmore. What happened along the way?
How about Ramses II? He's kind of the equal of Alexander, Hitler, and Napoleon. He's a man of immense proportions who saw himself as a god. I could still write about Napoleon if I were willing to do the research. It doesn't appeal to me. As you get older you realize that to do truly good work on any given subject you've got to put in the hours, the years. The amount of research it would take to do something good about Napoleon gives me pause. But the psychology of Napoleon doesn't. I feel I understand him to a degree. Now, you can be wrong about it. I thought I understood Gary Gilmore very well, that's why I began that book. But as I began to do the research I came to the conclusion I didn't understand him at all. So, you can start with the premise that you're on top of it and discover you're not.

In the end, did you feel you understood Gilmore?
He was a very complex man to me. On the one hand, he was virtually a mediocrity and disappointing. His mind was not that remarkable, he had a lot of ordinary ideas and small-minded prejudices. But he

was at least as complex as I was, and that was curious and humbling. The thought of people being so simple that you can comprehend them and deal with them is depressing. If all of us are complex, it will be that much harder for machines to take us over.

You believe that in Hemingway's time there were great writers like Faulkner, Steinbeck, Wolfe, Fitzgerald, and, of course, Hemingway. But that's not true today. Why not?

We're getting to questions that are too large to answer. It's probably because of the prevailing currents of the age. Hemingway and Faulkner between them captured profound elements in the American soul. At that time, reading was the most profound way to deepen your knowledge of existence. So writers were respected more. They were more important. We're moving from writing into electronic circuitry, television, computers. Print, as such, is going to disappear. It's a long way from going away, but there is a point where the act of reading a book may become a rare luxury, equal to eating Russian caviar. People now read off word processors on screens, where not only are the letters abominable but the image is full of flickering. If you could normally read a hundred pages without stopping, will you be able to read ten or fifteen under those conditions? It's as if the very sensuous qualities of reading are being taken away from us. In other words, reading's become an effort, equal to, say, having a pair of uncomfortable plastic earphones on, the sort they give you in an airplane, where it hurts your ears and your head and the sound's not very good. So you've got to work for the movie that you're seeing.

Of the writers in your time, who are the most important?

Borges and Márquez. After that, take your pick, there are about forty of us. I say forty because I don't know enough about foreign writers. I'm thinking ten American writers and I'm concealing my ignorance by hiding behind thirty writers from other countries.

In the early stages of your career you were obsessed with being the number one writer in America. Have you rethought that?

You could have writers who are first in the people's mind, but I don't know if that has any literary value. If you had an election tomorrow there would probably be five of us who would be in contention, and you could have a runoff. The results wouldn't matter because each of us would walk away thinking, "I was the best." I don't think it's important.

Is it important for you, though? To drive yourself?
So long as there's no election, I don't give a damn. It's not important anymore. If there was an election and somebody else won, I'd be annoyed.

How envious have you been of other writers?
By now I don't think I'm envious at all. When I was younger I would fight feelings of envy at times. But I've never felt envious so much about writers as I have about freedom. Since I've been married all my life, I've always envied the great freedom that certain men friends of mine would have.

But each time you've divorced you've gotten married again.
That's right. Once a philosopher, twice a pervert.

You've admitted envy for Truman Capote's ability to get invited to the right parties.
That was twenty years ago, when I wanted to get invited to those parties, because I could have written about them. Those parties had a wonderful feeling they don't possess now. When you're young is the time you should go to parties like that. Truman went to those parties at the right time.

What's your opinion of Capote?
Very, very talented man. I was misquoted in a magazine story that bothered me a great deal, had me saying that he was through.

That his life was wrecked.

I felt very bad about it, because what happened is the reporter led me down the garden path. She said, "Wouldn't you say that Truman is through?" And I said, "Off the record, I'll tell you that even if I thought he was through I would never say it, because I don't have the right to sit in judgment on another writer and decide they're through. People said I was through when I wasn't. I used to laugh inside. But they had no right to say it about me, and I have no right to say it about anyone else." She said, "But what do you *really* think?" I said, "If you push me I'll say that I don't think he's through." Well, she was reading all these qualifications, and in her mind she decided the bottom line was that he was through, so she put the words in my mouth. I never said it. No, I don't think he's through, I think he's not well and is going through a very tough time. We never know when we're going to get out of our troubles. He may not, but he might. The bits of *Answered Prayers* that he's published have been interesting.

Think he'll ever finish it?
I don't know how much of it he's done. And I don't know what kind of shape he's in.

What do you think of James A. Michener's remark that if Capote ever finishes it, *Answered Prayers* will be the book most remembered fifty years from now?
It's a remark. But authors' remarks are never terribly interesting. We're all self-serving in our subtle ways. As are politicians. Authors' theories are the same as politicians' theories. Writers advance those theories which are best for their own latest work.

Let me give you Capote's remark about your *Ancient Evenings*, spoken before it was published. He said it couldn't possibly be a good book, because you're only good at writing about what you know, and you didn't know anything about ancient Egypt, any more then you knew about Gary Gilmore.
Truman's very upset about *The Executioner's Song*. He feels that I should have made a pilgrimage and gotten down on my knees and

said, "Oh great Cardinal Capote, do I have your blessing? May I proceed to write a book about a killer?" And I didn't. He went around saying that I never gave any credit to his *In Cold Blood*. Well, I just thought that book was so famous that you didn't have to give credit to it. I reread *In Cold Blood* after I finished *The Executioner's Song* and it's a very good novel, as much of a novel as *The Executioner's Song*. Maybe more. It's very nicely written and it may end up being a classic because it is remarkable. But I don't know what he's talking about, it just struck me as a dumb remark. Truman is canny as hell but he's not the brightest guy in the world.

You and Truman Capote share a dislike for Gore Vidal. Why?
I don't want to get into it. We had a feud that went on for a few years and I don't care whether we ever make friends again.

Would you agree with Vidal that we live in a time where the personality of the writer is everything and what he writes is nothing?
No. There's a tendency in that direction but it's a vastly overexaggerated remark.

Vidal has called you a messiah without hope of Paradise and with no precise mission. How does that strike you?
As twelve years old.

You've come to blows with Vidal, haven't you?
No. I knocked a heavy cocktail glass out of his hand and that was the end of the fight.

Didn't you head-butt him?
That's not a fight, that's just head-butting.

You've butted heads with Hemingway's son, Gregory. Was that your way of connecting with his old man?
I head-butt with a lot of people. People have the wrong idea about it.

It isn't that you head-butt and somebody drops. For me, it's a touch of affection. You just butt heads once lightly.

Is it always lightly?
No, not always. It wasn't lightly with Vidal that time. But it's always fair for one writer to butt another in the head. Writers have hard heads. The hardest heads you'll ever encounter will be a writer's head. It's just like an erect phallus. All there.

During the making of your film *Maidstone*, you punched out a young actor and bit open Rip Torn's ear. Are you aware of what you're doing at such times?
No, it's just all fanciful, like a dream. [*Laughs*]

Were you trying to put yourself in a situation where Rip Torn might kill you on camera? Were you in that kind of frame of mind?
We don't have enough time to talk about the making of *Maidstone*. A comparatively complex set of notions went into it.

Then let me ask you, why are violent men always religious?
I don't know if they're always religious, but they tend to be. Violence is one of the existential states. So very often in a violent act you don't know how it's going to turn out. It's different from the way that it seems in the movies or in books. It's indefinable. Anyone who's been in an automobile accident knows how the moments before the accident have some exceptional time changes. I once got hit by a car many years ago and it was an extraordinary experience. I bounced off a couple of rocks and ended up wrapped around a tree, but it all took place very slowly.

Were you knocked unconscious?
No, but it was odd. It was a sports car, and it just bruised my hip. But it's just so different from the normal and the given that it leaves you with an echo that has a touch of the cosmos in it.

For decades you've been pushing violence as existential, hip, and heroic. Is the criminal, in your mind, the true artist?
No, most criminals are not very interesting guys.

You once told Mike Wallace that violence and creativity have a twinlike relation. Do you still believe that?
I think it's still true. That's part of the problem: if you cut all the violence out of society, you also cut out all the creativity. In fact, that's just what we're doing now: working for a law-and-order society that will not have any violence in the streets. At the same time, things are getting less and less creative. I've never taken myself so seriously as to speak of Mailer's Law of this or that, but I finally have one. It's Mailer's Law of Architectural Precedence in American Universities. Go to any university in the country and you have no problem determining the order in which the buildings were erected on that campus. The more atrocious the architecture, the newer the building. If the building next to you is less atrocious than the one you're in, it was built before. The oldest building on the campus is invariably the nicest. That says something about creativity going out of life. It also says something about violence going out of life, because there's a tendency in American life to become more and more safe.

Do you think American life is safer now than in the past?
No, of course not. Because it can't be done. It's a vain, false enterprise. A pious enterprise. We're doing it as a cover, which politicians talk about all the time, in their efforts to legislate it. Concomitant with the growth of technology there's a sort of spiritual software that accompanies technology, and that is control over our lives. You push a button delicately here and a button delicately there to adjust the situation. Those people detest violence because they keep breaking up the patterns, and the control. More than half the people in this country opt completely for control of their lives. What they don't control is their death, and that drives 'em right up the wall. One big reason why I'm so obsessed with Egypt and decided to write *Ancient Evenings* is precisely that I wanted to write about a culture that gave great pref-

ace to death, that lived for it, prepared for it, dwelt within it, in which virtually all of one's acts in one's life were steered toward one's death. It seemed to me that this is much more profound than what we have now. That's why people have such extraordinary reactions to *Ancient Evenings,* they love it or they detest it. Because people, without exception, who hate it are people who love a lot of control and high tech in their lives and don't like to talk or think about death.

In *Ancient Evenings* you've written that none fear death more than the most clever of the scribes. Being the most clever of scribes, do you fear death?
I'm not the most clever of the scribes at all. I don't consider myself clever. I consider myself rather dumb, simpleminded, when it comes to cleverness.

In other words, you don't fear death?
No, not particularly.

Have you ever envisioned your own death?
No, I don't think about it a great deal, because the one thing I'm sure of is that it won't be what I'm expecting. I'm not much on Hindu philosophy, but there's one notion from the Hindus I do like a great deal: never worry about something you can't effect.

Do you still reflect much on the horror of modern life?
We're in danger of a nuclear war until we get to a point where the sustenance of existence is almost entirely leeched out. About the time that we live with too many people on earth, all living in high-rise buildings, all utterly colorless, dull, and oppressive, and every building put up is as ugly as the one before, and when we drive we breathe nothing but polluted fumes on superhighways and there's smog everywhere, and all the palm trees are as wilted as they are in Mexico City, and the rivers are filthy, and everything is flat and dull, and sex is merely an extension of herpes, et cetera, et cetera, and people are dying of AIDS all over the place—at that point, the nuclear bomb is

going to seem welcome to people. Because at least it'll be their last shot at transcendence. We'll all go up together in that great white light. And at that point, we're in danger.

Is this your vision of the future?
No, it's a possible vision of the future. I don't think it's that automatic. If it were, why would I bother to talk about these matters?

You've predicted an extraordinary holocaust where we may all die off in a mysterious fashion.
I meant that metaphorically. One doesn't want to be prophetic about these matters at all. We have intimations of such horror with AIDS, for instance, where people are dying because their immunological faculties are atrophying or not functioning.

You've used the metaphor of cancer to describe our nation. Are we a cancerous nation?
Things are going to have to happen. There are going to have to be positive ideas emerging. I can offer you a simple few. One of my most fundamental beliefs is that the government has the right to tax people, but we have a right to say what we're taxed on. I'd like to see all sorts of referendums. I'd love to lead the crusade to tax the hell out of plastic. It would make it too expensive for them to make that crap anymore. So it would tend to disappear. Where plastic was indispensable it would still remain, because people would just pay the tax on it. If the only decent fishing rods or skis would be made out of plastic, we can pay a little more.

Another thing I'd absolutely be for is, we're just surrounded with meretriciousness and mendacity in every aspect of our immediate life. So I'd opt for taking away the tax deduction from advertising and let those businesses that need to advertise pay for the privilege, because what they're selling is not their product but a pile of horseshit. They're attaching values that have nothing to do with the product. It's attached to the entertainment that they give you on TV, which is mediocre entertainment at best. So why should that go into the price of a product? Why do we need to have the three major automobile manufacturers all advertising like crazy when we know they're all equally mediocre? Does it really matter? Is there any American who doesn't know that Ford, Chrysler, and General Motors products are all on the same level every year? That finally you're gonna pick it for the paint job? Why do you have to have a helicopter drop a car on top of a mountain peak? The millions that are spent on that, for what? To increase the price of the product? So, take away the tax deductions in advertising. You say that'll put a lot of people out of work? Well, great. They'll have to scuffle.

Are these among the stupid people?
I wouldn't say the media people are the stupid people, they're the clever people. It'll be hard times for a few of the clever people.

Regarding yourself, you said you may be one of the most wicked spirits in American life today. Are you?
I was preening. That day I had feathers and I was fluffin' 'em.

Oriana Fallaci wrote that the taint of insanity has been following you for years. Is there any truth in that?
No, but that's Oriana Fallaci, making a story.

In 1942, you worked for a while in a state mental institution in Boston. Some years later, after you stabbed your second wife, you wound up in a mental institution in Bellevue for a while. Did you feel in any way that you came full circle from that experience?
No. I mean, I thought of it. One could not think of the fact that one worked in a mental hospital earlier on the other side, as an attendant. That may have been of some help for me to get out of that place after seventeen days.

Because?

When I worked as an attendant, I learned one thing: don't make the guards pay attention to you. The less attention the guards pay to you, the better your chances of getting out are.

Were you crazy at that time?
Let's say I was highly strung and let it go at that.

I don't think you're going to answer me, but why did you stab your wife?
You made your try. Why do you want to get into something that personal?

It's a subject that you really haven't discussed, except in a poem you wrote, where you said, "So long as you use the knife . . . "
A knife.

". . . a knife, there's some love left."
The poem was written after the fact.

I know it was.
It's not a lively topic of conversation for me.

The doctor who treated your wife, Adele, said you were having an acute paranoid breakdown with delusional thinking, and that you were both homicidal and suicidal.
Well, since I didn't kill anybody after that and I didn't commit suicide or have a mental breakdown, my guess is that he wasn't too accurate.

But you later wrote that had you not done that act you might have been dead in a few years yourself.
Yes.

Have you ever contemplated suicide?
No, I never have.

When a movie is made of your life, who would you like to play you?
Larry Grobel.

You're getting angry at me now.
No. Edgy.

Okay. You blamed early success as the reason for the breakup of your first marriage . . .
I'm not getting angry, I'm getting offended. You want to discuss my life. I'm not going to give away my life. My life is my material. I would give you my life no more than I would give you my mate. That belongs to me, not to an interviewer.

Let's stay then with your work. What you do is often based on your need for money. The need for money is because you have to support a number of ex-wives. Germaine Greer called you an alimony slave.
I wonder how Germaine Greer came up with that? That was one of her bright days, huh?

Have your marriages influenced your career?
Of course they have. A marriage is a culture.

You've said that there isn't a man alive who doesn't have a profound animosity for women.
I also don't think there's a woman alive who doesn't have a profound animosity for men. But that's half of it. I would continue that remark by saying that there's not a man alive who doesn't have a profound need and love for women. That's part of the human condition. One of my favorite remarks is that the only time you ever do anything with great energy is when the best and worst motives in you are both involved at the same time. Or let's say the most love-filled and the most hate-filled motives reengaged at the same moment. Lust is a perfect example of that. When one feels and makes lust for a woman,

it's precisely because the love we feel for her and the hate we feel for her are both being fully expressed. And those would-be sexual relations really come from just one side or another of oneself being expressed.

Do you regret saying on TV in the early seventies that women should be kept in cages?

I said it in jest on a show with Orson Welles. One of the troubles with the media is that they are horrendously humorless. They might as well be human walking computers, because whatever you say, it's always assumed that you said it in a deadly earnest voice. We were chatting. He said, "Norman, you wrote recently that women are low, sloppy beasts." This was all pre-woman's lib. And I said, "The rest of that quote is that they're goddesses." What I was trying to get into was the fundamental male viewpoint towards women: on the one hand we see them as goddesses, on the other hand, as low, sloppy beasts. And he said, "Beasts?" I started thinking of a few fights I'd had with the ex-wife and began to laugh. And I said, "Oh come on, Orson, women should be kept in cages." If I had known what that remark was gonna cost, I'd of really bitten right through my lip before I ever said it. It was a stupid remark in terms of its cost. A moment's fun, which I'm paying for ever since.

There's a wonderful remark that a fellow once made with respect to *Women and Their Elegance*. It was that a woman got married to a man who's much beneath her, so she went to a family party, and the head of the family looked at her and said, "Thirty days of pleasure and thirty years at the wrong end of the table." That remark is equal to the one that I made.

There's another remark you made: That it's very dangerous to stick it up a woman's ass, it tends to make them more promiscuous.

Yeah, that was a rule of thumb remark. [*Laughs*] A pole-vaulter's remark.

Is it any wonder that when the Women's Movement started you were singled out as a great male chauvinist?

I was singled out because I was the last man in America to realize how big and powerful a movement that was. I saw all these men running for cover and paying this great respect to women and I'm such a fool, I said, "What are they doing that for?"

Why do you feel that masturbation cripples people and leads to insanity?

Why do you ask me a question when you know the answer?

Because not everyone who may read this will have read what you've written.

The tendency of masturbation is insanity. In the same way that the tendency of driving ninety miles per hour in a slow speed zone is a crash up. It doesn't mean it's going to happen. But you can't cheat life—which is about the only remark I made that I still hang on to. There's no objective correlative in masturbation. It encourages one's fantasy life in the weakest fashion possible. The tendency for masturbation nine times out of ten is to push people further and further into loneliness and into a fundamental sense of defeat about not getting what they really want sexually.

But can't that also be a release for them?

It's a release, in the sense it keeps them from something worse happening to them. But to see masturbation as something marvelous and part of a healthy sex life is dubious in the extreme.

You don't write as much about masturbation as you do other sexual acts, including buggery.

Buggery was much more common in ancient times than it is now. The Romans talked about it all the time. The Greeks lived with buggery, it was sort of a staple for them. It's my guess that in the Middle Ages you didn't have an extraordinary amount of buggery, because it was a form of contraception between men and women. And people lived much closer to excrement in those days. The smell was everywhere in the air. I had the experience once of being in Japan after the war, and people lived very close to the excrement of animals and to their own excrement. American soldiers were far more horrified by the fact that the Japanese would carry their human excrement in these honey pots through the cities or use them in gardens than they were at seeing battlefields with fifty dead soldiers. We seem to have separated ourselves from excrement a long time ago. It may be that you can't build a modern, technological civilization without keeping the shit out of the machines. But in ancient times that's the heart and core of it. You can't conceive of life in those days without a lot of buggery and a lot of living in and around excrement all the time.

In *Ancient Evenings* you have the chief charioteer getting buggered in a cave by the pharaoh, first in the ass, then in the mouth. Was this a way a pharaoh behaved?
It's the way pharaohs did behave. That was the toughest moment in the writing, because I felt as if I was crossing my own Rubicon at that point. I thought the book demanded it. I had an instinct that this was the great hinge of the book, because the charioteer was a very strong man. When he's buggered by his pharaoh it changes his life entirely. It dominates not only that life, but his remaining three lives, because he was born three times. He never comes out from under the shadow of that buggery. I feel it works well as a symbol of power and what power means. Power is buggery. People say that the sex drives in *Ancient Evenings* exhibit power relationships; I don't think it's true. There is more love there than you'd expect. The queen, Nefertiti, does bare the charioteer's child, which is only explainable in that she had enough love for him that she didn't abort the child or destroy it when it was born.

In the book, the moment of reincarnation comes through the sex act.

It's not proper reincarnation. He has himself reborn directly into the belly of his woman. As he dies, so his seed enters her belly and he's reborn. That's not true reincarnation. I always felt reincarnation means that you die and then some cosmic agent looks you over and decides your next life. In other words, there is a moment of truth, where your life is judged and you're sent out to improve the condition of the cosmos by the trials and joys you're going to have in your next existence.

Is that what you think will happen to you after you die?
I think reincarnation is the natural way to do it.

What would you like to come back as?
I don't have a clue. I feel great modesty before the Lord. I wouldn't dream of saying what I'd come back as, that's about the fastest way I know of not getting it. I think the Lord takes one look at you and that's it. I have a working joke on this: since I've contemplated these matters, I find that I'm killing cockroaches less and less often.

Do you literally believe in God?
It's much simpler than not to accept Him or Her.

Her?
I learned my lesson. I'll make my peace with the women libbers yet.

Is it true that your publisher was worried that they wouldn't make their money back on *Ancient Evenings,* so they put you under the gun to write another, shorter novel?
Is that the general interpretation of it?

It's the interpretation I've given.
You're clever. Yeah, they want me to do a short book because their feeling is that their chances of doing well with a short book are fine. I expect they're right. But why do we have to have this evil interpreta-

tion of it? I'm not under the gun. I agreed. I wanted to do a short book [*Tough Guys Don't Dance*] after I finished *Ancient Evenings*.

***Ancient Evenings* is the first of your planned trilogy. Do you think you'll write the next two books?**
I hope I will. I've got two huge books to do, one about a spaceship in the future and one about modern times. But it's not automatic. Maybe I'll do it and maybe I won't. *Ancient Evenings* was written to stand by itself, it does not need the other two to fulfill it.

How has *Ancient Evenings* been received?
It made me a prophet for too little. I said I was going to get the very best and the very worst reviews I'd ever gotten and that's been true. On the one hand, I've been called the best writer in America; on the other hand, two reviewers used the same word: *disaster.*

After the dust settles, will it rank among your most important work?
I think it will. If you work eleven years on a book and you take yourself seriously, as I do, how could I possibly not think it's my best book? I could be wrong, but I don't think I am. I think it is my best because I know what went into it. It's a very difficult book to get a hold of and seize and control. The prevailing mode in American letters is for high-tech writing. Writing that has a sheer command of the surface.

Tom Wolfe?
He's a very good example of that. But any number of writers are admired for their ability to capture the surface of things. They do it with skill and wit and irony. Irony is terribly important and crucial to modern writing. The kind of books that we like best are books where we're on top of three-quarters of the book, because we know and recognize it, we're comfortable with it, and one-quarter of it is new enough to give us pleasure. That's a very good working mixture. With

Ancient Evenings you've got a novel that's brand new, there isn't anything familiar, there's nothing in psychology we can count on, because it's a profoundly different psychology from our own. It owes nothing to Freud. Or to the Judeo-Christian tradition. As a result, it's a book that inspires an awful lot of irritability in people who like to be in command of what they're reading. For some people it's impossibly long, dull, and boring. For others it's rich, fabulous, and sensuous. There is a fundamental division of opinions.

Why are good novels so painful to read?
That's an excellent question. Name me any great novel you've ever read that didn't bore you in part while reading it the first time. A great novel has a consciousness that's new first. And any time we undergo that, we get bored because we have to withdraw and digest this new consciousness before we can go back to it. I've been bored in part by *Moby-Dick, The Red and the Black, Anna Karenina, The Scarlet Letter.*

Your editor compared you to Picasso in terms of your range, your refusal to age or to lose energy. Is that an agreeable comparison for you?
It's a little on the grand side. Picasso's a great artist who made huge changes in the world. There are two kinds of artist. There's the artist who essentially has an identity, and we turn to that artist to feel the resonance of that particular identity. Matisse, Renoir, Cézanne, to a lesser extent van Gogh. We know what we're going to get when we look at their work. But with Picasso, he was interested in throwing away his own identity in order to find a new one. Style for him was not something that was attached to his identity, style was a cutting edge with which he attacked the nature of reality. So he went through a whole series of phases and changes. I find literary style is that for me. But don't trust what I say because it's self-serving, as all writers' remarks are. The negative aspect of that is, "He can't write good anymore so his new style is a departure." Take your pick.

Any other artists or writers you wouldn't mind being compared with?

I don't know. I could say no. Yes. Maybe.

What about Gabriel García Márquez?

Oh, Márquez is wonderful. He may be a great writer, but we're not at all alike. I've read *One Hundred Years of Solitude* after I was halfway into *Ancient Evenings* and I was getting blissful when I read it. I thought, God, this guy covers family with ten people in it and they go through twenty years and he does it all in five or ten pages. In ten pages I'm lucky to get around one bend of the Nile. He writes very quickly about a great many things, he has that gift. If I have a gift it is in the opposite direction. I want to catch the slow movement of that Nile.

Márquez won the Nobel Prize. The opening of your *Prisoner of Sex* dealt with your obsession with winning that prize. What would it mean to you now if you got it?

I fully expect not to get it. It's the kind of thing that's not going to come my way.

Honestly?

Well, there's always a shot at it. But one of the things it depends on is your popularity in your own country with the most respected academics in the country. From what I've gathered, the Swedish Academy listens carefully to the literary curators of a country. I don't think my stock would be particularly high with them.

Do you feel that you've succeeded in creating a revolution in the consciousness of our times, as you once declared it was your ambition to do?

If we can use an image from buggery, I think I've gotten halfway up.

JOYCE CAROL OATES

I Can't Stop Taking Notes

JOYCE CAROL OATES IS ONE OF THE MOST PROLIFIC
writers in America. Her critics even complain that she writes too
much. She has written more novels than Nobel laureate Saul Bellow, more short story collections than John Updike, more books
of essays than Norman Mailer, more words of poetry than Emily
Dickinson, and more plays than Chekhov. Critic Harold Bloom
considers her "our true proletarian novelist," and favorably compares her with Theodore Dreiser, D. H. Lawrence, and Flannery
O'Connor. Author and critic John Gardner called her "an alarming phenomenon . . . one of the great writers of our time." James
A. Michener seconds that belief. And *Newsweek,* more than twenty
years ago, described her as "the most significant novelist to have
emerged in the United States in the last decade."

She has been described as shy, mouselike, intense, perceptive,
brilliant. She can cook, play the piano, and quote James Joyce,
and she writes about boxing with style and authority (in her *Life*
magazine piece on Mike Tyson she couldn't resist quoting
Thorstein Veblen, Henry James, George Santayana, and Wallace
Stevens). She writes about troubled lower-class people and the often vicious way they sometimes brutalize one another. She's been
criticized for being too fascinated with violence and praised for
writing about life as it is. She doesn't shy away from rough lan-

guage, and in her imagination she can commit the most horrendous crimes: murder, incest, self-abortion.

Both the critical and academic communities have embraced
Oates, as have a loyal cadre of readers who line up outside bookstores whenever she's signing, usually with half a dozen favorite
titles under their arms. "Nobody else writes nearly as much as she
does," said critic Bruce Allen in the *Hudson Review*. "The really
alarming thing is that so much of what she writes is good." Adds
book reviewer Marian Engel in the *New York Times*, "It has been
left to Joyce Carol Oates, a writer who seems to know a great deal
about the underside of America, to guide us—splendidly—down
dark passages."

UCLA English professor Calvin Bedient, in the *New York Times*,
calls her novels "grinding, brutal, harsh" and fiercely claustrophobic, and believes Oates writes "from within psyches that are
like prehistoric organisms." Carnegie-Mellon professor G. F.
Waller notes that through the ordinary settings of her urban
poor and suburban rich "erupt the latent terror, violence, obses-
sive sexuality, [and] religious strife Oates perceives lying close to
the surface of contemporary life." As Yale's Harold Bloom observes, what Oates has written about Flannery O'Connor is
equally true of herself: "Her world is that surreal primitive land-
scape in which the Unconscious is a determining quantity that
the Conscious cannot defeat, because it cannot recognize. In fact,
there is nothing to be recognized—there is only an experience to
be suffered."

Recognition is not a word one would apply to Oates's writing
style. What differentiates her from most other writers of her dis-
tinction (and what may be keeping her from having the huge
popular readership of, say, Stephen King or Larry McMurtry) is
that Oates doesn't have any particular style. Like some virtuoso
coloratura, she changes her voice according to her subject. One
doesn't pick up a Joyce Carol Oates novel, as one does a novel by
Ernest Hemingway, William Faulkner, or Elmore Leonard, with

predetermined familiarity. Oates's writing, like her subject matter, is neither predictable nor comforting. *Foxfire* is written from the point of view of a high school female gang member from upstate New York. *Black Water,* Oates's short novel that preceded it, is written from the point of view of a far more sophisticated young woman who happens to be drowning. *Zombie* comes at you from the chillingly mundane mind of a serial killer.

Hers is an intellectual life. When she isn't writing, she is the Roger S. Berlind Distinguished Professor of Humanities at Princeton, teaching graduate students about writers and writing. (She has also taught at the University of Detroit and the University of Windsor in Canada.) A friend, critic Elaine Showalter, once noted that, "In the midst of a quite ordinary conversation about the news or television or the family, Oates often inserts remarks whose philosophical penetration makes the rest of us feel like amoebas in the company of a more highly evolved life form." Oates is married to a teacher and editor, Raymond Smith, and they often spend time together reading each other poetry. Together they founded the *Ontario Review* and the Ontario Review Press, which publishes work by up-and-coming writers.

There is no other writer in America, male or female, who quite compares with Oates. In 1970, she won a National Book Award for an early novel, *them,* and she has been inducted into the American Academy and Institute of Arts and Letters. In 1990, she received the Rea Award for Achievement in the Short Story, the Bobst Lifetime Achievement Award, and the Heideman Award for One-Act Plays.

Born in the small town of Millersport, near Lockport, in western New York, on June 16, 1938, Joyce Carol Oates came from a working-class family. Her father was a tool-and-die maker and neither of her parents graduated from high school. Her grandfather was murdered when her mother was a baby, an act of violence that indelibly altered Oates's development.

She began writing as a young girl, throwing away novel after novel as quickly as she completed them. When she was fourteen her grandfather bought her a typewriter and she continued to churn out her stories. One of them, "In the Old World," written when she was nineteen, was a cowinner of *Mademoiselle*'s college fiction award. After graduating as valedictorian and Phi Beta Kappa from Syracuse University in 1960, she went to graduate school at the University of Wisconsin, where she received her master's degree and met and married her husband. While enrolled in a doctoral program at Rice, one of her stories was given an honorable mention in Martha Foley's annual *Best American Short Stories.* That was the acknowledgment she needed to convince herself that she was, truly, a writer. She dropped out of Rice and never looked back.

Her first book of stories, *By the North Gate,* was published in 1963 when she was twenty-five. A year later came her first novel, *With Shuddering Fall.* Then another book of stories, *Upon the Sweeping Flood,* followed by her second, third, and fourth novels in as many years: *A Garden of Earthly Delights* (1967), *Expensive People* (1968), *them* (1969). While living in Windsor, Ontario, she also managed to squeeze in two books of poetry in 1969 and 1970. This prodigious beginning was only an indication of things to come. In the seventies she published seven novels, nine books of short stories, four volumes of poetry, and two collections of essays. She also wrote shorter and more experimental work for various small presses such as Black Sparrow, Louisiana State University Press, Lord John Press, Pomegranate Press, Santa Susana Press, Rook Society, and Sylvester & Orphanos. Nine more novels were written in the eighties, including her trilogy of gothic, romance, and mystery novels: *Bellefleur, A Bloodsmoor Romance,* and *Mysteries of Winterthurn.*

In the thirty-eight years that she has been a professional writer, Joyce Carol Oates has written a total of thirty-three novels (her latest: *Middle Age: A Romance*), twenty-one collections of short stories, seven books of poetry, seven volumes of essays, eighteen plays, and more than two dozen works published by small, independent presses. She has, by her own estimate, written more than 300 short stories, most of which have not been collected in book form, and other novels that she has not seen fit to publish. She has edited numerous volumes of essays, story collections, and interviews with other writers on their craft. She has also written seven psychological suspense novels (*Lives of the Twins, Soul/Mates, Nemesis, Snake Eyes, You Can't Catch Me, Double Delight, Starr Bright will be with you soon*) under the pseudonym Rosamond Smith.

What is astounding about her output is the breadth and depth of her subjects as well as the quality of her prose. *With Shuddering Fall* deals with cars and leaving home; *them* with corruption, race riots, and death. *Wonderland* deals with family murder and the psychology of medicine; *The Assassins* with politics; *Son of the Morning* with religious fanaticism; *Do with Me What You Will* with irrational, possessive, adulterous love and the legal profession; *Angel of Light* with revenge; *Unholy Loves* with faculty life in an American college; *Solstice* with female love; *American Appetites* with turning fifty; *You Must Remember This* with coming of age and loss of innocence; *Because It Is Bitter, And Because It Is My Heart* with racism and alcoholism; *What I Lived For* with a man's psyche and moral ruin; *First Love* with sexual awakening and abuse; *We Were the Mulvaneys*—which became an Oprah Book Club selection—with the rise, fall, and ultimate redemption of an American family; *Broke Heart Blues* with a teenager who becomes a national obsession; *Blonde* with Marilyn Monroe. Her book *On Boxing* was an insightful look at an often brutal sport.

Here's Oates from her essay on boxing:

> Boxing as dream-image, or nightmare, pits self against self, identical twin against twin, as in the womb itself where "dominancy," that most mysterious of human hungers, is first expressed. Its most characteristic moments of ecstasy—the approach to the knockout, the knockout, the aftermath of the knockout, and, by way of television replays, the entire episode retraced in slow motion *as in the privacy of a dream*—are indistinguishable from obscenity, horror.

Here she is on test driving a Ferrari:

As the Testarosa was accelerated I felt that visceral sense of an irresistibly gathering and somehow condensing power—"speed" being in fact a mere distillation or side effect of power—and, within it, contained by it, an oddly humble sense of human smallness, frailty. One of the perhaps unexamined impulses behind high-speed racing must be not the mere "courting" of death but, on a more primary level, its actual pre-experience; its taste.

And on the exhausting preparation it took to turn Norma Jean Baker into Marilyn Monroe:

The day of the [*Gentlemen Prefer Blondes*] premiere, a half-dozen expert hands laid into the Blond Actress as chicken pluckers might lay into poultry carcasses. Her hair was shampooed and given a permanent and its shadowy roots bleached with peroxide so powerful they had to turn a fan on the Blond Actress to save her from asphyxiation and her hair was then rinsed another time and set on enormous pink plastic rollers and a roaring dryer lowered onto her head like a machine devised to administer electric shock. Her face and throat were steamed, chilled, and creamed. Her body was bathed and oiled, its unsightly hairs removed, she was powdered, perfumed, painted, and set to dry. Her fingernails and toenails were painted a brilliant crimson to match her neon mouth. Whitey the makeup man had labored for more than an hour when he saw to his chagrin a subtle asymmetry in the Blond Actress's darkened eyebrows and removed them entirely and redid them. The beauty mark was relocated by a tenth of a fraction of an inch, then prudently restored to its original position. False eyelashes were glued into place.

Her novel *Black Water* is a fictionalized account of Senator Ted Kennedy's incident at Chappaquiddick, where Mary Jo Kopechne drowned in a car accident that spoiled any chance Kennedy had of becoming president. The reviews were mostly raves. The *New*

York Times said it was as audacious as anything in recent fiction, "a brilliant vision of how a culture has learned to associate political power with sex. . . . Taut, powerfully imagined and beautifully written [it] ranks with the best of Joyce Carol Oates's already long list of distinguished achievements."

Oates is a powerful, unflinching writer who isn't afraid to take on the most searing issues, from the rotten morality of our politicians to the self-abortion of one of the "invisible" and powerless people she so often champions. Here is part of Oates's abortion scene from the conclusion of her novella *The Rise of Life on Earth,* so raw it barely uses punctuation:

> . . . a third time she bore the knife up inside her, now jamming it half-angrily into her and dropping it in nearly the same motion as her insides suddenly loosened, gushed hotly out between her legs *Oh oh oh* . . . her body heaved with pain like a bell clapper inside a bell, blood running down the drain of the tub as she'd planned but the sight of it confused her and she was shivering violently so naked but sweating too and the panicked thought came to her that she should not be sweating after the scrub, fresh bacteria were being flushed to the surface of her skin and she was helpless to prevent the contamination. Darker strands of blood began to appear inside her bleeding, now bits of tissue, cupping her gloved hands under her between her legs she saw suddenly the tender skinless thing, the tiny fetus about the size of her palm, part of it jelly, part liquid running seeping through her fingers *Oh oh oh.*

« «   » »

The street Oates lives on is quiet and idyllic, the area exclusive and privileged, the nearby university elite and prestigious. Her study and living spaces are lined with books on shelves, tables, and floors. There is a healthy garden outside where fresh vegetables are tenderly cared for by her husband. There is no indication that in such a town, on such a street, in such a house a writer of such prodigious and turbulent powers resides.

She appears fragile, this tall, lanky, bespectacled woman with the short curly hair and enormous eyes. During the week of our talks in 1992 she tired each day after a few hours; but that was because the focus was on her and her life, and she prefers putting her energies into the lives of her characters, who are endlessly vying for her attention.

What she seemed to look forward to each day was the time when we stopped and went out for dinner, or to a party hosted by one of her Princeton friends—a time when she could relax and enjoy the food and conversation, especially when the talk wasn't zeroing in on her. Yet during the days we taped—at her home, in a limousine taking her to and from a book signing, at a restaurant, and eight years later in Los Angeles—Joyce was all business: concentrated, thoughtful . . . and very, very smart.

Since you seem to be a compulsive writer, what is it that most excites you about putting words on paper?
The challenge of making an internal vision external. Getting the inner vision out. I love to write. I feel I have something to say. It's exhilarating once in a while, but most of my experiences are fraught with frustration because I always feel dissatisfied. A whole day can go by and I feel I haven't accomplished anything. My husband was asking me about this. He said, "You get a lot done in a day." I guess I do, but I don't feel that I have. I have a feeling always, which is subterranean, of being profoundly dissatisfied with what I'm working at.

Does dissatisfaction lead to compulsion?
I don't want to emphasize any morbidity or pathology in speaking of compulsion, but probably compulsion does account for virtually any achievement. There are people who say they are envious of me, who write "I wish I were you. I envy you." These people don't know how hard I work. You have to have a driving, almost feverish energy. It's like the tremendous hunger you saw in the young Mike Tyson. How

many other men who fantasize being a boxer would really want that kind of burning passion, hunger, and desire to hurt other people that a great boxer must have? To be a professional is really to be in a state of feverish commitment to your art or sport. If you don't have the will and you're not hungry and you're not almost compulsive about it, you can't succeed. To be a writer you have to be compulsive, eccentric. You have to want to stay up all night just writing because you have some brainstorm. The energies are demonic. You can't be a normal, happy, contented person and be a great novelist or a great filmmaker or actor. You've got to be a little "crazy."

How "crazy" does it get for you?
Well, I write all over, sometimes I can't stop taking notes. Maybe I shouldn't say this, but I've actually been writing while I'm being introduced to give a talk. It's a good way of using time. I really begrudge the hours that I have to go to sleep, because sleep is a waste of human energy. Think of all the hours you spend asleep! When I travel sometimes I just don't sleep at all. It's like a chaotic rush of images, a kaleidoscope, that keeps me awake all night.

Is it this inner chaos that drives you to be as prolific as you are?
I don't know how it adds up. I must have a different time zone. People ask me how do I find the time? I have the same amount of time as anybody else, I just try to use it. It might have to do with the tachycardia that I have, where with every tick and every heartbeat, if I'm not getting something done, I feel I've just wasted that moment. Whereas a more normal person would feel, well, why not relax for the whole afternoon, go out and do sailboating? I would always feel a residue of guilt if I did that. So perhaps I do inhabit a different time dimension, where clocks are ticking faster for me than for other people.

What exactly is tachycardia?
It's a little malformation of the heart valve. It's often associated with people who are tall and lank, a physical type. A tachycardia attack sends a person into hyperventilation, the heart speeds up and it

pounds very hard. A person may faint or feel they can't breathe. Then the extremities of the body start turning icy cold because the blood's not going down, so it's like a mimicry of death and it makes you feel terrified because you feel you are dying.

Do these attacks happen often?
I've probably had fifty attacks over my life. I've been admitted to the emergency room at Princeton a couple of times, but not for a while. I take digitalis every day of my life. If I have a mild attack I can take some other medicine, but it's so powerful that it leaves you exhausted and depressed for two or three days, so I hate to take it. It's because of these attacks that I have a very heightened sense of mortality and time. That's why I'm always working and why I'm concerned with wasting time. Almost every minute of my life is plotted very carefully. Thoreau said, "You can't kill time without injuring eternity." Probably that's part of the reason that I seem to be prolific.

So vacations or time at the beach are out of the question for you?
I would go crazy. I could sit on the beach for maybe three minutes. I was even wondering before you came if we could do this interview while jogging, but I realize that's absurd.

When did you first learn about this heart problem?
It started when I was eighteen and it scared the life out of me. I was playing basketball at Syracuse University and I was knocked down. I started having this attack and I scared everybody else, including my gym teacher, who almost fainted. She thought I was going to die in front of her eyes. That was the most terrifying attack. After that I'm more able to see that it's just a heart problem, but it's not supposed to be fatal. I don't want people to be thinking that I'm self-pitying or pathological. It's simply been absorbed in my life.

Nonetheless, your output is Promethean. Do you see yourself as successful?

No, I don't think of myself as successful. I experience dissatisfaction or relative degrees of failure more than success because I'm always rewriting. I have to be very careful not to put too low an evaluation on myself. Probably the people who are successful are only people who are dissatisfied. Because what else pushes them on? Some people are quite content, and they were content when they were eight years old, affable, happy people who are not going to be very successful but they don't care. And none of them are writers or creative artists because they don't have that push. All art begins in conflict. Even situation comedy.

Has any of your success, such as winning a National Book Award in 1970, created the kind of conflict that might get you to disavow success?

I was young when I won that, about twenty-nine or thirty. It got me much more exposure but it turned many people against me. People don't like someone being successful. Norman Mailer is the most classic example, where he started very big and then he got terrible reviews of his next novel. Since then Mailer has always been a kind of punching bag. There's some personal animosities.

Have you lost friends as your career took off?

There was a male writer whose career I'd helped—I got him my agent, gave him a quote for his first novel—and he really turned against me. He just couldn't take my winning that award. He threatened my life and did all sorts of strange things. He wanted me to write a review for the *New York Times Book Review* and I said I couldn't do it. He just went crazy. For years he would write me letters. It had to do with the National Book Award. He felt that suddenly I had fame and power and I could get a review published. I tried to explain that even if I wanted to do it, I wouldn't do it. He wrote a story called "How I Killed Joyce Carol Oates" and sent me the manuscript. I don't know if it ever got printed. It was pretty extreme. I once talked at the Modern Language Association and he was in the audience, and at the end he

came toward me. He was going to throw something at me. I don't
know what it was. Somebody found it on the floor and wouldn't let
me see it. I think it was a razor.

**Since your work often deals with violence, was that the only time
you've been threatened?**

I get a lot of letters from people in prisons—always men, never
women. They obviously haven't read anything of mine, but they see
stuff about me in *People* magazine. I can't be bothered.

In what other ways has fame affected you?

It's very complex. If one is famous one has a certain amount of
power, but maybe power is corruptive and corrosive. Look at the phenomenon of Marilyn Monroe, who had celebrity and extreme fame
yet had seemingly no personal life nor any control. Fame exacerbates
one's personal failing. Celebrity, if one doesn't have inner strength,
can be corrosive. It's as if the flaws in your character, like cracks in a
facade, become magnified in the public eye. And you can't hide them.
I feel my heart sink a little when people recognize me, because then I
have to put on this identity. At the supermarket I've sometimes had
to sign autographs on people's grocery lists. It's embarrassing to me.

**Yet yours is a modest kind of fame compared with a Monroe or a
Madonna.**

That's probably true. The outsider looking in would have thought
Marilyn Monroe was a tremendous success. It must have been keen
and sharp and terribly ironic for a person like her to realize that her
image was out in the world and she scarcely shared in that. It's a
bizarre, almost schizophrenic experience. I recently saw *The Misfits* on
video and I was really struck by Marilyn Monroe as a kind of female
impersonator. There were real women in that movie and they walked
around in regular shoes and then she would come on the screen completely confectionery, her hair, her manner, her walk, her physical being. It was as if she were a female impersonator in a way that we don't
experience women now—stuffed into a dress, teetering on high heels.

It's kind of like being an anthropologist and going back in time: was this really an ideal of female beauty, or was it, even then, very exaggerated and a little absurd? She said to one interviewer, "Just please don't make me a joke." So she was aware of that.

Did Norma Jean believe Marilyn Monroe was a joke?
Norma knew that Marilyn Monroe was her creation, that she played roles in two or three movies, and one of them was Lorelei Lee of *Gentlemen Prefer Blondes*. But not the characters in *Niagara, Don't Bother to Knock, Bus Stop,* or *The Misfits*. It wasn't a joke, necessarily; it was more like something she could do.

Why has our fascination with her lasted so long?
She may be the only female screen star of the twentieth century that's going to endure on an iconic level, like Elvis Presley, James Dean, Muhammad Ali. It must be because of her special qualities of extreme physical beauty and at the same time vulnerability and innocence mixed up with sexual glamor. Also, in a role like Sugar Kane in *Some Like it Hot*, she's very childlike. The world loves children.

There are probably more books about Marilyn Monroe than any other film star; what inspired you to add to this particular canon with *Blonde*?
My work is fiction and it's imaginative, so I was freed from any kind of biographical or historical constraints. I was particularly interested in writing about Norma Jean Baker, beginning with her childhood, moving into the young woman who becomes a photographer's model, a starlet under contract, and then is given the name Marilyn Monroe. I was going to write a novella of about 175 pages and end it there. But then it became an epic. I felt I wanted to give her a little more depth and poetic significance than she has been granted.

You describe her high school years trying out for cheerleading, singing, drama—and failing at everything. Was she a normal girl growing up?

Yes and no. The difference between a normal girl and her was that she just kept trying. Instead of slinking away she'd say, "Let me try again." And they'd let her and she'd still fail, and they'd tell her to try next year. Marilyn Monroe didn't take dancing lessons until she was, in a sense, too old. And she didn't have singing lessons until she was even older. But somehow she managed to sing and dance in movies like *Gentlemen Prefer Blondes.* She had a desperate will, and that will is analogous to the terrible hunger that you find in some athletes, like the young Mike Tyson, who are so hungry and so yearning to succeed that they just wipe away all the competition.

When you were growing up, did you ever fantasize wanting to look like her or any other movie star?
No, then you'd have to deal with so many men being attracted to you. And it's hard to deal with that. In Arthur Miller's *After the Fall* the figure who represents Marilyn Monroe can barely walk down the street without three men following her, accosting her, talking to her. Who would really want that? Unless basically you liked men or wanted to make some money off this power, it would be quite a distraction. The most attractive girls in high school were the ones who ended up getting married and having babies right out of high school. And in a sense their lives are finished. So being very beautiful and having a strong appeal for the opposite sex is quite a handicap, although it's not perceived that way when one is young.

So you've always been satisfied with who you are?
I don't really identify with my physical self that much. My spiritual self, my inner self, my imagination is probably my deepest self, and that expresses itself in language in my books. My physical and social self is just another person. I don't like the idea of being isolated or singled out. I'm very self-conscious about that.

Why do you feel being a woman allows you a certain invisibility?
Another complex question. A woman is judged often by her physical appearance or the phenomenon that she's a woman. But a man

would be judged by his work. It would never be said about a male novelist that he was very handsome. You don't say, "Hemingway, a male novelist, has written some good books." But people do write about women writers in such a way that we are all in some strange category that's very heterogeneous and a kind of promiscuous category where people are lumped together. I have books of literary criticism which lists "women novels," and I'll find myself in that chapter along with women who write about romantic experiences or domestic life or children. And my real kinship would be with someone in the realistic novel who's a man. But I'm not put in that chapter because I'm a woman, so as Ralph Ellison said about being black in America, one is an invisible man. So women very often are perceived as invisible.

And yet you also believe that this is the best time in history for a woman to be a woman.
I think so. Women are being published in great numbers, women are being read, women support one another—and this was not always the case. Women are directing plays and having a role in the organization and administration of theaters, which has been very, very male dominated. There are women's studies programs at universities. Young women are going into medical school, there are women doctors and lawyers. They still encounter sexism, of course, but it's not the way it used to be, when women couldn't get in at all. To me, it's by far the best time for women professionals.

Think we'll see a woman president in our lifetime?
I seriously doubt that. Vice president, possibly. Perhaps if the very best people ran for public office, we might see some women in them.

Do you take the radical feminist attitude that men are the enemy?
No, I have never felt as some feminists have felt, though I am a feminist, that men are the enemy. I've also never had any real animosity toward men. Some radical feminists have attacked me in the past because I write about men with a certain amount of compassion, or

even defend men. They feel that I've betrayed them. I was attacked in a women's journal because I'd written a novel called *Solstice,* and the woman who attacked me was a lesbian and she said that this was a thinly disguised novel about an evil lesbian. In fact the novel doesn't have a lesbian in it. She was projecting into the novel her own propagandistic vibes. I'm a counter-puncher, so I wrote back, "If I want to write a novel about a lesbian who is evil or a silly lesbian or a brilliant lesbian, I will do it. This is my prerogative as a writer and I don't ascribe to any ideology except writing." It didn't make me any friends within the feminists, but I'm not writing propaganda for feminists. Feminist literature per se is propagandist literature. And feminism, like any ism or ideology, exacts too high a toll. You can be politically incorrect and people get angry with you. I will always place a much higher value on aesthetic integrity than on any kind of political correctness, including feminism.

How do you define feminism?
In a very root way: that everyone should receive equal pay for equal work. To me feminism is basically economic. Women are only paid a fraction of what men are paid for the same work.

Are there differences between the sexes?
I really have to go against some feminist thinking. No, I don't think that the two sexes are that different. There's an intensification of aggression, especially sexual aggression, in the male. But it's an intensification: sexual feelings, instincts, and desires of the male are in many cases more intense than in the female. For instance, virtually nonexistent are female rapists or sex offenders. There are nineteen times as many male criminals as female criminals, and sexual component has a lot to do with that. But it's a continuum. If you got rid of all men and had only women left behind in some bizarre dimension, you would then find clustered toward one end of the continuum these very adversarial and aggressive women. And they would be the "new men." So I don't feel the sexes are different in kind, only in degree.

Camille Paglia, the author of *Sexual Personae*, believes that male aggression and lust are the energizing forces of culture, and that if civilization had been left in women's hands, we'd still be living in grass huts.

That's ridiculous! She obviously hates being a woman. And she's identifying with what most men would consider the worst traits of maleness. The men whom I know in Princeton and elsewhere, and the men in my family, are not marauding males energized by lust and aggression. No, they're energized by desire for creativity. Norman Mailer once said that nobody says to a woman, "Come on, be a woman!" But to be a man, either it's explicit or implicit: "Come on, be a man!" And that admonition to be a *man* is fraught with a good deal of anxiety. What does it mean? Be a man like Mozart? Like Einstein? No, it really means to be a tough man, a very physical man in terms of other men. Does it mean you risk your life? You should have joined the armed services to be in at least one war? Many men feel that way, even though they are pacifists. A young man who didn't want to go to war in World War II would be considered a coward and would have considered himself a coward. That's very difficult.

You don't think there are true differences between men and women, but what about the area of sports?

Sports, playing games together, this may be an area in which women and men are different. And that's too bad. The men whom I know who play squash or tennis or poker, it's a celebration of friendship. They love each other and they love what they're doing. And men experience sports that way. Women don't have the same thing. I don't know why not. When I watched a lot of boxing, virtually everyone I was with were men, it was a male experience, and when I was in it, it was as if I were a male. But other women experience it differently and they put their hands over their eyes: "Oooh, this is awful! How can you look at this?" As if by watching boxing I'd abrogated my femininity.

What is it about boxing that so fascinates you?

It's a paradigm of life, where you don't know what's going to happen. It's a mimicry of a fight to the death, mortal combat. Whereas tennis or chess is a stylized mimicry of a fight—the chess players are the kings and their pawns are soldiers and they're fighting on a board, but it's only a game. Boxing is not a game. It is the real thing. It inhabits a special dimension in the history of sports because it arises out of mortal combat in which one man would die. It's different not in degree but in kind from other sports. To me, boxing is mainly about failure. It's about getting hurt, but doing it with nobility and courage and not complaining. I tend to be sympathetic with boxers. I'm *not* sympathetic with the managers and the business side of it, because they exploit boxers.

You've written that boxing is "the quintessential image of human struggle against not only other people but one's own divided self."

Definitely. That's why writers are so drawn to boxing. They look and they see two ideally, almost evenly, matched opponents and they have such an identity with that, because it's like when we are creating our own work, we have a shadow self that we're fighting with in some strange shadowy struggle that we can't articulate. Like writing a novel: it's like you're doing battle with this other self. And boxing is such a silent sport, too. It's so mute, there's no language.

Are men fascinated by boxing because it suggests that masculinity is measured in terms of other men?

That's true. And boxers have a camaraderie with other boxers and with the history of boxing that excludes women. Women have nothing to do with it. Women could admire boxing, as I do, but boxers are basically boxing for other men and in terms of other boxers.

Was Mike Tyson surprised by your interest when you were interviewing him?

I was never really interviewing Mike Tyson in a formal way and I didn't have a tape recorder. I was doing it by hand. We were in [his then-comanager Jim] Jacob's apartment in New York sitting on a sofa, talking about fights, seeing boxing tapes. Mike was from a world in which everybody knew boxing, including women. To him it wouldn't have been surprising that a woman could talk about Jack Johnson or any other fighter.

Had he read any of your writing?
He wouldn't have had time. He had his karate videos and splatter films, he didn't have time to turn the pages of a book and move his eyes.

Did Tyson surprise you in any way?
Mike always surprises people when he comes in a room because he's so short. He's not a Sonny Liston or a Muhammad Ali. When I knew Mike he was only twenty years old. He's not the same person anymore. He was soft-spoken and much younger. After he got married and all the things that happened to him and his involvement with Don King, it accelerated his aging process. He's a much older person physically. He's probably abused his body, his reflexes may be gone. Also, he's been with people who have not had his best interest at heart.

Do you think what Tyson did to that young woman that landed him in prison was a terrible act?
I don't really think what Mike did to this young woman was the worst thing he's ever done. It was a case where he or his manager couldn't buy the person off. They tried to, but they failed.

Do you feel Tyson got the punishment he deserved?
It's hard to know what anyone deserves. Do we get what we deserve? Or do we deserve what we get? I'm not a person who judges very happily. I guess that's why I'm a novelist; judgment is usually suspended in a novel.

Do you think Tyson was an artist in the ring?

He was getting there. He never had a great fight. He wasn't an artist like Sugar Ray Robinson, who was the greatest boxer, even beyond Ali. He won his title five times.

What other boxers and fights do you admire?

One of the things I liked about Sugar Ray Leonard was that, like all great boxers, he was most dangerous after he'd been knocked down. The average boxer, once he's knocked down, he's shaken, something goes out of him. But when Leonard was knocked down and then would get up, he was much more dangerous than before. I liked Leonard near the end of his career a lot more than I liked him earlier. I had always sort of not liked him, he seemed a "yuppie," he seemed too clever. Like many people, I wanted [Marvin] Hagler to win their fight and couldn't believe when Hagler lost. Looking back, we might say that Hagler's finest moment—when he fought Tommy Hearns—turned him into a lesser boxer because of the beating he took from the man whom he beat. If Hagler had fought a different fight, he might have beat Hearns anyway, but he would not have been hurt as much. They both took terrible beatings. That was a fantastic fight.

What about the heavyweights?

I don't like heavyweights that much, except for the outstanding ones, like Ali. But most heavyweights, like Jerry Cooney, what can you say? I don't even want to see them. I've never seen George Foreman since he made his comeback. I refuse to look at a boxer whose physical being is an insult to a great sport. I don't want to see an overweight boxer in the ring. The sport is too important and has a history that the men who are in it should respect. That's why I was so shocked when Tyson came in out of condition with Buster Douglas. I couldn't believe that he would demean the heavyweight title. I found it very hard to watch Mike fight, because I knew him, and when I saw him lose the title to Douglas, I was so stunned. I literally couldn't believe my eyes. I could see when he came into the arena that night he was dry, he hadn't been sweating, he didn't look good. He hadn't done training. Intellectually, I saw that. Emotionally, when he came in the ring, I couldn't believe what a bad fight he was fighting. To me, that's much more profoundly disturbing and bizarre than the things that he did in his private life, which I can understand. I don't condone raping a young woman, but I can understand that a lot more than I can a heavyweight champion coming in at a young age and not being trained. That was very shocking to me.

Was it also shocking to you that your book *On Boxing* was praised by so many aficionados, including Norman Mailer?
Yes. Norman has said he feels a kinship with me. It was nice of him to say. He introduced me at Lincoln Center for a benefit evening and he said, "This person wrote an essay on boxing that was so good I thought I'd written it myself." And he didn't know why people were laughing. He meant it sincerely as the highest praise. I came out and said, "It's considered very high praise to be told you write like a man, but to be told that you write like Norman Mailer is off the scale!" And in my novel *You Must Remember This,* I'm really inside a person who's a boxer. I just love that part of the novel, that whole masculine ideology and the camaraderie of men in the gym. I don't suppose any other women novelists would even want to write about that.

How do you compare a boxing film like *Raging Bull* to Stallone's *Rocky* movies?
Anybody who likes boxing likes *Raging Bull,* and nobody who likes boxing likes the *Rocky* movies, because they're not about boxing, they're about weight lifters pummeling each other in the ring. I couldn't believe those *Rocky* movies—terrible.

Have you ever been approached to do a movie about boxing?
Dustin Hoffman spoke with me about my book on boxing. He wanted me to do a movie with him on a great trainer. I wasn't able to get together with him, but we talked over the phone once. He said

that he had wanted to be a boxer as a teenager. Boxing and acting—there is a real kinship.

Because both are so vulnerable?

I really admire actors who put so much of themselves in their work—they're so compulsive and perfectionist and physically present. They also seem to have such an ill-defined sense of themselves. They don't really know if they're good. They have to be told, more than most of us. They need applause, they need the constant adulation.

You're working on some screenplays based on your works now. Are you ever asked to write original scripts—not based on your stories—for actors?

I was asked for HBO if I would write the Jeffrey Dahmer story. I thought it was a strange invitation. And I was invited to write something on Mike Tyson for HBO and I declined. I don't have much time. I'm usually working all the time, sometimes up to midnight. I was so immersed in *What I Lived For,* a novel I'd been planning for a couple of years. It was my attempt to get inside the skin of a man, to deal with male sexuality in a very candid and nonjudgmental, realistic way. It was a challenge, because I certainly could have failed. I can't fail writing about women—I've written about women's sexuality many times—but this was something that I'd never really done before. The whole novel is completely this man going through four days of his life. It took me about two years to get the voice for this man—a lot of profanity, obscenity, but funny. I wanted him to be an average man.

What male writers have best captured the way a woman thinks and feels?

D. H. Lawrence is one of the pioneers in the male attempt to write about women. Lawrence had a sensibility that was perhaps androgynous; though he was a heterosexual male, he was also possibly homoerotic. He was attracted to men, too. He was an ideal artist in that he had an erotic feeling for much of nature. This kind of intense identification with some other living presence probably is necessary to be a writer. But I can't think of many of my male colleagues who've written very compellingly or convincingly about women. Faulkner is an example of a truly great talent who could not create any women characters of any depth; they tend to be caricatures. Melville has no women characters. Saul Bellow is a great writer who's concentrated on male portraits. His female portraits in some cases are compelling, but it's the male portraits that are really brilliant and memorable. Shakespeare was a great writer whose masculinity is pretty evident. He's created some great women like Cleopatra, but they tend to be somewhat mannish women.

Aren't you worried, then, that your male character might be considered a female-ish man?
Absolutely not. I feel that I know men from the inside. I've created a lot of male characters.

Why do you suppose that your contemporaries have such difficulty capturing women, but you don't have any difficulty capturing a man?
It's just a measure of what one's trying to do. I don't value one achievement over the other. Faulkner and Melville are great writers, it doesn't matter that they couldn't capture women as well as F. Scott Fitzgerald or D. H. Lawrence. The measurement of genius is *sui generis*. Geniuses are not compared with one another. I mean, it's not held against Chopin that he never wrote an opera.

Do you measure yourself against other writers?
No, it would be discouraging to do that. I don't like the idea of competition. We have great writers living today. It's very difficult for contemporaries to accept one another. Virginia Woolf said it's impossible. I agree.

What's the biggest compliment you've ever received as a writer?
I've been compared with the most extraordinary people like Bach, Melville. . . .

Since Melville is often considered to be America's greatest writer, isn't that comparison somewhat overwhelming?
Melville lived for years as a complete failure. That a man of such genius would think that he'd been a failure is just heartbreaking. That's one of the saddest stories in American literature. When he was writing *Moby-Dick* there was no prototype for it, it was an adventure story, it was a Shakespearean tragedy, it was metaphysical and philosophic speculation. Nobody had ever done that before in America. And then it got published and got the most vicious, ignorant, jeering reviews. Obviously his heart was broken, he didn't make any money, and after that his life took another turn. I kind of identify with him. Many writers do. It's like we've done the same thing but we're more lucky. When he died, his obituary in the *New York Times* was about *Henry* Melville—it even got his name wrong. Faulkner, too, was denigrated at home and treated very, very badly. Then he won a Nobel Prize and belatedly, a Pulitzer. Faulkner got his reputation in France and in Europe and then he got recognized at home. That might have happened with Melville in the twentieth century, but he was too early—essentially he was from a pioneer society, and there wasn't any place for those kinds of writers.

Hemingway said American literature starts with *Huckleberry Finn*, and Mailer said that William Burroughs changed the course of American literature. Do you agree?
No. In terms of history, Walt Whitman changed the course of American literature. He was saying things that nobody ever said before. Not William Burroughs, because very few people have even read him. But Whitman came along with *Leaves of Grass* in 1855, and he was saying things in his poetry, and he had a musical, incantatory voice in which he talked about being both male and female, standing up and talking

about homoeroticism, talking about having a baby. This is really profoundly contemporary and was so deeply disturbing to his contemporaries that he was considered extreme. And yet he has affected so many people.

Can a major writer alter, as Mailer called it, "the nerves and marrow of a nation"?
Not the United States. But definitely individuals are affected. Whitman. Charles Dickens, Dostoyevsky, Tolstoy, Solzhenitsyn. Harriet Beecher Stowe and Upton Sinclair had effects upon legislation in America. Emily Dickinson had effects upon individuals. People have told me that their lives have been changed by things I've written. A nun actually left the convent after she'd read a story of mine. Obviously she was inclined to feel that way, and then the story gave her a push. She just became the person that she maybe should have been.

You've harbored a Balzacian ambition to get the whole world into a novel, haven't you?
It's an ongoing ambition. It isn't possible, one can't do it, but . . . Balzac had such a magnitude of vision.

Which is your most Balzacian novel?
Maybe *Because It Is Bitter, And Because It Is My Heart.* Because it deals with a strata of society.

How much of a class society is America?
Oh, very much a class society. It's getting more and more self-evident. Segregation is more marked than it was in the 1960s. We have a new division between fundamentally illiterate people and the rest of our society that's educated and has knowledge of computers and the electronic medium. Along with other problems of poverty, the ghetto, drugs, I don't know what's going to happen. Los Angeles demonstrates that.

You dealt with an earlier city riot, the one in Detroit in 1967, in your novel *them*. Did you actually experience the riot?

We were only one block away from some of the burning and looting, and I'd never been in any situation like that where your physical being is at risk. You never forget it, and as a writer, you want to deal with it. It was not an easy time. Living in Detroit changed my life completely. I'd never lived in a city like that. I would still be writing a different kind of work right now had I not have been there. I came from this rural background, and suddenly I was thrust into the city in the 1960s that was so alive and fraught with excitement. There were boom times, a lot of building and expansion going on. We became acquainted with all kinds of people, including automobile executives, professors, writers. We even got to know two young people in [the radical group] Weatherman, who later went underground for being involved in that bombing in the state of Washington that killed somebody. Then there was the riots.

Were you yourself ever in physical danger?

Once I was leaving my friend's studio in the inner city and was walking to my car, and these guys were right behind me. A police car came around the corner, so these guys dropped back. You never really know what might have happened. But I miss Detroit, the excitement, the adventures. Now it's a different city. It's really depopulated.

Do you also miss the rural background of your youth? Or was that a little too country?

I don't want to make my childhood sound like something out of *Tobacco Road*. It wasn't. But I went to a one-room schoolhouse and the other students, particularly the boys, were very rough, really cruel kids. A lot of things just frightened me, but I had to face it day after day. At one point there were eight grades, and some of the boys were very big, like six feet tall, farm boys, very crude. We heard tales of things that had been done to other girls, acts of incest of an older brother forcing himself on a younger sister, then boasting about it. And I certainly was the object of molestation of one kind or another.

Verbal or physical?

Verbal is nothing, who cares about verbal? No, really physical. Being chased, being mauled. I was molested. I was not raped, but it would be considered sexual molestation today, when I was about nine or ten. And I couldn't go to my mother and say I was sexually harassed today at school. I was threatened not to tell. However, I never forgot it.

Did you have anyone you could talk with?

There was no consciousness. Molested, battered children were in a category that was like limbo, there were no words, no language. If you tried to talk about it, you'd say, "I was picked at." Then there was a certain amount of hesitancy, if not actual shame, to say anything about your body, so you wouldn't want to say where you were harassed. So a lot of this was never spoken. It was extremely important for me, retrospectively, to have these early experiences of being quite a helpless victim, because it allows me to sympathize—or *compels* me to sympathize—with victims. I know what it's like to be a victim, but I also know what it's like to get away and not have been damaged or scarred. I was part of a world where almost everybody who was weak was victimized. This seems to be the human condition: to be picked on, to be a victim.

Did this drive you inward, turn you to writing at an early age?

I was always writing little books when I was five or six, I would use a tablet and do drawings. I was never interested in dolls, I gave my dolls away. I was reading books like *Alice in Wonderland* and *Through the Looking Glass* when I was very young. I obviously was greatly influenced by Alice as a character who was a little girl but has some of the courage and resilience we associate with adults. And, of course, she's a female protagonist, and that made a strong impression on me. After sixth grade, I went on a bus into the city and I was more alone. I used to eat alone in a diner when I was eleven, and I liked that.

Wasn't this around the time your family returned to the Church?

My family became religious when my grandfather died of emphysema. He worked at a foundry and his lungs were filled with bits of metal. Our household was completely traumatized by that. My parents had been Catholic and they had been lapsed. That's a joke to other people, but to Catholics you are never not a Catholic. You're born Catholic and you're baptized, then you become a lapsed Catholic for the next ninety years. It's like an alcoholic, you're never not an alcoholic. So they went back to the Church when I was about twelve. You have to be no older than seven for the Church to do some work on you. I'm not a person who feels very friendly toward organized religion. I think people have been brainwashed through the centuries. The churches, particularly the Catholic Church, are patriarchal organizations that have been invested with power for the sake of the people in power. And they happen to be men. It breeds corruption.

I found going to church every Sunday and on holy days an exercise of extreme boredom. I never felt that the priest had any kind of connection with God. I've never felt that anyone who stands up and says, "Look, I've got the answers," has got the answers. I would look around in the church and see people praying and sometimes crying and genuflecting, saying the rosary, and I never felt any identification. I never felt that I was experiencing what they were experiencing. I couldn't figure out whether or not they were pretending.

Yet haven't you had some mystical experiences?
I actually had some experiences that were electrifying to me and changed my way of looking at life. But I haven't had them for a long time.

Can you describe what happened to you?
I can't talk about it. A mystical experience is ineffable and you can't put any language to it, because as soon as you do you demean and reduce it. You wouldn't have a mystical experience in a Sunday mass, you'd have it out in the wilderness. You'd have to be alone. It may not have any God involved, it would be more like an activation of the

deepest psyche. I've been interested in religious experience and the spiritual side of all of us, and mysticism. But organized religions such as the Catholic Church are the antithesis of religious experience. They take experience away from people and it's projected onto a hierarchy, and the priest or the cardinal or the bishop or the pope will say, "We will tell you what your experience is. We will tell you who God is and we will tell you how to get to heaven and how to avoid hell, you can't do it yourself." That's just the ground for extreme corruption and contamination.

Do you feel the same way about astrologers, numerologists, Tarot card and Ouija-board readers?
The persistence of crackpots, pseudoscientists like astrologers, suggests the tragic failure of science and education. How can we have people still being superstitious, still believing in nonsense and astrology and demonic, grotesque religions of every kind, every fundamentalist religion crowding us on all sides? How can we have this phenomena and say that science and education have not failed? From the Greeks to the present time. That's just embarrassing. Even in women's magazines, where there are some high ideals—they run horoscopes. People ask me what my sign is. This is a completely discredited pseudo-science, it never had any validity. These things come from the right hemisphere of the brain, they are primitive and childlike and I don't see why we should accommodate them; it's nonsense.

Tell that to the basketball coach who wears the same socks when his team is winning in the playoffs.
Well, it's just silly. If it were that easy to win, everybody would have aged dirty socks.

Sounds like you're not the kind of person who would seek out therapy to solve any problems.
I can't begin to imagine going to a psychotherapist. You're just going to another person who has some dogmatic ideas and his or her own agenda. Why go to somebody else anyway? Theoretically they're lis-

tening, but in fact they're not, they're looking at the clock, thinking, How can I bend this person to my own theories? I have friends who have done so, and I just think that you don't need to do it. Go for a long walk or go jogging, take a retreat and meditate and think. Or read Walt Whitman. Instead of doing that they run to a psychotherapist and/or they get prescription drugs without even trying.

Would it be fair to categorize your philosophy as: Shut up, don't complain, and get on with it?
I have strong interior models coming from my parents and grandmother of how a human being should behave with dignity. Not that I always live up to it, but I sure know how you die, how you deal with life without complaining, with as much strength as possible. I'm in a profession where people are so quick to complain about the smallest things, and their vanities and egos are easily bruised. To me, this is just absurd. The harshest facts of life have to do with the economy, with one's own economy. If you are poor, if you are living at or below the poverty line, then you're right up against life in a way that literary and academic or professional people are not. I come from a world where there was a fear that there wouldn't literally be enough money. Not enough to eat. I remember that. Now I'm in a world where somebody fears they'll get a bad review.

You also come from a world where one relative was murdered and another committed suicide.
My mother's father was murdered in a saloon fight when she was a baby, the youngest of eight or nine children. Their family was extremely poor, so she was given away to relatives. I only found out about it as an adult. Then I found out, many years later, that a relative put a gun in his mouth and shot himself while my father's mother was with him. This took place before I was born, however it's part of my parents' life. I'm pretty close to my parents, and a lot of my writing draws on their experiences. They really had adventurous and arduous lives growing up in the earlier part of the century, in a

rough part of America. And then coming of age as adults in the 1930s in the Depression. They were brave, strong people.

Their lives weren't made any easier after you were grown and your sister was born autistic. Being as verbal and articulate as you are, that must be something you've given much thought to.
I've written about the phenomenon of one person living in language and the other not having any language. My sister has not really ever spoken. She was born at a time when virtually nothing was known about autism. An autistic person has a little bit wrong with the brain chemistry. It's a mystery. She's now in a special home.

Given your history, it's understandable why you lean more toward tragedy than comedy and stories with happy endings.
I'm always struck by that wonderful remark of Henry James, how what's bliss for one person is bane or evil or pain for another. That's so true in life—that what's happy for one person can be painful for another. If you have a happy ending in a novel, it's probably not going to be happy for everyone.

Why are difficult and troubling works of art more beneficial than happy ones?
Well, the classic theory of tragedy is that it allows people to be ennobled, and we see people pushing to the limits of their courage and their involvement. King Lear, for instance, rises to a stature by the end of the play that he didn't have in the beginning. If it were a situation comedy and Lear was just dealing with a funny daughter, he would always be on the same level. Serious works of art push people to the extreme. That's why creative artists try risking things that could fail, because they feel that's how they learn more about themselves.

Can fiction show a person how to survive?
Oh, definitely. We pick our models from art. In the past, prose fiction and drama provided models for people. I'm sure many young people

get their role models from the movies and television, which may not always be good.

Are there any programs on TV that interest you?
I don't watch television. I don't have time.

What about news events such as political conventions or the Olympics?
No. If I wanted to know about the conventions I read the *New York Times.* And I'm sorry to say that I was no more interested in the Olympics than those athletes are interested in my writing. As many athletes are crowding one another at the bookstores to get hold of my books, that's as much as I watched that. I like to read. Television is a different kind of medium: it's for people who are skimming along on the surface of life.

Were you skimming yourself when you joined a sorority when you went to Syracuse University?
That was an unfortunate part of my life. I sort of gravitate along the lines of least resistance, not always thinking about what I'm doing, because I'm thinking so much about something else. This may be characteristic of so-called creative people. So I woke up and I was in this sorority and I couldn't get out. If I started skipping meetings, I would be fined $25 an evening. It was really expensive for me, so I was trapped. I certainly would not do that again.

With the way you work, would you have felt trapped if you had children?
I wasn't ever driven by a strong maternal instinct. Nor does my husband have a strong paternal instinct. We never really thought about it much.

Did you think about marriage before you met Ray?
I grew up in a time when young women were very conscious of wanting to be engaged as soon as possible. This was in 1960. To get mar-

ried was the ideal. But I was very different. I had no interest in getting engaged or married and not having a career. I was always bent on either teaching or being a writer. I had a very steady boyfriend all through college, but in retrospect we were just good friends. I don't think the romance was very strong on either side.

How old were you when you met Ray?

I was twenty-one and he was thirty, so he was an older man. This had a certain romance about it. He was getting his Ph.D. and I was beginning my M.A. I guess it was love at first sight. Or love at first conversation. We met at a social gathering and we started talking. I think of marriage and/or love as a long conversation that has many modulations to it. Ray's a very stabilizing force in my life. When I have trouble writing he is just a voice of calm.

Is that the secret to a successful marriage: stay calm and have long talks?

The secret is that one is closest friends with one's spouse, and it's a relationship that deepens with time. People have asked him how he can tolerate being married to a person like me, that he would be lonely because I'll be working so hard at my work, and the assumption is that he's not working at his. But he works just as hard and sometimes longer than I do in a given day. We're both workaholics.

Does Ray ever appear as a character in your books?

No, I'm so close to him that in a way I don't see him. I have assimilated him, which is typical for people who have been married quite a while. There's a kind of pronoun *we* consciousness.

Do you share with the housework?

I do all the housework and Ray does all the outside work—the lawn, the garden. I start making dinner at eight, which is pretty late. My take on cooking and housework is that it's part of my writing. Sometimes my brain is like a computer screen, and I can do my revisions and copy editing of the whole day's work while I'm preparing a meal.

When I'm done I'll go to my desk and make those corrections, then the whole thing's erased in my head.

Is it true that your husband never reads your work?
I have always felt that I didn't particularly want people close to me—my parents, my husband—to read my work. I wanted freedom and I didn't want people peering over my shoulder. I didn't want them to feel they had to like it. I'm not a person who gives my writing to my friends to read. I would feel very embarrassed to do that. Joan Didion and John Gregory Dunne read each other's work all the time. That's a very healthy, symbiotic relationship they've worked out. But Ray has so much of his own life to do, he just wouldn't have time to read any of my work. It's a little tricky or touchy or sticky to have a spouse reading one's work.

Who takes care of the finances in your house?
Ray is in charge of the finances. When he married me many years ago he could not have anticipated that he'd spend a lot of time dealing with accountants and investors and money men. It's nothing that he's interested in. We're both very literary people and interested in culture.

Are you also very rich?
How can you ask a question like that? If I said yes to that question, I'd have a burglar visiting immediately. I don't have much idea of how much money we have, but we're not really wealthy people. We don't spend money, put it that way. We live quite modestly. I'm not very concerned with money.

Still, with all those books still in print, you must constantly be receiving royalty checks from around the world.
Over the years I'm surprised by checks that come in because I don't expect them. I could probably live very comfortably on my income just from Germany and Sweden.

What does money mean to you?

Money is kind of a burden, because one feels that one should spend it intelligently. You can spend money in a consumptive way and just waste it, but to spend money intelligently, to direct it toward meaningful goals, to give to charities that are not going to be exploitive, that's difficult. We subsidize our friends in terms of publishing ventures. James Michener has given away millions of dollars. Giving away that amount of money has probably caused him creative angst.

Are you very uncomfortable talking about money?
When I grew up, sex was not talked about—it was a classic taboo subject. Now I think money may not be talked about. If a child were to ask his parents, "How much money do you make? How much is in the bank?" that might be the taboo subject today.

So let's talk about sex. Norman Mailer says that great sex makes one more religious.
How does Mailer know what is great? Maybe what he's experienced is very puny, but he has only his own experiences. Norman has a sense of being an entertainer. He's like a boxer—he feels you get in the ring and you want to put on a show and it's adversarial. I'm not like that. If I were a man, maybe I would be more like that.

Was sex a scary subject for you growing up?
Girls were and probably are afraid of sex—for a good reason. Getting pregnant was always the fear that girls had. It was a sense of public humiliation. For most young women in my generation it was a combination of reading novels and experience.

For many boys of your generation the novels to read were usually written by Henry Miller. Did you read him as well?
I read some of Henry Miller, but it's on the level of a comic book. People seem shallow, nothing that has any appeal to me. I do remember going to a library in the adult section when I was about twelve and I pulled *Ulysses* off the shelf and the whole book seemed to glimmer with a sort of forbidden glow, it was erotic and forbidden and ex-

citing and sacred. Now when I look at it I feel this identification with James Joyce, who was thirty-eight when he finished it. But he was a struggling writer, and that's the effort of his great struggle.

How seminal a work is *Ulysses* in modern literature?

What we call modern literature begins around the turn of the century. It explodes outward into a formal experimentation of language and structure. It had been anticipated in art in the nineteenth century by Cézanne and Monet and Manet and van Gogh. A good model would be *Ulysses,* because it's basically a work of a naturalistic intention in which Joyce wants to recapture it with voices of his childhood, predominantly his father. But he doesn't give it to us in a conventional form. It becomes a work in which the language is shimmering and musical. But Dublin is very real, it's a historically valid work, so it's a realistic novel. It became a sort of surreal novel in which the interior of the self is explored as well as the exterior self, so it's a watershed novel.

Which of your own novels are watershed in terms of your career?

Evidently *them*—it's the one people talk about. Maybe *Because It Is Bitter,* and *You Must Remember This*—so much of my own life and heart went into them. I can't tell, it's hard to get a bead on one's own self.

You omitted *Wonderland*, which caused you quite a bit of anxiety when you wrote it.

Probably the closest I ever came to cracking up was writing *Wonderland.* Appropriately enough it's about the human brain, examining a crisis in American society by way of one representative man. I had a large metaphor that was the brain. It's very hard to talk about. I thought that I had this neurological problem and had to see a specialist, but it was more a biochemical problem caused by stress. I put so much energy into that, it was such a monumental novel, very daunting to write. It left me kind of breathless. I felt when I was done that I didn't want to write any more long novels.

That didn't last too long. By the early eighties you were off and writing what has become your Gothic trilogy: *Bellefleur, A Bloodsmoor Romance, Mysteries of Winterthurn.* **Was that your attempt to show America as viewed through its most popular genres?**

Yes. And I still am much interested in that. Those novels are very surreal in their plans. It's like fables and folk tales and legends and myths, much of it from a woman's perspective. These are feminist rewritings of history. Seeing, for instance, Mark Twain from the perspective of a woman. I want to do two more postmodernist Gothic novels that will take American history up till about 1940. I started way back with *A Bloodsmoor Romance* that goes back to before we were a nation, to the colonies. Then I moved up with *Bellefleur*, which on one level was about the idea of empire, and *Winterthurn* takes us up to the administration of Teddy Roosevelt. I have two more novels planned that go through the Woodrow Wilson era and into Harding and up into FDR and ends with Roosevelt's election. These very big, massive, grandiose American history novels were all part of a plan, very definitely.

In 1985, you claimed *Mysteries of Winterthurn* **to be your most difficult and favorite novel. Has that changed?**

It's certainly one of my very favorite novels. I don't know why I love it so much. I can't imagine that I would ever love writing a novel more than that. It's so wild, kind of tall tales about women committing crimes.

How is writing a detective mystery novel different from other kinds of novels?

It's an intensification of other novels. You have to know where you're going. You have to begin with the ending. It's like a spiderweb. Like mathematics or solving a problem. It's not the kind of novel that Henry James would write.

What about the novels of Rosamond Smith; are they the kind of novels Joyce Carol Oates would write? Or did you choose that pseudonym to escape from your identity?

I wanted to write psychological suspense novels that are more cinematic than my other novels. However, as time has gone by, they have gotten more intellectual and analytical, more Jamesian, more interior. All the Smith novels are about twins of one kind or another.

How strongly did you want to keep your identity a secret?

I wanted very badly to keep it a secret. It was like being eleven years old again, like a little girl. I would have had reviews that were for a first novel, and everything would have been new and fresh and untried. But then the secret got out. My editor was very upset, and had reason to be. I didn't think it was that important if I wrote a novel under a pseudonym. Why would anyone care? But it's very hard to have a secret identity, because one has to have a Social Security number, income tax forms. . . .

Why'd you feel the need to go undercover?

Because people don't judge the new work as new work. In my case they say, "This is Oates's twenty-fifth novel, or fiftieth book." Whereas with my new identity it would have been, "Here is a new novel by a writer we haven't heard of." And the attentiveness would have been for the text.

Were you very disheartened when you were discovered?

It was sad. Disappointing.

Do you think the Smith novels are more accessible than your others?

Some of them have been mass-market paperbacks. And the first one, *Lives of the Twins,* was a made-for-television movie with Isabella Rossellini and Aiden Quinn. They changed the title to *Lies of the Twins* and changed the plot quite a bit. I didn't watch it.

Critic Alfred Kazin said that you write to relieve your mind of things that haunt us rather than to try and create literature that will live.

Well, Kazin doesn't know. It's sort of a statement like, "Does she dye her hair?" It's a haphazard pomposity that one gets from people who have no idea what they're talking about.

Do critics *ever* know what they're talking about?
It's very unpredictable. I get extremely good reviews or very angry reviews. People have said to me that they admire that I keep going. They have a very different reading of the enterprise of being a writer. My worst problems are inner-generated, they come from my own self.

You've said that a writer who has published as much as you have has developed a skin like a rhino. How necessary is it to be thick-skinned?
It's scar tissue over the years. I started writing before women's liberation, publishing since 1963, so I came under a lot of attack just because I was a woman writing about subjects that men usually write about. John Updike once said that I really took a lot of hostile criticism. Some writers stay down in the mud. D. H. Lawrence called it the scrimmage of life. I consider myself still down there. I'm fair game for the attack.

How wary are you of the New York literary community?
I guess I'm part of it. I review for the *New York Times Book Review* fairly often. And many of the people are people whom I know.

Let's talk about some of those people. Your opinion of Norman Mailer?
If anyone has literary presence and power in New York it would be Mailer. He has been very courageous and adventurous, he obviously loves the craft of fiction. He also gets negative reviews. People are either jealous of him or they have an ax to grind. Norman and I try different things all the time, different voices. We are much more vulnerable than many writers who repeat the same formulas for success. But Norman has taken a good deal of abuse. And it's good for him, he's a fighter, a counterpuncher. One should defend oneself.

Doris Lessing.
She's in the tradition of George Eliot—she's trying to write about society in a very ambitious way. Lessing's more like Norman Mailer and like me, for better or worse. She's tried different things.

John Updike.
A great writer, a major, important writer. I write to John Updike and he writes to me quite often. He's a wonderful letter writer.

Iris Murdoch.
I have read a lot of Iris Murdoch and I have written about her. There was a time when every new Murdoch novel came out I would be asked to review it. Her novels are somewhat repetitive.

Tom Wolfe.
He's obviously a satirist and a social critic. I don't think of Tom Wolfe as a literary figure, but he's amusing.

Flannery O'Connor.
She's an American classic. A very special, very individualistic, very idiosyncratic and, in an odd way, very Catholic writer. She had a gift for satire and treating character very quickly.

Eudora Welty.
She has a broader humanity than Flannery O'Connor. O'Connor was very narrow and good at what she did—she never wrote about romantic love, perhaps knew nothing about it. Welty tried many more things. She's more ambitious.

Saul Bellow.
Bellow's brilliant. Bellow is a genius. A great writer. Brilliant themes. Saul Bellow is off the scale of even Capote, Pynchon, or Thomas Wolfe. You can't compare him with these others.

How about Philip Roth?

Roth is not as ambitious as Bellow. He hasn't tried as many things. But what he does he does brilliantly. Philip is very self-conscious as a stylist. At some point in his life he needed to write like *Augie March,* which Bellow did. Over the top, pages and pages of description and melodrama and people talking . . . exaggeration. There's something about what Bellow is willing to do, it's a little like Mailer, let it all out and write things that you'll be criticized for. But Philip has been very self-conscious as a craftsman and his writing tends to be faultless.

Katherine Anne Porter.
She's a classic, but she basically didn't try very much.

T. Coraghessan Boyle.
Tom Boyle is a wild writer, very inventive, surreal, funny. He's a serious person.

Gabriel García Márquez.
I've enjoyed him very much. My favorite Márquez is the Faulknerian *Autumn of the Patriarch.* It's his best novel.

You're a big Faulkner fan, aren't you?
Faulkner was very ambitious and very courageous in what he did. And that accounts for a lot. The South American writers were immensely influenced by Faulkner. Without Faulkner, Márquez wouldn't have been Márquez. To speak of greatness, we're speaking of Faulkner.

How about J. D. Salinger?
He was, or is, a very winning and appealing writer who had a strong appeal at a certain time. But there's no comparison with Faulkner. I wouldn't even put them in the same room together.

Who influenced Faulkner?
He derives partly from Flaubert, partly from Joseph Conrad, very much from James Joyce, and a bit from the Southern tall-tale tellers like Mark Twain.

You're a friend of Anne Tyler and Joan Didion, aren't you?

Yes. I've read all of their work. I like Anne's writing very much. It's certainly different from what I'm doing. I think the way I'm writing is probably the way Joan Didion writes, where she does a lot of revision. Her prose has that feel, a Hemingway tautness to it. And her ironic vision is one that I feel comfortable with.

Are you familiar with Cormac McCarthy?

His last novel, *All the Pretty Horses,* was wonderful. That will have an effect on younger male writers, probably not women writers. Here was an unabashedly and shamelessly romantic novel about the coming of age of a young man. And no serious writer has written about this in a long time. I actually wrote him a note and sent him a book of mine, which I thought related to what he was doing, called *I Lock My Door Upon Myself*—the language and the use of tall tales and going into the countryside and the mysticism of nature is similar to what he was doing in his novel.

Toni Morrison, who teaches as well at Princeton.

Toni is a technician, a born writer, an artist of language. She's like the black writer John Edgar Wideman, whose prose is like music. Toni is very flamboyant and very Faulknerian in the good sense of the word.

F. Scott Fitzgerald.

He was a brilliant, gifted, somewhat limited writer who needed to live longer. He simply didn't develop.

Virginia Woolf.

I like her journals and letters immensely. I think her fiction has been sentimentalized by women and feminists. She's become a heroine, but some of the prose fiction is hard to get through, it has a lot of problems. She's like Hawthorne in a way that the journals are so much more interesting than the fiction.

Ernest Hemingway.

I've always read Hemingway for his prose. I've never thought his characters were very interesting, they seem to be very flat and childlike. His dialogue seems infantile, but his eye for nature and his ear for language were breathtaking. If you want subtleties of character you don't find them in Hemingway, you find them in Henry James.

Henry James.
A great master, he's up there, he's like Shakespeare.

Bernard Malamud.
He was a wonderful short story writer, just brilliant, the use of the vernacular. And Malamud was very different from his narrator. He spoke in very formal, even clipped English, very precise, so that when one met Bernard one was usually surprised at how different he was from his own writing.

Isaac Bashevis Singer.
Very experimental. My favorite Singer stories are the fabulous ones that have magic in them. He's a remarkable writer.

Susan Sontag.
Another friend. She's very ambitious, very smart, analytical, intelligent.

Samuel Beckett.
I virtually stopped reading Beckett because he seems to me somewhat repetitive.

Harold Brodkey.
Oh, I can't talk about Harold Brodkey. He was terribly victimized by a grandiose reputation that no one could have lived up to.

Danielle Steele.
I've never read her. There are people who are looking for entertainment, and women read Danielle Steele because they are romances and

they can identify, they have happy endings. I guess. Stephen King is more interesting as an American phenomenon than a romance writer. I have read some of his work and I did like it. King is a naturally gifted, compulsive artist who is exorcising private demons that, happily for him, have hooked up with public demons. And he's able to write in a popular mode. I would guess he's not a person who fusses over his prose and does the sorts of things that Henry James or T. S. Eliot did. But he's hooked in with popular culture, so he makes references to television and to brand names.

The Russians: Tolstoy, Dostoyevsky, Chekhov.
These writers are just unquestionably great. I prefer Dostoyevsky to Tolstoy. Tolstoy had a misogynous strain with the Christian dogmatism, which hasn't held up very well. Dostoyevsky is in some ways a careless writer. Can a great work of art be sloppily written? I think it can. Shakespeare did things pretty fast, he could have revised a bit, but when you're on that level of great genius it scarcely matters. The prototype of all genius, the naturally gifted genius, is Mozart, who never revised. But for those of us who revise a lot it might be Beethoven, who, in some people's imaginations, was a greater composer than Mozart.

Do you read many biographies?
There are a lot of very, very good biographies. We're all fascinated by personalities and by lives perceived as narratives with beginnings, middles, and ends. And many contemporary novels and works of fiction don't satisfy that desire. The writing is much more elliptical or experimental, so you're not getting the full panoply of the richness of a life that we would expect from the great novels of Dickens or Thomas Hardy or George Eliot, so we go to biographies for that.

Is the novel the most moral of art forms?
For me the novel is the hardest art form that I work with. But any art form can be very moral. And there are some art forms like the movies that are very curious, because they can have moral intentions but

they've seemed to glorify immoral or antimoral activity. I was reading about some young boys who murdered a playmate. They had been influenced by one of the *Godfather* movies. The morality of those films is really that this is a vicious life and it consumes the people who are in it, but these kids saw the movie and took away none of that, and they were left with certain images which they imitated. So art is a very curious phenomenon in that it can have moral intentions and yet it works against them.

What would you say has been your most influential work?
One short story, "Where Are You Going, Where Have You Been?" has been anthologized a good deal and made into a movie called *Smooth Talk,* and everywhere I go, people ask me about that.

Martin Scorsese plans to produce *You Must Remember This,* which Martha Coolidge will direct from your script. Are you excited about this?
Excited is a word that's not in my vocabulary, but I'm very hopeful.

When the movie is made of your life, who would you like to play you?
Oh, that's really science fiction.

Capote thought the ghost of Eisenhower would be right for him.
Oh well . . . the ghost of Henry James.

We haven't talked about how you write. Do you use a computer?
I don't have a word processor anymore. I write in longhand first, that's the only way I can be in touch with the emotions that the people are going through. Then I go to the typewriter and it starts to be something different. Much more in control and meticulous. That's a different process. Ninety percent of what I do now is revision. The task before me is very much organizational and structural. It has to do with language. I have the characters all there, the plot, and now

it's up to me to build the bridge to have the structure that will take them over to the other side.

Have you ever written a story in one sitting?
Never. I was very upset when somebody said it in the *Times Book Review*. It's the most insane thing.

Do you often work on two novels simultaneously?
No, I never do that.

How important are names for your characters?
Absolutely important. I spend a long time naming names. If I can't get a name right, I can't write, I can't begin. I have a lot of people's names that begin with J, especially men. It's like my alter ego. I always go for the J if I can get away with it.

What about a journal—do you keep one?
I've kept a journal for about twenty years. It may one day be published in some severely edited form. It's more of a journal than a diary.

Have you ever used drugs to stimulate your thinking?
No, I'd no more do that than I'd take a bottle of ink and pour it on my rug. What if you stained your consciousness permanently? It's not a gamble that I would consider significant.

Does it bother you that your books rarely make the best-seller lists?
Popular writing appeals to great masses of people and my writing doesn't. I don't have a wide readership, but I've sold over a long period. They can be horizontal best-sellers rather than vertical best-sellers.

You teach two writing classes at Princeton. Can writing be taught?
We're not teaching writing, we're teaching writers. I believe in helping gifted students get published. I really want to be like a trainer, where

you keep pushing and pushing the gifted writer. I'm looking for my Mike Tyson.

Why study novels, poetry, art?
To gain insight into civilization, cultural history, the human spirit. It can be a profound experience. It's like you're going inward into your own being as well as dealing with the language. The thing that I'm most interested in, or would be if I had the ability and time, is the history of the universe. That interests me immensely.

Are you familiar with Stephen Hawking's *A Brief History of Time*?
No, but people say it's really incoherent. My astrophysicist friends say it's really not very good, that people are reading it and pretending to understand it but it's incomprehensible. When people are talking on that level it's impossible for those of us who are laymen to even know what they're talking about.

Some feel that way about the themes of novelists. *Newsweek* **declared your subject to be "passion and its irrational power over human destinies." Would that be accurate?**
That may be part of it. I certainly do feel that we're guided by subterranean impulses. And I don't just mean individuals, I mean the collective. I mean entire nations. Completely subterranean, unacknowledged desires. You see it in countries like Iraq and Iran. It seems like a wave of irrationality just rushes through a whole people and could carry them almost to suicidal behavior. And then you see it in individuals. Nietzsche said that madness in individuals is a rarity, but in nations it's the norm. It's a good point.

In *Black Water* you attack former President Bush as being evil, exploitative, hypocritical, shallow—would he qualify as a mad Nietzschean individual?
You're being too meticulous. I'm just amazed that Bush has gotten away with such blatant falsehoods. He says things that are screamingly untrue, like Clarence Thomas is the best person, male, female,

black or white, to sit on the Supreme Court, and nobody would believe that, including Clarence Thomas!

We take it you voted for Clinton?
Yes. As long as I don't have to listen to him speak. Or listen to Al Gore go on and on shamelessly about his son.

You once sat next to Henry Kissinger during a meeting of artists and intellectuals with then Soviet Premier Gorbachev. You also wrote critically of Kissinger in the past. Was it awkward?
It was a funny situation, because people are always saying, "I admire your work." Kissinger actually said something like that to me, and it's so hypocritical. I guess it's just courteous. He's a very dangerous megalomaniac, the very Claus von Bulow of statesmanship.

What was your impression of Gorbachev?
I truly admire Gorbachev. Here was this wonderful, intelligent statesman who came to talk to us and our own president was such a fool. Gorbachev addressed this group of people for two hours, very spontaneously, without any notes . . . compared to our President Ronald Reagan, who arguably could not have spoken for twenty seconds without a teleprompter, and even then might have read it inaccurately.

You obviously lean more toward the downtrodden and invisible sectors of our society than those in positions of power when it comes to your writing. Do you feel a responsibility to be a voice for the powerless?
Yes, I do. There are a lot of people whom nobody cares about. They work at the minimum wage, they're exploited, they exist all around us, but they're invisible. They can't write about themselves, they don't have any language, sometimes they're illiterate. So if anybody's going to write about them, it's got to be someone who can feel sympathy for them. And I've always felt the sense of "there but for the grace of God go I."

It seems ironic that among the powerless you have championed was a woman who was not illiterate or invisible but surely exploited. I'm coming back to *Blonde* and your tour de force fictionalization of Marilyn Monroe. Do you feel that her greatest desire was to be wanted?

Yes. To be loved. She didn't feel she deserved to live, or to be born. There are many people like that. These people are often very creative, very energetic, they're workaholics, they're trying to prove that they deserve to be alive. Then there's a whole large category of other people who don't feel that way, they just live ordinary lives, completely happy being unknown.

You write that one could see the doom in her by the time she was nineteen. Was she fated to be destroyed?

She came of a certain class, she's like the Okies in California. The photographer who takes her pinup shot thinks she's one of all these thousands of girls who come to Hollywood to be used and then tossed out

What would you say were the three greatest disappointments of her life?

The first great disappointment would have been losing her mother, being put into an orphanage and then a foster home. Then the prevailing disappointment was never having a father who would acknowledge her. Then the third would be a combination of a failure to have a happy marriage and a failure to have a baby. They're all very personal and have nothing to do with her career.

How much of a victim of the casting couch was she? Did she have a choice?

She was absolutely a victim of the casting couch . . . that expression is valuable. She never had any choice about that. It went on for years and years. It's because she came from such a lower economic level.

You describe her attempting to kill herself after discovering her lover, Cass Chaplin, in bed with Edward G. Robinson's son. In real life, apparently, it was Cass Chaplin who walked in on Marilyn with his brother, Sydney.

Yeah, I got rid of some of these extra men.

That's a pretty drastic change, though, going from a heterosexual to a homosexual scene. What made you change this?

I know the three of them were seen together, they were young, attractive people in Hollywood, a bit on the margins. One of them, it may have been Chaplin, introduced Marilyn to drugs. I'm just assuming this kind of drug, promiscuous sex life that I'm writing about.

How did she see her marriages to Joe DiMaggio and Arthur Miller?

She didn't really want to marry DiMaggio, he talked her into it and it only lasted a few months. He was very much attracted to her as a beautiful blond girl. He had a taste for starlets and models. But the Arthur Miller marriage was much more stable, it lasted four years. He was much more thoughtful about the relationship. He obviously loved her as a person. He did feel that she was marrying him for reasons that were partly unconscious. He's a smart man, a substantive man. He must have understood that she was idolizing him and that ultimately it wasn't a realistic relationship, it was more like fantasy. But he's a very subtle thinker, much more subtle and sensitive than Joe DiMaggio.

You say that Arthur Miller "would not bend truth even in the service of art." Is this a major failing in his work?

I do admire his work, though I don't think he's on the level of Chekhov, but who is? He's more of a moralist. If you compare him to Tennessee Williams, Williams is the greater artist because he could go into poetry and fantasy, whereas Arthur Miller is pretty dogmatic. But he's intelligent, he's a considerable playwright.

After the failure of her marriage with Miller, she got involved with President Kennedy. How sordid was that relationship?
It was pretty bad. I didn't talk about her relationship with Frank Sinatra, Dean Martin . . . I guess all these men sort of passed her around to one another. It was kind of disgusting.

Your Marilyn is murdered by an injection to the heart from The Sharpshooter. Who does The Sharpshooter symbolize?
I was thinking of the extreme right-wing, which was very active in California and elsewhere in the 1950s, aligned with the FBI and J. Edgar Hoover. There was a terrible fear and paranoia about communism and Communist sympathizers and homosexuals, Marxists, Jews, that would breed a figure like The Sharpshooter, who basically is just up for hire, he's a patriot. I was thinking of people like Timothy McVeigh or Lee Harvey Oswald. But also, he may well be her imagination. She has this somewhat hallucinatory imagination near the end of her life. She thinks somebody is spying on her. Historically, in fact, there was surveillance on Marilyn Monroe. Her phone was tapped and it may have been the FBI because of her involvement with John F. Kennedy.

Do you think the real Marilyn was murdered?
There are three general theories: one that she committed suicide deliberately; one that she took an overdose of barbiturates in a befuddled state, didn't know what she was doing, and died accidentally; or that she was murdered by the FBI or the Secret Service, maybe the Kennedys, maybe J. Edgar Hoover.

You combined all three in your novel.
I did, that's what I wanted to do, to make it like a poem or a dream sequence in a movie, where people if they thought about it could have different interpretations.

What kind of life and career might she have had had she lived?

If she stayed in New York and worked in the theater she could still be acting, playing older roles in Chekhov, Ibsen. She didn't try hard enough with that side of her career.

Do you feel you've given her back her humanity?
That's what I hope, her inner poetic self that has been lost. The spiritual self that we all have.

What actress today might you compare with her?
People say Madonna or Julia Roberts, but they're nowhere near her. Madonna seems very shallow and two-dimensional.

Do you think *Blonde* might be your most widely read book?
I don't know, but if so, it's because of Marilyn Monroe.

With such a body of work already behind you, what are your thoughts about immortality?
It's just a word, a wishful word. People are not immortal.
Why do we feel haunted by the dead or by thoughts of death?
It's all very sad how we love people and they are so fiercely individual and so priceless and they pass away and then as we in turn pass away into oblivion their memories are gone. It's the eternal drama of a species, of time burying the dead. The wheels keep turning.

Do you feel you've accomplished much of what you wanted to do if your life ended suddenly?
I will never live long enough to execute all the ideas I have. Probably everybody has serious work to do and wild stories to tell, but life gets in the way. Everybody has a novel to write.

But not everybody who writes one has a chance for a Nobel Prize. How would you feel if you were so honored?
It would be a great honor, and it would bring honor to a body of work and to a group of people—American women writers. And it

would probably change my life irrevocably. If it comes too soon it can have an adverse effect, like with Albert Camus, who was the youngest Nobel Prizewinner. When he won it I think he was only forty-four. He seemed then to have felt that he could not live up to it. But if it comes at the end of a career, obviously that's very different.

So it's still something a long way off in your dreams?
I'm sure I have a long way to go. I won't hold my breath.

NEIL SIMON

"Ssshh, He's Writing"

FOR TWO HOURS ON AN OCTOBER AFTERNOON IN 1985, IN an empty theater in Los Angeles, Neil Simon talks about his life. This is before he's written the last of his "Jerome" trilogy *(Brighton Beach Memoirs, Biloxi Blues, Broadway Bound),* and before he twice married and divorced Diane Lander and had a daughter (his third) with her. He lost his first wife, Joan Baim, to cancer in 1973. His second marriage to actress Marsha Mason lasted ten years. There'd be another wife, Elaine Joyce, after Diane. But at this moment in his life, years before either of his 1996 and 1999 memoirs have been written, he's a single man enjoying enormous success and willing to reflect on how he came to be the "Shakespeare of his time."

He's not a very imposing figure, but then neither is Woody Allen or Alan Greenspan, and neither was Napoleon or H. L. Mencken. He doesn't suck the air out of a crowded room the way Orson Welles or John F. Kennedy did, but he towers like a Colossus over the American Theater. When Neil Simon's time comes to be judged among successful playwrights of the twentieth century, he will definitely be first among equals. No other playwright in history has had the run he has: fifteen "Best Plays" of their seasons, three Tony Awards, a Pulitzer Prize, a Broadway theater named after him. And when he's not preparing a play (he's written thirty) he's writing a movie (twenty-five of those) or his memoirs.

Is there a person of moviegoing age who hasn't seen at least one of Neil Simon's films, from the 1967 *Barefoot in the Park* starring Robert Redford and Jane Fonda to Walter Matthau and Jack Lemmon as *The Odd Couple,* Charles Grodin, Jeannie Berlin, and Cybill Shepherd in *The Heartbreak Kid,* Matthau and George Burns in *The Sunshine Boys,* Richard Dreyfuss and Marsha Mason in *The Goodbye Girl,* Lemmon and Sandy Dennis in *The Out-of-Towners* (remade with Goldie Hawn and Steve Martin), Matthew Broderick in *Biloxi Blues*?

But movies are secondary to the plays, which began with *Come Blow Your Horn* in 1961, followed by *Little Me, Barefoot in the Park, The Odd Couple, Sweet Charity, The Star-Spangled Girl, Plaza Suite, Promises, Promises, Last of the Red Hot Lovers, The Gingerbread Lady, The Prisoner of Second Avenue, The Sunshine Boys, The Good Doctor, God's Favorite, California Suite, Chapter Two, They're Playing Our Song, I Ought to Be in Pictures, Fools, Brighton Beach Memoirs, Biloxi Blues, Broadway Bound, Rumors, Lost in Yonkers, Jake's Women, Laughter on the 23rd Floor, London Suite, The Dinner Party.*

Simon was born in the Bronx, N.Y., on the 4th of July, 1927. His father worked in New York's garment district selling piece goods to dress manufacturers. He wasn't always a presence in his two sons lives because he kept leaving their mother. The person closest to Neil was his eight-year-older brother, Danny, who became his first writing partner. The brothers worked together and apart on some popular television shows, among them "Caesar's Hour," "Sergeant Bilko," and "The Garry Moore Show." Yet Simon believed there was more to life than sitting in a room with a half dozen frenzied comedy writers competing for the brightest quip, and made the decision to leave the sitcom world to try his hand at playwriting. It didn't come easy, but it came, and once he had a taste of his name in lights, opening nights, and laughter in the dark, he knew he had found a home.

In the first volume of his *Collected Plays,* Simon compares himself to Lon Chaney's portrayal of Lawrence Talbot—a monster who turns back into a man. The writer, especially the comic writer, he says, is a creature who at the first sign of personal, human involvement (like a fight with his wife) transforms into "the most feared and dangerous beast on earth, the observer-writer." His wife throws a frozen veal chop at him and whacks him above his right eye and he responds by smiling—she has given that great gift: material! His behavior is monstrous, he admits it; but he can't help it. He's cursed to be a part of those "strange breeds called writers." They get involved, and then step back to watch the proceedings. He observes, he records, he creates. And then he turns the light inward. "Not content to prey on his fellow creatures, the Monster eventually turns on his Alter Ego, the Human Being, and dissects himself unmercifully."

The dissection continues in the introduction to the second volume of his *Collected Plays,* where he writes of being in a perpetual state of a "no-man's land of self-evaluation. On a Tuesday I see myself as so gifted that I think the cornflakes I left over for breakfast should immediately be wrapped and sent to some Literary Museum for bronzing and held for posterity. . . . Come around on a Thursday and I will grovel at your feet to take me on as a shipping clerk in a dockside factory that manufactures 'I Love New York' ashtrays. My confidence not only blows with the wind but is susceptible to the currents caused by a butterfly at rest."

More self-doubts end his introduction to volume three. He's just completed *Lost in Yonkers.* He loves it. But his previous experience with *Jake's Women* makes him acutely aware how much of a crapshoot each new opening night is. "We've already seen what my confidence or lack of it can lead to. Betrayal, betrayal, time and again."

Not this time. *Lost in Yonkers* would bring Simon his first Pulitzer. It would bolster his confidence to go on, into his seven-

ties, to write more plays, more movies, even books. He had finally
learned to live with his insecurities—and has probably found security in them.

**You're considered to be the most successful playwright in
history. Is that a blessing or a burden?**
Both. It's only a blessing in terms of your ego, to think that that's
happened. I don't know how it helps me in any other way. I don't
think people go to see my plays just because I wrote them. They wait
to see the reviews, to hear the word-of-mouth. I've had a few plays the
audience didn't like and they disappeared after two months. They
judge me play by play. There are critics with their prejudices. John Simon saying, "I can't believe it, I actually like Neil Simon's *Biloxi Blues*"
sort of threw me, because it meant I couldn't hate him completely
anymore. I do happen to think he's a very intelligent critic who does
have his prejudices.

**How does it feel to be the only living playwright to have his name
on a Broadway theater?**
That was a thrill. I have a hunch that it will start to happen more to
other people in the theater. Certainly if anybody deserves his name
up on a contemporary theater now it would be Stephen Sondheim. I
once owned the Eugene O'Neill Theater in conjunction with another
man, but the fact that it had O'Neill's name on it was like a dream
come true, because I remember reading about Shakespeare having his
own theater. So I knew I could always bring my plays to my theater. I
don't own the Neil Simon Theater, someone else does. But when I
drive by there and see the name up in lights, for however long it's going to last, it's thrilling.

I would think it's monumental.
It is.

Do you feel you've influenced the theater?

I hate questions like that because it pushes me to make an answer that is going to be filled with myself.

But a case can be made that every young actor who has tried comedy has probably done one of your plays.
I'm sure Truman Capote could have handled a question like this because he was so much easier talking about what he felt about his own work. I'm not that immodest or modest about it, I'm just not that sure about what my place is. I know that I've been very successful. Being very successful is not always the most gratifying thing in the world. You also would like to be recognized for quality. Once in a while it happens in both areas at the same time.

You've written nearly two dozen plays and another two dozen screenplays in the last quarter of a century—do you worry at all about drying up?
Sometimes I do, but there will come in a flourish four or five ideas. There have been times when I feel I just haven't the slightest idea about what I want to do. It's never that you don't come up with an idea, any prolific writer always comes up with ideas. Writer's block is: it's not good enough. But you never just see blankness.

Is it different writing a play versus a movie?
I always feel more like a writer when I'm writing a play because of the tradition of the theater. If you think of who was the greatest playwright, you say Shakespeare. And then you say, "Hey, I'm in the same business with Shakespeare." You think of screenwriters—not that there aren't great screenwriters, there are—but there is no tradition of the screenwriter, unless he is also the director, which makes him an *auteur*. So I really feel that I'm writing for posterity with plays, which have been around since the Greek times.

For every play or script that gets produced, how many are there that are unfinished or unproduced?

I only have one full-length play that I tried out in a regional theater but did not go on with it. It was called *Actors and Actresses,* about a troupe of actors traveling by bus and truck. It was about what their sordid, tawdry, unhappy lives were like. But I've written four or five films that are still in the drawer.

Why is drama considered a higher art than comedy?

Age-old question and controversy. I'm not quite sure. People think anything that is serious is more important. Maybe it is. Comedy is much harder to do. It's just not given the same respect. I don't write pure comedies anymore. The first thing that I think of in writing something is, What is it I'm trying to say? Whereas in the beginning I'd say, How can I make this funny? By and large my plays now are dramatic with a great deal of humor and comedy.

How did you get the nickname Doc?

My brother gave me that. When I was two, someone brought a toy stethoscope with little sugar candy balls in it. I started examining people and he called me Doc. What amazes me is a nickname like that would stick around for all of these years. Almost everybody I know who are friends calls me Doc. I think they assume it's because I'm a play doctor, I go in and work on other people's plays. I have rarely done that.

Do you prefer Neil now to Doc?

Yeah.

Was your family a good audience for you?

Not really. I wasn't very funny around my mother or father. I don't think they would appreciate the kind of humor I dealt with, they wouldn't understand it. My mother would laugh out of pure affection. She never got the joke, she just laughed because I was saying it. She did the same for my brother Danny. We both worked together for a number of years and she was our first audience. We would read the material to her and she would sit and laugh. When my brother would ask her, "Did you get it?" She'd say, "No, but I like the way you do it." She was a good mother.

Didn't your father used to boast that practically nothing could make him laugh?

Yeah. There were very few comedians that he laughed at. He found that a matter of some pride—I can't imagine why. One of the men that he thought was incredibly funny was a man that I, too, loved as a comedian: Bert Lahr. He was an acting comedian, he was enormously funny but could also do something like *Godot* and be quite brilliant in it. But my father thought it was foolish to go into show business because he never knew anybody personally who ever made it, and certainly not as a writer. He wanted us to go into the post office, where the civil service check came every week and you were sure to get your money. That's a Depression-period mentality. Once I started writing the plays—and he did not live to see many of them; he died shortly after my third play, *Barefoot in the Park*—he was the biggest seller of tickets of anyone I knew. He went all through the garment district in New York where he worked, saying, "You ought to go see this play."

So in the end, you were able to make your father laugh?

I don't know if he laughed . . . he did laugh at *Come Blow Your Horn,* because that was about the family. There was a man onstage, Lou Jacobi, playing my father. The ironic thing was that when the play was over my father said, "I loved it, it was just wonderful. And the thing is I know so many people just like that." He never saw himself. Just as he had seen *Death of a Salesman* and came home and said, "What a great play. It's so true to life. It's about this wonderful father who has two rotten sons."

There was a lot of disharmony in your family, wasn't there?

Yeah, it was sort of living on a yo-yo. My father and mother broke up maybe ten times, which was probably worse than breaking up once and being gone. This was getting to live with expectations and disap-

pointments. I would come home from school one day and my
mother had a beaming smile saying, "Dad is coming home." I'd say,
"Great! He's going to be here again." It meant security, it meant
money was coming back into the house, and also I liked being with
him. A year later he could be gone. To this day I never really knew
what the reason for all the fights and battles were about between the
two of them.

But your mother always took him back?
Always.

So this was really the pattern of their relationship.
Yes. I don't know if she knew he'd be coming back. She would swear
off it. She'd hate him and be very angry, but he would come back and
she would take him back. She really loved him.

Did it create a lot of anxieties for you and your brother?
As a child, yeah. It's partly why I became a writer, because I learned to
fend for myself very early. There was no sense of security and no one I
could depend on. I couldn't depend on my father. I couldn't depend
on my mother a lot, except for love. I got a great deal of love from her
and for her. What I couldn't depend on was her emotional stability.
She would panic and fall apart when these things would happen. She
did manage to get through it all and provide for us, though I don't
know how she always did it. She would work a little bit here and
there. But I began to think early on, at the age of seven or eight, that
I'd better start taking care of myself somehow, emotionally. It's
worked for me and against me. It made me strong as an independent
person, but sometimes it isolated me, because when you depend on
yourself so much, you tend to cut off other people. I found that my
circle of friends and family was always very small. I didn't trust lots of
people.

Have your early friends lasted?

The friends that I've had have lasted over the years. Maybe there's ten or twelve really good friends.

Did you go to a lot of different schools growing up?
When the family started to break up, I started to go to a lot of junior high schools, maybe four of them. At one point my mother and I moved in with a cousin, so I had to move to another section of New York. Then we moved to another place. So I never developed a lot of friends in school—they were all from the neighborhood that I grew up in.

Were you the only Jewish kid in any of your schools?
There was one school in Queens where there was one other Jewish kid. It's where I felt the first experiences of anti-Semitism, which I didn't understand. They would hear the name Simon and laugh. I never thought that was a particularly Jewish name, I always thought it was a rather English name. In this particular school there was some harassment and I felt isolated, like I was a Martian. They didn't know what to expect from a Jew—what one looked like or sounded like. It was crazy. I grew up in a neighborhood that was all Jewish, Italian, Spanish, black, Irish. The only thing that saved me was I went out for the baseball team and I made it. I was a pretty good athlete, and being a good center fielder they took me in, but they didn't take in the other Jewish boy. And I didn't go to bat for him. I didn't know how to deal with it, so I felt a great deal of guilt about it. I eventually wrote about this in *Biloxi Blues*.

Was it Charlie Chaplin who inspired you to be funny?
Everybody has an influence on you. I don't know if he inspired me to want to write, because most of the movies I saw of his were silent films and I never thought that they were written. I thought they turned the camera on these people and they did all that stuff. But it was the appreciation of his ability to make people laugh—that was the only thing that I saw in the future for myself as a connection with people. I knew I was never going to be an athlete or a doctor or a

politician. I said, What am I going to do with my life that I can do well and that I'd like to do? My brother encouraged me early on in terms of my sense of humor, my observation of things, which was slightly offbeat and oblique. With Danny's encouragement and the people that I saw in films and listened to on the radio I felt that's where I belonged. Then I started reading the humorists a lot. Mark Twain, Stephen Leacock, Robert Benchley. I used to do my own versions of their style of writing, because I didn't have a style. And I found I could imitate theirs until gradually I started to write my own.

Your brother was the inspiration for *The Odd Couple*, but didn't you suggest that he write that himself?
Yeah, I saw him living it. He lived with a friend of his, Roy Gerber, who was an agent. They were both recently divorced. They would frequently invite girls to have dinner at their house rather than go out, and Danny was a pretty good cook. I would go over there occasionally and be witness to this. I would hear the fights that Danny and Roy would have, it sounded like a husband and wife fighting. I said, "Danny, you've got to write this as a play." So he started it, but Danny was never comfortable writing alone. He liked writing with me or with other writers. Danny's an incredible editor. He teaches comedy writing now all over the country. Woody Allen said he learned more about comedy writing from Danny Simon than anyone he ever worked with. I did, too, but I didn't learn it as from a teacher, we did it together, but he was always ahead of me. He's eight years older than I am and he seemed to have an intuitive feeling for it. Where I was coming up with lots of funny things, he was shaping them. His grasp of what made funny things funny helped me to edit my own work, so when I eventually left Danny he left his impression on me.

Before the plays there was radio and television. Did it all begin in the mail room at Warner Bros.?
Well, that was the first job I had getting out of the army. My brother had preceded me there. He worked in the New York office of Warner

Bros. Pictures, first in the mail room and then in publicity. He got me a job there. But that did not lead to anything in show business. There was a press agent there, Sid Garfield, who told us about Goodman Ace, who was a wonderful radio writer. CBS started a stable of young writers. They wanted to invent a program for them to write on, and then use these people to fill up the needs of their future radio and TV shows. We got on a show they created for an actor named Robert Q. Lewis. They put it on Saturday night at six o'clock when they knew no one would be watching or listening to it. But they knew it was a good way for us to learn to fail. We worked on it for about a year and got a lot of good experience out of it.

When you wrote for TV it was called the Golden Age. Was it really?
Some was bronze, some tin. This, today, will eventually be the Golden Age of somebody else's period in TV. But there were a few landmark shows back then—"Playhouse 90" for drama, and in comedy, "Your Show of Shows"—which eventually turned into "Caesar's Hour"—and "Sergeant Bilko," which I was lucky enough to work on both. Between the two of them I spent five years and learned more about what I was eventually going to do than in any other previous experience.

How do you compare TV then to today?
I don't watch situation comedies today. I watch sports, movies, special events.

Why did you dislike working on the Jackie Gleason show?
He wasn't very nice to us. We only worked a couple of weeks and never got to meet him. I remember working with the other writers, one was Harry Crane, who was very, very funny. He had a baseball glove and a baseball and he would throw the ball to one fellow, Walter, and Walter would throw it to another writer named Marvin, and back to Harry. The ball went around the room as they were tossing out ideas for Jackie's show. My brother and I sat on the sofa in the room and pitched ideas, but they wouldn't listen to us. Finally I said

something that was really good and Harry threw me the ball. I said, wow, I'm in. Eventually Danny got his ball, too. But we never met Gleason. The sketches that we wrote would go upstairs to this ivory tower where Jackie lived. Then the script would come sliding under the door with a big NG on it, meaning Not Good. So I didn't learn anything from him.

It was different when you worked with Sid Caesar, wasn't it?
Yeah, because Sid loved the writers. He knew his career depended on them. Sid paid the writers better than anyone else. He lived with them. From the moment he came in in the morning until the end of the day, he worked there. We would break up in groups. There were about seven writers plus Sid, Carl Reiner, and Howie Morris, so that's ten people in the room. Larry Gelbart and myself, say, would go into another room and write a German professor, and two others—Mel Brooks and maybe Woody Allen—would write one of the other sketches. Then when we had all the sketches done we would bring it in to the central meeting place and everyone would pitch in and rewrite it. So we all had a part of it. When I would watch it on Saturday night I didn't have the slightest inkling about what my contribution was. You forget, in the heat of battle. You're just throwing lines into it, guys are shouting at each other. It was not only the best learning experience for me, it was probably the most enjoyable time I ever had in writing with other people.

Was Caesar jealous or bitter after the show was canceled and most of the writers went on to greater success?
I never spoke to Sid about that. I don't think he was jealous because he loved those writers. He was very proud of our success. Maybe Sid was bitter that the time had passed him by. He wrote a book about the problems he had with alcohol and pills, he had a long way to come back, but he did come back.

Is Mel Brooks one of the funniest men you know?

Yeah. He could annoy me, drive me crazy, but he could make me laugh almost any time he wanted.

Who else is like that?
Larry Gelbart is probably the wittiest of any of the writers I know. I can come up with lines fast when I have to, but not as fast as Larry. He's the fastest in the West. And probably in the East.

After Woody Allen's *Manhattan*, you said you were jealous of his success. Why were you jealous?
It was just a frank and honest thing to say. I don't know anyone in any business who isn't jealous of their colleagues who make an enormous success. I thought *Annie Hall* and *Manhattan* were incredible, just wonderful films. There was Woody on the cover of *Time* and it said, "America's Comic Genius." It would be hypocritical of me not to feel jealous. You would have to be a saint. But there is no rancor in it. I don't think jealousy is a negative trait, unless it gets out of hand. Sometimes it can stir you on to say, "Well then, I'm going to try and do that."

Do you feel competitive as a writer the way, say, Norman Mailer does?
I don't feel competitive, no. But I feel sometimes that I wish I were doing something better than I did, or I did do something better and someone who did something less good got a better review. They're all natural feelings and you deal with them.

When did you realize that television wasn't fulfilling for you?
I felt if I stayed in television I wouldn't get past the point of situation comedy. Maybe I might branch off and write a film. I was as well-known and well paid a writer as Mel Brooks or Larry Gelbart, but when I was with the William Morris office—they were my agents—I would go to them and say, "I want to do a film, can you get one for me?" They would say, "No, you have no experience." So it was

Catch-22: you couldn't write a movie unless you had written one. So I said, I see how it works now, I've got to do it myself. But I didn't know anybody on the West Coast, I had no ins to break into film, so I thought I'd be better off writing a play, because I liked the theater more. So I spent three years writing *Come Blow Your Horn*.

Why did it take so long to write?
Because I was working in television at the same time. I was writing the "Bilko" show and "The Garry Moore Show" after that. Those shows, especially the "Bilko" show, were enormously demanding. We worked six days a week and sometimes at night. So to try to write a play and having no experience—I didn't know how to get actors on or off the stage—it was different than it was working in television. The craft of the theater had escaped me at that point and I had to learn it. That's what took three years.

How many times did you rewrite that first play?
At least twenty. And I mean from beginning to end, without a single word of earlier drafts in some of the later versions.

You must have had a supreme belief in yourself that you would eventually get it right.
It was the *lack* of belief in myself. I said, This isn't good enough. It's not right. That doesn't mean I believed I could make it better, but I felt I had to try. Those twenty versions were shown to at least twenty different major producers in New York, all of whom were interested in it, but none of them wanted to produce it. But each of them gave me a hint about what was wrong, so I picked up a little here and there. It was the equivalent to three years of college. Then I was also saved by the fact that I couldn't get it produced on Broadway. Had I gotten it on Broadway it would have failed and that would have been the end of it and I'd have been writing on a sitcom for the rest of my life. What happened was, since I couldn't get a producer, the agent I had, Helen Harvey, suggested I try it out in summer stock some-where. The fear was if that didn't work, it was the last you ever heard

of it. But there was about forty percent of the play that was good enough for Broadway and sixty percent that needed rewriting, so I had the advantage of seeing it in front of an audience every night, seeing what worked and what didn't. Then we took six months off and I rewrote it again. Tried it in Philadelphia and it was a big hit. It was not a big hit in New York, but there were enough people who started to come and talk about it that it subsidized me for the next two plays. I was able to write the musical *Little Me* and after that, *Barefoot in the Park*.

I read that you invested the money from *Come Blow Your Horn* in sick cattle that eventually died.

Well, I learned that from Moss Hart's autobiography, *Act One,* in which he said, "Be prepared to lose all the money you make on your first play, because you won't know how to handle it." And that's what happened. I had a semihit, so I had semimoney, so I put it in semistocks, and became semibroke. [*Laughs*] Yes, a business advisor advised me to put my money in cattle. I did, they froze in Montana, and I got a check with a lot of zeroes with no numbers in front of it and said, That's the end of that. I better learn how to handle money if any more comes in. A little came in on *Little Me,* but a lot came in on *Barefoot in the Park*. I learned to manage it a little better.

After the success of *Barefoot in the Park,* did you feel you found your profession?

I needed a lot more hits to feel accepted. Luckily the next play was *The Odd Couple,* and that really solidified my reputation. But still, you have to keep on proving yourself. You take a couple of steps forward and then have a flop, it's a couple of steps backward.

Did you feel after *The Odd Couple* that you had your finger on the pulse of America's funny bone?

For a while. But I knew I had to keep my finger on the pulse and try to understand what would make a successful and good play. There's a big difference between successful and good.

How did you handle success when it came?

It didn't affect the work, but it did my personal life. It isolated me even more. People root for you in the beginning, then when you have a lot of success people say, "Why? Why is he doing that? His stuff isn't that good." It's like my being jealous of Woody Allen. Oscar Wilde said, "Success isn't really, truly enjoyable unless your friends fail as well." I remember a friend of mine threw a party for me after *The Odd Couple,* he raised his glass in toast and said, "This is to Neil, this is the last night he's going to have any friends." It's not a very likable trait in all of us, when we do that to the people who become very successful. You can imagine how many people are waiting for Steven Spielberg to fail. These people suddenly become gods when they're so successful and you want to shoot them back down to earth. Once they're down long enough, then you don't mind if they rise up again. We're such a success-oriented country. People treat successful people as royalty and yet they also want to shoot them down at the same time.

After *The Odd Couple* I began appearing on Merv Griffin and Johnny Carson and all those shows, which I didn't think I was equipped to do. I would feel very self-conscious about it. I felt obligated to be funny. And when you're that tense you're not going to be funny. It's kind of pushy to be funny when there's no reason to be. What got me through it was more work. I've been called a workaholic. To hide myself in a room working on another play or movie was a way of not dealing with some of the other things that were happening to me. It was also a very productive and healthier way to do it. I'm not really a workaholic, because I don't work that many hours in the day—I work maybe four hours a day, and I don't know many people who have a job that you can work only four hours a day and get well paid for it.

Is *The Odd Couple* your most successful work? It's been a play, a movie, a TV series, a play for women, for blacks . . .

It depends on how you define success. In terms of how long it ran or in financial terms. In financial terms, no, *Brighton Beach* has far surpassed that.

You didn't get any money for the TV series of *The Odd Couple*, did you?

Not a penny. It's a shame, but we didn't know how to deal with that. I had people representing me who made a bad deal. We sold the rights to *Barefoot in the Park*, but with that went the television rights for *The Odd Couple*. Part of it was my own fault because I was so naïve. I thought, *The Odd Couple*'s never going to make a TV series. I never think they are. I never think anything I do is going to be successful.

Do you still feel that way?

It sounds a little facetious to say that, but I'm still doubtful all the time. But things generally even out. I sold a couple of plays to the movies that didn't turn out to be very good movies.

Was it difficult changing *The Odd Couple* from two men to two women?

It wasn't difficult once you make up your mind to make women funny as well. But you have to ask yourself: Is this basic premise as funny for women? I'm not sure about that.

Right from the beginning you made a change: from the males playing poker to the women playing Trivial Pursuit.

We tried it with poker and got totally no laughs with the same material we used for the men, which I didn't think at first had any gender to the humor. But they didn't believe six women sitting around playing poker. They believe Trivial Pursuit, which does happen and is more contemporary.

Did you learn about the differences between the sexes after rewriting that play?

No. I know more about the sexes by writing about them in other plays.

Are women easier to share feelings with than men?

In life? I don't know. Some feelings, yes. I have much longer conversations with women because I spend more time with women. There are certain in-depth conversations I don't have with men, but because I've been married, my wives also became my best friends. The major conversations in my life took place between us.

Chapter Two dealt with the guilt feelings you had remarrying four months after your first wife died. How different was that second marriage for you?

I don't know how to answer that without getting into personalities. It was basically a pretty good, and at times a wonderful marriage. I have a different philosophy now that some time has gone by since we divorced: some things are meant to run just so long. My first marriage ended because Joan died. Which is not to say that we would have lived the rest of our lives married together. I have no idea where it would have gone. But Marsha and I were very happy and compatible, and then we reached a point where we went separate ways.

Marsha Mason being an actress and having a career of her own, did that lead to difficulties?

The only problem it led to for me was I don't like long separations. When Marsha did other films there would be long separations. But that was not the basis of our breakup. In the beginning I had asked Marsha not to work for a while so that we could solidify our relationship, because we met while we were doing *The Good Doctor.* And to her credit she gave up three years of her career at a very important time for her. She had just made *Cinderella Liberty* and gotten an Oscar nomination. After those three years, not only did I change my idea of her not working, I started to write for her. Mostly because I thought she was a terrific actress. She got three Academy nominations in the pictures that we did together, purely on her own merits. *The Goodbye Girl, Only When I Laugh,* and *Chapter Two.*

When that marriage ended, you said that perhaps you hadn't made enough of a sacrifice. Did you blame yourself?

When the breakup happens you say a lot of things. And you need some history between the breakup and where you are right now to really see things. Of course, Marsha was at fault; I was at fault. We also were both responsible for the good times. Breaking up is as indefinable as trying to figure out why you fall in love with somebody. You just do. There are so many intangibles.

Did Marsha's spiritualism cause any problems for you? She would appear on talk shows chanting or talking about her guru Muktananda.

I didn't find fault that she took it very seriously, because it meant a lot to her. What I didn't like was the amount of time that she spent with it. It became somewhat of a threat. But I also learned from Marsha and through Swami Muktananda—there was something in the Eastern philosophy that helped me a lot. But I started that before I met Marsha. During Joan's illness, in my search for some way to deal with it, I found a way to keep going in some of the sayings in Eastern philosophy.

Are you able to write when you're depressed?

Yeah, I could write at any time. I even wrote *The Sunshine Boys* during Joan's illness. I have this facility, which started when I was a young boy and things were not good at home, I was able to block out things by going into a dark room by myself and letting my thoughts wander. I could isolate myself from the rest of the world, so that when I write—and the reason that I'm prolific—I don't hear noise, I don't know what room I'm in, sometimes I don't know what country I'm in. I wrote *The Heartbreak Kid* in Spain, and the room that I was in was New York City as far as I was concerned.

What's your take on marriage? Do you feel you need to be married?

My feeling about that is, I never even thought about marriage from the very beginning. When I first met Joan I didn't think I wanted to get married. I just fell in love with her and she was such an incredible girl. I just wanted to be with her every day. So marriage was a natural evolution. Wanted children as well—and we had two daughters, Ellen and Nancy. Same thing happened with Marsha.

How old were your children when Joan died?

Nancy was ten, Ellen was fifteen. It affected Nancy more than Ellen, because Nancy was the younger one and she didn't have those years with Joan, and those are five very important years. Ellen is very strong and I leaned on her a lot, in a positive way for me, sort of a burden for her. They were the reason for me wanting to go on with my life. It sounds very tragic, but you needed something to answer, How do you deal with all of this? They were always the reason for dealing with everything for me.

What was their reaction when four months later you remarried?

I never would have gotten married if they resented it. I brought them to rehearsals of *The Good Doctor* and it was the first play that they had ever come around to watch. We went out to a restaurant afterwards and Ellen and Nancy said, "Marsha's terrific, why don't you ask her for a date?" They pushed me.

How did they feel ten years later when that marriage split up?

I never asked them that question. They were bystanders, observers to this wreckage that was going on. But they weren't really there because they were away, Marsha and I were alone.

Do you see humor in all situations, no matter how grim?

I might privately. With friends the humor can get very black. It's a self-defense against warding off a lot of problems in life. You can make jokes about death and illnesses. The more lightly you treat it, the less frightening it may be. But it's something that I wouldn't always put on the stage. I don't want to censor myself that much, but there are certain things that cross over the boundaries of bad taste. Sometimes I'm guilty of it.

Are there things today that offend you?

It's bad quality that offends me. It's not scatological humor, because I would use it myself. Certainly it's not nudity, we're past all of that. Bad taste is not the villain; it's bad quality.

What was the most difficult play for you to write?

Star-Spangled Girl. I didn't believe in it. I didn't like it. It's a play that would have been in the bottom of the drawer after forty pages, but the producer, Saint-Subber—who produced Tennessee Williams, Carson McCullers, William Inge—was the one who got me through *Barefoot in the Park,* and the same thing with *The Star-Spangled Girl.* I said, "This play has no validity." And he said, "No, I'm telling you it's even better." So he helped me through it, though I should have left it in the drawer.

Who are the actors who best understand the rhythms of your writing?

Any really good actor. I never thought that George C. Scott would be so good for my material, but when we did *Plaza Suite,* I never saw anyone on stage as funny as he was in the third act. I could barely watch it, it was so funny. Because he played it like King Lear. He's one of the best farceurs anywhere. Walter Matthau and Jack Lemmon, it goes without saying, because I've worked with them so often. The women, like Maureen Stapleton—but she's good for everybody. Marlon Brando has none of the rhythms that I write in, but maybe he would be wonderful. The ones that I would love to work with are Dustin Hoffman and Jack Nicholson.

You worked on *Bogart Slept Here* with Robert De Niro and Mike Nichols, but it didn't work out, did it?

It was aborted after a week. There was only one time I worked directly for two actors and that was for *The Goodbye Girl.* I knew who was going to be in it before I wrote it: Richard Dreyfuss and Marsha Mason. Because that was a spin-off of *Bogart Slept Here.* When I discarded that I started to use that story and went back to the origins of it. But before we went ahead with it, I had Dreyfuss and Marsha read *Bogart Slept Here.* They sounded wonderful, but I saw the problems with it. Seeing and hearing the chemistry between them, though, propelled me to want to write *The Goodbye Girl.*

Dreyfuss won an Oscar for it, then soon after seemed to disappear. Did that surprise you?

Yeah. It did. He's enormously gifted. He did *Jaws* and *Close Encounters* too. He started to try a lot of different things: Shakespeare, other plays. But it did surprise me that he fell off the cliff so suddenly. Anybody who becomes very famous and very rich in a short amount of time, and is fairly young, can't handle it.

In *The Gingerbread Lady* you wrote about a singer who was self-destructive. And you said you've seen a lot of actors who are that way.

But I never thought it was a play about alcoholism, it was just about somebody who couldn't explain why she was unhappy. One of the reviewers wanted to know what made her unhappy. Well, there are people who are self-destructive, who are alcoholics or on drugs, who spend a lifetime trying to find out what started it. I don't think you ever find out. I don't think it's more prevalent with actors than with anyone else.

Is it true that Bob Hope offered you $1 million for *The Sunshine Boys* so he and Bing Crosby could make the film?

Yeah. But I was writing about a particular milieu in the theater that I had grown up with. It was basically Jewish vaudevillian. The play was written in that style. Bob Hope and Bing Crosby were wrong for it. I needed two dramatic actors to play it. It worked better that way than with comedians. When I see George Burns's performance I say that's an actor doing it, not a comedian.

Is *The Sunshine Boys* the best film translation of any of your plays so far?

I think so.

You didn't feel that Jack Lemmon was cast right for *Prisoner of Second Avenue*, did you?

It was written with a certain New York sound to it that Jack doesn't have, but Jack is such a fine actor he gave a brilliant performance in it.

Didn't you also prefer Diane Keaton over Jeannie Berlin for *The Heartbreak Kid*?

I did, for a very valid reason. I didn't think that Jeannie Berlin was as attractive as Cybill Shepherd, so it made the story too simplistic: that this guy marries a rather plain-looking girl and meets this out-and-out beauty. I thought it seemed pretty obvious that he's going to want to make that change. Diane Keaton, before she had hit it with all the other films, she looked every bit as good as Cybill Shepherd. I thought that was more interesting.

How protective are you of your words? You don't allow any of them to be changed, do you?
That's not true. Allow them to be changed arbitrarily. I wouldn't like to come into the theater one night and hear the actors saying their own words and saying, "We think it's better this way." That's happened in rehearsals. And sometimes an actor will stumble on something much better and I'll use it, because if it's good I'll get the credit for it anyway. It happens in the movies sometimes, too. But I don't want anybody rewriting me, because I think I can rewrite me better than someone else can.

Do you have the same control in films as you do in plays?
Up to a certain point. Once we agree with what the words are, no one is going to rewrite it. But what does happen in film is the editing room. In a play they cannot, by contract between the producers and the Dramatist's Guild, cut or rewrite or change anything without your permission. But with a film, I'll see things that I had written that do not appear in the film that I think are integral to the film. *The Slugger's Wife* is a very good example of something that was completely bastardized. Music was interjected and chunks of dialogue and scenes came out of it. I ended up, along with the public, disliking that picture a lot.

Could you have gotten your name off that picture?
There were too many problems within the creative group itself, and you have to take the good with the bad. I was not going to make a case about taking my name off, because that meant I was going to blame everybody else. There were a lot of people to blame, but I was one of them. So, I had a failure.

What happened to the script you wrote for Eddie Murphy?

I still have it. I thought he behaved rather strangely, if not badly. I had written fifty-four pages. He read them and was so delighted that he went on his own, without telling me, on "Entertainment Tonight" and said, "I found a script, it's the best thing I ever read, it's Neil Simon's *Mr. Bad News,* and I'm doing it as soon as he finishes it." I was upset about that because I said, "Wait, you may not like the next fifty-four pages." I finished it and never heard from Eddie Murphy. Never heard from his managers. They just disappeared. It was one of the strangest experiences. He didn't say, "No, I don't like it." Or, "Can we meet?" I was bewildered. I'm never really upset about something once I write it—it's the experience of writing that's the most important thing for me. Once it's done, most of the joy of it is gone. I put this one aside for four months, then read it again and liked it. It's a good idea. Pure farce.

But not for Eddie Murphy, who's basically out of it?

Not basically, definitely.

Truman Capote told me that you wrote *Murder by Death* for him. True?

No. It wasn't even my idea. I just wrote the character. When I spoke to Ray Stark, who produced it, we both agreed that since this man was playing a literary character, it would be good to get somebody who we could believe. Ray came up with the idea of Truman Capote. I was nervous about it, because I said actors are actors, and you have to be a good actor to do anything. I don't think a personality can get their way through a film. There's no doubt that Truman had an enormously strong, impressionable personality, but I had mixed feelings about him doing it.

Was Capote the genius that he felt he was?

It's hard to think that anybody is the genius that they think they are, because the really true geniuses don't think they are. Maybe Mozart thought he was, I don't know. He must have had grave doubts later

on in his career when he couldn't work. Or van Gogh. Truman had
an enormous ego, but he also was enormously talented.

He said he learned more from failures than successes.
Yeah, because you learn what not to do again. It's very hard to learn
what to do again.

**He felt all his failures had to do with the theater. He blamed that
more on the producers and investors than on his writing.**
I think you've got to lay the blame at your own feet. Mike Nichols and I
had a very good relationship for four plays, mostly because our attitude
toward the work was, anything that I saw on the stage I blamed on myself if it wasn't working, and he felt the same way about himself. So we
never blamed each other. Truman was a good enough prose writer to be
accepted, but maybe he didn't understand the theater as well.

**How many plays and films that you've written would you like to
disown?**
A lot of them. But less than half.

How autobiographical a writer are you?
Very, when I'm writing autobiographical plays. In a sense, everything
you write is autobiographical because it is going through your brain,
so it comes out like litmus paper, it always catches some of who you
are. But even when you write the autobiographical plays, they are not
specifically autobiographical. When people see plays like *Come Blow
Your Horn* or *Brighton Beach* and *Biloxi Blues,* they'll ask, "Did that really
happen? Did he say that?" Well, sometimes it's true, sometimes it's
not. Sometimes I've given aspects of my life to somebody else, like my
girl cousin, who had aspects of what I went through as a child. It's
hard to discuss that writing process. It's like you throw it into a bowl,
mix it up, and pour it out. But everything of you is in there.

**Are *Brighton Beach Memoirs* and *Biloxi Blues* your best work to
date?**

Yeah. *Brighton Beach Memoirs* took nine years from the inception of the idea, but only four months to write. It was a big breakthrough for me. Not because it was autobiographical, but it was the first time I wrote a tapestry play. I said to myself in writing it: there are seven characters, I am going to make each one of them the star of the play. Because people always say, Who's this play about? I say, it's about each of them. So the audience watching can pick up any person in the play and identify and say, yes, that's what this is about. *Biloxi Blues* is pretty much the same thing, even though it's seen through the eyes of the narrator, Eugene Morris Jerome—my alter ego.

In that play you deal with your character's encounter with anti-Semitism and his loss of virginity. Do those events parallel your own life?
Sure.

Sure? Let me be more specific: Was your first time with a prostitute?
It was.

Was it memorable?
Oh, it would have to be. How could you not remember the first time?

A lot of women don't.
Liars. I never met a woman who wasn't able to talk about her first time. More say it was pleasurable than not pleasurable. Because generally speaking, they either very much wanted to do it to have the experience, or there was a boy who was very important in their lives at that time.

Many actresses I've spoken with about this remember it as a horrible experience.
Maybe they don't want to admit it was wonderful. Maybe they think it's sinful to say they enjoyed it the first time, because maybe they weren't married.

Did your brother take you to lose your virginity?

Yes. He took me the first time, which I've written about in plays in various forms. He took me up to a place and I didn't know what to say or do. There's the line I use in *Biloxi Blues,* which I literally said: "I don't care if this is a memorable experience or not, I just want to get it over with." I don't know sexually if it was a wonderful experience or not, it was your initiation into manhood. What I did, mostly, was talk to this woman. I thought she'd like me if I talked to her. That's all I cared about: did she like me? Then I asked her who was her most memorable experience with. She surprised me. I was nineteen and she said it was with a fifty-four-year-old man. I said I couldn't wait to be fifty-four.

You also said when you were in your forties you missed the entire sexual revolution.

I didn't miss it, I saw it go by from my window.

With regret?

Yes and no. Because whatever I did get in terms of my experiences I seemed to enjoy. I get the feeling that when it becomes so available and accessible it loses its value. I don't know if it's all that available anymore, but it's what I seem to hear and think that goes on with young kids. The latest event in our society, in terms of diseases [AIDS], has suddenly halted that and made people think twice about it now.

The revolution is over.

Oh, for sure. Heterosexually speaking, people are saying, "Be careful who you go with." It has nothing to do solely with homosexuality. But it was very difficult when I was a teenager, even my early twenties, but for different reasons. It led to such frustration and repression that I didn't think that was so hot, either. I don't think sex ever is an easy subject for anybody except two people who are in love with each other.

You're a romantic.
Extremely.

You've compared writing plays to the sex act.
I would compare anything to the sex act. I would compare the sex act
to almost any form of music. Not a song as much, but a symphony. We
all know what a symphony sounds like, and if that doesn't feel like the
sex act then you either haven't heard a symphony or had the sex act.

**Let's talk about something more painful than sex. How torturous
is an opening night for you?**
It's not anymore. Opening nights have changed. There is no opening
night anymore. It was torturous for the first three plays—I thought I
couldn't do it again. After *Come Blow Your Horn* I said I'll never write
another play because I can't go through this. My mouth was drier
than the Sahara Desert. I couldn't talk, the actors seemed eighty
miles away when I was standing in the back of the theater, and my
heart was pounding. I said, "My life depends on this night. If I fail,
and fail real big, I'll have to creep away in the night and go someplace
else to try and make my living." I was fortunate that that did not happen to me, even though I was also fortunate in not being an overwhelming success, because that would make your second attempt unbearable. How would you live up to that? So I was in the middle of
the road. But the second play, *Little Me,* was just as nerve wracking. I
started to feel that way on *Barefoot in the Park,* but within five minutes
of that play you could tell it was working. At that time, all the critics
used to come on one night and all your eggs were in that one basket.
Now the critics come over a period of four preview nights, so it's broken up and you get three or four good chances at it. I like it better
that way; it's a much fairer and easier process.

**Nonetheless, isn't it true that a Broadway opening is still
dependent upon what the *New York Times* says the next day?**
Yes and no. *Brighton Beach* got a pretty good review from them, and
I've never had a play as successful in terms of financial reward. Frank

Rich's review of *Biloxi Blues* was a wonderful review, and that success came much quicker. But previous to Frank Rich's coming on to the *New York Times* there were other critics there who just lambasted my plays, and they were big successes anyway. Conversely, I've had some good reviews in the *New York Times* and that didn't impress the people, who didn't like it.

Do critics bother you, or are you able to be like George Bernard Shaw, who supposedly once wrote a critic saying, "I'm sitting on the toilet reading your review of my play and soon it will be behind me"?

Well, he was a critic himself so that must have applied to him. No, I can get very angry with them but I can't ignore them. To me the most important function of the critic is what I learn from them. That generally takes place before you ever open in New York, because I still have time to fix the play. I've done a number of plays in Los Angeles, and I don't read just one critic, I try to read twenty reviews and see if they all have the same opinion, then I'd put some validity to it. By the time it gets to New York, the critic is really telling the audience what they should do. What I might learn there is what to do with the next play I wrote. Frank Rich gave me a mandate to go write the second play, which I never contemplated. It was just going to be one play, *Brighton Beach,* but at the end he said, "One hopes that there is a chapter two." So I wrote the second play. And then the third.

Has it gotten too expensive to see a Broadway show?

It's changed only in that people will now only go to see the hits, where as in the old days when they could afford to see almost anything, they would go to see almost anything.

What do you see as the future of Broadway?

I'm always optimistic. I don't think Broadway's ever going to go away. It's why people basically still come to New York. They always think of going to the theater. What bothers me more than the prices is the lack of playwrights right now. We always seem to depend so much on

English imports. Maybe there is a slight turn happening now because of regional theater. Plays are starting in different places than they used to. Audiences are much more receptive to experimental plays. Off-Broadway is becoming more and more important. So there will always be theater.

Being a bicoastal writer, what do you dislike most about California and New York?
What I dislike most about California is that everything is centered on the business. There's not a restaurant I go to that I don't meet people in the business; it seems like one big company town. The other thing that I miss a great deal is accessibility to people. You really only meet people at red lights, driving around. In New York I meet them all on the streets, and you renew old acquaintances. After a while in New York I can feel it crowds in on me, that there's no space. But it's still a much more exciting and vibrant city. I've been more prolific in California because I have less things to do there. There are more distractions in New York.

Are you also a bad traveler who gets sick wherever you go?
I used to. After my divorce it hasn't happened so much—not saying that marriage is conducive to all sorts of ailments. I feel less stress.

Does anything frighten you about getting older?
Just physically. That I can't do the things I used to do. Not being able to play tennis or run, I would miss that. But I run as fast on the tennis court today as I did when I was younger.

Do you think about death much?
Yeah. I have strange feelings about it. Sometimes it doesn't make much difference to me. I don't think it's out of a despair that I feel that way. If I were to suddenly pop off, the only thing that I would regret are certain personal things. I don't necessarily want to live to be ninety-two.

Didn't Shaw live into his nineties?

Yeah, but he ate vegetables and I hate them.

Have you thought of an epitaph?

"Ssshh, he's writing."

INDEX